Applied Ethics and Human Rights

Applied Ethics and Human Rights

Conceptual Analysis and Contextual Applications

Edited by
Shashi Motilal

ANTHEM PRESS
LONDON · NEW YORK · DELHI

Anthem Press India
An imprint of Wimbledon Publishing Company India Private Limited (WPCIPL)
WPCIPL is a subsidiary of Wimbledon Publishing Company Limited

This edition first published in 2011
by ANTHEM PRESS INDIA

Distributed by ANTHEM PRESS
www.anthempress.com

ISBN-13: 978 93 80601 15 1 (Pbk)
ISBN-10: 93 80601 15 8 (Pbk)

Dedicated to the memory of Professor Pranab Kumar Sen,
my most revered teacher of philosophy

TABLE OF CONTENTS

Part Two: Human Rights Issues 127

PREFACE

Few ideas have engaged the thought of philosophers for so great a length of time and occupied a momentous place in its history as the idea of human rights and human moral obligations. Much has been written on almost every aspect of these two ideas, so, in a sense, this book, which addresses questions concerning the concepts of human rights and human obligations, the relations between them, the conflicts which arise when there are flagrant violations of each and the impact each has on decisions and actions undertaken (individually or collectively) in real life situations, cannot claim to be discussing things that have not been discussed before. However, philosophical enterprise being what it is, there is always room for another 'point of view' and that is justification enough. A different point of view brings to light new and distinct perspectives which may help provide a better understanding of morally perplexing problems. Many papers in this volume are an attempt to deal with the question of human rights and obligations in an Indian context, and herein lies its claim to novelty, its *raison d 'etre.*

Philosophical problems have this die-hard quality about them that they remain the same at the core; only the context in which they are presented provides a distinct perspective to them. The different context demands a review, revisiting and rehearsing of existing solutions to suit its present needs. The Indian context – a context that is a reflection of various socio-cultural, linguistic and religious hues of a multiplicity of diverse groups poses a host of ethical dilemmas that make a demand on the sagacious intellect of the moral philosopher.

It has been argued by many philosophers and sociologists that the notion of 'human rights' is a 'western notion' rooted in western political values. When we turn to traditional non-western societies (Indian, Chinese, Japanese, Islamic), we fail to find a corresponding notion of human rights. Instead, the notions of responsibility and community prevail. Respect for obligation, duty, moral and social responsibility towards the community, are considered more important than individualistic ideas of rights. In ancient Indian philosophy and ethics we find that the notion of dharma plays a pivotal role in understanding moral life. The point of view of dharma may be regarded as an Indian point of view, though not the Indian point of view. Perhaps, there cannot be a pan Indian point of view and no such claim is being made in the book. The question is – what solutions can this specific Indian point of view provide to some common problems relating to issues of human rights that have been tackled from the western point of view? Can the notion of dharma, which in one of its interpretations is the notion of 'moral order', do the job that the notion of 'human rights' accomplishes in the western discourse on morality? Can a parallel notion of human rights be derived from the notion of dharma?

Part I of the book includes papers that deal with the conceptual analysis of issues relating to human rights. An understanding of these issues is a prerequisite to any endeavour in undertaking Applied Ethics. Some of the questions dealt with in this section are: What is involved in applying ethical principles to real life situations? What are the limits of the legal and why one needs to go beyond the realm of the legal to the moral? Can one claim that there exists only one uniform set of moral principles that will uniquely determine what is right or wrong in every society irrespective of differences amongst them? What is the logical justification for such a claim? Can there be a mid-way between the metaethical views of moral relativism and moral absolutism that will satisfy the need for moral objectivity? The conflict amongst competing human rights and between rights and obligations underlies many moral debates. This calls for a clear understanding of the notions of 'rights', 'human rights', and 'moral obligations and responsibilities'. The question of how the notion of 'dharma' squares with the notion of rights and obligations is also taken up here.

Part II of the book is devoted to the contextual applications of the concepts of human rights and human moral obligations. It comprises of papers that deal with the problems arising out of violation of human rights. It discusses the rights of various groups of people (e.g., people belonging to minority communities, gays, lesbians and other members of the transgender community, criminals, people afflicted with mental illness, the future generation, the unborn foetus and women) and the specific contexts of the violation of these rights. It includes papers on the right to violence for survival and on the right to freedom of information *vis-à-vis* the right to private (intellectual) property in the context of the Internet. The issue of globalization and how it impacts human rights is also discussed in this section.

Applied Ethics is a 'do-it-yourself' exercise. Anyone who is willing to think hard about moral matters has to discover his/her own solutions for which he/she needs adequate training. This training involves intellectual wrestling with the finer points of moral theory and practice. The book seeks to approach some typical moral problems keeping the above questions in mind, with the aim that a new approach may help understand the problem in a different light and may also help provide morally viable solutions. It is restricted in its scope and does not claim to have dealt with all aspects of human rights and obligations. Even with respect to those aspects that have been discussed, no final conclusions have been offered. The main aim has been to state the problematic, provide a context of reference, raise relevant questions, examine logical arguments and direct the mind to think of satisfactory solutions. It provides food for thought, and would be useful for students taking a course in Applied Ethics or in the Philosophy of Human Rights, researchers in these areas, and for the general audience, provided it is philosophically discerning and willing to contemplate hard on these issues.

This book has been long in the making. It started as a volume under the 'Book Project' of DIVA-INDIA (Development of Integrated Value Applications), which was a registered society for Applied Ethics. I am extremely grateful to the Ford Foundation for financial support without which this project could not have taken off. I am especially thankful to my friend and colleague Dr. Deepa Nag Haksar who first thought of bringing out few volumes in different areas of Applied Ethics under the auspices of the 'Book Project', and whose enthusiasm encouraged me to think about editing a volume on Applied Ethics and Human Rights.

Editing a book which thematically binds together over twenty papers seemed to have taken longer than I thought it would. Also, being my first endeavour in this direction, it received, like one's 'first born', somewhat extended care and concern. For some time, other pressing professional and personal commitments occupied me and work on the book had to be put aside. I am happy that things have fallen in place and the book will finally see the light of day.

In the long journey with this book, I have many to be grateful to; people without whose support the journey and this book would never have happened. They are first and foremost the contributors who have so patiently borne with me, never losing confidence in my effort and commitment to bring out such a volume. I am deeply indebted to them all.

When working on the chapters I have benefited a lot by discussions held with the graduate students of my Philosophy of Human Rights class both at Delhi University and Carleton University, Ottawa, Canada, where I took a few guest lectures. I am also thankful to Professor Bijoy Boruah of the Department of Humanities and Social Sciences, IIT Delhi for his very valuable comments and suggestions on the Introduction of the book. For stylistic 'fine tuning' I am thankful to my son Arpan and close friend and colleague Bijayalaxmi Nanda. Their frank and free comments helped me see mistakes which would otherwise have gone unnoticed. Despite their help to make the book better, I am wholly responsible for any shortcomings in it.

Special thanks are also due to my friends Debjani Datta, Manidipa Sen, Franson Manjali and Pragati Sahni whose help and support saw this book through some difficult times during the course of its publication. Heartfelt thanks are also due to my friend Bijayalaxmi, who in many 'big' and 'small' ways helped uplift my sagging spirits when things were not progressing well with the book.

Ms. Pramila Kardam and Ms. Suchitra Singh deserve a very big 'thank you' for their tremendous help with the computer work throughout the preparation of this volume. Their efficiency, patience and above all their willingness to work any time made my task much easier.

I express my deepest gratitude to Mr. Tej P. S. Sood, Publishing Director of Anthem Press, London, for offering to publish my work, and to Ms. Janka Romero and the Anthem Press team who very enthusiastically took up the publication of this work. I am also appreciative of Mr. Partha Mallik of the Kolkata office of Anthem Press for his timely help and advice.

I am grateful to late Prof. Daya Krishna, Ex-editor of JICPR (Journal of the Indian Council of Philosophical Research) for granting me permission to reprint the paper by Rajendra Prasad, "Applying Ethics: Modes, Motives and Levels of Commitment" JICPR, XIV: 2, Jan – April, 1997, and to the Indian Council of Philosophical Research for the paper by S.R. Bhatt, "Dharma: The Overriding Principle of Indian Life and Thought" which was presented at the International Conference on Indian Philosophy, Science and Culture, organized by ICPR during March, 2003.

Last but not least, I would like to express my heartfelt gratitude and indebtedness to my family for their help, support and encouragement, especially during times when I thought I could not make it.

INTRODUCTION

I

Applying Ethics

Morality, our sense of the morally right or wrong act, finds expression in individual claims of what is of moral value, for example, honesty, loyalty, fidelity, and what ought to be done or avoided in general and on particular occasions, e.g., always help others in need, never cause unnecessary harm to others, be fair in your dealings with others, etc. More often than not, one may not know why, what is morally right or wrong, is so, except for the very general reason that the morally right action is beneficial for all and the morally wrong act is not. A moral/ethical theory purports to answer the basic question – why are certain acts morally right and certain other acts morally wrong? Of course, one can make moral claims and more generally possess a morality without having a moral theory. Furthermore, the same moral claims may be compatible with different moral theories. Thus, one may hold that lying is wrong without having a systematic account of what makes it wrong and this moral claim may be justifiable by quite distinct moral theories such as those of Consequentialism, Deontology or Divine Law. The level at which moral claims and judgements are made is the level of substantive ethics, and the level at which theories are adduced to explain these claims is the level of normative ethics. There is a third level, that of meta-ethics, which constitutes a discerning enquiry into the fundamental logic of the language of morals. The question 'Is there a single sense of moral correctness', for example, belongs to this realm.

Applied Ethics, which is the practical aspect of Ethics, consists in the systematic application of moral theory to particular moral problems. It is ethics applied to cases of morally dilemmatic situations where a person must act but does not know the morally correct course of action. The cases may be actual situations involving real (present or past) events, or may be possible future situations (e.g., when considering the moral implications of drawing up certain legislation), or the situation may be wholly fictitious, taken as a 'thought experiment' to provide a paradigm for a class of cases which may include real ones. Substantive, normative and metaethical considerations do enter into Applied Ethics in the sense that a moral theory which is applied to resolve a moral dilemma may itself be a product of the combination of the three, but these considerations are not the primary concern of Applied Ethics. The primary concern of Applied Ethics is more of a practical nature rather than theoretical. In the words of Brenda Almond, co-founder of the Society for Applied Philosophy, Applied Ethics is, "the philosophical examination, from a moral standpoint, of particular issues in private and public life that are matters of moral judgment."[1]

Moral dilemmas, situations where an individual is faced with the question 'What ought I to do', are situations which on analysis are seen to be, at the core, a conflict between rights either of two individuals or two groups, or an individual and a group, or a conflict between equally demanding obligations (duties), or again, a conflict between a right which one has, and an obligation one is bound by. These conflicts are to be encountered in various fields of human life, and Applied Ethics attempts to resolve these conflicts.

In Medical Ethics such moral dilemmas abound in number. The issue of abortion brings forth the dilemma between the right of the mother and that of the foetus. Euthanasia or Mercy killing raises the question whether one has the right to die with dignity *vis-a-vis* the doctor's moral obligation to respect this right of the patient. There is also the question whether some circumstances endorse a 'duty to die'?

In the area of Ethics and Governance, policy decisions are affected by what accord is given to minority rights versus majority rights, what stance is adopted in case of a conflict between the larger interests of society and violation of minority rights. These issues come up in an important way in policy decisions which need to be taken in developmental projects affecting large sections of society.

There is no dearth of examples of such conflicts in Business Ethics. Conflicts between the rights and the obligations of the consumer and the producer of goods, the employer and the employees take various forms. The right of managers to profit and limits imposed on that, the duty of 'whistleblowers' to the general public as opposed to their employers, are issues which clearly express conflicts of rights and duties.

In Journalistic Ethics there are many issues that are at root clashes between the consumer's right to information and the provider's obligation to exercise restraint and avoid sensationalism. Other areas where the rights-obligation conflicts are encountered are Environmental Ethics, Legal Ethics, Computer Ethics, Neuroethics and various areas in public and personal life.

It is therefore important to be clear about the concepts of human rights and human obligations, before applying normative ethics to solve moral dilemmas in personal, professional and social life. At the same time, conceptual clarity is better achieved only in and through understanding the inter relations in a contextual setting. Applied ethics serves the purpose of providing rational and moral guidance for human action. In fulfilling this primarily practical purpose, applied ethics also – in passing as it were – serves to test moral principles at the tribunal of real life. In applying moral principles, we are called upon to question and, if need be, criticize and revise them. The first part of the present volume aims at developing conceptual clarity about notions of 'applying ethics' or 'applying the principles of ethics', 'human rights' and 'human obligations'. Some papers, which delineate the concept of *Dharma* as it is found in ancient Indian Philosophical texts, lead one to questions about the possibility of understanding the concept in the traditional Western human rights and obligations discourse. Alongside this endeavour to achieve conceptual clarity some discussion also centres around certain meta-ethical questions, such as whether there can be a universal and absolute concept of moral values. Since human rights are human values, the question whether there is or can be a single notion of human rights also becomes relevant.

When we talk of applying a moral principle to a concrete morally dilemmatic case, what exactly are we doing? What exactly are we effecting and how? Rajendra Prasad, in his paper **Applying Ethics: Modes, Motives and Levels of Commitment**, talks about the logistics of applying ethical principles to morally conflicting situations. He speaks of the modes of applying ethical principles, the motivation behind the application and the levels of commitment involved in such application. He maintains that ethical theory can be applied at various levels – the level of judgement, decision or persuasion. Taking examples from the great Indian epic the *Mahābhārata*, Rajendra Prasad shows that a sub-committal or a hyper committal attitude to applying moral principles is not correct. In applying moral principles, the commitment of the evaluator must be strong and firm. He must believe in the moral rightness or wrongness of the principle and his evaluation (judgement) or decision (to perform or not to perform the act) or persuasion, must follow from this belief. Claiming that neutrality has no place in applying ethics, Prasad argues that although it is possible to be non-religious, it is not possible to be non-moral, thus highlighting the distinction between religiosity and morality. Such a stand allows the co-existence of being secular and being morally judgemental with respect to religion.

An issue that is very important to any discussion of ethical questions is the distinction between the legal and the moral. The ethical is closely bound up with the legal and the religious, and yet it is distinct from both. Many things that are morally prohibited are legally forbidden as well. However, most philosophers would insist on the autonomy and higher authority of ethics. This means that moral principles are neither reducible to nor derived from legal rules. The ultimate justification for moral principles, most philosophers would argue, is in human reason or human understanding or in human experience. In his paper **Jurisprudence and the Individual: Bridging the General and the Particular**, Abhik Majumdar puts forth various views adduced for and against the separation of law and morals and discusses the consequences this separation entails for the ordinary individual. Tracing briefly the history of the debate on Legal Positivism, the author shows that the debate does not provide a satisfactory answer to the question of why it is obligatory for an individual to comply with the law. A higher law prescribing obedience to the law would be pointless. It would clearly beg the question presupposing the very thing it was intended to justify viz., the general obligation to obey the law. This obligation must be moral since without it obedience to law would amount to prudence and not to doing the morally right thing. A system of positive law can come into being only in a community where most people acknowledge that they have a moral obligation to obey the law. Majumdar concludes that without the moral obligation to obey the law, there could be no legal obligation. We are forced to look beyond the realm of the legal into the realm of the moral. But the realm of the moral is not easy to comprehend.

At this point a pertinent question can be raised. We ought to consider whether the very idea of applying ethical theories is misguided, since it assumes that we can use ethical theories to determine what is morally right and wrong. But, is there any single theory of ethics which can claim that it gives us a set of moral values that are universal in the sense that they are universally accepted by all cultures of the world and strongly still, by all cultures there possibly could be? In applying ethical principles to real life situations, there may be a tacit presumption that there is a set of universally accepted moral values and that we can make moral judgements based on our understanding of these moral values – further still, that these judgements of right and wrong are objective assessments that will be universally accepted. This presumption has been widely challenged from many quarters, one of them being Moral Relativism. It is common to hear people say: 'what is right for one person is not necessarily right for another' and 'what is right in one circumstance is not right in other circumstances'. If this were true – that is, if moral values were relative to different cultures and contexts – then it would not be possible to make any general or objective moral assessments. In the absence of universally acceptable moral standards Applied Ethics would be a meaningless enterprise, unless one was prepared to admit that Applied Ethics is itself relative.

On the other hand, there are staunch believers in Moral Absolutism who have given arguments to show that Moral Relativism as a theory about morality cannot stand logical scrutiny. The debate between different forms of relativism and absolutism has gone on for decades with no conclusive answer. R. C. Pradhan in his paper **Why Moral Relativism Does Not Make Sense** argues why Moral Relativism cannot be the correct and final theory about morality. He argues that moral values are not the products of cultural differences; rather they are the preconditions of every culture. If moral values were determined by culture then ethics would no longer be a normative study; it would be reduced to an empirical study like sociology or anthropology. Further, moral relativism undermines the possibility of moral truths, and even moral emotions and prescriptions need evaluation in the light of moral truths. He claims that the entire enterprise of Applied Ethics can make sense only if we accept the presupposition of universal and objective moral truths.

Moral Relativism and Human Rights

Relativism with regard to morality can take on various forms – there can be relativism about moral virtues, moral goods, moral rights and obligations. Moral Relativism with respect to moral rights would see the rights people have as relative to their society, state or governmental system. It would be totally opposed to the idea of a 'universal' 'transcultural' right. But what is a right? Or, more specifically, what is it to have a right? What are the sources of rights? Why should there be rights at all? The key notion in the concept of a right is 'entitlement'. To say that one has a right to something is to say that one is entitled to it, e.g. the right to vote gives one the legitimate entitlement to exercise one's franchise and so with other rights. But what entitles one to a right? There are three ways by virtue of which one becomes entitled to something. These are – law, custom and morality. A moral relativist maintains that all the rights that we can have are derived from either law or custom or both, and since these differ from one society to another, there can be no universal rights. There are no rights that are derived from a common sense of morality since there is no single morality common to all societies. It is a-historical to hold that there is/has been a single morality. The moral absolutist, on the other hand, believes that despite multiculturality, there is a core sense of morality (the inviolable sense of right and wrong) which forms the basis of certain rights and obligations, rights which are possessed by all human beings and obligations which bind all human beings despite myriad differences amongst them. These rights are moral rights and have come to be called 'human rights'.

If the adjective in 'human rights' is to have any significance, the idea of human rights must be the idea that there are certain rights which, whether or not they are recognized, belong to all human beings at all times and in all places. These are the rights which they have solely in virtue of being human, irrespective of nationality, religion, sex, social status, occupation, wealth, property, or any other differentiating ethnic, cultural or social characteristic. Article 2 of the United Nations Declaration of Human Rights appears to support this claim. Human Rights are general (holding for human beings generally), and they are moral rights (not bestowed or given by a legal document or by legal action). The important feature of human rights is that they are entitlements we have independent of our standing in social institutions. Indeed, since social institutions should respect and/or promote human rights, they constitute a test of social institutions. An institution is judged to be adequate or inadequate, good or bad, in terms of its support of human rights. Human rights are moral rights because the arguments made on behalf of them are moral arguments.

Krishna Menon in her paper **Human Rights – A Theoretical Foray** traces the origins and development of the concept of rights to its present day form expressed in the notion to be found in the Universal Declaration of Human Rights. In tracing the development of the idea of rights she discusses the theoretical and practical difficulties involved in admitting rights that are taken to be universal, inviolable and absolute. She points out that there is a conflict between the doctrine of human rights and what nation states claim they need to do to guarantee them keeping in mind their own distinctive culture and religious practices. Above all there is the great difficulty in agreeing upon a common universal profile of human nature and what constitutes 'quality of life'. The basic difficulty with the doctrine of human rights is that it is individualistic and a-historical. Even a constructivist approach fails to answer the question of the contents of human rights. Notwithstanding this difficulty about content, most thinkers are inclined to accept human rights that are universally binding although they differ in the manner in which they claim to apprehend these rights. The author concludes with accepting what she describes as minimal universalism so far as rights are concerned.

The concept of human rights, the moral rights that human beings are said to have by virtue of being human, has its groundings in the Kantian principle of respect for persons. The foundationalistic approach to understanding human rights maintains that there are basic or primary values shared by human beings by virtue of their common humanity. As Amartya Sen observes, 'The notion of human rights builds on our shared humanity' (Sen, 1997: 39). Such rights and the duties they entail would be universally binding even if not universally acceptable. Hence, the important point is not whether such moral values are actually accepted by one and all but that they are binding on one and all. And they are binding in this manner because we share a common humanity. Shashi Motilal in her paper **Moral Relativism and Human Rights** considers the debate between the foundationalists and anti-foundationalists on justifying universal human rights. The former proceed on the assumption that human nature is homogenous. They do not believe that the humanness of human beings is to be sought in and through the differences that are expressed in the forms of varying cultural beliefs and practices. Humanness, whatever that may be, is the basis of human rights, but takes on different forms in differing socio-cultural backgrounds. To consider only the commonalities in abstraction and make it a basis of human rights will be to ignore the multi-cultural and plural dimension of human society. A view that seeks to reconcile Moral Relativism with the demands of moral objectivity and moral universalism is required.

Moral Rights, Obligations and Responsibilities

Philosophers and jurisprudents have commonly suggested various forms of relationships between rights and obligations (or duties) (White: 1984). Rights and obligations differ both in what can be the objects of one or the other and what can be the subjects of one or the other and also in their scope. We have rights and obligations to separate sets of things. We can have an obligation, but not usually a right to persons; and rights, but not usually obligations to things; for having an obligation to someone implies having a duty to do something for him, whereas having a right to something implies having a legitimate/fair/justified claim to its possession. Also, whenever we have an obligation to do something, it makes sense to say that we have a right to it, e.g., when I have an obligation to speak the truth I also have a right to speak it. But, the converse is not true. I can have a right to do something but from that it does not follow that I have an obligation to do it. For example, I can be said to have a right to receive parental guidance, but no duty to do so, in the sense that I may very well decline it. Our duties or obligations are confined to what we can be said to be capable of doing.

The question who is a proper bearer of rights and who can be said to be bound by a moral obligation is extremely important and one that needs to be settled before taking cudgels with philosophers on issues involving rights and obligations. What can have a right and what can have an obligation are in some cases definitely and in some cases contentiously different. Adult human beings can have both rights and obligations. But, whereas it may be, and has been argued, that rights may be possessed by other than adult human beings, whether they are the future generation, human fetuses, animals or objects in nature, it is never suggested that these have obligations of any sort. Most discussions about the kind of things that can possess rights center on the kinds of capacities (either necessary or sufficient, or both) these things have for their possible possession. These range from having interests, rationality, sentience, capability to experience suffering, the ability to claim, etc. Sometimes the criteria (in terms of the above) are too narrow so as to exclude children and the feeble minded and sometimes too wide so as to include inanimate objects, artifacts, abstract conceptions within their fold. In deciding what qualifies as a rights holder, a question that may sensibly be asked is – is it the sort of subject of which it makes sense to use what may be called 'the full language of rights'?

A right can be described as something which can be said to be exercised, earned, enjoyed, given, claimed, demanded, asserted, secured, waived or surrendered. There can be rights of action and rights of recipience. One can also have a right to have a certain feeling or adopt a certain attitude. Further, a right is related to and contrasted with a duty or obligation, a privilege, a power, or a liability. A possible possessor of rights is, therefore, whatever can be properly spoken of in such language. Only a *person* can be the subject of such predications. In other words, rights are not the sorts of things of which non-persons can be the subjects, however right it may be to treat them in certain ways. This criterion will not exclude infants, the feeble minded, the comatose patient or the future generation from having rights. So long as they are persons, i.e., so long as we can speak of them as 'feeble', 'unborn', 'incapable' or even 'dead' persons, they can be said to have rights. It is a matter of unfortunate contingency, not a tautology, that these persons cannot exercise or enjoy, claim or waive their rights, or do their duty or fulfill their obligations. Even the law links the notion of a person and the bearer of rights. The charge of 'speciesism' does not apply here since it is not being contented that it is right to treat one species less considerately than another, but only that one species, that is a person, can sensibly be said to exercise or waive a right, be under an obligation, have a duty, etc., whereas members of the other species cannot, however unable particular members of the former species may be to do so.

The question about the logical relation between rights and obligations can arise either when it is one and the same person's rights and obligations or when it is the right of one person and the obligation of another. In the first case, it is quite clear that there are instances where a person may have both a right to do something as well as an obligation. For example, the judge has both a right and an obligation to direct the jury on certain points. On the other hand, there are examples where a person may enjoy a right without having any obligation, e.g., infants, children, persons with physical and mental disabilities, etc. Philosophers have usually been more interested in the second kind of logical relation, viz., the relation between one person's right and another's obligation since moral dilemmas about rights and obligations generally involve inter personal relationships.

With respect to the right of one and the obligation of another, it is generally held that rights and duties or obligations are correlatives or two sides of the same coin. If rights are claims then, to accord or ascribe a right to an individual implies that someone or something other than that individual has an obligation to uphold or respect that right. This is definitely true of legal rights where the legal right of the right holder is to be respected by others who are also bound by the same law which confers the same legal right to them as well. The law of the state or of any institution is binding on each and every citizen or member of the institution as the case may be. Every one enjoys the benefits of the law because every individual while having a legal claim to something is also obliged to respect the same claim which others belonging to the same state or institution have. So, if X by virtue of being a bonafide member of an institution has a claim to something, then other members of the same institution have an obligation or responsibility to uphold that claim of X. This is true of every member of that institution.

There is, however, no *logical* connection between rights and obligations *per se* such that every right entails a positive duty on the part of someone else to do something. In one sense, however, there is a correlation between a right and an obligation and this is from the point of view of negative duties. If I have a right to something, it is an obligation upon everyone else to refrain from doing anything that would violate that right. Everyone else has an obligation not to prevent me from doing it and not to penalize me or make me suffer for having done it. If I have a right to receive something then there must be someone/something who/which is under an obligation to provide it to me. Conversely, it is wrong for someone to stop that person from meeting his/her obligation to me. But, if it is right both for people to have what they are entitled to and also to meet their obligation, what is the difference between a right and an obligation? A *prima facie* difference is that an obligation may be supervened by another more pressing obligation in which case you must meet the latter. There is no choice about it. But, when you have a right, you have a choice not to exercise it.

Since there is no logical relation between rights and obligations *per se*, there are examples of rights without reciprocal obligations on the part of someone and similarly, there are examples of obligations that do not entail any reciprocal right had by someone. Notwithstanding the fact that there are instances of human relationships where rights and obligations are not reciprocal, it is important to note that the concepts of rights, privileges, responsibilities, obligations, duties, all hold together and not one in isolation from the others. To consider them in isolation is, perhaps, the source of many moral/ philosophical dilemmas.

An excerpt from the proposal on A Universal Declaration of Human Responsibilities put forward by the Inter Action Council in 1997 highlights the importance of considering rights and responsibilities together.

> Although traditionally we have spoken of human rights, and indeed the world has gone a long way in their international recognition and protection

> since the Universal Declaration of Human Rights was adopted by the United Nations in 1948, it is time now to initiate an equally important quest for the acceptance of human duties or obligations.
>
> This emphasis of human obligations is necessary for several reasons. Of course, this idea is new only to some regions of the world; many societies have traditionally conceived of human relations in terms of obligations rather than rights. This is true, in general terms, for instance, for much of Eastern thought. While traditionally in the West, at least since the 17th century age of enlightenment, the concepts of freedom and individuality have been emphasized, in the East, the notions of responsibility and community have prevailed. The fact that a Universal Declaration of Human Rights was drafted instead of a Universal Declaration of Human Duties undoubtedly reflects the philosophical and cultural background of the document drafters who, as is known, represented the Western powers who emerged victorious from the Second World War.
>
> The concept of human obligations also serves to balance the notions of freedom and responsibility: while rights relate more to freedom, obligations are associated with responsibility. Despite this distinction, freedom and responsibility are interdependent. Responsibility, as a moral quality, serves as a natural, voluntary check for freedom. In any society, freedom can never be exercised without limits. Thus, the more freedom we enjoy, the greater the responsibility we bear, toward others as well as ourselves. The more talents we possess, the bigger the responsibility we have to develop them to their fullest capacity. We must move away from the freedom of indifference towards the freedom of involvement.[2]

The Preamble of the Universal Declaration of Human Responsibilities expresses that an exclusive insistence on rights can result in conflict, indecision and endless dispute, neglect of human responsibilities with a possible outcome of lawlessness and chaos. Rights and responsibilities are to be treated as two sides of the same coin. If exercising of a right is an expression of freedom, a freedom to a claim of a sort, then this freedom must come with its share of responsibilities too. In other words, we need to exercise our freedom "sensibly", and "sensitively". It is only when rights are tempered with responsibilities that we can be said to truly have a right to something. The 19 articles of the UN Declaration of Human Responsibilities manifest a deep and rich progression of legal thought treating rights and responsibilities as complementary to each other.

Moral Responsibility, unlike causal and legal responsibility, is not an easy concept to comprehend. Ascribing moral responsibility becomes more difficult when collective action is involved. Pratap Bhanu Mehta, in his paper

Complicity and Responsibility, discusses the intricacies of attributing individual responsibility to a person based purely on the causal relation between him/her as an agent and the act he/she causes. To do so amounts to identifying a trivial element in the context of guilt and moral wrong doing, and this is supported by the phenomenon of counterfactual guilt, from which people suffer occasionally. How should we then hold individuals responsible in contexts where the outcomes are products of a large number of actions undertaken by other people? Ascribing 'collective responsibility' really amounts to saying that no one is responsible and this, in a sense, does not nullify the question of individual responsibility.

Taking a series of examples, Mehta shows that an individual may become responsible in many ways going beyond direct causal responsibility. All these ways point to an expanded notion of responsibility, which, in his view makes responsibility a 'political' concept. According to him, questions of responsibility turn not simply upon our conception of the person, but upon our relations to others, which are determined by the fair terms of interaction between the concerned parties. To consider only the person, his actual involvement, his intentions and inclinations, tends to sever the link between responsibility and our interpersonal relations in terms of what we owe others. Allocation of responsibility centres on issues of distributive justice and is not merely a matter of figuring out the relation between agents and the consequences of their acts. Mehta's notion of responsibility draws heavily upon the distinction between act and omission or 'positive' and 'negative' conceptions of duty. Failing to do the right thing in a given situation is on a par with wilfully doing the wrong thing. Therefore, complicity also amounts to responsibility.

Dharma as Moral Obligation or Righteousness

When we turn to the Indian context, particularly to the ethical philosophies of ancient India and look for a concept corresponding to the western notion of 'rights' or 'human rights' we are faced with a peculiar situation. There is no term in Sanskrit that is perfectly cognate with the term 'right' as a 'natural/ moral entitlement'. Most thinkers who have dealt with the question of human rights in the context of ancient Indian Philosophy will readily agree that there is no notion of 'human rights' to be found there. It appears that in the traditional Indian context, one cannot speak of rights without giving priority to duty. Austin Creel cites B.N. Chobe saying that there is no Sanskrit word that means rights and goes on to remark, 'Rights are present in the system, but as the obverse of duties, the reciprocal duties of groups and individuals to each other, and never in any sense separated in status. To the extent that one not only owed duties to another but was owed duties by others, rights are bound up with duties, any duty involving a corresponding right or claim.' (Creel, 1997: 19)

'Adhikāra': A Right in Classical Indian Philosophy?

At this juncture, it is interesting to note an attempt made by a scholar to read a rights discourse onto a certain interpretation given of the term '*adhikāra*' which occurs in a verse in the Mīmāmsā texts of Jaimini. In the popular vernacular usage, the term has stood for what are called rights. Taking the term '*adhikāra*', which occurs in certain Mīmāmsā texts, Purushottama Bilimoria explains how the term can be construed, through a series of derivations as coming closest to our current use of the term 'rights'. (Bilimoria, 1993) According to Bilimoria, the term '*adhikāra*' as used by Jaimini of the Purva Mīmāmsā School specifies the eligibility criteria for being a proper subject of the *vidhi* or injunctions regarding sacrificial performances. There are four major criteria that are mentioned. These are *ārthītva, sāmarthya, agniman* and *vidvan.*[3] Detailed specifications and requirements of the fourth criterion, however, restrict these entitlements to only one class of people, viz., the Brahmins. In a similar vein the Mīmāmsāka understands a text in the *Mahābhārata*, '*śrāvayet caturo varṇan*', as stating that the four castes[4] have the '*adhikāra*' to acquire knowledge of the *smrti* scriptures (*Itihāsa and Purānas*). This is reiterated in Samkara Vedanta too (*śrāvayet caturo varṇan iti ca itihāsapurāṇadhigame cāturvarṇasya adhikārasmaraṇat*). This offers concessional entitlements to the non-'twice-born' (non-brahmins) in respect of performing rituals derived from non-vedic injunctions.

It is quite evident that the *adhikāra*s spoken of in these texts are at best social or conventional rights as they are based on social stratification. They are not rights in the sense of 'natural' claims or moral entitlements. Bilimoria makes an interesting remark about one occurrence of the term '*adhikāra*' in the *Gītā*. According to him, the term '*adhikāra*' as it occurs in the verse "*Karmanyevādhikāraraste māphaleṣu kadācana*" (11.47) is best understood when the verse is translated to mean 'You have entitlement indeed to actions, never though to the results.' Arjuna here is being told that, since he is a *kṣatriya* (soldier) his *adhikāra* is only to the act performed by a soldier, not to the consequences which may or may not follow. Further he is also being told that he has no *adhikāra* to desist from the action that is incumbent on him as a *kṣatriya*. Bilimoria remarks: 'While it may appear that the *Gītā* is confusing the locution of duties with that of rights (understood as entitlements, let us concede), the move is deliberate, because the author(s) here is attempting to introduce the idea of 'negative rights', which effectively states that no one, including oneself, can rightfully interfere with what is one's due or desert by virtue of the law (of *dharma*)... It is almost as though to say that the *Gītā* was tempted to speak of the 'right to duty' (just as we speak of the right to employment).' (Bilimoria, 1993: 43) Bilimoria's suggestion is that the *Gītā* seeks to apply the notion of *adhikāra* beyond the Mīmāmsā framework of sacrificial and religious rites to the wider context of social dharma but does not go beyond that for then it would have to accept the idea that all persons are born equal and that there are no 'natural' differences among human beings which translate into social differentiations. This, perhaps, it was hard for the author(s) of the *Gītā* to accept considering the overbearing weight of the *varṇāsramadharma*. In conclusion, Bilimoria says, 'Thus the response of the *Gītā* is restrained and calculated; it merely suggests the possibility of a discourse of universal human rights (*mānavasarvadhikāra*) but does not develop it.' (Bilimoria, 1993: 44)

As mentioned earlier, there is no word in Sanskrit or even Pali which conveys the idea of a 'right' understood as a subjective entitlement. Does this mean that the concept of 'rights' is alien to Indian Philosophy? Alan Gewirth has pointed out that cultures/traditions may possess the concept of rights without having a specific vocabulary for it. He says it is 'important to distinguish between having or using a concept and the clear or explicit recognition and elucidation of it ... Thus persons might have and use the concept of a right without explicitly having a single word for it.'[5] This is, perhaps, true of the Indian context. In the Indian context, the concept of *dharma* does 'double duty' for the concept of rights and obligations. *Dharma* determines what is right and just in all contexts. It determines what is 'due' in any situation. It tells us not merely 'what one is due to do' but also 'what is due to one'. This reciprocal sense of obligation ensures that justice is met.

Thus, when A performs his 'dharmic' duty, B receives what is 'due' to him or that to which he is 'entitled' in and through *dharma*. The duty of one corresponds to the entitlement of the other. If the husband has a duty or obligation to support his wife, the wife has a 'right' to seek support from her husband. If the wife has a duty/obligation to look after her husband's property, the husband has a 'right' to safe keeping of his property by his wife. Similarly, the king has a duty (*dharma*) to look after the subjects (citizens) and they have a 'right' to be looked after by the king. The king has a 'right' to collect taxes and the citizens have an obligation to pay it.

Thus, under *dharma*, human relationships are entrenched in bonds of reciprocal obligations that can be analyzed into rights and obligations. However, it must be noted that in the Indian context, *dharma*, the moral guiding principle, delineates these bindings only in terms of obligations, not rights. It states what is due in the form, 'A husband should support his wife' rather than 'A wife has a right to be maintained by her husband'. So, in a sense, rights are not recognized as discrete 'dues' under *dharma*. A right is a useful concept that provides a particular perspective on justice. Its correlative obligation provides another. Both may be considered as windows onto the common good, which is justice.

It is widely acknowledged by most scholars of Indian philosophy that philosophy in India was a way of life rather than an isolated intellectual enterprise. Most scholars also acknowledge that Indian philosophy has been duty-centric rather than rights-centric, that the emphasis has always remained on duty than on rights. The welfare of the group, whether it be, the family or community or any larger group, was always placed higher than that of the individual. And this obligated the individual to perform actions that were conducive to the growth and welfare of the group. It was held that the individual's moral and spiritual progress could only be achieved in and through actions that are in accordance with the larger social and moral order of the cosmos and the principle governing that order was a form of *Dharma*. The concept of *Dharma* has been translated in many ways to mean Moral Obligation or Duty, Righteousness, Justice, etc. It is believed that this multi faceted concept has determined the moral, cultural and spiritual life of India ever since the Vedic period and continues to do so even now.

In his paper ***Dharma*: The Overriding Principle of Indian Life and Thought** S. R. Bhatt shows how the concept of *Dharma* forms the foundation of moral philosophy in India from Vedic times to the present day. He writes that the concept of *Dharma* has its genesis in the Vedic intuition of '*ṛta*' from which it has flown into and permeated every form and facet of Indian life. *Ṛta* conceptualizes the vision of the Vedic seers of an inexorable, unswerving and pervasive order prevailing in the Reality and the cosmos. The Vedic seers apprehended an immanent teleology in the Reality and 'telosembeddedness' in the cosmic process. In Bhatt's view the concept of *Ṛta* and *Dharma* are cognates and so in time they got conflated and the word *Dharma* got currency and popular acceptance. It retained the full meaning of the word *Ṛta* and also acquired new and additional meanings.

Shashi Prabha Kumar discusses the notion of *Dharma* as the moral foundation of the social order as it is given in the *Vaiśeṣikasūtra* of Kaṇāda in her paper **Moral Foundations of Social Order as Suggested in the *Vaiśeṣikasūtras***. She maintains that despite differences in their metaphysics, the Indian philosophical systems, except the materialist *Cārvākas*, are unified in their views about morality. For all, the highest aim of life is liberation from the material world, which is achieved by realizing the true nature of the self. All the systems maintain that human being is a manifestation of a deeper central reality and at the root of this is a cosmic moral principle that is *Dharma*. *Dharma* serves the dual function of facilitating one's own well being as well as the well being of others, the former being the spiritual development of man towards self realization or *nihśreyas*, and the latter being worldly progress or *abhyudaya*. Shashi Prabha Kumar points out that though many thinkers are of the view that there is a basic opposition between *moksa dharma* and moral and social *dharmas* because the former repudiates the moral and social aspects of human existence, this is not so in the Vaiśeşika system, and this is a point to be appreciated. Kaṇāda deals with the moral values concerned with social harmony first and later on with those that lead a person to *nihśreyas*, his individual spiritual progress.

Saral Jhingran in her paper **Modern Western Conception of Justice as Equality before the Law and *Dharmaśāstras*** is of the view that the *varṇa vyavasthā* accepted in ancient India was based on birth and hereditary professions and not on psychological inclinations and voluntary professions as is claimed by some thinkers. Beginning with the notion of justice which incorporates the idea of equality before the law, Jhingran argues that in one interpretation of *Dharma* where it is taken to mean justice, (the concept as is found in the *Dharmaśāstras*, the Hindu law books of collective duties of human beings), it does not admit of the idea of being equal before the law. According to Jhingran, the notion of *Dharma* in the *Dharmaśā*stras is far from the Modern western conception of justice, which incorporates within it the idea of being equal before the law. Even if equality is understood in a limited sense, which she elaborates in her paper, such a limited notion cannot be admitted in the *Dharmaśāstras*, since the *varṇa* of a person is based on the contingent factor of birth.

There have been scholars who have maintained that although the *varṇavyavasthā* eventually degenerated into the much despised caste system, in itself it was a classification determined not by birth but by psychological inclination and the profession voluntarily adopted by an individual. All orthodox systems of Indian philosophy, the *Vedās* and the *Upaniśads* as well as the *Bhagvadgītā* unequivocally accepted the *varṇāsramadharmas* or socio-individual duties as necessary and indispensable for the ethico-spiritual development of individuals and society. In the Bhagvadgītā, Krishna, having attained true knowledge of *Brahman*, says:

> *Cāturvarṇya mayā sṛiṣṭam guṇakarmavibhāgaśah* (*Bhagvadgītā*, IV, 13)

That is, 'The four divisions of society have been created by me on the basis of inclination and profession'. It is evident from this statement and other statements disclaiming the spiritual difference between the high caste Brāhmana and the low caste Caṇḍāla that until the time of the *Bhagvadgītā* there was no rigidity in the caste system and the classification was based not on birth, but on the voluntary profession or occupation. Once a person had adopted a particular profession it was necessary for him/her to adhere to the duty enjoined upon that profession even at the cost of his/her life rather than change professional duty. This is expressed in the following

Svadharme ninhanam śreyad, paradharmo bhayāvahah (*Bhagvadgītā*, III, 35)

Along with the four fold stages in life, the *varṇaāsramadharma* offered complete guide to right conduct. Deviation from dharma was regarded as immoral or wrong conduct. But it must be noted that the concept of dharma incorporates both empirical and spiritual duties and each is given equal worth. It would be wrong to overlook the instrumental value of social and professional duties, as it would be to neglect spiritual duties (complete self surrender to God). The *Bhagvadgītā* throughout emphasizes the importance of performing one's duty or moral obligation and provides guidance to resolve conflict of duties.

The social context in which the dictates of dharma prevailed in ancient India was a context based on the hierarchical structure of *varṇa* and the *dharma* to be followed was appropriately called *varṇāsramadharma*. In this structure of categories, the lowest caste, that of the *śudras*, did not enjoy any privileges. They had no claims but only obligations to fulfill. Can it be maintained that the obligations of the upper castes (the Brahmins, the *kşatriyas* and the *vaiśyas*) towards the *śudras* took care of the 'rights' of the latter? It is difficult to comprehend how that could happen, except on one assumption. The assumption being that the principle of *Dharma* worked in tandem with the retributive principle of Karma. The *śudra* by virtue of being a *śudra* was entitled to only that much or nothing at all. And, to the question why a *śudra* should be born a *śudra* the answer was because of his past karmas. The doctrine of Karma as the retributive principle of justice is appealed to which along with the principle of *Dharma* bestows only those privileges that are due to one. In other words, even if the *non-śudras* tried to bestow more on the *śudras*, they could not have done so because that would have gone against the Law of Karma. In such a society, justice could not possibly mean 'equal in the eyes of the law', for the law of Karma required that every body bear the fruits (good or bad) of their karma (deeds). So, it is bound to be the case that some people would suffer on account of not having any rights or only minimal rights, but in each case they would be receiving what is rightly due to them. So, one may argue that even in ancient Indian society where the *varṇavyavasthā* prevailed, people did have rights although it appeared that some did not have them at all.

In due course of time, this justification of the non-egalitarian distribution of rights and privileges came to be rejected by modern 'rights based societies'. One's position in society was no longer seen as the appropriate basis for the distribution of rights and privileges. Comparing traditional non-western contexts with contemporary rights–based systems Uma Narayan observes that 'the contrast lies in the greater distribution of a great number of legal claims, powers, liberties, and so forth across the individuals who comprise the subjects of a contemporary "western" legal system. In many "traditional" systems, both "western" and "nonwestern", a few individuals had a great many legal powers, immunities, liberties and claims, while the rest primarily "enjoyed" no-claims, duties, disabilities and liabilities!' (Narayan, 1993: 189) She further remarks that the 'highly unequal distributions of Hohfeldian advantages within these systems was grounded in the rationale that such a distribution was the one most conducive to the ideal of "social harmony". Thus, while the ideal of "social harmony" did not function so as to invalidate all rights claims in such a context, it might very well have functioned to normatively de-legitimize demands for more egalitarian distributions of rights within that context on the grounds that any significant change in the existing distribution of Hohfeldian advantages would be destructive of "social harmony"'. (Narayan, 1993: 191)

The question is whether the stake of preserving 'social harmony' is so important that it justifies unequal distribution of rights and privileges. The answer to this question can, perhaps, be found in the following thoughts. Even in a society without social hierarchies, natural differences among people resulting in benefits to some and disadvantages to others will have to be explained. One way of explaining these differences is by taking recourse to the Law of Karma as a retributive principle of justice. This helps maintain the 'natural harmony' in the world. Perhaps, the same explanation can be adduced to explain the in-egalitarian distribution of rights and claims, now for the sake of 'social harmony'. What is more important and incumbent on all is that we recognize our responsibilities and obligations to one another which will ensure that 'rights' of individuals are not flouted, although it will not ensure that there will be no inequalities that will bring advantages to some and deprivations to others.

II

Part I of the book takes us through a conceptual analysis of some fundamental concepts of ethics. An understanding of these concepts is crucial, rather a necessary prerequisite, for any ethical enterprise, particularly, the applying of ethical principles to provide solutions to morally perplexing problems in real life situations. The moral philosopher not only needs to be clear about ethical concepts, she also needs to know what exactly she is aiming to do in applying ethics, to what extent her purpose can be fulfilled and how. She must also be prepared to encounter challenges put forward to her by the moral skeptic and the moral relativist.

Most moral dilemmas involving interpersonal relationships are at the root conflicts of rights and obligations in some form or the other. In majority of cases the problem arises due to a flagrant violation of some human right or conversely, the non-fulfillment of some moral obligation. As we saw between persons of equal moral standing, there can be no rights without obligations and therefore if one person's rights are being violated, then, there is some other person who is not fulfilling her obligation towards that individual. But, moral perplexities abound in such contexts also, where one individual has a moral obligation to fulfill towards another who/which does not have a moral right in any clear sense (the unborn, the future generation, animals, nature, etc.). The converse may also invite moral speculation; the cases where the fetus, the future generation and animals are said to have rights (in some sense) but human beings because of their superior position have no obligations towards them. Part II contains papers that discuss moral issues that arise when there is a conflict between rights people enjoy and obligations that bind them. Rights belong to people and people fall into groups, sometimes naturally (by way of biological differences, spatial-temporal differences or differences due to traits contingently possessed by them) and sometimes not so naturally (by way of social differences e.g., caste or racial differences). The papers dealing with issues pertaining to human rights belonging to these groups of individuals have been classified separately. The underlying idea, however, remains that of rights and obligations. The first set of papers concern rights of minority groups or the 'marginalized' sections of society.

Rakesh Chandra in his paper **Fragile Identities and Constructed Rights** raises interesting questions that place the problem of the identity of the minorities in a context that relates it to the discourse of ethics and to the discourse of philosophy of language. The question he addresses is – how do twentieth century discourses in philosophy of language and discourses in moral philosophy interface with the twentieth century struggle for identity that marks the movement of the socially marginalized? His query is that if one accepts Nussbaum's capability theory as the basis of human rights then why, if capabilities are same, two individuals cannot, or rather, do not as a matter of fact, belong to the same group despite their different social identities? He maintains that it is how we understand basic humanness that will determine whether a particular use of a certain referring expression ('dalit', 'gay', 'lesbian', Marxist') identifies the person as human being *per se* (the Kripkean use of rigid designation or Donellan's referential use of description) or *the human being as belonging to a certain group, clan* etc. (non-rigid designation or Donellan's attributive use of descriptions). According to Rakesh Chandra it is because of their universalism that branches of philosophy (philosophy of language, epistemology and metaphysics) have not concerned themselves with questions pertaining to conflicts of personhood and identity among particular groups. But such universalism cannot afford to be exclusionary. Rakesh Chandra's attempt at understanding the problem of fractured identities is an attempt in this direction.

Another paper grappling with the issues of identities is **Ethics, Human Rights and the LGBT Discourse in India** by Ashley Tellis. The paper is an examination of the history and development of the Same-Sex Movement in India. The area it traverses spans from the Indian Women's Movement Studies/Women's Studies diluted and hesitant efforts to address the issue to the donor-driven NGO initiatives. Tellis's analysis wrestles with complex social realities taking into account the influence of class, individual and group identities as well as the shifting and heterogeneous character of the state itself. Through a series of compelling arguments, each centered round either the Indian Women's Movement's efforts or the NGO initiatives, this paper demonstrates the present inadequacy of their commitment to same-sex rights by exposing the contradictory position of the parties to the issue of same-sex relationships. It is a powerful critique of the addressing of the issue by the Indian Women's Movement/Women's Studies and the NGO initiatives. In the opinion of Tellis, Indian feminism has simply jumped over the knotty problem of how to conceptualize sexuality. According to him, the internationalization and globalization of gay/lesbian/transgender/queer identities, is closely tied to economic and market processes and by buying into the global speak of LGBT discourse we are unable to recuperate the richer and more complicated understandings of same-sex relations and their trajectories in India.

Tellis unfolds a two-pronged argument: (a) the language of rights and citizenship advanced by feminist politics in India cannot be unproblematically available to the same-sex rights movement since it continues to sustain 'woman' as a category of analysis; (b) the 'politics of funding' leaves the NGO's with very little scope to do justice to the issue. The paper concludes by emphasizing the issue of human rights and ethics in this case. In order to ensure the application of a human rights and ethics based approach to the same-sex rights movement, the author suggests the creation of a democratic, emancipatory space where there is dialoguing between people, keeping in mind the intersectionality of class, caste, ethnicity, religion, gender and sexuality. This continuous and sustained dialoguing can lead to a dynamic, vibrant and energised same-sex rights movement in India.

When it comes to the marginalized sections of society, an intriguing problem triggering an ongoing debate among moral philosophers relates to the rights of the 'discriminated against'. 'Affirmative action' or 'preferential treatment' seems to go against the very egalitarian spirit underlying the Universal Declaration of Human Rights and yet there has been support for it amongst moral philosophers who have argued that it is a form of 'compensation' for those whose rights were initially violated by society. 'Is affirmative action a form of compensation, or another form of discrimination' is the question taken up by Madhucchanda Sen in her paper **Affirmative Action: Compensation or Discrimination?** Do discriminated social groups have a right to compensation? Do affirmative action policies provide compensation to those who truly deserve compensation? Does reverse discrimination violate the right of an applicant to equal consideration and equal opportunity? Can reverse discrimination be justified as an unwanted consequence of a benign act/policy. Madhucchanda Sen takes up these questions while critically appraising the arguments and counterarguments in the debate. In her opinion one cannot say that affirmative action policies are all morally right or wrong. Several factors including the political history of the society where such policies are being adopted have to be taken into consideration. She also thinks that one should not ignore the fact that beneficiaries of affirmative action policies feel thwarted when due credit is not given to their own efforts in their achievements, everything being attributed to desert from such policies.

Affirmative action policies and the resulting reverse discrimination are often seen to be a part of the program of retributive justice against injustices done to certain groups/sections of society where the grouping was determined by birth and ideologically based social constructs. At the same time affirmative action is a move in the direction of achieving distributive justice that to a large extent is a State affair and is intended to enhance upward mobility of a group, tribe, caste or community. Despite the reasonableness of its aims, distributive justice has its own merits and demerits in its practical application and fulfilment. Bhagat Oinam in his paper **Distributive Justice: Locating in Context** highlights some of these merits and demerits while also pointing to an inconsistency in the very concept of distributive justice. Oinam, takes off from Dworkin's formulation of distributive justice which includes 'equality of welfare' and 'equality of resources', and considering the Indian context, adds a third factor which is 'equality of opportunity'. He contends that though distinguishable, the three are not separable, inasmuch, as the first cannot be achieved without the second and the third. Here much depends on who is given the priority – the individual or the group to which he belongs though only contingently. In other words, it is only when an individual has free access/opportunity over resources in and around her that she can utilize these for the enhancement of her welfare. Not withstanding the variable differences in individuals (including state of mind, needs and capabilities) basic infra structure facilities should be made available to every citizen of the State. The dual standards of the State in accepting the inalienability of private property rights on the one hand, yet promoting group-centric programs will not help fulfilling the aims of distributive justice. There is no justification in counting *individual* political participation of citizens in the existence of adult franchise and disregarding the individual when chalking out programs of welfare. Plurality, in the opinion of the author, should not stop short at the group but percolate down to the level of the individuals. The question to consider, which Oinam admittedly avoids, is the relation between retributive justice and distributive justice and whether they should be seen as two sides of the same coin. In the debate on affirmative action the two must be seen as the same thing. It is only when group centered affirmative action programs are seen as retribution that they can make any sense and there can be some justification of the resulting 'reverse discrimination'.

But, does 'reverse discrimination' really need to be justified? In the first place, is it discrimination of any kind to exclude from consideration some one who fails to meet the requirements of a certain institution or program, the institution having a legitimate right to set its requirements as per its aims, motives and needs? Many thinkers do not believe so. Discrimination in its negative sense becomes intelligible only in a certain context, the context where 'discrimination' (i.e., reverse discrimination) is regarded as a form of punishment. And yet, many people do think that being excluded as a result of Affirmative Action Policies of the government, amounts to punishment; that they are being 'punished' for no fault of theirs. Punishment in any form is legitimate only when given to an offender. In what sense are those who are (reversely) discriminated against, offenders? Punishment presupposes responsibility for the offence. Therefore, the question is – in what sense can we hold them (the reversely discriminated) 'responsible' thereby justifying 'reverse discrimination? Can reverse discrimination be justified on the expanded notion of responsibility where it includes complicity as suggested by Mehta in his paper? Even on this understanding of responsibility, it would be odd to hold the present generation responsible for the deeds, rather 'misdeeds', of their ancestors in causing the initial acts of discrimination that now call for compensation.

Retributive punishment requires at least the identity of the offender and the punished, even if time and space conditions are not adhered to, as in the case of explanations of suffering given on the basis of past 'karma' by the doctrine of Karma in some systems of Indian philosophy. Also, it is important that if punishment is to reform the offender, he/she must know the offence he/she has committed. This also does not square well with reverse discrimination as a form of retributive justice. Moreover, if a particular group (caste, or tribe) has suffered in the past, no one individual has suffered on account of any one individual. People belonging to one group have suffered because of unjust social practices adopted by people belonging to another, supposedly 'higher' group. It is difficult to attribute collective responsibility and punishment, since the notion of collective responsibility is very complicated and not very clear. There is also the point of view of the moral relativist who would not regard the initial act to be wrong in the first place. The subscriber of Moral Relativism need not regard the deprivation of equal opportunities suffered by the lower castes to be wrong, since that was accepted by the then society. If the initial suffering is not considered wrong, no question of compensation need arise. It therefore seems that because reverse discrimination cannot be regarded as a form of retributive punishment it is not wrong.

In the context of punishment the rights of the punished raises interesting moral issues. Does a person committing a moral offence have any claim to human rights that are by nature moral rights? Ruplekha Khullar in her paper **Punishment and Human Rights** takes up the question of how punishment impacts the issue of human rights. According to her, no punishment can claim legitimacy unless it adheres to the inviolability of the human person and is bound by the spirit of the Preamble to the Universal Declaration of Human Rights that emphasizes the inherent dignity of human beings for freedom, justice and peace in the world. The blatant violation of human dignity and growing awareness of human rights issues brought about a shift from corporal torture as a form of retribution to more 'humane' forms of retributive punishment. For the same reasons, excess punishment for stronger deterrence gave way to moderation and economy. However, it is reformation that provides the most spirited defense of human rights because it is based on the firm belief in the inherent dignity and worth of human life.

If rationality distinguishes human beings from other sentient beings (as is traditionally presupposed) and thereby is responsible for human worth and dignity, which in turn are the necessary and sufficient conditions for human rights, what happens to the rights of the mentally ill/ distressed, of people who are labeled as 'mad'? Can they be said to have any rights at all? Ranjita Biswas and Anup Dhar in their paper **Rights of the 'Mad' in Mental Health Sciences** address this all important question relevant to a large section of society. What does one mean by the rights of the mentally ill/distressed? Is it the right to informed consent? Does the very fact of mental illness/distress preclude/ foreclose the possibility of 'informed consent'? Would 'informed consent' also mean 'consent to restriction of movement', consent to the limitation of the freedom of the very person who gives the consent? Can the mentally ill be truly informed and be in a position to give consent? In the paper, the authors take up theoretical critiques that have come up against mental health science – both at the level of 'institutional operations' as well as at the level of 'epistemology' and try to understand the notion of insanity. According to them, the positing of one-way causal processes of 'labeling' both in dominant psychiatry and in anti-psychiatry does not offer any agency to those labeled 'mad'. The biology *vs* society logic remains central to most debates surrounding the origins and phenomenology of mental illness. The authors believe that attempts at placing 'mental illness' within the realm of history, culture and politics and tracing the multidimensional relationship between 'knowledge', 'structural oppression' and the 'phenomenological being' could perhaps make possible a dialogue with mental illness (a dialogue that was broken off in the classical age by the Cartesian interdiction) and an engagement with the constructed complexity of human suffering. The authors look at both mainstream (the discourse of rights) and non-mainstream (ethical relation with unreason as the other of the Knowing Other) efforts to open a dialogue with Unreason.

From the realm of unreason we turn to the realm of potential reason – the realm of individuals who have the potential to reason – the human foetus. Does it have a right, not a potential right, but an actual right to life – the most basic right? Anirban Das in his paper **Choice, Life and the (m)Other: Towards Ethics in/of Abortion** tackles this all important question which has vexed philosophers engaged in the pro choice – pro life debate for decades. Taking into account the techno-scientific practices and instruments that shape the definitions of both, the foetus and the mother, and their relationships, Das goes on to ask how do relations of gender, race or economy take part in the process of formulating positions in the debate. He, however, maintains that a critical look into the terms and metaphors at work in the formulation of the matter in legal, medical, and philosophical texts, as also multiple intricacies of the situation, makes it difficult, if not impossible to comment on the desirability of a 'stance' with regard to the problem – a veritable 'aporia' in the Derridean sense. The question of an ethico-politics of a 'responsibility to the other' complicates the problem even more. A feminist position, sensitive to the predicament of the 'woman' in the gendered and (class, caste or ethnicity) divided society, can hardly afford to remain deaf to the 'call of the wholly other', to the other within her body. The paper tries to work out certain tentative ways to approach the violent impasse for the woman and the social institutions. Falteringly, it tries to whisper some conjectures to 'face' the foetus in a world made by nature and the nurturing and violating acts of science, technology and the (wo)man.

From considering issues related to rights of people who are living on the 'fringe' of society as it were, we turn to the rights of another section of society, the rights of women, a section of society that has not exactly been in the margins but nevertheless has remained deprived of its rightful space. Undoubtedly, the right to be able to live one's life with dignity, free from domination and violence, with full respect for autonomy, is a human right that women all over should be able to enjoy. To this, perhaps, one can add the right not to be 'idolized', a right, the lack of which has been the cause of many afflictions of the Indian woman particularly in ancient and modern Indian society.

How the 'deification' of a woman is in violation of her rights is the subject of the paper by Rekha Basu. In her paper **The Nationalist Project and the Women's Question: A Reading of *The Home and the World* and *Nationalism*** the author takes up some issues of women's rights in the very specific context of the *Swadeshi* movement in India as it is represented in Rabindranath Tagore's novel *The Home and the World* and four essays published under the rubric Nationalism. The author of the paper analyzes the character of the protagonist of the novel Bimala who has been portrayed as a site for two warring masculinities – Nikhilesh, her husband's gently persuasive humanism and Sandip's ultra chauvinistic form of nationalism. Basu sees Sandip's ostensive elevation of Bimala into the essential woman in the novel as a violation of her rights as a person. Her subjectivity, her autonomy is superseded by a grand image of her person as representative of Indian Womanhood. In Basu's opinion both Tagore's Nationalism and *The Home and the World* are anti-people in the sense that they are not sensitive to questions of caste, minority and gender. The nobility of the goal in each case failed to pay attention to the means employed and that was the reason why the projects misfired.

A morally perplexing issue in this context concerns the rights of the future generation, a class of people who do not exist when they are talked about. The issue is interesting because if we can talk about the future generation, we can talk about its needs, its expectations and perhaps, its rights. But, the matter is not so easy when it comes to the question of rights. For, rights as we saw imply obligations. So, if, in any strained sense, the future generation can be said to have rights then we are under an obligation towards it. Nirmalaya Narayan Chakraborty's paper **On the Idea of Obligation to Future Generations** calls into question this very idea throwing us back into the debate whether every right entails an obligation and *vice versa*. In fact, it takes us beyond the debate to consider the question whether not fulfilling this 'obligation' would amount to an immoral act on the part of an individual. This question is important because it impacts many policy decisions that affect people in the future, e.g., what should be our relation towards our environment and natural resources? Should we plunder, or preserve nature for the future generation? The author argues that though there may be other reasons why we, who technically are responsible for the existence of the future generation, may feel inclined to fulfil this causal responsibility, there cannot be any moral obligation to do the same.

According to Chakravarty, an obligation is always to some one, here the future generation. But by definition the future generation does not exist. So, it is only in a vacuous sense that we can talk of an obligation to it. Can we absolve ourselves of the responsibility of the welfare of that which presently does not exist, but for whose existence we are causally responsible? In a sense, since my own existence in the future is by definition presently non-existent can I say that I do not have a moral obligation to myself e.g., to keep myself safe as far as I can? If we denounce our moral obligation towards the future generation then we must also denounce any moral obligation we have towards our future selves. In that case, all programs that aim to preserve and conserve nature for our own future use and that of the future generation will become futile.

From papers addressing problems and issues relating to certain groups of individuals as rights holders, we turn to a set of papers addressing the question how the conflicts amongst some basic human rights and obligations influence our individual, collective and global lives. The first paper in this group discusses the sensitive issue of the 'right to survive' which sometimes hinges on violating or infringing upon the very same right enjoyed by another individual. Taking up one such instance, Anup Dhar in his paper **Violence – A Right to the Survival of the Self?** raises the question whether this conflict can be solved from within the rights paradigm or whether one needs to move beyond rights to seek an ethics of survival where the desire of the 'self' to survive 'neither devours nor annihilates the other'. The author discusses the views of those who believe that survival is inherently violent – something that impinges on the survival of the other. It is in the very nature of the 'genes' to survive anyhow and therefore, the theory of the survival of the fittest. This idea affects us in the way we organize our lives, creating subjectivities of structures and layers of identity as we go along. An ethics of survival must transcend such pettiness of ideas to enter into the world of peaceful co-existence.

From violence as a 'right' to survival we can turn to violence, which becomes part of a duty – the duty to fight injustice – what is called *dharmayuddha* or *dharmārtha yuddha* (war for the sake of restoring justice). Here not only is there a right to use violent means for a justified cause, there is a moral obligation to do so, albeit contentiously. Contentiously because it is not altogether clear that the obligation is moral in nature. In ancient Indian society, where the class system (*varna vyavasthā*) prevailed, it was the *kṣatriya* *dharma* to fight against injustice. But this may be regarded merely as a 'social duty' with no moral bindings attached. Just as it was the 'occupational duty' of the Brahmin to study the scriptures and impart knowledge, so, it was the 'occupational duty' of the *kṣatriya* to fight for justice. In her paper **'Moral Obligation' to Fight for the Prevention of Greater Calamity: A Debate Between *Sādhārana Dharma* and *Sva Dharma*** Malabika Majumdar traces the meaning of the qualifying term 'dharma' in '*dharmayuddha*' in three different contexts: the context of the Bhagvadgītā, the context of the writings of nineteenth-century

Renaissance thinkers of Bengal and the context of the Gandhian resurrection of the *ahimsā dharma*. According to her, the term lacks uniformity of meaning and application because its link with the conservative meaning of the term '*dharma*' as found in the *Śruti* and *Dharmaśāstras* is not very clear. Both sets of texts formulate rules of *dharma* that have served as quasi-legal rules governing the kinship behaviour till as late as the eighteenth century. Taking a close look at the debate between the notions of *Sva dharma* and that of *Sādhārana dharma*, the author concludes that in all the three contexts there seems to be no conflict between the two, that in some special contexts it becomes part of the duty (moral obligation) of the individual to fight for the prevention of a greater calamity.

Another instance of a conflict of rights is that of the conflict between the right to freedom of information and the right to intellectual property. A context in which this conflict is glaring is the context of Cyberspace or the Internet. The moral issues defining this conflict have been addressed by Maushumi Guha and Amita Chatterjee in their paper **Morality in Cyberspace: Intellectual Property and the Right to Information.** Against the backdrop of a two-fold distinction drawn between rights and goods, the authors argue against the right to profit from intellectual goods which in their opinion is a commodity right. According to them, the creator of intellectual goods has only a moral right over his/her creation, meaning he/she can only lay a claim to be appropriately acknowledged. It would be immoral for the creator or any other 'middle man' to make profit from that intellectual good.

Just as a conflict of rights impacts the life of an individual (my right to life being the reason of another's death) or a collective (the collective of internet users), it also impacts life 'globally'. R. P. Singh in his paper **Globalisation and Human Rights** tries to reassess the realm of human rights in the wake of globalization. His contention is that 'globalization' which has affected human life in multiple ways has also given rise to a dilemma. On the one hand it creates obstructions to the progress of human rights and on the other hand it enhances sensitivity towards their practice. The author feels that globalization of technology, trade and commerce and the optimization of these factors will not be of much help unless we revitalize local identities. At the same time he admits that globalization provides avenues to enhance people's sensitivity to local identities. According to Singh, globalization hinders the rightful expression of human rights at two levels – at the top (where powerful nations are placed) and at the bottom (where the weaker nations are placed). As far as India is concerned, the author feels that there is a need to expose our selves to our own cultural traditions in the context of India's all round development in the global market. He rejects the idea that the State has withered and feels that it is the responsibility of the State to come forward and provide a framework where without marginalizing local identities, the reward of globalization can create equity between nations.

III

Concluding Remarks

The issues of human rights and obligations which these papers try to bring forth in their specific contexts come across as moral dilemmas in Applied Ethics demanding a moral resolution. Human rights conceived as moral rights have always appealed to the human mind as a homogenizing, unifying and binding force cutting across contingent differences of caste, class, gender, ethnicity, religion, nationality, etc. However, this unifying effect is marred by the individualistic nature of these rights, as when the rights of one individual conflict with that of another or a group, forcing us to review the status of human rights vis-à-vis human responsibilities or human moral obligations in specific contexts.

Each human being has a human moral obligation (*dharma*) to himself as well as to other beings (both human and non-human) to treat each with dignity and respect, as every being is an integral part of the cosmic whole. This is every human being's basic moral obligation or dharma. If and when this basic moral obligation is fulfilled towards all, then perhaps, there would be no need for individual claims to be treated with respect and dignity. It must also be kept it mind that besides human beings no other being is capable of making such claims, and yet, in a sense, every such being has a place in the cosmos. Besides this basic human moral obligation, which all human beings have *qua* human being and which affords life and meaningful existence to all beings, there are other moral obligations which one has by virtue of the personal/social roles that one enters into throughout one's life. For example, as a parent, I have the moral obligations associated with being a good parent and my child must eventually learn about his obligations towards me. When we each fulfill these obligations, there would be no need for individual claims of human rights.

Obligations determined by social roles are affected by cultural determinants and since cultures differ in different societies, the social role determined human moral obligations would be different in different cultures. They would not be absolute in the sense of admitting of no exception. Like *dharma* admits of exceptions, so also our moral social obligations are *prima facie* duties which can be overridden by other duties depending on the nature of the exceptional circumstance. The special contexts of the various marginalized groups of people and the exceptional circumstances which life sometimes throws us into call for a rethinking of human moral obligations.

If our actions (*karma*) are guided by appropriate human moral obligations (*dharma*) then we can dispense with the troublesome language of rights. The rights of all would be served by the fulfillment of the moral obligations of all. *Dharma* in the Indian context is not only an end (*puruṣārtha*), but also a means of *moksha* or liberation. I do not wish to say that the complete fulfillment of the moral obligations we have will lead us to the attainment of liberation in any transcendental sense but if a world in which there are no violations of the so called human rights is a 'universally' desirable world, then fulfilling our moral obligations is a sure means of attaining such a world.

I believe that we can do without the language of human rights conceived as moral rights since it carries with it the baggage of individualism and morality cannot be practiced in an isolated individual context. The main opponent of this approach would be one who believed that there is something lacking with the language of obligations which is well afforded by the language of rights. Richard B. Brandt thinks that the language of rights 'encourages the patients of right-infringing actions to feel resentment, to protest, to take a firm stand. To say "You have a right to this" seems to imply that these attitudes/behaviours are justified'. (Brandt, 1983: 44–45) But one can protest or feel resentment and take a firm stand and express the immorality of the right-infringing action without using the rights vocabulary by showing that the immoral action goes against the violator's human moral obligations by which he is bound even if he is in a denial mode. History is witness to many a silent and non-violent protests where it is by the sheer force of moral pressure that the party in the wrong has yielded.

Thus, it appears that the language of rights has no special advantage over the language of human moral obligation. On the contrary the latter helps us to keep at bay problems which the rights language implies. All that we need are legal rights afforded by the laws of the State. One of the reasons why the concept of human rights was admitted was because it was thought that the law of the land itself could be unfair (e.g., the laws that allowed apartheid) calling for basic moral rights which every human being had by virtue of being human. In my opinion if the law of the land is in conformity with our human moral obligations it would not be unfair. And where individuals fail to abide by their human moral obligations, legal rights could be appealed to rectify the wrong done. Cultures which justify so called human rights violations on grounds of cultural and moral diversity and on grounds that there is no universal and uniform notion of human right, have laws which are morally wrong in the first place because they are not in conformity with the basic human moral obligations which transcend all cultural differences.

The language of 'rights' will have to give way to the language of 'responsibilities and obligations'. What is required is that each individual discover for himself/

herself his/her personal, professional and social '*dharma*' and act accordingly. In cases where there is a conflict of duties, one duty would supervene depending on the context and that would be the duty to be performed in that context. It is possible that, that duty supervenes because doing it produces the larger good for society or that it is an intrinsically 'good' thing to do. In matters of choice and action, conviction is of utmost importance. Unless a person is fully convinced, no amount of external pressure can get him to continue to choose the right course of action although he may do it once. Since, conviction comes from within the self, one must ensure that the conviction is not of a paranoid self but a rational conviction of a reflective and emotive self.

Notes

1 From Wikipedia. Source: http://en.wikipedia.org/wiki/Applied_ethics

2 Report on the Conclusions and Recommendations by a High-level Expert Group Meeting, Vienna, Austria (20–22 April 1997) on A Universal Declaration of Human Responsibilities. Source: www.asiawide.or.jp/iac/UDHR/EngDell/.htm

3 From Jaimini *Mimāṃsā Sūtra*. Adhyāya 6 pada 1. This is from footnote 17 of Bilimoria's article.

4 The word 'caste' refers to the four categories of Brahman, Ksatriya, Vaisya and Sudra which comprised the Varṇavyavasthā. This was the hierarchical social stratification of society in ancient India and it is a contentious matter whether a person belonged to one of these castes by virtue of being born into it or by virtue of one's psychological dispositions.

5 Quoted in Richard Dagger, Rights in Terence Ball et.al *Political Innovation and Conceptual Change* Cambridge: Cambridge University Press 1989. p. 286.

References

Alan R. White, *Rights*, Oxford: Claredon Press, 1984, chapters 5 and 6.

Amartya Sen, Human Rights and Asian Values in *New Republic* in 14–21, July, 1997.

Austin B. Creel, 1997 *Dharma in Hindu Ethics* Columbia: South Asia Books.

Purushottama Bilimoria, 1993 Rights and Duties: The (Modern) Indian Dilemma in Ninian Smart and Shivesh Thakur eds. *Ethical and Political Dilemmas of Modern India* New York: St. Martin's Press.

Uma Narayan, What Do Rights Have To Do With It?: Reflections On What Distinguishes "Traditional Non-Western" Frameworks From Contemporary Rights-Based System in *Journal of Social Philosophy* Vol. XXIV, Number 2, Fall 1993.

Richard B Brandt, The Concept of a Moral Right and its Function, *The Journal of Philosophy*, Vol. 80, No. 1 (Jan., 1983).

Part One

RIGHTS, OBLIGATIONS AND RESPONSIBILITIES

Chapter 1

APPLYING ETHICS: MODES, MOTIVES AND LEVELS OF COMMITMENT

Rajendra Prasad

Ethics and the World

'Ethics does not treat', says Wittgenstein, 'of the world. Ethics must be a condition of the world, like logic.' (Wittgenstein, *Notebooks*, 1914–16, 77e) He seems to suggest that ethics must be a condition of the world in the same sense in which logic must be. Logic must be a condition of the world, as I take him to mean, in the sense that it determines what the world may or may not contain: the world can contain only that which is logically possible and cannot contain anything which is not. This does not mean that it contains, or must contain, all that is logically possible. It means that any x it contains, or may contain, must be logically possible. X's logical possibility is a necessary condition of its being contained in the world.

But no sense can be given to the corresponding terms 'ethically possible' and 'ethically impossible'. Ethical principles do not determine the possibility or impossibility of anything they are relevant to; rather, they determine its desirability or undesirability. Of course, they are not relevant to anything and everything, but only to certain types of things, like individuals, their groups, their actions, motives, intentions, attitudes, plans and policies, projects and projections, etc. Let us then speak of ethically desirable and undesirable things, that is, things which are in accordance with, or violative of, ethical principles, and not of ethically possible and impossible things. But even then we cannot say that ethics must be a condition of the world in the sense that the world must have only ethically desirable things because it cannot have any ethically undesirable thing. To say that would be flying in the face of facts because the world does contain at least a few ethical evils, that is, ethically undesirable things. However, we definitely can say that the world should contain ethically desirable things. It is (almost) a logical truth that a desirable world, a world living in which would be worthwhile, must contain ethically desirable things. Negatively speaking, if a world does not contain any ethically desirable thing or contains lesser number of ethically desirable than ethically undesirable things, it would not be a desirable world, or would at the most be only a marginally desirable world.

To make ethical desirability a condition of the desirability of a world does not imply that a world's being ethically desirable would make it desirable on the whole. For example, a miserable world in which poverty abounds, whose inmates lead by and large a moral life though eating only half a meal a day, would not be a desirable world even if it is an ethically desirable one. On the other hand, even if it is desirable in other, say, political, economic, etc., but not in ethical, respects, it would not be a desirable world. Ethical goodness is foundational to all other kinds of goodnesses in the sense that its presence in any one of them heightens the latter's natural or distinctive value, and its absence in the latter, or the latter's having been polluted with some ethical evil, does the contrary. It can also be asserted with a good amount of reasonable force that no non-ethical goodness can sustain itself, or its dignity, unless it is accompanied, or fortified, with some kind of ethical goodness. A necessary component of our ethical concern is a concern, or care, for the welfare of others. In a world, whose inhabitants completely lack this concern, any non-ethical goodness, like economic, political, etc., can have, if at all, only an anaemic existence. No wonder that life in it would become 'nasty, short, and brutish'.

The things which a world may contain can be classified into the following types: things which it ought to have, things which it ought not to have, things which it may or may not have, and things whose absence in it would not make it ethically poorer but whose presence in it would add some lustre to its ethical value. Slightly stretching the use of a terminology meant to be applicable to human actions, when considered from the ethical (or even some non-ethical evaluative) point of view, we can call the above four types of things obligatory, forbidden, permissible, and recommended. In an ideal ethical world the number of forbiddens would be nil, but all the other three types it can very well accommodate. In any actual world, all the four types of things exist. The normal way to improve its ethical quality is to minimize the number of forbiddens and increase that of the obligatory and the recommended. The permissible are ethically indifferent, and therefore their status, that is, any plan or policy about encouraging or discouraging the existence of one or more of them, is determined, in any society by some other, non-ethical, consideration or considerations. For example, the direction a house should face is generally determined by considerations which maybe climatic, spatial, situational, economic etc. and seldom by some ethical consideration.

Anyway, a desirable world should have as few of the forbiddens as possible and definitely fewer than any one of the three others. This is only to assert that in a desirable world undesirables should be less than desirable, or even morally indifferent, ones. The obvious implication here is that it is empirically possible for an actual world to have all of the four types of things. This implication is true because it is a matter of fact that our world contains all of them. Here the analogy with logic breaks. No possible (therefore, actual) world can have what logic forbids or disallows, that is, what is logically impossible, and no world can miss or avoid to have what is logically obligatory for it to have, that is, what is logically necessary. Corresponding to the ethically permissible, we have the logically possible which may or may not be empirically possible. Nothing in logic corresponds to the ethically recommended. Logic allows, disallows, or requires, but does not do any of these things in a more or less manner. Therefore, there is no place in logic for anything which may be called the logically recommended, that is, something more logically possible than the merely logically possible and less logically required than the logically necessary. The concepts of logical possibility, impossibility and necessity do not admit of degrees. In the ethical context, on the contrary, we have the concept of recommendation which applies to a thing of which we cannot say that the desirable world ought to have, but only that it would be good if it has it. Its importance becomes clearer if we contrast it with the permissible, the ethically neutral. It does not matter to the desirability of a world whether or not the world has it, but it does matter to it if the world has what it is recommended to have. Having the recommended carries more credit than having the permissible, less credit than having the obligatory, and not having it carries no discredit, and definitely less discredit than not having the obligatory.

From the granting to ethics the status of being a necessary condition of the desirable world, that is, of being necessary to its very structure or constitution, two very important lessons follow: one about the relation of ethical theory to the desirable world, which I would call the build-in applicability of the former to the latter, and the other about the relation of the ethically desirable to other kinds of desirables, which I would call the primacy of the ethical.

An ethical theory primarily aims at telling us what is ethically desirable and thereby what is ethically forbidden, permissible, or recommendable. If it tells us what is ethically desirable, or what makes a thing ethically desirable, by implication it tells us what is, or what makes a thing, ethically undesirable or forbidden, and obviously we can then determine what is permissible or recommendable. If something is neither ethically desirable nor undesirable, neither obligatory nor forbidden, it is permissible. The ethically desirable is basic or necessary to the very being of a desirable world. Therefore, the connection of ethical theory with the desirable world must be very close. It must be true of the latter, of course, but not in the sense of being accurately descriptive of it, because it 'does not treat of the world'. It should be true of the latter in the normative sense; it should tell us what is involved in being ethically desirable, or, what makes a thing ethically desirable and distinguishes it from the undesirable, the permissible, and the recommended.

A thing could be desirable from the ethical as well as from many other points of view. For example, economic, political, prudential, religious, strategic, etc. Since ethical desirability is the condition of a desirable world, it occupies the place of primacy in the sense that any world, to be desirable in any way whatsoever, must first be ethically desirable. That is, to be desirable economically, politically, etc., it must first be ethically desirable. This would perhaps look more persuasive if it is said negatively or contrapositively: if something is not ethically desirable, it is not desirable economically, politically, etc. The vice versa of it is obviously not true because no other kind of desirability, economic, political, etc. can be said to be a condition of ethical desirability.

Ethical reasons for considering something undesirable (or desirable) would thus override, or supersede in merit, other reasons for considering it desirable (or undesirable). Similarly, if ethical and non-ethical reasons point in the same direction, i.e. if both tend to show that something is desirable (or undesirable), the former would very greatly increase the normative force of the latter.

Applicability of an Ethical Theory

Without prejudging anything about the nature or possibility of non-human ethics, like animal ethics, environmental ethics, etc., I shall limit myself in this essay to human ethics. The term 'ethical theory', therefore, would mean an ethical theory concerning the human things relevant to ethicizing, that is, relevant to constructing an ethical theory. This is also, by and large, its traditional sense.

There is another clarification that I need to make about the term's use. A large number of philosophers have used it restrictively to stand only for a normative ethical theory and distinguish the latter from what they call a metaethical theory. I myself have done that in more than one writing of mine. But here I am using it in a liberal sense to include both normative ethical and meta-ethical theories. I am doing this because in claiming that that an ethical theory has built into it its applicability I am claiming that it is true of both of them.

Some professional philosophers as well as non-philosophers complain: (i) present-day ethical theorizing has become very technical and sophisticated, and (ii) therefore, cut-off from the practical affairs of life, meaning that thereby it has become inapplicable to real life situations.

The first part of the complaint is true but there is no reason at all to grieve over it. Becoming technical and sophisticated is a sign of advancement and growth. Even a folk song, to be sung well, has to be sung in a technical and sophisticated manner. De-sophisticating even a practice, and not only a theory, tends to make it inelegant. The attempts made by some Indian politicians of the post-Nehru period and more enthusiastically by some recent ones to de-sophisticate Indian political practice, in the name of bringing it nearer to the grassroots, have made a large part of it inelegant, uncouth, and crude. A sensitive and neutral observer may as well say that they have made it much more backward, or uncivilized, than what it was in the Gandhian period of pre-Independence, and even in the early years of post-Independence Nehru period.

The second part of the complaint is invalid because the technical sophistication of a theory does not make it inapplicable if it is not otherwise inapplicable. A general understanding of the broad aspects of an ethical theory is enough for applying it in normal situations. Only in a tricky situation one needs to take into account its technical, sophisticated, precisified version. And, there may occur a problem, in which case even an acknowledged possessor of ethical knowledge may fail to see how the relevant theory or theories are to be applied to yield a satisfactory solution. This would not necessarily imply that the theory or theories concerned are inapplicable. Rather, it may simply imply that the problem is unusually complicated and human intelligence is finite on account of which the application of ethical knowledge has become so difficult. When Draupadī asks Bhīṣma whether Dharma allows Yudhiṣṭhira, even after his having lost his freedom and therefore his agency, to have the moral right to put her, who is not a thing but his wife, on the stakes, his saying that, because the meaning of Dharma is extremely subtle and deep, he does not know how to answer her question, very well illustrates this truth. It would, of course, mean assuming that the reason which Bhīṣma gives for not answering Draupadi's question is his real reason.[1]

Comprehending properly the applicability of a sophisticated theory is itself a sophisticated job, and actually applying it to a concrete, difficult, or unusual situation still more sophisticated. There need be no wonder, therefore, if the people, who complain against the alleged inapplicability of recent ethical theorizing, are generally those who have not cared to read seriously even a single technical work in the area.

But we are not always in a Bhīṣma-like situation. In the majority of cases we know how to apply the available ethical knowledge, or which part of it to apply. We do apply it and solve our ethical problems, which may sometimes require immediate action, and sometimes only taking a decision to act in a certain manner at some appropriate time in the immediate, or not too immediate, future. Solving an ethical problem either way involves applying an ethical principle, or a point of view, to the situation concerned. More often than not the application takes place in a smooth and effortless manner. Sometimes it is so smooth that we feel no pressure at all on our moral nerves. Had it not been the case, life would have become, if not impossible, definitely much more difficult than what we in fact find it to be.

A tenable theory of any sort has to be applicable to the field it is a theory about. A psychological theory of human learning, for example, has to be applicable to our learning behaviour in the sense that it should be able to explain how we learn and also in the other sense that it should be usable in making us better learners. These are two different types of traits or features which its applicability has. This sort of complexity, or one similar to it, is present in the applicability of any theory, though it may not be obvious in the case of a natural, scientific or mathematical theory. The physical theory, that heat expands and cold contracts a metallic body, not only enriches our understanding of the behaviour of the metallic bodies concerned but also enables us to expand or contract any one of them if we need to. Similar is the case with a mathematical theory. The geometrical theorem, that the straight-line drawn from the vertex to the base of an isosceles triangle, bisecting the base, also bisects the triangle, not only explains how an isosceles triangle can be divided into two equal parts, but also enables a father to equally divide among his two quarrelling sons his isosceles triangular drawing room.

An ethical theory (of the normative variety) also has some sort of a built-in applicability, and that it has to have it is *not an ethical but a logical* requirement. It is a requirement for its being an ethical theory. An ethical theory is one about what is worth doing, achieving, or cultivating; that is, about what sort of actions we should do, what sorts of experiences or things we should try to have, and what sorts of character traits we should have or cultivate. It tells us in a systematic, conceptually organized, way what could be a moral duty, a value, or a virtue, which, in fact, amounts to telling us what sort of life would be a good life from the moral point of view, a life we should live.

An ethical theory can be applied in more than one way, or on more than one level. I shall mention here only three such ways or levels: judgemental, decisional and persuasional. Take, for example, the consequentialist theory that an action is right if the majority of its consequences are more likely to be useful than harmful to personal and social well-being. We apply it in the judgmental way when we judge an action of an individual, or of a group, say, a political party or a university's syndicate, right or wrong on the basis of its actual or probable consequences. We call booth-capturing by a candidate or his party men wrong on this ground. A theory is applied in the decisional way when an individual uses it to decide what he should do in a concrete situation. This he does when he is not sure which way he should go, and then seeks help from the ethical theory or theories he is acquainted with, or has already accepted.

The use or application of a theory, as I have said, is not always made in a conscious, effortful manner. One does that only when the alternative he should choose is not obvious, or when he finds more than one course of action claiming execution. Almost every normal individual possesses some ethical knowledge, partly inherited from his cultural heritage and partly acquired through his own reflection on certain situations he has been directly or indirectly involved in. This ethical knowledge stands by him in most of the cases in which he has to take a moral decision. Only occasionally does he need to make an effort to apply an ethical theory, or to explore which ethical theory can be relevantly applied, to the then situation. He may then even have to decide with how much rigour or stringency the relevant theory is to be applied in order to have a fit between the situation and the theory (or principle), without either sacrificing the spirit of the latter or ignoring the distinctive demands made by the former.

It does not mean, however, that one would always abide by the theory or principle he considers relevant to his decision-making. A decision to act, or one which is acted upon, can be taken on more than one ground, and not only on a moral ground. The application of an ethical theory would give him only a *moral* ground for doing, or forbear doing, something, which may or may not be sufficient to motivate him to do, or avoid doing, the action concerned. Some other motive or motives may overshadow the moral consideration. But this does not mean that the theory concerned has not been applied or is inapplicable. The fact of the matter is that it has been applied but not acted upon in spite of its having clearly shown what the agent should have done. After considering whether or not he should get a certain booth captured, a candidate may find it morally impermissible on account of its likely consequences, but he may still go ahead with his plan of capturing it if his moral will or determination is weak, or if he is overpowered by his strong desire to win the election by hook or by crook. This example does not show in any way that the consequentialist theory is inapplicable in decision-making. It is applicable because it is conceptually possible to have a good idea or assessment of the overall utilitarian value of a large number of the likely consequences of booth-capturing, of the good or bad effects of the move on social well-being, as well as on the future of the candidate and his party.

A theory is used in the persuasional way when it is used by an individual, who is himself convinced of its viability, to convince another individual (or a group of individuals) to accept it and make his (its) behaviour conform to the theory wherever it is relevant. Here again it is not necessary that he succeeds in convincing his subject, or his subject acts accordingly even though he has become convinced of the merits of the theory. Jai Prakash Narayan was himself convinced of the theory that the electorate which elects a certain individual to represent it in a public body, a legislature or a panchayat, has the moral right to call him back, to de-elect him, even before his term has expired, if it finds that he has conspicuously failed in promoting the legitimate interests of the electorate, which was his moral duty. He became a hyperactive moralist, in a laudatory sense, because, instead of limiting his moral conviction only to himself, he started a moral movement to convince the then Indian society of the moral necessity of de-electing some elected representatives: his was a moral move to change the then political and legal or constitutional ethos of Indian electoral practices or conventions. It is a pity that Jai Prakash and his movement failed. It is a greater pity that a moral (re-armament) movement was misconstrued as a political movement for destabilizing the social order and, therefore, was politically opposed and crushed, using all types of political and pseudo-legal might. Almost all of Gandhi's political movements had a moral component and largely on account of that he got domestic as well as international support. But because of the changed political and moral set-up of the country Jai Prakash could not have this advantage though his movement was as moral, or even more so, than any of Gandhi's.

A normative ethical theory has to be, at least in principle, applicable in all the above three ways and only then could it be called so. Almost all of the available ethical theories satisfy this requirement, maybe with more or less ease. It would be in the fitness of things to reject a proposed ethical theory by exhibiting that it is in principle inapplicable in any of the above three ways. One may say, for example, of the divine theory of ethics, that it is inapplicable and therefore not an ethical theory, or not a sound one. The theory says that an action is right if God approves of it. But there is no way to know in a definitive, conclusive way whether or not God approves of a certain action, or what are the features which an action must have in order to be approved of by him. Therefore, we cannot apply this theory in judging whether or not what someone has done is right, or in deciding whether or not we should do something.

The three ways of being applicable are not completely independent of, or unrelated to, each other. The judgemental and decisional uses are almost identical, or very much the same. To judge that something should be done, as per the ethical theory one accepts, is to have a very good, or the best, reason for deciding to do it, or for doing it, if the judger is also the agent groping for the right decision. Similarly, and rather more obviously, to decide what to do, or not to do, in the light of the theory, is to judge if the theory approves, or disapproves, of doing it. The third way is also not unrelated to them. To try to persuade someone to x on the ground that x-ing is the moral thing he should do would be pointless, both logically and ethically, if the persuader himself does not judge it to be the moral thing, and is not prepared to do it though it is also his moral duty as much as it is of the person or persons he is trying to persuade. Such a move would signify the persuader's ethical hypocrisy as well as meta-ethical insensitivity to the logic of the ethical concepts involved in the game. Although aware of all this, I have mentioned them as *three* ways only to make the modes of an ethical theory's applicability clearer.

To apply a theory, or a principle, to a given situation is, in effect, to apply a concept, and every theory has a concept, or a set of concepts, which may be called its root concept or concepts. For example, the root concept of consequentialism is the concept of utility, or well-being, in terms of which it explicates other concepts. When, on consequentialist grounds, one judges that x-ing is right, or decides to x as the right thing to do, he applies the consequentialist notion of rightness to x-ing. This for him is the correct notion of rightness because he has accepted consequentialism. Similarly, to try to persuade someone to x on a moral ground is also to apply some moral concept to x-ing. It is obvious then that a theory can be applied if and only if it tells us clearly what are the conditions which x-ing should satisfy in order that a moral concept, say, that of rightness, can be applied to it, and its failing to do that would make the latter inapplicable to it.

Bhīṣma expresses his inability to answer Draupadī's question, already referred to, on the ground of Dharma's meaning being too subtle, and is not prepared even to openly condemn Duḥśāsana's attempt to derobe her. This inability of his can be interpreted to mean that the then theory of Dharma does not, according to him, clearly specify the conditions whose satisfaction by an action would make it congruent with Dharma (धर्मानुकूल) and whose non-satisfaction by it would make it incongruent (धर्मविरूद्ध). On the other hand, for Vidura and Draupadī it does and therefore makes amply clear that an action like Duḥśāsana's to de-robe a woman like Draupadī is against Dharma. What all this means is that a theory would be inapplicable if it does not clearly state the conditions or criteria for applying its basic concept or concepts. And, even if it does, it would remain inapplicable for him who does not know what these conditions or criteria are, or believes that they do not exist, or questions their validity.

A theory would also become inapplicable if, though the criterion given by it is clear and precise, it is not possible to decide whether or not x-ing satisfies it. This seems to be the case with the divine command theory of, say, rightness. According to it, one ought to x if and only if God has asked or commanded him to x. The notion of God's command is quite clear, or at least tolerably clear, but it seems impossible to know whether or not God has commanded one to x, whether or not x-ing satisfies the criterion laid down by the theory. When confronted with this difficulty, theological ethicists, by and large, appeal to some scripture or scriptures which, they claim, have been revealed by God. The sum and substance of what they claim is that God has revealed his prescriptions and prohibitions in some scripture, for example, in the Vedas according to some Indian theologians. Apart from the problems of deciphering what exactly is the purport of a scriptural injunction, of two injunctions incongruous with each other, or of an injunction seemingly immoral, to say that one should always consult some scripture to ascertain what he should do when he has to make a decision concerning a matter to which scriptural consultation is relevant, has a derogatory implication for God himself, namely, that God stopped thinking after revealing his commands in the scripture(s). By demonstrating the failure of the scriptures in giving any help to experts in deciding a trivial-looking matter, namely, what sort of rites (*saṃskāras*) should be performed to dispose of the dead body of a Brāhmin who, in his lifetime, led an un-brāhamanical life, Ananthamurthi's *Saṃskāras* very convincingly shows that God still needs to think.

There is also another factor which makes an ethical theory inapplicable, unattractive, or forbidding. An ethical theory may be formulated, and generally it is, by a highly gifted individual, a versatile thinker, a savant, or a man of extraordinarily noble and elevated character. But it is meant for normal people who have normal abilities to do moral things but are also liable to commit some immoralities. Therefore, if a moral theory keeps moral norms so high that they become unreachable for the common man, prescribes principles he cannot emulate, or recommends actions he cannot perform, it is bound to be dissuasive. The common man may not dare to try to follow it, or apply it, to solve his moral problems. Moral norms, principles, criteria of rightness, etc., do not have to be so easy and soft that no effort is ever needed to live up to them. But living up to them must be possible not only in the logical but also in the empirical sense. That is, human nature being what it is and the human world being what it is, it must be possible for a normal human being to desire living a good moral life and to actually live it, maybe with more or less of his own trying, or procuring direct or indirect assistance from education, social surrounding, cultural heritage, etc.

In brief, what an ethical theory presents as the desirable in the ethical sense, as that which is worthy of desire must also be desire-able, that is, capable of being desired in the psychological sense. If what if offers as worthy of desire cannot be desired by the common man, it cannot function as a goal or norm of action for him. If it can be desired only by a set of extraordinarily gifted individuals, it can be used only by them in leading a good moral life. It would not then do what an ethical theory should. Ethical guidance, which it aims at giving, is needed more by ordinary than by extraordinary people. The latter may lead a good moral life even without any guidance from a theory; they may not need to be told what they ought or ought not to do. A medicine which could be available to those who need it very rarely, and unavailable, or only rarely available, to those who need it most often, would not be worth manufacturing. It was the realization of this fact which inspired Buddha to present an ethical code he called *madhya mārga* (middle path). He realized that there was no point in laying out a road on which only the extremely sturdy could walk.

The human world and human nature are extremely complex and non-static. They keep raising, and therefore have to face, newer and newer ethical problems. These problems can be looked at in more than one way, and that is why different moral philosophers, looking at them from different points of view, have offered a number of theories and principles. But the theories and principles are not so different, or incongruous, as to make it impossible to decide which one to apply in which situation. Sometimes it may be difficult to make a choice of the relevant principle but the demands of life almost always show the way if one has the will. On the theoretical level it may not be possible to say with full confidence which theory is the best, or which principle the most comprehensive. But in practical life the situation is not so bad. The situation one is in quite often forces, which is also a way to help, him to select a principle of action. He may, some time later, consider it to have been a wrong move, but that can happen with any move whatsoever. Still, this remains true that whichever principle he selects and considers to be a moral principle, it will have for him an authority which no non-moral principle of action can have.

Primacy of the Ethical

That an ethical consideration has the primacy, or an overriding authority, is clear from the fact that no non-moral consideration can take away, or curtail, for example, the moral rightness of an action, if the latter is otherwise morally right. On the other hand, a contrary moral consideration can cancel, or very greatly reduce, the non-moral rightness of an action, that is, a rightness grounded in some non-moral consideration.

Rather, the moral rightness of an action can be a very good ground, or some would say, the best ground, for attributing to it some other kind of rightness, say, political rightness. But the vice versa is not, or need not be, true. All this is obvious from the common-sense fact that we consider it quite in order to call, for example, an action politically right, or prudentially right, because of its being morally right, but not the vice versa. This is true even of actions considered to be right on some religious consideration. It may be said that no action can, or should, be said to be right, even from the religious point of view, if it is morally wrong. In fact, one of the methods quite frequently adopted by religious reformers to purify or improve the functioning of a religion is to suggest dropping or modifying those of its prescriptions or proscriptions which they consider morally wrong, unjustified, or insignificant. Religion, like politics, is also a social institution and therefore cannot be exempted from the requirements of morality. It cannot make a morally wrong action right because it is in accordance with one of its prescriptions, and a morally right action wrong because it goes against the latter.

But despite its overridingness, a moral principle is itself sometimes superseded, or rather overpowered, and in more than one way. This should not make one raise his eyebrows because to say that it is overriding is only to say that it has the authority or moral right, to supersede a non-moral principle, and not that it has the power to do that. I shall discuss below some of the ways in which, or occasions on which, such a thing may happen.

(a) Let us take the principle of truth-telling. One may be in a situation in which telling the required, or relevant, truth is very likely to get an innocent man killed. He may then not tell the truth and save the innocent man's life and justify his action on the ground that the principle of avoiding harm to an innocent man (*ahiṃsā*) is a higher-order moral principle than that of truth-telling (*satya*). Here the principle of truth-telling is superseded, overridden, by that of saving an innocent man's life. The latter is also a moral principle, rather one taken to be of a higher order, and therefore, this would not be a case of overriding a moral principle by a non-moral one.

Or, he may modify the principle of truth-telling, as the classical Indian tradition did, by incorporating in it the clause that malevolent truth ought not to be told. Even this modification or expansion would not offend the overriding character of the principle of truth-telling because it has been done in the moral direction, or on a moral ground. The reasoning behind the expansion very well could be that if a malevolent truth, because it is as much true as is a benevolent or neutral one, is made as tellable as the latter, the ethical practice, in which the principle of truth-telling operates, would tend to cause social ill will or ill being.

It is some such thinking which must have prompted the classical Indian thinkers to phrase the principle of truth-telling in the form 'The truth be told, the pleasant truth be told, but not the unpleasant truth, nor even the pleasant untruth.' (*Manusmṛti*, 138: 65)

This process of expanding a principle, making it more specific, declaring something (for example, a malevolent truth) to be an exception, a case to which it does not apply, is not unusual in the practice of applying it to a concrete situation. It is not that *any* exception to, or modification of, a principle would be as good as any other. For example, when one tells an untruth to save an innocent man's life, he would not be considered guilty of violating the spirit of the principle of truth-telling, because saving an innocent man's life would be considered a good moral ground for telling the untruth. On the other hand, in such a situation, if he tells the truth and thereby helps the killer in killing the innocent man, we would say some such things as 'He followed the principle blindly', 'he is (in a bad sense) a moral fanatic', etc. What actually happens when we make a genuine exception is that we do not make an exception to the *morality* of the principle but to the scope of its application. This we do on the ground that granting to it unlimited *scope* may sometimes sanction a move which is obviously immoral. But when an exception to a principle is made on a non-moral ground, for example, prudential, political, religious etc., it would hurt the morality of the principle. It is obviously valid to say of an action that it is desirable from the prudential, political, or religious point of view, but it ought not to be done because it is undesirable from the moral point of view. But we cannot say the reverse of it.

It is in no way intended here to suggest that it is always so easy to solve, as the above example may suggest, the problem of choice when two different moral principles are relevant or applicable to a case. Sometimes the two principles may be so incompatible with each other that one finds it extremely difficult, or almost impossible, to modify any one in the light of the other, or even to decide which one to choose and which one to reject. But this is not the place to discuss the problem, practical or logical, which such dilemmas pose. I have mentioned the above example only to illustrate the case in which a relevant moral principle may give place to another, or be modified in the light of the latter, without letting the morality of the resulting action be watered down.

(b) There is another type of case in which there is no doubt in the agent's mind about the relevance or applicability of a moral principle, but still he does not put it into practice because of the weakness of his (moral) will. He knows very well what he ought to do, but does not do it, or does something else which he knows he ought not to. He may do the immorality in a huff, or because he is so overpowered by the desire to do it that he is not able to pay adequate attention to the immorality of what he is doing. To put it metaphorically, he is not able to smell the stink the immorality of the act emits. Or, he may not be in a huff, or overpowered by a contrary desire, and may even try to think out whether or not he should do the immoral act. He does the immoral act because the motivating power of the desire to do it is stronger than that of his moral will. It is this kind of immorality which Yudhiṣṭhira commits by telling the celebrated untruth about Aśvathāmā's having been killed.[2] He knows that he ought not to tell it, still he tells it, of course on Kṛṣṇa's persuasion. But he tells it because he wants to win the battle. His wanting to win exercises a greater motivational pull than his moral will to tell the truth, though his will to tell the truth does not become extinct as is evinced by the feeling of compunction, the prick of conscience, he experiences in performing the immoral feat.

Kṛṣṇa's argument can be put as follows:

1. You, Yudhiṣṭhira, want to win the battle.
2. You can win the battle only if Droṇa withdraws from the battlefield.
3. Droṇa will withdraw only if he believes that his son, Aśvathāmā, has been killed.
4. Droṇa will believe it only if you, Yudhiṣṭhira, announce that Aśvathāmā has been killed.
5. Therefore, you, Yudhiṣṭhira, ought to announce that Aśvathāmā has been killed.

Yudhiṣṭhira's moral will to tell the truth and only the truth is not strong enough to enable him to resist the argument, and to reply to Kṛṣṇa that he would prefer loosing the battle to winning it by telling an untruth. Rather, he buckles down and he tells the untruth, though to console his conscience he adds in a subdued voice that the killed is the elephant, and not the man, named 'Aśvathāmā'. His subdued utterance of the added clause can be said to be an act of self-deception or bad faith.

An important feature of an immorality done by a morally weak-willed person is that the latter knows, or at least believes, that he has done something wrong. He may even repent a little later, or even in the very process of doing the wrong thing. And, when some suffering, or punishment, is inflicted on him on account of it, instead of grudging the infliction, he may feel relieved, or atoned, because he would think that he has deserved it. All this is true not only of a Yudhiṣṭhira but of a good number of ordinary mortals as well.

An immorality done by a weak-willed, *akratic*, agent is no doubt an immorality, and examples of it, involving minor as well as major lapses, can be very easily located in every society. But they need not make us feel pessimistic. The agent's awareness or acknowledgement that he has failed to act according to his own moral principle, his feeling of self-repentance, may be used, along with some other devices, to strengthen his moral will and thereby to minimize immoralities attributable to a weak will. A very common way to motivate a man to stop committing an immorality he is prone to, adopted by moral reformers, even parents when dealing with a wayward child, is to generate in him a feeling of shame for it, or to intensify the feeling if it is already there though in a feeble form. I have my views about some of the ways in which the moral will may be strengthened but discussing them would take me beyond the scope of this essay.

(c) There is a third kind of infringement of a moral principle which the agent commits neither in a huff nor in a state of mind in which his moral will has lost completely, or almost completely, its power to determine the nature of his actions. Of an immorality committed in such a state of mind we may sometimes say that it was beyond him to have done something else. But this is not true of the kind of infringement I have in mind because the agent commits it with full self-control, with a will fully operative. He may even commit the infringement in accordance with a well thought-out plan. Take, for example, the case of a candidate in an election who gets the booths favourable to his opponent captured, or looted, and never repents for what he has done; rather, he repents when he fails to get the booths either captured or looted. A friend once reported to me that a person, known to both of us, was very sorry when his muscle men could not capture his contestant's favourable booths because, on account of having taken too heavy a doze of *tawdi*, they overslept in the night in which the operation was to be carried out, whereas his contestant's muscle men succeeded in capturing his favourable booths because they had taken only a moderate doze of the liquor and therefore did not oversleep.

This kind of immorality can be described more accurately as an expression of a strong immoral will than as one of a weak moral will. Its agent does not feel in any way ashamed of having done it, and may even feel proud of the prowess in doing it. And, it does not matter whether he does the immorality to promote his, or his group's, or party's interest.

An immorality of this type is not the result of the agent's failing to apply, or misapplying, a moral principle, nor of his inability to apply one because of being confronted with a moral conflict or dilemma. It is the result of his having bad, perverted moral principles. The principles which well-meaning citizens of his society cherish he does not cherish, and the ones he cherishes are considered by the former uncherishable, or unmaintainable. A perverted moral principle can be shown to be perverted by an argument and one may thereby hope to give a good reason to the holder of the former to stop acting in accordance with it and committing the immorality resulting therefrom. But this can be done only if there is at least some point of moral agreement between him and the person opposing the perverted moral principle. Moral argumentation works successfully only when both the sides have a common stock of principles, however small the latter's number may be. Therefore, if the booth capturer's principles are entirely different from mine, if he is morally thick-skinned, or completely insensitive to my principles, I cannot convince him of the immorality of booth-capturing by using any one of my principles as a premise howsoever sound a moral principle it may be. It is to handle such cases that we have the machinery of the legal enforcement of morals. If a moral principle is converted into a juridical law, then it can be enforced on an offender of it, no matter whether or not he accepts it as a law. But if legal machinery itself becomes indolent or corrupt, the situation becomes extremely frustrating for morally or legally sensitive citizens. It is not impossible then that they resort to the use of violence to stop immoralities. The latter may beget further violence. The result may then be complete social and moral chaos. That chaos leads to construction, or re-construction, maybe a soothing belief but the risk involved is too great to justify frequent use of violence. Once in a while it may yield some good results, and therefore, individuals as well as societies do sometimes use it. But it cannot be adopted as a dependable or safe method of checking violations of moral principles either in private, or in public, life.

Ethics and Metaethics

The view that a moral consideration has built into it an overriding authority over any non-moral consideration can be held as a meta-ethical and also ethical position. One may assert it on the basis of a logical analysis of a moral judgment, or of some specific moral concepts, such as those of moral obligation, moral rightness, moral reason for doing something, being morally commendable or preferable, etc. But equally cogently he can offer it as a substantive ethical thesis. For example, he may say that human nature and the human world being what they are, human well-being, or a desirable and meaningful existence for all, or at least for the majority of human beings, can be ensured only if moral considerations are considered as having the authority to override all other considerations. The thesis of overridingness simply means, as already explained, that if at any time there is a conflict between a moral and a non-moral consideration, the former has the authority to override, or supersede, the latter. Suppose a person is morally undesirable because of his proneness to take bribe from industrialists, but is politically useful because of his shrewdness in silencing some members of the opposition in the legislature who are extremely hostile to his party. Then, obviously, there is a strong moral reason against, but also a strong political reason in favour of, giving him a ministerial berth. What could be the response of one, who holds the thesis of overridingness, to this situation is obvious.

Call the overriding thesis ethical or meta-ethical, as it pleases you. Whichever way you go, you cannot deny its practical importance. There is something in the very logic of the word 'moral'; to have a moral reason for doing something is to have a conclusive, sufficient, reason for doing it, and this is not the case with other types of reasons. After admitting that there is a moral reason for x-ing, one cannot ask for another reason for doing it, though even after admitting that there is some other kind of reason, say, prudential, political, or religious, for it, he very well can. With a moral reason against x-ing and a non-moral reason for x-ing, if one chooses to x, he may be accused by the metaethicist of logical stupidity, meaning thereby that he is logically too dull to understand what is involved in the concept of moral reason, or too irrational to forbear doing that against which there exists a conclusive reason. The ethicist may, on the other hand, accuse him of moral stupidity which would mean that he is morally too insensitive to feel the pull of a moral reason, or too wicked to avoid doing what is morally wrong. Both of the accusations are serious, no matter whether or not they sting the stupid.

To accept the overriding thesis as a guiding principle of one's life is to become committed to lead a moral life. And, if it becomes an operative principle in the life of a society, it would not only ensure social harmony and prosperity, but will work as an Occam's razor to cut off some socially irksome, or apparently insoluble, problems. For example, the best way to soften the rough edges of religious fundamentalism, which erode social cohesiveness and peace, is to convince the fundamentalist that some of his doctrines go against moral common sense: since it is morally right to treat men and women as equal, it is wrong to debar women from studying the Vedas, even if the Vedas say so; since all women, irrespective of their religious affiliation, are equal, it is morally wrong to debar some from some of their rights because they belong to this or that religion. Similarly, one can tell the political fundamentalist: since its is morally wrong to prefer a less meritorious person to a more meritorious one, it is wrong to do that even if the two belong to two different castes or religions; when there is a moral reason to treat A and B alike, they ought to be treated alike even if there is a political reason to treat them differently. The Indian politician is not solving the classes of problems these cases exemplify because he is not willing to attach due weightage to moral considerations; rather, he prefers to act more on political than on moral considerations, and, whether he admits it or not, the political for him is amoral.

It is clear from the above discussion that even a meta-ethical view can have some practical applications. It is true that some early metaethicists were very forthright in claiming that a meta-ethical position has no normative implication. I myself once did that, but in a qualified manner. The early metaethicists were vocal on this issue because they were, of course falsely, accused by some unwary critics of having propounded meta-ethical view having some pernicious implications for moral life. What I have so far claimed in the present essay is that some meta-ethical view(s) can also be used to yield some practical lessons. This is true even of some very technical ones. For example, when a metaethicist says that no set of factual assertions can entail a moral judgement, even though factual assertions are relevant to its acceptance or rejection, the obvious lesson is: do not expect to give a rock-bottom argument for a moral judgment from a set consisting only of factual assertions. In the same way, from the view that when a person judges something morally right it only means that he likes it, one can draw the lesson: be prepared, if you hold this view, to admit that the same move may be both morally right and morally wrong (because you may like and I may dislike it).

It is a well-known fact of the history of ethics that the latter lesson has been used by the objectivist as a *reduction ad absurdum* argument against subjectivism and as a clear signal to the common man of the danger involved in accepting and using subjectivism as a guide in making his choices.

The above are, one may say, though connected with practice, mainly logical applications of some meta-ethical views. It may be true, but it cannot be an objection to what I have been trying to show. Moreover, I have not yet told the whole story. A meta-ethical view can also be used in a more earthly, substantive manner to help one out of an agonizing situation.

Suppose B unnecessarily keeps rebuking and humiliating his neighbour A. A then decides to become completely indifferent to B, thinking there is no way to have any friendly relation with him. But on the New Year's Day he picks up courage, goes to his house and wishes him a happy new year. Instead of being softened, B again rebukes him. Now, instead of reacting to him, A starts blaming himself for having wished him, knowing fully well the kind of person B is. He blames himself for having shown weakness of the will by acting against his own best judgment that it is impossible to befriend B, against his own determination to be completely indifferent to him, etc., etc. He thus suffers intensely from a feeling of self-repentance a feeling of guilt for having himself been responsible for his own humiliation.

At this point he recollects the meta-ethical distinction between obligatory and recommended or supererogatory actions, and realizes that what he has done is a supererogatory action for which he deserves moral merit, or admiration. He argues with himself as follows: 'I have gone out of the way to wish a happy new year to a man who hates me, I have responded to hatred by love and thereby have shown greatness. Therefore, if I have shown weakness of the will, I have shown it in having done something good and great which should make me feel elevated and happy, and not guilty and repentant.' He thus backs himself up and becomes his normal self, and he does all this by making use of a meta-ethical distinction.

We make the distinction between meta-ethical and normative ethical ideas to enable us to comprehend better the phenomenology of moral life, its conceptual and contentual aspects. In actual moral practice we keep using ideas from both the stocks as and when we need them. Therefore, it should not at all be a matter of surprise that meta-ethical ideas or analyses are also sometimes used for practical purposes. It is true, however, that when philosophers speak of applying an ethical theory, they generally have in mind a normative ethical theory. That is why 'applied ethics' has become (almost) synonymous with 'applied normative ethics'. Mainly to correct this imbalance I have given in the preceding few pages examples of applying some meta-ethical ideas.

Application and Motivation

Applying an ethical, or a meta-ethical theory, is a voluntary action. Like any voluntary action it can be done with any sort of motive, ethical or unethical. To illustrate what I mean let me turn to the example of the two neighbours, A and B, already given.

Suppose A asks C if he should go to B's house to wish him a happy new year. C, who knows the background very well, may do either one of the following:

(a) Himself believing in the ethical principle 'Love thy neighbour as thyself' and intending that A and B should also follow it, he may advise A to go to B and wish him a happy new year, his motivation being to get started the process of establishing the relation of good neighbourliness between the two. His motivation would then be ethical and, therefore, his application of the ethical principle, in his advice to A, would also be an ethical application.

(b) Suppose A returns rebuked and starts blaming himself for having gone to B and blaming C for having advised him to do so. C then may tell A that he has done nothing wrong. On the contrary, he has done something noble by returning love for hatred, by doing something supererogatory, something highly recommended, something he was not obligated to do. Therefore, neither is he blameable for having wished him a happy new year, nor is C himself for giving him the advice. C would now be using the meta-ethical notion of a supererogatory, or ethically recommendable action, with an ethical motivation.

(c) But C could have advised A, with an unethical motive, to do what he did, for example, with the motive of getting him humiliated by B and thereby arousing in him intense hatred, which was so far nonexistent, for B, hoping that then each one would try to physically assault the other. And, C could have told A to go to B on the New Year's Day in the name of the same principle 'Love thy neighbour as thyself'. He may not himself then be believing in the principle. One *does not have to* believe in an ethical principle to apply it, and particularly when he makes an unethical use of it, as C would in this case be doing. But, it seems to me, one *may* even believe in a principle and still apply it unethically. The way Vālmīki depicts Kaikeyī's pressurizing Daśaratha to keep his blanket promise of fulfilling two of her wishes, whatever they may be, gives a good ground to the reader to assume that she herself believes in the principle of promise-keeping. She uses this principle, a venerated one of classical Indian ethics and of Raghukula (Daśaratha's ancestors), with blatantly unethical motives of getting her son, who was not the rightful claimant to the throne, enthroned and getting her step son, who was, exiled. Some of the *Purāṇas* depict Yudhiṣṭhira—and this can be supported by reading in between the lines of the *Mahābhārata's* account—as having used the ethical principle 'A mother's instruction ought to be obeyed by her children' unethically in getting Draupadī wedded to all the five brothers including himself. And, obviously, Yudhiṣṭhira believes in the ethical principle of children's respecting their mother's instructions.

(d) C may as well use the meta-ethical notion of the supererogatory to dissuade A from going to B with the unethical motive of keeping alive the existing hostility between A and B. He may tell A that his wishing B a happy new year would certainly be a good gesture. But it would be a supererogatory action, an action he is not obligated, or morally required, to do to a man so hostile to him. He would not, therefore, be doing anything wrong in not wishing him. And, why to do something morally not required, but only recommended, to a person like B?

All this is true of applying any theory whatsoever. One need not therefore think that applying ethics, or applied ethics, is congenitally infected with a dangerous virus when he is told of the possibility, particularly, of a (normative) ethical theory's being used, or applied, with an unethical motive, that is, unethically. To do anything, theoretical or practical, in an ethically upright manner one has to have an ethically upright motive, a good moral will to do what he thinks to be morally right. It may seem a plain and simple verbal truth to a stickler of the orthodoxy of the analytic–synthetic dichotomy. But it is not. One does not first apply ethical principles ethically and then becomes ethical. But he first has, develops, or cultivates the ethical attitude, what I have called a concern for the welfare of other, which is another name, may be a non or anti-Kantian name, for the moral goodwill, or simply, the ethical will. What are the conditions congenial to, or necessary for, having, or acquiring it, is an important topic, quite tricky and complex, like other important ones. It is a topic in the discussion of which the entire corpus of ethical studies, normative, meta-ethical, applied, and empirical facts have to cooperate with and be assisted by one another.

Application and Levels of Commitment

Our comprehension of the act of applying an ethical principle, whether with an ethical or unethical motive, would definitely become richer if it is imbued with a proper understanding of at least some of the important levels on which one's commitment to the ethical principle or principles he applies, or is required to apply, to a certain case, could be operative. Whenever he sincerely holds an ethical principle, he has a sense of commitment to uphold the dignity of the principle in whichever way he thinks appropriate. This is not the occasion to dilate upon the nature of hypocrisy, though it is a very good topic for philosophical scrutiny. It would not, however, be amiss to say that it is his complete lack of commitment to the principle, or principles, he says he holds, which makes him a hypocrite. But a fair philosophical deal to him I may give at some other time.

Sense of commitment admits of levels or degrees. One who has no ethical principle at all, and therefore no sense of commitment to any, would be a hypothetical, completely amoral, person. I call him a hypothetical being because I do no think it is empirically possible for any human being to be completely amoral, that is, completely indifferent to all moral principles he is aware of. The hypocrite is not without any moral principle. His is the interesting case of a person whose real principles are different from those which he publicly declares to be his.

Assuming that every normal person has some ethical principle or principles and that to have one is to have a sense of commitment to it, I will discuss what seem to me the three important levels on which the latter may be operative. I shall call them (a) sub-committal, (b) committal and (c) hyper-committal.

(a) The sub-committal person has his principles and is committed to them like any other normal person. But in a certain case he has, for some reason or reasons, private or public, suspended, subdued, or made inoperative, his sense of commitment to the principle or principles which otherwise he, or any other applier, could relevantly have applied to the case. His sub-committal attitude does not, however, make him morally neutral.

Moral neutrality is by and large an untenable notion. If to be morally neutral means to be neutral to both morality and immorality, that is, to take a neutral stand between two issues one of which is morally right and the other morally wrong, then it is not to be morally *neutral.* One cannot be neutral to immorality without himself becoming immoral. To be neutral, in the natural way, should mean to have no leaning towards either one of the two sides. To be unwilling to approve of the moral, as well as not to disapprove of the immoral, is to be immoral, and therefore to cease to be (morally) neutral. To be neutral between the moral and the immoral is like keeping one's mouth tight-lipped in a congregation one is attending and is supposed to participate in when a controversy is going on between two persons of whom one is pleading the cause of justice and the other opposing it tooth and nail. The tight-lipped neutral and the open-mouthed champion of injustice are, Manu rightly says, equally contemptible from the moral point of view.[3]

If on the other hand, the morally neutral is said to be one who, of two morally right issues, does not favour either one more, or less, than the other, then he is not *morally* neutral. He is, in fact, one who approves of both the issues, and therefore is not really neutral, or indifferent, to either one of them.

If we still want to call him neutral, we can do that in an attenuated sense, meaning thereby that he does not mind which one of the two issues is acted upon. For example, of the two proposals, one to found a free primary school for the children of the poor citizens of an area and the other to found a charitable hospital for the same people, a person may say he is neutral to them, simply to indicate that he equally approves of both of them and not that he is equally indifferent to both them.

It is possible, on the other hand, to maintain some other sorts of neutrality, for example, religious neutrality or a religiosity. One may be neutral to all religions in the sense that one is neither in favour of, nor against, anyone's following, or not following, any one of them, and may oneself not follow any one of them. This is so because it is possible to be completely non-religious or a-religious, but not to be completely non-moral or amoral. I can very well say to a neighbour that I do not care whether he is a Hindu or a Christian, etc., or has no religion at all. But I cannot say that I do not care if he entices small children of his neighbourhood into smoking five cigarettes every morning. The latter is an immoral act and one cannot be indifferent or neutral towards one who does it.

The sub-committal individual may suspend his commitment to a moral principle for more than one reason.

(i) For example, he may do that because he thinks its application to the present case conflicts with another principle to which also he feels committed. Gautama asks his son Cirakārī to kill his mother because he believes that she is guilty of having committed adultery with Indra. Cirakārī is committed to the principle 'To obey his father's commands is a son's sublime duty'. But he finds it difficult to implement it because its implementation would come into conflict with another principle, 'It is a son's duty to protect his mother', to which also he is equally committed.[4] He suspends his commitment to the former and keeps thinking how to solve the dilemma. His dilemma is ultimately dissolved by his father who withdraws his order when he realizes that his wife is not really to blame because Indra, by appearing before her in the garb of Gautama himself, made her believe that he was her husband. She offered her body to him under the false impression that she was offering it to her husband.

(ii) One may also suspend his commitment to a principle, even though there is no conflict between it and another principle, if he is not sure of the case in hand being the right case for the principle to be applied to. Gautama would have suspended his commitment to the principle 'A woman ought to be beheaded if she commits adultery', had he been unsure of his wife's being a clear case of adulterous behaviour. As mentioned above, after realizing that it is not, he withdraws his order to kill her, repents for having given it, pardons her, and thanks Cirakārī for having taken so much time, as was his wont, in thinking what to do. ('Śānti Parva', *Mahābhārata*, Vol. V, 11–12: 5109–11)

(iii) There is also a third way of being sub-committal. I shall call it the strategic way. To reply to a moral question, to suggest a solution to a moral problem, is to apply a moral principle. Its application in the proper way may yield a reply against the self-interest of the replier, and its misapplication a reply against his dignity as a morally respected person. When put in such a situation, if one suspends his commitment to the principle involved, or concerned, and becomes non-committal, saying that he cannot reply this way or that way, or that he does not know the reply, I will call him a strategic sub-committal person.

Bhīṣma's response to Draupadī may be described as strategic. He is a man committed to Dharma, to leading a Dharmic life. Being well-versed in the *Dharmaśāstra* (sacred literature), he is expected to know what is, and what is not, in accordance with Dharma. That he knows all this and a lot more, he himself owns and demonstrates when, lying down on his deathbed of arrows, he teaches Yudhiṣṭhira, on his and Kṛṣṇa's request, all kinds of moralities, private, public and political. Kṛṣṇa, who, as per the tradition, never errs, calls him 'the great knower' (महाप्राज्ञ) and 'the great repository of Dharma' (धर्मयोनिधिः).[5] It is very unlikely that such a Bhīsma really found the meaning of Dharma so subtle or deep that he could not use it to answer Draupadī's question. Therefore, it would not be unfair or incorrect to interpret his expression of inability to give the reply, which is the same thing as the suspension of his commitment to Dharma, as strategic. This needs some elaboration which I will give right now.

To say that the meaning of Dharma is so subtle that it is sometimes not clear whether or not something is in accordance with it is to make a meta-ethical claim. In modern terminology it means that the necessary and sufficient conditions for the application of the concept of Dharma are not definitively and exhaustively stateable. Therefore, there may be occasions when we cannot categorically say whether or not something is Dharmic. But Draupadī's case is not an ordinary, humdrum, or trivial one: a woman has been put on the stakes as if she were a chattel, and lost, by a husband who has already lost his free agency, and that woman is being derobed in public. If the existing concept of Dharma is not usable or applicable to this case, if it does not give to an expert applier of it like Bhīṣma, a good moral ground to condemn the act of derobing, it is an unviable, incompetent concept. What is needed, therefore, is to make it usable by properly analysing and precizifying it. It is such occasion which necessitates the analysis and precizification of concepts. Bhīṣma should have proceeded to do that because he is not only a scholar but also a repository of Dharma. But he does not do any such thing: he simply uses the meta-ethical claim about its extraordinary subtlety as a reason for not replying to Draupadī's question whether or not, as per Dharma, she has been lost by Yudhiṣṭhira to the Kauravas.

One may say that he uses the meta-ethical claim as a device, or strategy, to circumvent his responsibility to reply. It is not implausible to call it his strategy because both the affirmative and the negative answers to the question are likely to be embarrassing for him: suppose he says it is unDharmic for Yudhiṣṭhira to have put her on the stakes because he has already lost his freedom, or because a wife is not her husband's chattel or property, or because Yudhiṣṭhira is not the sole owner of her, and therefore the attempt to derobe her is unDharmic; or, that the derobing attempt is intrinsically so abominable that in itself it is unDharmic, whatever may be Yudhiṣṭhira's own status, or claim on her. He knows he would then anger Duryodhana which he does not obviously want to. On the other hand, he also knows that, if he says that all this is Dharmic, he would lose the respect people have for his moral stature. Therefore, he uses the meta-ethical defect of the concept of Dharma to justify his silence, which is very much similar to that of Manu's silent man in a court of justice where injustice is being manoeuvred by some vocal members of the court. Vidura minces no words in saying things which justify the appropriateness of this analogy.[6]

Some of the things which Bhīṣma actually says in this regard are really revealing. He not only reminds her of his earlier statement about the hyper-subtlety of the concept of Dharma and his consequential inability to answer her question, but even tries to pass the buck to Yudhiṣṭhira. He tells her that, being an expert in Dhārmic matters, Yudhiṣṭhira alone can give the correct answer.[7]

This is an ethical, and not a meta-ethical, device as is the earlier one, since it is an advice to refer the matter to a moral authority. But it is not as innocent or flawless as it may seem to be. According to the then acceptation, the grand-nephew (Yudhiṣṭhira) is not a higher moral authority than the granduncle (Bhīṣma), and this is not unknown to the latter. Even history supports it, as is testified by the former's taking, after the war is over, his final moral lessons from the latter. Moreover, it does not seem fair at all to ask the harassed lady to turn to Yudhiṣṭhira who, largely due to his own doing, has placed not only her but also himself in the tortuous situation they are in. These devices by Bhīṣma must have made morality wail more helplessly than even Draupadī herself. Kṛṣṇa does save Draupadī from being derobed, but not morality. Morality does get derobed, and that is the greatest tragedy, or at least one of the greatest tragedies, of the *Mahābhārata*.

(b) The committal attitude is the normal man's attitude towards his moral ideas, principles, or theories. If he holds a moral principle, for example, the principle of truth-telling, whenever telling the truth is relevant or required, he feels committed to follow or use it in one or more than one of the three modes, judgemental, decisional, and persuasional, discussed earlier, as per the demand of the situation he is in. All this he may not, of course, do when he is afflicted with a conflict between this principle and some other principle, or some opposing desire, or with *akrasia*. When dealing with someone else, the committal person does try to persuade him to follow the principle he holds and considers it appropriate for him to follow. But what needs to be underlined is that he goes only up to a certain point, and then leaves the latter to decide according to his own judgement and moral common sense.

A very good example of the committal attitude is Vidura's. Whatever his own moral understanding convinces him to be right or wrong, he tries to abide by it, expresses his judgement fearlessly, frankly and honestly, and tries to persuade the relevant persons to act according to the principle he thinks they ought to follow. This he does even with Duryodhana and Dhṛtarāṣṭra whose moral integrity he does not have much faith in. He is the only person who openly pleads for immediately stopping Duṣsāsana from trying to derobe Draupadī, as it is, according to him, an immoral act. But he too proceeds only up to the point of pleading, persuading and arguing, and stops there even when his efforts are not met with success. He complaints and cajoles, frets and fumes, but does nothing beyond that.

Vidura represents the ideal type of a normal committal, or moral, person. To say this does not mean or imply that every normal moral person always does, or would do, whatever Vidura does. Vidura is not a strategist like Bhīṣma. What the latter calls the hyper-subtlety of the notion of Dharma does not bother him, nor does it deter him from unambiguously declaring that the derobing attempt is immoral. It may even be said that the notion of Dharma is not for him so subtle, as it is for Bhīṣma according to his own confession, that it becomes unusable in the present case. That is why he finds no hurdle, conceptual or normative, in calling the act unDhārmic. He categorically says, addressing all the great men assembled there, that because of their not answering Draupadī's question, who is crying like an unprotected woman, Dharma itself is being injured, that is, violated.[8] This means a lot, particularly in view of the admission by the tradition that his knowledge of Dharma is in no way inferior to anyone else's.

(c) The hyper-committal individual is a hyper-active moralist. His commitment to his moral principles, to his way of looking at what is and what is not morally desirable, that is, to his moral perspective, is so great that he is not merely satisfied with trying to convince, or even with convincing, someone of its worth, and leaving it to him to act according to his own best judgment which may or may not be congruent with his. His mode of thinking is something like this: I am convinced on irrefutable grounds that any A ought to x in any situation S. Since A is in S, he ought to x. Therefore, I ought to convince him that he ought to x and see that he actually x-es. If I do not try to convince him that he ought to x and see that he does, I would be failing in my duty: since x-ing ought to be done by A and I know that it ought to be, it is my duty to see that he does what he ought to. If I do not make him x, he would be failing in his duty, I in mine, and I would be doubly guilty because I would also, to some extent, be responsible for his failure. On the other hand, if I make him overcome his unwillingness to x and make him x, he would be doing his duty, I mine, and I would have the additional moral satisfaction or credit of having made, or helped, him perform his duty, of having guided him in leading a moral life.

The hyper-committal moralist does not make a distinction between persuading and pressurizing, between what W D Falk calls, guiding and goading. He does not see any conceptual gap between 'ought' and 'must'. He finds it not only natural but perfectly in order to glide down from 'ought' to must': since I am convinced that A ought to x, I ought to see that A x-es; since I ought to see that he x-es, I must; since A ought to x, he must.

After giving his moral advice as to what one should do in a particular situation, or after expressing his moral opinion about what ought or ought not to be done in a certain case, the hyper-committal individual would not withdraw from the scene, as Vidura used to do. It is true that in the Kaurava household he did not have the status of one who could put any moral pressure on Duryodhana or Dhṛtaraṣtra. But he did not even take such steps as going on prolonged fast, in the Gandhian manner, as Gandhi sometimes did when he wanted to get his moral–political views accepted or implemented, or starting a public agitation in the Jai Prakashian manner. Nor did he go to the marketplace to argue with the common people and the youth to create public opinion against Duryodhana, in the Socratic manner, though he had the Socratic skill, to mould their views in his favour by practicing midwifery on their natural, implicit, embryonic, moral–political ideas. This was so because all of the three, Socrates, Gandhi and Jai Prakash, were hyper-committal and therefore hyper-activists in applying their moral (or political) views. But Vidura was not: he remained only a good, flawless, normal moralist, or what I have called a committal individual.

Many times when Gandhi wanted to get some of his moral–political views accepted or implemented, and felt that no other method was likely to persuade the dissenters to change their views, he went on fast which lasted for several days and was broken only after his objective was fulfilled as per his satisfaction. His adoption of the fasting method was a pressure technique. The Indian people, and even the people of some other countries, if they considered it a moral method, it was because they believed that Gandhi's motive behind the adoption of the fasting method was morally pure. Gandhi was a hyper-committal individual, and he applied his moral principles on many occasions in the manner of a hyper-activist. His fasting method did exert some pressure on some of the people concerned and made them feel, of course, out of their love and respect for him, that their freedom was being curtailed and they were in a sense made, or forced, to take the steps he wanted them to take. This made some neutral observers of the then Indian scene doubt, and not without good reason, the fully non-violent character of Gandhian fasts.

I may, as an aside, say that only a few years after Independence, when his pre-Independence disciples had got themselves well-seated in their ministerial chairs, Gandhi seems to have realized that his hyper-active moralism was not likely to yield the fruits it had yielded earlier. Perhaps it was on this account, or largely on this account, that he became a recluse, a *mahātmā* in the traditional sense, contenting himself with addressing prayer meetings. The conversion of a hyper-committal, hyper-active, moralist into a peripatetic preacher is a pathetic comment on the too early commencement of the process of moral dehydration of Indian political practice.

The best example, however, of a hyper-committal, hyper-active moralist, in the Indian tradition, is found in Kṛṣṇa. I will mention only two episodes in his life to corroborate my claim.

(i) As already discussed, he himself is convinced that it is morally right for Yudhiṣṭhira to announce that Aśvathāmā has been killed even though it is untrue. He not only argues with and persuades him to do it but uses all the influence he has on him to remove his unwillingness and finally succeeds in making him do it. He does not leave it to his own moral discretion. He even sees to it that Yudhiṣṭhira's later part of the announcement 'It is the animal Aśvathāmā who has been killed', is uttered in such a low, subdued, voice that it is not heard by Droṇa, or any other person of his side who may inform him of the truth. Kṛṣṇa gets an untruth actually told by an otherwise truthful person and also believed by the person for whom it was meant. It is worth nothing that this is the only untruth which Yudhiṣṭhira utters in his whole life and he utters it under Kṛṣṇa's influence (कृष्णावाक्य प्रचोदितः, 'Droṇabadha Parva', *Mahābhārata*, Vol. IV, p. 3692)

(ii) The dialogue between Arjuna and Kṛṣṇa in the *Gītā* is another example, rather a more forceful one, of the latter's hyper-committal hyper-activism. He is himself, here again, fully convinced that Arjuna ought to fight the battle and tries his best to convince him that he ought to. To persuade him to fight he offers the theory of *niṣkāma karma* to the effect that no sin accrues from an action done only out of one's sense of duty, without any desire for anything resulting from it, though he gives no reason why this is so. He tries to refute Arjuna's

> arguments against fighting, and perhaps Arjuna thinks that he really refutes them. In fact, he does not succeed in refuting any one of them conclusively, but this is not the occasion to show that, since I am here concerned with his hyper-activism and not with his good or bad logic. His hyper-active morality is visible all along in his conversation with Arjuna, but it becomes glaring when he shows to the latter his expansive, majestic, divine form which excites and terrifies Arjuna. He starts trembling (*भयेन चप्रव्यथितं मनो मे*) and does not dare to raise any further doubt or question. Rather, he starts praying to him to re-assume his beautiful human form, tenders his apologies for having mistaken him to be an ordinary mortal, and seeks his protection as a child seeks from his father, etc., etc. (*Gītā*, Chapter II, p. 9–16)

Kṛṣṇa's may be the divine way to apply an ethical principle or theory to help Arjuna out of a difficult moral situation, to assist him in making a right moral decision. But it is certainly not the human way. The human way of applying ethics is to make to the agent the relevant aspects of the problem clearer, to make available the relevant ethical principles, if they are not already available to him, to assess, with his cooperation, in a rationally coherent way, their strengths and weaknesses, etc. But to leave it ultimately to the agent himself to make his decision, without generating in him a fear to lose something important if he decides one way, or a hope to get something important if he decides in another way. The heart of a moral decision lies in the agent's freedom. It must be *his* decision, and to be a moral decision it has to be taken on moral grounds. By applying an ethical theory, the applier can only prepare the ground for the agent's making a right decision; he is not to force or tempt him to take a particular decision. It is more than a mere truism to say that only the agent can take his moral decisions. Applied ethics, being a philosophical exercise, can be done well, in keeping with the human dignity of the moral agent, only if it is done with full awareness of this truth.

Notes

1 'Dyūta Parva', *Mahābhārata*, Vol. I, Gītā Press, p. 898. For a little more detailed analysis of Bhīṣma's attitude to the derobing episode see section 'Application and Levels of Commitment', of this essay.

2 'Droṇabadha Parva', *Mahābhārata*, Vol. IV, Gītā Press, pp. 3692–3. See section 'Application and Levels of Commitment', of this essay.

3 सभां वा न प्रवेष्टव्यं वक्तव्यं वा समंजसम् ।
अब्रुवन्वि ब्रुवन्वापि नरो भवति किल्विबी ।।13

One should either not attend the congregation, or if he attends, he should speak what is congruent with justice. The silent, as well as the speaker against justice, deserves to be condemned.

Manusmrti, Vaidika Dharmaśāstra Prakāśana Saṃsthā, Delhi, p. 121.

See also 'Dyūta Parva', *Mahābhārata*, Vol. I, Gītā Press, p. 904 for a similar remark by Vidura.

4 पितुराज्ञा परो धर्मः स्वधर्मो मातृरक्षणम् ।
अस्वतन्त्रं च पुत्रत्वं किं तु मां नानुपीडयेत् ।। **11**
स्त्रियं हत्वा मातरं च को हि जातु सुखी भवेत् ।
पितरं चाप्यवज्ञाय कः प्रतिष्ठामवाप्नुयात् ।। **12**

It is the son's highest duty to obey his father's order and to protect his mother. He is never independent, but always under the control of his parents. Therefore, what should I do to avoid the anguish resulting out of dutylessness? Which son can ever be happy after killing a woman, and that too his mother? Who can remain dignified even after flouting his father's order?

'Santi Parva', *Mahabharata*, Vol. V, 11–12, Gītā Press, p. 5107.

5 संहारश्चैव भूतानां धर्मस्य च फलोदयः ।
विदितस्ते महाप्राज्ञ त्वं हि धर्ममयो निधिः ।। **19**

Ibid., Chapter 50, p. 4549.

(Kṛṣṇa says to Bhīṣma:)

The great savant, because you are the great repository of Dharma, you know all such things as when are living beings destroyed, what is the result of Dharma, when does that arise.

See pp. 4548–4550 for Kṛṣṇa's high regards for Bhīṣma's erudition, purity of life, and moral wisdom, excelled by no one he knows of. The largest part of Volume V is devoted to recording Bhīṣma's replies to various types of Dharmic questions asked by Yudhiṣṭhira.

6 यो हि प्रश्नं न विब्रूयाद् धर्मदर्शी सभागतः ।
अनृते चा फलावाप्तिस्तस्याः सोऽअर्ध समश्नुते ।। **63**

The knower of Dharma who goes to attend a congregation but does not answer the question asked, shares half of the (demeritorious) consequence of telling an untruth.

'Sabhā Parva', *Mahābhārata*, Vol. I, Gītā Press, p. 904.

7 उक्तवानस्मि कल्याणि धर्मस्य परमा गतिः ।
लोके न शक्यते ज्ञातुमपि विज्ञैर्महात्मभिः ।। **14**
न विवेक्तुं च ते प्रश्नमिमं शक्नोमि निश्चयात् ।
सूक्ष्मत्वाद् गहनत्वाच्च कार्यस्यास्य च गौरवात् ।। **16**
युधिष्ठिरस्तु प्रश्नेऽस्मिन प्रमाणमिति मे मतिः ।
अजिता वा जिता वेति स्वयं व्याहर्तुमर्हति ।। **21**

Blessed Draupadī, I have already told you that the way Dharma works is very subtle. Even expert saints in the world cannot accurately know it.

I cannot give a definite and correct solution of this question of yours because of the nature of Dharma being extremely subtle and deep and the question of deciding what is and what is not Dharmic being extremely important.

In my opinion, Yudhiṣṭhira alone, whose knowledge of Dharma is perfect, is the most authoritative person to answer this question. He himself should say whether or not you have been lost in the game of dice.

'Sabhā Parva', *Mahābhārata*, Vol. I, Gītā Press, p. 907.

8 द्रौपदी प्रश्नमुक्त्कैवं रोरवीति हत्यनाथवत् ।
न च विब्रूतं तं प्रश्नं सभ्या धर्मोऽन्त पीडत्यते ।। **59**
After putting her question to you Draupadī is crying like a woman who has none to support her. But you are not answering it. Therefore, Dharma suffers in this congregation.
'Dyūta Parva', *Mahābhārata*, Vol. I, pp. 904–6.

References

Manusmṛti, Delhi, Vaidika Dharmaśāstra Prakāśana Samsthā.

Wittgenstein, Ludwig, 1979, *Notebooks*, 1914–16, Wright Von, G H, and Anscombe, G E M, eds, Chicago, University of Chicago Press.

Mahabharata, ed. and trans. Ramnarayan Dutta Shastri, (Gorakhpur: Gita Press) 2004.

Chapter 2

JURISPRUDENCE AND THE INDIVIDUAL: BRIDGING THE GENERAL AND THE PARTICULAR

Abhik Majumdar

Positivism has often been compared to the revolution brought about in the natural sciences by Galileo, Newton, Dalton and their ilk. Before them, scientists confined their attention to the question 'why' – why, for example, did things fall down and not up, why did a moving body come to a stop, why did a stone fall faster than a feather, and so on. Philosophers like Aristotle sought to answer the questions by saying that it was the inherent nature of bodies to fall and stay at rest, and that heavier bodies tended to fall faster than lighter things.

Around the time of the Renaissance, however, thinkers realised that their insistence on the question 'why' was misplaced. They instead began to examine the question 'how' – as in how bodies fell, how moving bodies came to a standstill, and so on. Doing so, they came up with a set of rules explaining natural phenomenon that were both logically consistent and in agreement with observed facts.

Similarly, prior to the advent of positivism, legal thinkers tried to construe the law in terms of its purpose. They postulated that it was a means to give effect to divine will, justice, morality and so forth. Consequently, many held that laws that did not conform to these purposes were not laws at all, that is, they were devoid of legal sanction.

The positivists, on the other hand, realised that a law's objective has little bearing on its validity. A law may be blasphemous, unjust or immoral and yet retain the character of law. They stated that objectives like the divine will, justice and morality at best indicated how the law *ought to be*, which they distinguished from law as it *is*. The latter, they felt, was the proper subject for the jurist; the study of law as it ought to be they dismissed as the work of ethical philosopher.

Understanding the law as it was entailed two fundamental approaches. The first was an analytical approach to the study of law in much the same fashion as scientists sought to study nature. The second was the separation of laws from morals. Inevitably, it evoked and still evokes considerable debate. Some criticise it as amoral; others charge its proponents with indifference towards society's welfare, and so on.

At the same time, even positivism's severest critics have admitted to being influenced by certain aspects of it, such as its reliance on logic and analysis of everyday notions. Hence, positivism's impact has been much more pervasive as compared to other theories. It has not merely given us a fresh viewpoint in legal theory, it has in fact altered the very manner in which we view the law.

Strictly speaking, the present paper is not about positivism as such. It relates more properly to the ongoing debate on positivism, i.e. to the various points of view adduced for and against the separation of law and morals. Moreover, I feel that although a broad consensus exists on what these various points of view mean per se, a question remains unanswered as to what they actually *imply*, that is, what consequences they entail for the ordinary individual. Consequently, in this paper I attempt an overview of the debate on positivism in terms of its implications. I shall begin with a brief discussion on the tenor of jurisprudence before the advent of positivism. This will give us a good idea of what precisely positivism was up against. From here, we shall scrutinise Bentham's utilitarian philosophy, and then move on to positivism per se. We shall deal with two types of positivism, namely the classical version as epitomised by Austin, and its modern iteration of which Hart is widely recognised as the finest proponent. Next, we shall look at two powerful challenges mounted at the positivist conception, one by Fuller in the course of the Hart-Fuller debates, and the other by Dworkin. Finally, in the conclusion, I shall examine positivism in the light of these discussions, and attempt to understand what the positivist conception of value-neutrality holds for the individual.

Legal Theory Prior to Positivism

Before the nineteenth century, two broad doctrines held sway over jurisprudence. Both concerned themselves with the justification or basis of law. The first sought to locate it in the laws of God, holding them to be superior to human ones. It asserted that the laws of Man were devised to effect God's will enshrined in Divine law. The natural law thinkers, on the other hand, based their jurisprudential conceptions on more rational foundations. Their fundamental beliefs centred on a universal and absolute conception of justice, which existed a priori to and independent of the law of the land. Moreover, the nature of this conception was perceptible to the mind and could be deduced from self-evident principles.

A feature common to divine law and natural law theorists alike was that their fundamental concern was with the ends or purposes of the law rather than the law itself. This approach assumed, as given, a consonance between the two. But what would happen if the consonance did not exist, i.e. when laws conflicted with their deemed objectives and purposes. They tried to answer this question in diverse ways, none of which, however, could be held entirely satisfactory.

One school of divine-law thinkers postulated that since the sovereign ruled by divine right, whatever laws he created had divine sanction. Hence the law of God was precisely what the sovereign held it to be, which precluded any conflict between the two. A group of natural law thinkers confined their self-evident principles to a few basic propositions, consigning the rest of the field to the domain of man-made laws.

Proponents of the divine-law theory are relevant to the present paper for another reason. They, more than natural-law thinkers, were of the view that man-made law was subordinate to the appropriate higher law (in their case divine law), and the former was valid only insofar as it conformed to the latter. Consequently, if a man-made law was inconsistent with divine law, it ceased to be legally valid altogether. This contention made divine-law thinkers a favourite target of the positivists. As, for example, Austin says:

> Now, to say that human laws which conflict with the Divine law are not binding, that is to say, are not laws, is to talk stark nonsense. The most pernicious laws, and therefore those which are most opposed to the will of God, have been and are continuously enforced as laws by judicial tribunals [...] An exception, demurrer, or plea, founded on the law of God was never heard in a Court of Justice, from the creation of the world down to the present day (Austin, 1995: 158).

Bentham: Precursor to Positivism

Bentham represents a halfway-house between two phases of jurisprudence. He recognised the legislative supremacy of the sovereign. At the same time, he was just as convinced as the divine-law and natural-law thinkers that the law was a means to a predetermined objective or purpose. According to him, however, the end of law was nothing more than securing the greatest good of the community (Bentham, 1945: 113; 1970: 31).

Though he believed in laissez-faire capitalism and the inviolability of private property, his emphasis on subsistence and abundance led him to become a rallying point for welfarists as well. In any case, throughout his life he campaigned for law reform, especially the repealing of outdated laws. For this, he felt, a thorough understanding of its conceptual framework was necessary, which led to his contributions to analytical jurisprudence. Much of his most important work on legal theory, *Of Laws in General*, is devoted to examining in detail what oft-used legal concepts actually mean.

As we saw, one point on which Bentham differs from his divine-law and natural-law predecessors is that he envisages law as a means to improving social and economic conditions rather than justice, morality and the like. In other words, if we go by Dworkin's classification of standards of conduct (1977: 22, 82), the ends of law are thus shifted from the realm of *principle* to that of *policy*. Indeed, Bentham's distaste for natural theory is well known. He is famous for having described the 'natural, inalienable, and sacred rights of man' enumerated in the French Declaration of the Rights of Man as 'nonsense upon stilts' (see Bentham, 2002).

Bentham, of course, made this shift with a clear objective in mind. In his view, a priori notions like justice, fairness and so on were inherently ambiguous, giving rise to needless confusion and speculation. On the other hand, the greatest-good-of-the-greatest-number principle was not just admirably clear in its meaning and implications, but also lent itself to precise quantification by means of the pain-pleasure calculus.

Unfortunately, Bentham's conjecture does not bear itself out on closer inspection. Given that short- and long-term good are often mutually inconsistent, and also the myriad interests of diverse sections of society, the greatest good of the community becomes just as intangible as the notions it seeks to supplant. Moreover, a priori concepts like justice and morality are useful in that the sovereign needs to provide at least some level of justification for his actions to meet their demands. On the other hand, once the illusion of objective calculability is removed, policy objectives that entail a posteriori justification bestow the sovereign, especially the absolute sovereign that Bentham envisaged, with considerable discretion in deciding what is desirable or not.

The distinction between a priori and a posteriori limitations assumes another dimension in the context of minorities. There remains every possibility that what constitutes the greatest good of the community is inimical to even the minimum legitimate interests of small groups falling outside the majority. The Nazi pogroms of the 1930s and the Gujarat riots of 2002 are grim reminders of how a body claiming to represent the majority can torment the minority with substantial state concurrence.

The Positivists: From Austin to Hart

Austin

Bentham laid down the groundwork for positivism. Unfortunately, the manuscript of his main treatise on jurisprudence lay unpublished for a long time. In 1945, Prof. Charles Everett discovered it and published it under the title *The Limits of Jurisprudence Defined.* Subsequently, Prof. H L A Hart published a revised and edited version as *Of Laws in General.* It is nonetheless a fact that his work on analytical jurisprudence covered much of what Austin had to say later. Some even hold the view that if *Of Laws in General* were discovered earlier, then people would have talked of Bentham as today they do of Austin (e.g. Hart, 1982: chapter 5). However, Austin must be given the credit for finally bringing about a separation between law and its ends.

To Austin's mind, the distinction was clear. He was an adherent of Bentham's utilitarian ideas, and believed that law should secure the greatest good of the community. At the same time, he was also shrewd enough to recognise that whether or not a particular law was intended to that end had no bearing whatsoever on its validity or status as a law. He resolved the situation by drawing a distinction between ethics and jurisprudence, relegating to the former all questions about how the law *ought to be,* and reserving the latter for the study of law *as it is.*[1] Hence, jurisprudence was for him by definition value-neutral. This, naturally, did not mean that according to him the law should be bereft of all values. It is just that whatever values it adheres to is a matter of complete indifference as far as jurisprudence is concerned.[2]

Austin's conception of law was simple. As mentioned before, he realised that a law does not depend for its validity on whether it is inherently just, moral and so on. History has shown us that a law can be none of the things mentioned, and yet retain the character of law. He further observed that a bare norm or standard of conduct becomes a law only if the sovereign deems it so. Hence he characterised a law as merely a command of the sovereign, to be precise a general one applicable to the entire populace or a section of it rather than a single specified individual or group of individuals. A command he defined as nothing more than an order to do or abstain from doing a particular act, accompanied with the threat of sanction in case of non-compliance.

Concepts such as divine right seek to *justify* rather than *characterise* the institution of sovereignty. To Austin, therefore, determining sovereignty in terms of such notions was meaningless. The only factor that mattered was the *fact* of sovereignty, i.e. the capacity for imposing sanctions, which existed independently of any justification. Accordingly, he defined the sovereign as one whom people are habituated to obey, and who in turn is habituated to obey no one.

In keeping with his rigid distinction between jurisprudence and ethics, Austin prescribed clearly demarcated roles for the student of each. Since jurisprudence exclusively concerned laws as they stand, he advised jurists to confine their study to only that and not venture into issues of laws as they ought to be. It is in this context that the analytical jurisprudence assumes such importance in the positivist framework.

Positivism in Its Modern Form: H L A Hart

H L A Hart is credited with having transformed positivism into something so powerful that even its staunchest critics are compelled to recognise its merits.[3] At the same time, he has arguably attracted more varied criticism than any other theory. Some even deny him the status of a positivist *stricto sensu*.[4] In the postscript to the second edition of the *Concept of Law*, Hart on his own part elucidates in the following manner:

> My aim in this book was to furnish a theory of what law is which is both general and descriptive. It is *general* in the sense that it is not tied to any legal system or legal culture, but seeks to give an explanatory and clarifying account of law as a complex social and political institution, with a rule-governed (and in that sense "normative") aspect (Hart, 1994: 239).

In any case, it is clear that Hart's theory has its roots in positivism. Specifically, it is born out of a dissatisfaction with Austin's conception of law as the command, i.e. order backed by threat, of the sovereign. To Hart's mind, this was not only too simplistic, but also inadequate to explain certain phenomena. For example, a revolver-wielding bank robber's order to a cashier was just as much an order backed by a threat as the law of the sovereign was (Hart, 1994: 19). How was it to be distinguished from the order of a sovereign?

Hart reasoned that the notion of command entailed a dimension altogether absent in the gunman's orders. When a general commands a sergeant to do something, the latter is supposed to comply not out of fear of consequences, but out of respect for authority (Hart, 1994: 20). That is, the very fact that a person in authority issued the command becomes the reason for compliance given to the sergeant (cf. MacCormick, 1977: 110).

So can law be identified with this new conception of command? Hart does admit that ' [...] the idea of a command with its very strong connexion with authority is much closer to that of law than our gunman's order backed by threats [...] (Hart, 1994: 20).' Surprisingly, however, he eschews any further development on these lines,[5] and instead prefers to dilate further on the insufficiencies of Austin's notion of law (Hart, 1994: 20).

Hart proceeds to isolate four such shortcomings (see Hart, 1994: 26–76). First, laws apply even to those who enact them; this cannot be true of orders backed by threats. Secondly, laws that confer powers (such as the power to judge disputes, or create or vary legal relations) cannot be construed in terms of orders backed by threats. Thirdly, some legal rules are not brought about by any explicit process akin to commanding. Fourthly, the sovereign cannot be identified with either the legislature or the electorate in a modern state. And finally, Austin's model fails to account for how laws persist even when the sovereign changes, since the new sovereign is not compelled to repeat the orders of his predecessor (Hart, 1994: 77).

Possibly Hart's most fundamental contribution to jurisprudence is his conception of law as a union of primary and secondary rules (Hart, 1994: 77 *et seq.*). This derives from his observation that all the problems listed above are a result of laws being treated solely in terms of rules that impose obligations on individuals, i.e. what he termed primary rules. A regime comprised *solely* of such rules cannot constitute a legal *system* in the proper sense of the term. Specifically, people governed by such rules have no standard or method to determine the precise scope and applicability of a specific rule (Hart, 1994: 90); a collection of rules merely conferring duties cannot contain within itself any procedure for altering or modifying such rules (Hart, 1994: 90–1); and such rules cannot empower any agency to adjudicate upon disputes concerning their violation (Hart, 1994: 91).

The way to rectify these lacunae lies in supplementing primary rules with what Hart termed secondary rules. These are essential to Hart's concept of law since only their presence can imbue a regime of rules with the attributes of a legal *system* (Hart, 1994: 91). In Hart's own words secondary rules:

> [...] may all be said to be on a different level from the primary rules, for they are all *about* such rules; in the sense that while primary rules are concerned with the actions that individuals must or must not do, these secondary rules are all concerned with the primary rules themselves. They specify the ways in which primary rules may be conclusively ascertained, introduced, varied, and the fact of their violation conclusively determined (Hart, 1994: 92).

Hart isolates three kinds of secondary rules, one in response to each lacuna mentioned above. Rules of *recognition* are intended to conclusively determine whether a standard of conduct is a legal rule or not; rules of *change* govern the way in which a legal rule may be introduced, modified or repealed; and rules of *adjudication* specify how disputes concerning rules and their violation are to be resolved.

Hart's conception of a rule bears further scrutiny. He has dealt with the topic at length (Hart, 1994: 49–56), but for our purposes, it is sufficient to highlight only one specific aspect. According to him, one factor that distinguishes a rule from a mere habit is that the former entails an *internal aspect* (Hart, 1994: 55). In simple terms, this consists in at least some people recognising that the rule in question is a general standard to be followed by the people governed by the rule as a whole (Hart, 1994: 55). Hart himself explained further in the following terms:

> There is no contradiction in saying that people accept certain rules but experience no feelings of compulsion. What is necessary is that there should be a *critical reflective attitude* to certain patterns of behaviour as a common standard, and that this should display itself in criticism (including self-criticism), demands for conformity, and in acknowledgements that such criticism and demands are justified, all of which wind their characteristic expression in the normative terminology of "ought", "must", and "should", "right" and "wrong". (emphasis added) (Hart, 1994: 56)

So what does all this mean for the ordinary individual? What reason is given to the man on the street to obey the law? Strangely, Hart chooses to be uncharacteristically obscure on the matter. As a matter of fact, the foregoing quotation contains indications to two separate reasons for compliance, since (external) criticism and self-criticism entail two very different sets of rationales and consequences.

The first reason for compliance derives from criticism by others. Hart mentions elsewhere that legal rules are characterised by the obligations they impose: 'Rules are conceived and spoken of as imposing obligations when the general demand for conformity is insistent and the social pressure brought to bear upon those who deviate or threaten to deviate is great.' (Hart, 1994: 84)

The second derives from self-criticism. What forms the basis for it? A plain reading seems to indicate that deviation from the rule directly leads to self-criticism. Which can only mean, therefore, that the rule itself forms the reason for compliance. That is, the individual is required to conform to the rule simply because it is the rule.[6] This takes us closer to the notion of command where, as we recall, the fact that a person in authority issued the command itself forms the reason for compliance.

To add to the confusion, as many (e.g. Morrison 1997: 372–3) have pointed out, Hart suffers from an inconsistency about how the internal aspect is to apply. He begins by holding that every society is comprised of those who voluntarily recognise their legal obligation (i.e. the internal aspect of law) and those who comply with the law only to avoid coercive sanctions (Hart, 1994: 88).

From this he postulates that the members of the latter class have to be in a minority, otherwise they will encounter too little social pressure (Hart, 1994: 89). At a subsequent point, however, he states that in proper legal systems, it is enough if only officials (i.e. upholders and implementers of secondary rules) subscribe to the internal aspect of law (Hart, 1994: 114).

If the latter is the case, what does the law require ordinary individuals to do? Merely comply with it without acknowledging its internal aspect? Does that not stray dangerously close to the Austinian notion of habitual obedience? Actually it does so in an indirect way also. Restricting the internal aspect only to officials (Hart, 1994: 114) means that they are motivated, by either the authority of law or the threat of social pressure, to properly implement the law as it applies to ordinary individuals, and especially enforce the sanctions devolving on the latter consequent to their violating the law. Hence the only factor acting on ordinary individuals is the implementation of the law by officials in pursuance of the internal aspect, specifically the imposed sanctions emanating from this implementation.

In other words, the only way in which the internal aspect affects the individual is through sanctions imposed on him as a result of officials' diligent implementation of the law. This serves to erode the distinction between law and coercive orders, at least as far as ordinary individuals are concerned.

To sum up, therefore, *The Concept of Law* seems to offer three distinct reasons for compliance with the law, viz. (a) out of social pressure, (b) simply because it is the law (i.e. due to its internal aspect), and (c) for no specific reason as such, except the threat of sanctions, i.e. the individual is required to merely comply with the letter of the law without referring to its internal aspect.

Challenges to Positivism: The Hart-Fuller Debate

The Second World War threw up in its wake a number of unprecedented legal situations. Former colonies became independent, governments changed, monarchies moved towards democracy, republics became socialist dictatorships. All these entailed massive legal upheavals. In the eyes of many, however, the most contentious debates involved the Nuremberg trials. These trials were instituted to punish German leaders and soldiers who had helped commit surely the grisliest atrocities yet perpetrated on humanity.

The legal debate here was this: the defendants claimed that irrespective of how barbaric the acts were, they were only following the law of the land and doing their duty as members of the armed forces. Punishing them now for acts committed at a time when they were legal would amount to retrospectively criminalising such acts. The prosecution's case was that the horrors perpetrated by the Nazi regime were so barbaric, so inimical to all that humanity stood for, that even though they were sanctioned by a sovereign state they could not be treated as anything other than crimes against humanity. Moreover, it was pointed out that each individual had the option of following their consciences and refusing to follow orders; that they did not automatically make them culpable in the eyes of humanity. In this manner the prosecution sought to parry the issue of retrospectivity.

In other words, the core issue was essentially whether a set of laws so patently unjust could be treated as laws at all. As a corollary, did the individual have any duty to obey a law of this nature.

Hart

H L A Hart's essay 'Positivism and the Separation of Laws and Morals' can be treated as a manifesto of sorts for positivist philosophy. Its first few parts are devoted to a lucid exposition of the elements of positivism. Indeed, he devotes as much attention to what positivism is *not* as to what it is, thereby seeking to clarify much of the misconceptions surrounding it. Interestingly enough, we find here a far more faithful adherence to the tenets of positivism than in the subsequent *Concept of Law.*

At present, however, we will confine ourselves to a narrower topic, viz. his perspective on the dilemmas thrown by the Nazi regime and its aftermath. The keystone of this was the possibility that a law may be too evil to be followed but yet may be a valid law:

> If with the utilitarians we speak plainly, we say that laws may be law but too evil to be obeyed. This is a moral condemnation which everyone can understand and it makes an immediate and obvious claim to moral attention. If, on the other hand we formulate our assertion that these evil things are not law, here is an assertion which many people do not believe [...] (Hart, 1958: 620)

In other words, he draws a distinction between the formal validity of a law and the necessity to obey it. To his mind the two issues are qualitatively different. A law's validity is dependent solely on its consonance with certain formal requirements. On the other hand, whether it is too evil to be obeyed (and presumably, whether one should obey it or not) is a question of morality (Hart, 1958: 618).

Hart sought to extend this thesis through by taking recourse to a specific example. For this, he chose a case where a woman in Nazi Germany sought to get rid of her husband by reporting to the authorities that he had made derogatory statements about the government (Hart, 1958: 618–19).

The husband was sentenced to death, but was ultimately sent to the front. After the war, she was prosecuted for illegally depriving a person of his freedom. Her defence was that she acted under what was then a valid law. The court, however, rejected this plea on the ground that the law in question was contrary to all notions of morality and justice, and therefore was no law at all; consequently, it did not justify her actions in any way.

According to Hart, the court had two other options before it. The first was to recognise the validity of the Nazi law and effectively allow the woman to get away scot-free. He readily admits that this would have made a most unhappy conclusion to the episode, as it would have enabled her to evade the consequences of what was clearly a wrongful act. The second option was to introduce a 'frankly retrospective law' to criminalise all acts committed under the previous law (Hart, 1958: 619). Hart acknowledged that retrospective criminal legislation went against the very grain of prevalent notions of justice and fairness, but nevertheless justified it on grounds that it was the lesser of two evils:

> Surely if we have learned anything from the history of morals it is that the thing to do with a moral quandary is not to hide it. Like nettles, the occasions when life forces us to choose between the lesser of two evils must be grasped with the consciousness that they are what they are (Hart, 1958: 619–20).

The retrospective legislation device bears further scrutiny. On the one hand, it does not refrain from recognising the legality of the earlier law. At the same time, just as a law binds individuals to a certain course of conduct, it also binds subsequent legislatures to not resort to something so inherently unjust as retrospective legislation. Furthermore, just as Hart envisages that individuals need not comply with an outrageously immoral legislation, so are legislatures free to legislate retrospectively if the earlier legislation were bigger threat to justice and morality than even the consequences of such retrospective legislation are. What is significant is that the act of retrospective legislation *ipso facto* implies the unjust or immoral character of the previous law.

Such a postulate is entirely in keeping with Hart's conception of laws being valid and at the same time so immoral that people need not obey them. It is therefore interesting to note the possibility of an inconsistency between this conception and Hart's subsequent work. As we saw earlier, Hart's idea of command revolves around a predetermined hierarchy. Extending this to the legal sphere, we find that a law derives its authority from its formal attributes. That is, the moment a law is formally enacted, it occupies a position of hierarchical superiority with respect to the individual and, moreover, this fact of hierarchical superiority *ipso facto* obligates the latter to comply with it.

In other words, the moment a law becomes a law, individuals become obligated to obey it irrespective of how immoral it is. This is in direct conflict with the postulate that when laws become immoral people need not obey them.

Of course, this does not apply to subsequent legislatures. The latter are by no means bound to the acts of previous ones, and are at liberty to legislate retrospectively. It does, however, throw doubt on the objective of such legislation. Punishment is meaningful when its subject acted reprehensibly in spite of having a realistic choice in the matter. Now if a person acts in the course of a legal duty, it means that he did not have a choice before him, since the moment a law is formally enacted (thereby attaining a hierarchically superior position), individuals become obligated to obey them. In other words, retrospective punishment implies punishing individuals for not exercising a choice they did not have in the first place.

Fuller

Just as 'Positivism and the Separation of Laws and Morals' laid the groundwork for *The Concept of Law*, we find the seeds of Fuller's *The Morality of Law* in his 'Positivism and Fidelity to Law – A Response to Professor Hart'. The similarity does not end there. As we observed, Hart sought to reconcile his value-neutral concept of law with his loathing for Nazi excesses by concluding that a law may be valid and at the same time too evil to be obeyed. Fuller attacks him on precisely this ground:

> Most of the issues raised by Professor Hart's essay can be restated in terms of the distinction between order and good order. Law may be said to represent order *simpliciter*. Good order is law that corresponds to the demands of justice, or morality, or men's notions of what ought to be (Fuller, 1958: 644).

Moreover, even if it is possible to separate order from good order, any order must feature characteristics such as consistency, comprehensible language, and so on. Fuller's contention is that such virtues lie outside the domain of law, and so must be treated as morality. 'Law, considered merely as order, contains, then, its own implicit morality.' (Fuller, 1958: 645)

At the same time, he talks of an external morality that law must display, for it is from this consonance with morality that law derives its legitimacy or, as he puts it, 'competency'. He readily concedes that external morality is not enough to ensure adherence to morals, as the sovereign can accord to himself the final authority to make laws. However, he contends that the internal and external moralities share a symbiotic relation and reciprocally influence each other.

That is, when the state ignores external moralities, it inevitably disregards the requirements of internal morality.

Fuller demonstrates his contention by going deeper into the case Hart referred to, viz. the one about the wife reporting her husband's remarks to the authorities. He points out that the husband's conviction rested on two statutes that concerned utterances made *in public*. Moreover, one statute expressly stated that a private utterance would be treated as public only if the speaker knew at that time that his utterances were likely to be made public. The facts of the case, on the other hand, disclose that the husband's remarks were clearly meant only for his wife, and that he had no knowledge that they might become public (Fuller, 1958: 654). In other words, the person was convicted on the basis of a clearly inapplicable law. According to Fuller, this can happen only when the internal morality of a system is sufficiently eroded to allow rulers to apply the law at their own convenience. This, in turn, becomes possible only when the regime is sufficiently divorced from notions of external morality.

So what is the legal status of laws made by such a regime? Fuller is highly critical of Hart's formulation that a law may be valid and yet too evil to be followed:

> So far as the courts are concerned, matters certainly would not have been helped if, instead of saying, "This is not law", they had said, "This is law but it is so evil that we refuse to apply it". Surely moral confusion reaches its height when a court refuses to apply something it admits to be law [...] (Fuller, 1958: 655)

Fuller, on his part, has no hesitation in declaring that if a regime sufficiently deviates from the internal morality of law, it loses the status of a legal system (Fuller, 1958: 666). This statement more than anything else marks the dividing line between positivists and their detractors.

Challenges to Positivism: Dworkin

Ronald Dworkin, arguably the greatest legal theorist alive today, has authored another powerful challenge to H L A Hart's version of positivism. His attack is concentrated on what he calls 'hard cases'. Hart himself had mentioned that laws were open-textured, that is, there were always some cases that did not fall squarely within any proposition of law, and thus could not be decided one way or the other merely by reference to legal rules. In such cases, he concluded that the judge of the issue had the discretion to settle it one way or the other.

We have already referred to Dworkin's classification of standards of conduct as principles or policies (Dworkin, 1977: 22, 82). (He himself preferred to address them by the generic term 'principles'). He examined cases of this type (i.e. hard cases), and concluded that judges decide them by referring to such principles (Dworkin, 1977: 23). Moreover, they are not applied haphazardly according to the judge's discretion, as positivists would like to make out. Their workings are admittedly different from those of rules. More than one principle may apply concurrently to a situation, but may carry different 'weights', that is, varying amounts of relevance. On the other hand, rules operate in an 'all or nothing' manner, where only one rule applies, and applies absolutely to a situation at one time. Dworkin contended that principles are also binding on the judge, since failure on his part to apply appropriate principles will attract censure just the way any failure to apply relevant rules would (Dworkin, 1977: 35–6).

He also challenged another possible positivist construct; to wit, that principles are binding on judges because they are formally similar to rules. The latter, after all, are enacted by a competent authority. Principles, on the other hand, gain their 'weight' because people gradually acknowledge their substantive correctness or appropriateness. Similarly, they lose weight also through a process of gradual rejection, in contrast to rules, which are repealed by a formal process. Hence principles and rules entail very different processes, viz. acceptance and validation respectively, for their significance. Clearly, then, the two cannot be treated as formally at par (Dworkin, 1977: 43).

To sum up, Dworkin established the following in instances of hard cases: first, judges take recourse to extra-legal standards of conduct such as principles and policies (collectively referred to as principles). Secondly, they are bound by such principles in the sense that disregarding them invites just as much censure as a similar disregard for legal rules; consequently, the judicial construct of judicial discretion is not borne out by facts. And finally, these principles are not formally similar to legal rules. The latter attain significance by fulfilling the requirements laid down by rules of recognition. Principles, on the other hand, are significant because of their content; they are considered binding because people accept them as materially correct or appropriate. Consequent to all this, Dworkin reasons, the positivist conception is inadequate to satisfactorily explain hard cases, for which referring to principles, i.e. extra-legal standards of conduct that are nevertheless binding on judges, becomes necessary.

Conclusion

In the introduction, we saw that the reason positivism had so deeply influenced legal theory was that it introduced an approach that can best be called 'scientific'. Its essence lay in that it sought to limit itself to issues of causation instead of normativity, that is, it looked only at how the law operates rather than why it is the way it is. Now, in the conclusion, we examine how this very factor is also responsible for positivism's greatest weakness.

To the individual, the legal system per se means little. Put simply, the only things that matter are his rights and his duties. Rights imply what he can expect from the law, and duties imply what the law obligates him to do. Attached to the latter is yet another matter of concern for the individual, namely the basis of his obligations, or the *reasons for compliance* with the law.

As we saw earlier, positivism limits itself to the question how. Reasons for compliance, on the other hand, necessarily entail the question why. After all, the purpose of these reasons is to explain why one should comply with the law. Hence, the moment we talk of reasons for compliance, we automatically step out of the domain of causation, which means that no approach on these lines will serve our purposes any longer. At the same time, examining the issue of reasons for compliance is necessary to the point of being unavoidable. Otherwise, the threat of sanctions will remain the only factor causing compliance, which, as Hart pointed out, will make a law indistinguishable from a gunman's order.

Theories that characterise the law as a means to an end avoid this pitfall. Logically, whatever is deemed to be the purpose of the law applies in equal measure to the individual. For example, if the law is intended to give effect to the divine will, then surely the individual is also under an obligation to uphold the same. Even Bentham's utilitarian objectives satisfy this requirement, as here the individual is bound to ensure the greatest happiness of the greatest number.

We cannot claim the same of positivism. Since the irrelevance of the ends of law is fundamental to it, naturally it has to look elsewhere for the basis of the individual's reason for compliance. As a matter of fact, our discussion on positivism reveals five distinct perspectives on the issue. The first, of course, is classical positivism's treating compliance purely in terms of threat of sanctions. We reject this outright, as it collapses the distinction between law and a gunman's orders.

The second confines the internal aspect of law only to officials, and enjoins upon individuals to comply with only its external aspect. As we saw, this also has the effect of blurring the distinction between law and coercive orders.

The third derives from pressure exerted by society in recognition of the internal aspect of the law. This cannot really be called a reason for action in the true sense. After all, it is not an intrinsic or inseparable element, or even an inevitable consequence, of the legal system. For instance, what happens when people generally do not recognise the internal aspect of law, and so are not inclined to exert pressure on the deviant? Is the individual then left with no reason for compliance except the threat of sanctions? Which, of course, leads us back to square one.

The fourth perspective can be gleaned from Hart's 1958 article (p. 620); this was reiterated in *The Concept of Law* (Hart, 1994: 203–7). It rests on the premise that a law may be valid and yet at the same time too evil to be obeyed. This implies that this reason for compliance exists independent of the fact of validity. Consequently, to understand this reason we need to look beyond the law and into extra-legal standards of conduct such as morality. The problem here is obvious. Relegating the issue of reason for compliance into the realm of morality amounts to admitting that positivism cannot provide such a reason. Further, since we agreed that the distinction between law and a gunman's orders stems from a reason for compliance other than the threat of sanctions, this in turn implies that positivism is in itself incapable of making such a distinction.

The fifth, which Hart hinted at but did not explicitly mention, treats law as similar to a command (see Hart, 1994: 20 *et seq.*). That is, the authority or hierarchical superiority of the law itself forms the reason for compliance. This is definitely closer to what we have in mind. At the same time, its consequences raise serious questions. We recall that when Bentham widened the ambit of the ends of law from divine will and a priori to the greatest happiness principle, it had the effect of also widening the scope of the sovereign's discretion. With Hart's viewpoint, this discretion becomes absolute. No matter what the sovereign may enact, the individual is obligated to obey it, since it is a valid law.

One may argue that such a construction is merely in keeping with the overall value-neutral tenor of positivism. In my opinion, this is not a valid contention. Positivism's value-neutrality derives from its purely descriptive agenda; it can afford to be value-neutral because it only considers what *is*, not what *ought to be*. But when it talks of a reason for compliance, it acquires prescriptive overtones, since it talks of why one *should* comply with the law. Hence now we have a framework that is at the same time value-neutral and prescriptive, since it gives a reason why one should comply with the law irrespective of its content.

Hart's earlier position conformed more closely to value-neutrality. There he drew a distinction between the validity of law (a verifiable fact) and whether it is too evil to be obeyed (surely a value-judgement). In his later position, on the other hand, he points to the validity of law, and from there asks the individual to comply regardless of how evil it is. In other words, in the former case, he acknowledged that law and morality may make their own demands on the individual. His value-neutrality derived from the fact that he saw the two sets of demands as independent of each other. In the latter case, however, what he asks the individual to do is in effect blind himself to the demands of morality. So far from treating the demands of law and morality as independent, he effectively makes the former supersede the latter. Consequently, in this iteration of positivism, morality is deprived of a role altogether, or at least made subject to the sovereign's inclinations.

What we discussed may well be called positivism's inherent dilemma. If the law's validity and the need to obey it are treated as separate, the law can no longer provide a reason for compliance. This renders the positivist framework inherently incomplete, since now to distinguish between law and orders backed by threats we need to refer to extra-legal standards as Fuller and Dworkin have done. On the other hand, if the law itself becomes a reason for compliance, then the value-neutrality of positivism degenerates into an absolute submission to the will of the sovereign. We may conclude, therefore, that even though positivism effectively transformed the study of legal theory, it is per se inadequate to satisfactorily describe the nature of demands imposed on the individual. For this purpose, moreover, we are forced to look beyond the law as such, and take recourse to standards of conduct that lie beyond it.

Notes

1 Austin draws a distinction between laws properly so called and improperly so called, reserving the former as the subject-matter of jurisprudence (Austin, 1995: 32, 112).

2 'The *science of jurisprudence* (or, simply and briefly, *jurisprudence*) is concerned with positive laws, or with laws strictly so called, without regard to their goodness or badness.' (Austin, 1995: 112)

Cf. 'Here we shall take jurisprudence to mean the simple contention that it is in no sense a necessary truth that laws reproduce or satisfy certain demands of morality, though in fact they have often done so.' (Hart, 1994: 181-8–2)

3 E.g. 'I want to examine the soundness of legal positivism, particularly in the powerful form that Professor HLA Hart has given to it. I choose to focus on his position, not only because of its clarity and elegance, but here, as almost everywhere else in legal philosophy, constructive thought must start with a consideration of his views.' (Dworkin, 1977: 22)

4 E.g. 'Without clearly locating his text, Hart joined legal positivism with wider currents of social writings – currents which presented our social institutions as comprising relatively durable sets of rules and social resources [...] which both constrain and enable social life.' (Morrison, 1997: 353)

5 Hart does mention in passing that when a rule upholding the ruler's power to make law is accepted, he '[...] will in fact be a legislator with the *authority* to legislate [...]' (Hart, 1994: 56–7) However, this cannot be construed as an explicit statement regarding the relation between legal rules and commands.

6 'The existence of the rule is a reason for action.' (Morrison, 1997: 370)

References

Austin, J L, 'The Province of Jurisprudence Determined' in Rumble, W E, ed, Cambridge, Cambridge University Press, 1995.

Bentham, Jeremy, 1945, *The Limits of Jurisprudence Defined*, Everett, C W, ed, New York, Columbia University Press.

_______, 1970, *Of Laws in General*, Hart, H L A, ed, London, The Athlone Press.

_______, *Rights, Representation, and Reform - Nonsense upon Stilts and Other Writings on the French Revolution*, Schofield, P, Pease-Watkin, C and Blamires, C, eds, Oxford, Clarendon Press, 2000.

Dworkin, Ronald, 1977, *Taking Rights Seriously*, Cambridge, Massachusetts, Harvard University Press.

Fuller, L L, 1958, 'Positivism and Fidelity to Law – A Reply to Professor Hart', in *Harvard Law Review*, Vol. 71, p. 630.

_______, 1969, *The Morality of Law*, CT: Yale University Press, New Haven.

Hart, H L A, 'Positivism and the Separation of Laws and Morals', in *Harvard Law Review*, Vol. 71, 1958, p. 593.

_______, 1982, *Essays on Bentham*, Oxford, Clarendon Press.

_______, 1994, *The Concept of Law*, second edition, Oxford, Clarendon Press.

MacCormick, D N, *Legal Obligation and the Imperative Fallacy*, in Simpson, A W B, ed, 1973, *Oxford Essays in Jurisprudence (Second Series)*, Oxford, Clarendon Press.

Morrison, W, 1997, *Jurisprudence: From the Greeks to Postmodernism*, London, Cavendish Publishing.

Chapter 3

WHY MORAL RELATIVISM DOES NOT MAKE SENSE

R. C. Pradhan

In this paper I would like to examine the presuppositions of moral relativism and suggest that moral relativism, like any other relativism, does not hold good because of certain conceptual oddities involved in it. To argue that moral values are relative to cultures and societies and that morality is culture-variant is wrong because there are moral values which cut across all cultures and societies. Moral ideals and principles are not products of culture because culture itself presupposes them. Hence it is more appropriate to argue that morality has a core that does not change with history and culture.

What is Moral Relativism?

Moral relativism is the moral theory that says that moral values are of cultural origin and that they are relative to the cultures in which they are expressed. That is to say, moral values are culture-variant and they cannot be shared by all cultures. This argument regarding the nature and origin of moral values admits the relativity of moral ideals and values and reduces them to certain cultural practices or at best to some cultural ideals which are specific to some historical contexts. This is how cultural relativism has been identified with moral relativism in recent times. (Matilal 1994)

The strongest argument for moral relativism is that moral values are man-centric and that they arise due to historical and cultural needs of mankind. Thus moral values are no exception to the general historical and cultural situation which controls and conditions our life. If morality is conditioned by history and culture, then there is no morality independent of culture and therefore there are only culture-specific moral systems which have nothing in common with one another. Moral relativists are thus sceptical about the so-called objectivity of moral values and they therefore seriously undermine the absolutism associated with the traditional concept of values.

Traditionally values have been taken as absolute and universal on the ground that values qua values are of universal significance and that they are absolute in character because they are not subject to change and destruction. The absolutistic view is found in the writings of Plato, Kant, Wittgenstein and many others precisely because in any investigation into the foundations of ethics, one encounters the basic human values which remain fundamental to human life. The defender of absolute values is likely to argue that values cannot be products of culture because culture itself presupposes the values which it expresses. Values are not only not relative to any society or group, but they are also not made by any group or society. If they were products of the social practices, then they are not values per se. As Wittgenstein argues, if values are found to be in the world in the sense of being produced by it, then they are not values at all. (Wittgenstein, 1961) Values in this perspective are the conditions of the world in the sense that they provide a framework for making the world intelligible. (Wittgenstein *Notebooks*, 77)

The absolutist believes that there is a moral fabric of the world which cannot be subject to change and history. The moral fabric is the original moral structure which *transcends* the contingent world-process and is therefore beyond the passing events and actions taking place in the world. Moral values belong to the basic moral fabric which can never be fragmented into contingent pieces. The relativists celebrate the fact that man can never be able to grasp the whole moral fabric and therefore they argue that there is no point in accepting such a totalitarian and absolute moral structure. But the fact remains that there are values which can never be shown to be culture-centric and so are found to be universal and objective without ceasing to be humanly graspable.

The relativists are not only sceptical about the moral fabric but also are not sure if there are any values which are objectively real. (Mackie 1977) Values as objective entities are considered to be products of human error because such a hypothesis leads us to postulate entities which do not exist anywhere in the world. (Mackie 1977)

What is Wrong with Moral Relativism?

Moral relativism goes wrong in reducing ethics to a social science, thus making values non-different from empirical facts about man. It takes ethics as a sociological phenomenon rather than as a normative discipline. Therefore moral relativists cannot see beyond what is happening in the social behaviour of man. Ethical pursuits are normative by nature and thus there cannot be any way by which ethics itself can be reduced to sociology. The domain of ethics is the domain of values which cannot be reduced to that of facts of any kind. Therefore the autonomy of ethics has to be admitted to safeguard values against the onslaught of the empirical disciplines.

The relativists believe that ethical ideals are matters of social and cultural preference and therefore there cannot be anything objective about them. Objectivity is a misnomer with regard to the moral values as the latter are based on our cultural tastes. Just as there cannot be any objective criteria for judging whether a particular taste is better than another, so also there cannot be any objective way of deciding whether a particular value is better than another, e.g. whether non-killing is better than killing. Those who profess relativism are likely to argue that there is nothing to choose between the two because each could be justified to be a value in some society or other. Thus the relativists find no justification for accepting one value-system rather than another. Thus, according to them, everything goes in morality.

The idea of 'everything goes in morality' undermines the normative character of ethics. If everything is possible in morality, then there will be nothing good or bad at all. Good and bad will be matters of indifference. This moral impossibility will lead to a denial of any ethical value at all. Putnam (1981) rightly points out that moral predicates cannot be applied to any human action if there is no objective basis on which such application can be made. Objective criteria are therefore needed for making morality at all possible.

Objectivity of the moral predicates is necessary if there is to be a genuine distinction between what is morally good and what is not. It cannot be the case that all moral actions are of the same status. Some are more appreciable than others; it is the appreciable ones which require to be based on a solid ground. That solid ground is none other than the objective and rationally justifiable ground. For example, why animals should not be unnecessarily killed or why the environment has to be protected has to be decided only on objective grounds and must be based on moral reasoning. Thus the whole idea of ethics is based on the idea of moral or practical reason which provides the grounds for moral actions.

Moral relativism undermines moral objectivity. It seriously questions the very idea of a universal moral reason. Therefore it comes into conflict with the moral theory which accepts moral principles beyond a specific cultural domain. What the relativists demand is that there should be no talk of moral law or ideal which has universal moral significance. Relativists are of the opinion that morality is itself a matter of contextual significance and so there is no sense in the talk of impersonal, objective moral truths.

Moral Truths

Now the question arises: are there moral truths which everybody accepts or can accept? The relativist's answer is that there are such truths but only in a limited context. That is, moral truths are of limited validity in that they hold good only in the context where they are practiced. For example, it is a moral truth in the Hindu society to give alms to a beggar. But in another society it may be considered immoral because it encourages people to remain poor. Such instances can be multiplied. What is important here is that according to the relativists moral truths change from society to society and so claiming universal moral truths becomes questionable.

Whether there are universal moral truths or not has to be decided only on the ground whether morality demands universality or not. To issue a moral command is to issue a rule for all in all similar situations. It means that all human beings in a particular situation have to follow that rule in order to be moral. Besides, the same rule should prevail in all similar situations. This is called the universalizability of the moral principles. (Hare 1952) Morality does not need only local conditions for validity. The more local a rule is the less moral it is. Hence, the demand for non-locality of moral truths.

There is an argument that morality has no truths and that it only issues prescriptions or commands. This is called non-cognitivism in moral theory. According to this theory, there are no moral propositions that are true or false. Thus we are told to accept the domain of morality as the domain of moral appreciations and condemnations and not truths regarding those appreciations. In this sense morality is a matter of moral emotions and of prescriptions. Both emotivism and prescriptivism, however, fail to tell us how to go about moral actions in the absence of moral truths. Even the so-called moral emotions and prescriptions need evaluation in the light of moral truths. Therefore there must be moral ideals as moral truths to guide our moral actions and evaluations.

However, once we accept moral truths it becomes clear that we are back to moral rules which must be objective and universal. That is, the moral rules must be absolute in the proper sense of the term. The demand of absolutism is that moral ideals or truths must be held as transcending the contingent conditions in which they are applied. Application of rules can be contingent but rules have to be non-contingent.

Does Applied Ethics Presuppose Relativism?

Admittedly, applied ethics requires the locality of the moral norms as in business and other professional ethics. A set of norms apply, say, in business, provided the business systems evolve those norms. To make profit is a business norm in the domain of business activity. It cannot be universalized. There cannot be any business motive in love and other personal relationships, for example. Thus one may argue that applied ethics accepts only locality conditions of morality. But the argument seems faulty because any moral norm whether in business or outside must be non-local. If a rule has no condition as this, then we may doubt whether it is a moral rule at all. Business itself has to be under such rules which are genuinely moral. Thus we are in need of moral rules which are non-local and unconditional.

If the moral rules would have been relative and subjective in character, even applied ethics will not be possible because we need rules that have objective application to a number of agents other than my or our cultural group in order to be moral rules. For example, if we intend to make it a rule that nature must be treated with respect, then this has to objectively apply to a number of cases across all cultural groups. If it is a rule for my cultural group, it cannot have that significance which it would have if it were a rule for all cultural groups. Thus objectivity is a *sine qua non* for applied ethics as for ethics in general. That is to say, applied philosophy must also disregard relativism.

All systems of ethics more or less admit objectivity of its moral values and norms. This is due to the fact that morality cannot brook any form of relativism and subjectivism so far as the latter tries to make moral norms situation or group-dependent Morality is the only science that can and should demand universality.

References

Hare, R M, 1952, *The Language of Morals*, Oxford, Clarendon Press.

Kant, Immanuel, 1987, *Fundamental Principles of the Metaphysics of Ethics*, Delhi, Orient Publications.

Mackie, J L, 1977, *Ethics: Inventing Right and Wrong*, Harmondsworth, Penguin.

Matilal, B K, 1994 'Pluralism, Relativism and Interaction Between Cultures', in Eliot Deutsch, ed., *Culture and Modernity: East-West Philosophical Perspectives*, Honolulu: University of Hawaii Press.

Putnam, Hilary, 1981, *Reason, Truth and History*, Cambridge, Cambridge University Press.

Wittgenstein, Ludwig, *Notebooks*, 1914–16, translated by Anscombe, G E M, Oxford, Basil Blackwell. 1961.

Wittgenstein, *Tractatus Logico-Philosophicus*, translated by Pears, D F, and McGuinness, B F, London, Routledge and Kegan Paul. 1961.

Chapter 4

HUMAN RIGHTS – A THEORETICAL FORAY

Krishna Menon

A commitment to human rights is something that all contemporary nation states are united by. No regime would like to be thought of as being opposed to human rights, all portray themselves as champions of human rights. Clearly it appears that human rights are very desirable and ought to be defended. The only murmur of disagreement comes from political theorists. This is ironical, for here is a concept that all practitioners of politics would like to identify with. And yet this is a concept not accepted uncritically by the theorists of politics. (Susan Mendus in David Beetham, 1995)

The extent of this philosophical scepticism can be gauged from the comparison that A. MacIntyre makes of human rights with unicorns and witches! (MacIntyre, 1981) This rather provocative comparison indicates the existence of very profound objections to the whole concept of human rights. However in the bulk of contemporary western political theory there is an acceptance of the concept of human rights although there are debates regarding the content of these rights. (Barry, 1992) The most obvious example would be the differences between the libertarians who see an almost insignificant role for the state, where individuals have rights whether or not recognized by the legal system, and the positive liberals who would insist that the state play a greater role in the regulation of the economy and the society in order to secure human rights.

Here in this paper an attempt will be made to examine these objections and understand the issues that are being raised.

Origins

The idea of human rights has emerged out of the idea of natural rights, a popular idea of the early modern period in Europe. (Heywood, 1994) John Locke, the English political philosopher, was securing the foundations of the modern concept of human rights when he argued that human beings by virtue of belonging to the human species are endowed by nature with three cardinal and inviolable rights, the right to life, the right to liberty and the right to property. Locke was thus suggesting that to be human means to possess these three rights granted by God. The natural rights framework implied that these God-given rights are obtained in the realm of nature and are prior both to the society and obviously to the state. Locke's famous account of the state of nature thus is characterised by the absence of society and state but interestingly by the presence of individuals who possess the right to life, liberty and property. Locke was not making a simple moral claim for these rights but was suggesting that these rights symbolize the most natural and fundamental human drives and desires, in the absence of which a truly human existence is not possible. (Heywood, 1994)

The twentieth century saw many changes in theoretical concerns, but an interest in natural rights remained, although now it appeared in the more secularised incarnation of human rights. Human beings came to be conceived of as ends-in-themselves and this Kantian notion suggested that they could therefore be bearers of rights. These rights invoked respect for human agency and autonomy, and honoured the notion of the autonomous individual capable of making independent choices and pursuing their own ends and values. (Ramsay, 1997) Thus today human rights are understood as those rights that people are entitled to by virtue of the fact that they are human beings. Thus human rights are defended as universal, fundamental and absolute. (Heywood, 1994)

While most people would try not to sound like opponents of the idea of human rights, the fact is that the term human rights itself raises many difficult conceptual issues that make its unequivocal advocacy somewhat difficult. There are also practical problems that emerge with the absolute, inviolable, universal and fundamental nature of human rights. In practice we discover that rights often need to be balanced one against the other, hence absolute rights are almost impossible. Norman P Barry illustrates this with the example of a conflict between the right to life and capital punishment or warfare. Besides he argues that the right to life would necessarily be limited once you acknowledge the right to self-protection.

Then of course there are the deeply philosophical issues of who exactly can be regarded as human and when does human life itself begin. Feminists would recall the difficulty this issue presents, for if life is taken to begin at conception then there can be no right to safe abortion, however if human life is understood to begin at birth then the scenario is different. The issue gets even more complicated for feminists in countries like India, where the right to safe abortion, far from emerging out of a discourse of women's rights over their bodies, is actually a part of the state's population policy. This right is further complicated by the existence of modern technologies like amniocentesis that are being used to determine the sex of the foetus and then perform selective abortion if the foetus is found to be female. In this context when women ask for the right to safe abortion would they not be facilitating female foeticide as well? (For an interesting examination of this issue see Nivedita Menon, 1999) Thus it is clear that the language of absolute and universal rights is far from being problem free.

Another kind of question that is being asked in this context is if human rights are to be granted to only individuals capable of independent life and thinking and possessed with a measure of self-consciousness, then what of the human rights of children and people with mental and physical disabilities?

A completely different objection is raised by a group of people who argue that the term human rights is too anthropocentric and assumes that only human beings should have rights; if life is the criterion for enjoyment of rights then why should animals and birds and fish and plants not have rights? This is the rhetorical question they ask, and in asking these and other similar questions the grand, universal assumptions of human rights appear rather limited and vulnerable upon close scrutiny.

And then of course there are pitched battles fought about the contents of the list of human rights. The traditional liberal hues of the list with its commitment to right to life, liberty and property has undergone a transformation during the twentieth century when another range of rights has been added, acknowledging the state's commitment to the social and economic well being of the people.

Utilitarians, Marxists and Human Rights

Modern nation states are based on the idea of citizenship rights that are inspired to a great extent by the doctrine of human rights. (Bellamy, 1993) Human rights are based on the idea of universality and are understood to be fundamental in nature. Hence, these rights must potentially be extended to all people regardless of social and economic divisions, race, caste, creed, gender and so on. However it is obvious that each nation state would institutionalise these abstract ideals differently given the distinctions in culture, history and practical constraints. It is therefore that international agreements like the United Nations Universal Declaration of Human Rights of 1948 become important. Such international agreements oblige governments to uphold certain basic rights enshrined in the Declaration. But often there are conflicts between the doctrine of human rights and what nation states claim they need to do in order to guarantee human rights. This conflict among many other limitations of the concept of human rights leads us to doubt the supposed fundamental and universal nature of human rights.

Two basic ideas that determine the human rights framework are that of a divinely ordained human natural law and human nature. Given the plurality of religious worldviews (and of course the existence of atheism), God is, as Bellamy says, a very contentious starting point for any theory. (Bellamy, 1993) And then, of course, is the great difficulty that we would experience in agreeing on a profile of human nature; the selection of what constitutes the basic human qualities is not easy. This would definitely involve making judgments about good life and morality and there are no empirical facts to base this appeal to uphold human rights. It is therefore reasonable to say that the fundamental and universal nature of human rights is a somewhat exaggerated claim given the plurality of views on what constitutes good life and what is morality and hence what are the absolutely inviolable human rights.

This discomfort with the concept of human rights is definitely not new. The unhappiness with the idea of human rights has been expressed both from a philosophical as well as from a political standpoint. The basic point that all collectivist criticisms of human rights make is that the doctrine is individualistic and a-historical. (Barry, 1992) Utilitarians like Bentham have very famously denounced the whole notion of natural rights as nonsense upon stilts. Thus Utilitarians have been intensely hostile to the idea of human rights.

Collectivists of all hues are unable to appreciate the idea of human rights as popularly understood for they argue that rights within the existing framework are guarantees for the individual against the state, this assumes that there can never be a relationship between the individual and the state that is not antagonistic. This is an idea that of course is unacceptable to the notion of an ideal society that is entertained by both socialists and communitarians.

It is often suggested that Marxists share this intense hostility with the Utilitarians towards the whole idea of human rights. A closer examination would reveal that this is not the case. Karl Marx was, it is true, rather ambivalent in his views towards human rights. Like every other enterprise that Marx undertook, his study of human rights was also from a historical perspective. It is in his 'On the Jewish Question' that Marx evaluates the history of rights. He is clearly appreciative of the progressive nature of the idea of natural rights with its strong commitment to the idea of universalism; he acknowledges the fact that these ideas more than anything else helped liberate Europe from the oppressive shackles of feudalism. Marx's reservations regarding human rights are well known, he argued that the concept of rights were skewed in favour of the bourgeois individual, meant to defend the egoistic individual separated from the community. Marx rejected the universal claims of the existing formulations on human rights; he rejected the idea of a universal human nature. Marx was thus unprepared to accept the construction of human rights that was in vogue in the Europe of his times for he saw this construct as being based on the ideology of possessive individualism.

Therefore, Marx was rejecting the universal claims of the liberal philosophical framework while acknowledging the liberating impact of the idea of human rights. Thus Marx's enterprise is rather interesting and fascinating for while he appreciates the emancipatory potential of the doctrine of human rights he is also quick to point out the limitations of its supposed universal claims. Perhaps Marx has often been misunderstood because of the rather sorry record of human rights that many of the erstwhile actually existing socialist societies had. While making proclamations about their commitment to upholding human rights they were guilty of some of the worst violations of rights, specially the right to freedom of speech and expression, and the right to freedom of faith and religion, among many others. But to set the record straight, these regimes by focussing on the right to health care, housing, cultural and sporting facilities and so on added a new dimension to the contents of human rights.

Can Human Rights be Universal – New Perspectives

More recently, MacIntyre and Richard Rorty are among the many philosophers who have voiced their deep suspicion of the doctrine of human rights. MacIntyre who is very aggressive in his denouncement of human rights bases his critique on a larger project, that of critiquing the whole concept of human reason which arose during the Enlightenment in Europe. This paper does not permit a detailed examination of that critique which he shares with many others, however to use a word that most of these critics would not like, the essence of the critique is that there is no such clearly identifiable thing as *human reason* and hence obviously there cannot be such a thing as *human rights.* (Mendus, in Beetham, 1995)

MacIntyre's rather persuasive argument is as follows: in the absence of a universal concept of reason, what exists is rationality constructed by and embedded in a particular tradition. Hence he argues that there cannot be a universal account of human rights. MacIntyre points out that the problem with much of the contemporary theories of human rights is that they are based on an understanding of human nature and reason that are themselves based rather narrowly (despite claims of universality) on the assumptions of a particular tradition. This immediately violates the most cardinal principle of the current doctrine of human rights, i.e. universality. (Mendus, in Beetham, 1995) It is not difficult to see here that once the central element of universality is abandoned then it would be impossible to talk of a limited set of basic human rights, for every need or interest could be interpreted as a basic human right.

Richard Rorty goes further to say that the search for foundations is a futile one and hence the search for human rights would also be a futile one since it is looking for universal foundations. In the face of these doubts about human rights, modern political philosophers who seek to defend the doctrine of human rights have moved away from the foundationalist approach towards what has come to be described as the constructivist approach. (Mendus, in Beetham, 1995) The early writings of John Rawls are perhaps the best illustration of this approach. Rawls steers clear of theological arguments as well as of extravagant assumptions, instead he argued on the basis of certain assumptions about rationality and appealed for human rights from this vantage point.

Critics were of course quick to point out that Rawls' assumptions regarding rationality is nothing but the representation of white, male, American sensibilities, which might appeal to people who respond to this description but would be of no relevance to others. This approach also faces the by now familiar problem that all theorists of human rights encounter, what exactly would the contents of the list of rights be? So then should the pursuit of human rights be abandoned? The intuitive answer would hopefully be a resounding no: the experience of life within a nation state would make our commitment to human rights stronger. Thus Raymond Plant is absolutely right when he says that concern for human rights is suggestive of our belief that the boundaries of nations are not boundaries of moral concern. (Plant , 1991)

The context of the decolonized twentieth-century world is a world where it is easy to argue that different countries have different cultures and requirements and therefore have specific rights that are appropriate for each country. It is often argued that the requirements and culture of Islamic societies or countries of South East Asia are very different from that of the West, so universality of human rights would be an impossible idea. (Brown in Dunn and Wheeler, 1999) Such a relativist position is assuming that beliefs and practices of a society are good for its members; this however need not be true. What we need to check is whether or not a belief or a practice is good for all the members of the society. For instance the practice of apartheid was clearly not beneficial to the people of colour in South Africa, or the caste system is not beneficial to the Dalits in India.

The question then is can we defend a set of rights as being basic to human life irrespective of national boundaries and culture? The enterprise is characterized by a search for a set of rights that can be declared universal, transcending national and cultural specificities. This would hopefully enable us to say with certainty that some things are wrong and violate human rights irrespective of the national or cultural boundaries involved. Such a response would have to start by saying that identities are not fixed, nor are cultural or national boundaries permanent. In fact there is nothing as notoriously fluid as identities. Prior to the 1984 anti-Sikh riots in Delhi, the Sikh identity was a matter of great pride, but it did not take for all this to change once the killings and the hate campaign began. An identity that was a matter of pride now aroused insecurity in the minds of the members of the Sikh community.

In this context it is useful to point out that identities are not homogenous either, what might seem like a monolithic, impregnable group would have its own differences. The Rashtriya Swayamsewak Sangh in India for instance talks of the insecurity that the Hindus feel in the context of the supposed increasing numbers, organization and strength of the Muslims. Here an assumption is being made about the monolithic character of the Hindu identity that is most certainly divided by caste, among many other possible divisions. A similar assumption is being made of the minority community as well. Muslims in India are vastly different; Tamil Muslims are very unlike the Muslims from Bihar and so on. So what is being argued is that cultural specificities need not be such a big barrier to the idea of universal human rights as argued by those who wish to establish the impossibility of universal human rights. Anyone who is familiar with contemporary international politics would agree that national boundaries and identities do not take long to change. Yugoslavia is an excellent reminder of this fact.

It is an undeniable fact that peoples and cultures are different but this still need not mean that we would be completely unable to judge other societies and cultures. As Bhikhu Parekh shows (Parekh, in Dunn and Wheeler, 1999), the way out is to ascertain whether their practices are consistent with their beliefs, which in turn can be examined for practical justification, and finally match the moral beliefs based on a particular conception of man and nature with the empirical beliefs on which these are based.

Criticism of rights violation thus need not necessarily take the form of denouncing a particular culture or identity. It is possible, as Michael Walzer has argued, to criticize by referring to the shared moral understanding of the community and its cultural roots, rather than on the basis of some transcendental moral standards.

Yet another hopeful voice comes from Rorty who while setting aside the foundationalist approach argues nevertheless for human rights. His suggestion is to move away from questions about human nature to focussing on the potential that human beings have of being able to live together and work in harmonious ways despite huge differences. Rorty's interesting prescription is to encourage people to see the differences between themselves as less significant when contrasted with the similarities. By doing this he hopes that men and women would easily accept the need for basic human rights such as they enjoy for others as well. Rorty is obviously uncomfortable with the idea of universal rationality hence he recognizes the impossibility of evaluating people's lives against such universal standards and condemning them as irrational or wrong. He would rather see them as being 'deprived' of the sense of security that might have extended to other people and cultures the opportunity to develop a different and, dare one use the word, more humane set of rights. Rorty thus is arguing that human rights are essential but only when they evolve out of a culture of human rights and not as a consequence of some moral or intellectual exercise. Rorty hence concludes that human rights are part of a cultural ethos and people need to be educated about the need for such a cultural fabric that makes the existence of human rights possible.

Bhikhu Parekh makes an interesting distinction between relativism, monism and minimum universalism. (Parekh, in Dunn and Wheeler, 1999) Relativists would argue that since different societies have different histories and backgrounds there is no way that we can talk of universal rights. Monists would see the obvious diversity that surrounds them but would unhesitatingly put it down to ignorance and lack of intellectual rigour and continue to uphold the idea of an absolute and true human way of life against which all other practices are to be judged.

Minimum universalism on the other hand holds that while there are bound to be different ways of living, these however can be judged on the basis of some universally held values. Minimum universalists differ among themselves about the manner in which they arrive at these universally held values. Some appeal to human nature, others to the nature of human agency and still others construct a hypothetical veil of ignorance from behind which human beings would, it is assumed, choose values that are universally valid.

The minimum universalists base their observations on a framework that acknowledges the fact that all human beings belong to a common species and hence share certain attributes in common. Yet at the same time they are culturally different and this difference cannot be dismissed as being insignificant.

What seems to be the need of the day is the creation of an international ethos which while being supportive of a democratic culture is also free of ethnocentric biases. Such a process, Bhikhu Parekh, is convinced will lead to the possibility of a cross-cultural dialogue and would definitely lead to the creation of universal values. On the basis of a very interesting discussion and examination of human nature and society, Parekh arrives at five universal moral values of human unity, human dignity, human worth, promotion of human well being and equality. He argues that these values can be defended across cultures. And these values, if we take the argument further, would be basis, according to Parekh, for any framework of human rights.

A universal discourse on human rights has been subject to increasing scrutiny and often this is associated with the arrogance of the west, almost suggesting that non-western societies have no need for human rights.

It is in this context that that there is much talk of the so-called Asian values which many South East Asian politicians have been defending. They argue that these values might not be in keeping with the western notion of human rights however they are as legitimate as the latter. Of course the standard western response to these reservations is that there are no uniquely Asian values that are found across Asian countries. Any invocation of Asian values is therefore simply a means to justify their subversion of human rights.

At the core of the Asian leaders disquiet with the doctrine of human rights is the belief that the doctrine of human rights in the contemporary world is nothing but a defence of the western, liberal-individualistic framework of democracy and a neglect of traditional, communitarian networks of rights and obligations and duties.

Conclusion

On the international stage today there is a growing support for human rights, simultaneously however there is great deal of philosophical and political discomfort with the idea as well. Edmund Burke and other conservatives argued for rights based on a clearly identifiable national tradition and legal order. Utilitarians like Bentham saw only those rights as valid that were derived from the principle of utility and not from some vague moral principles. Marxists of course have always been sceptical of universal ideas, criticizing them for being a historical and, worse still, a defence of the bourgeois individual. Feminists have serious reservations because the human rights framework ignores the specificity of belonging to the female gender. Added to this is the more contemporary feminist criticism of the discourse of human rights that accuses this discourse of being patriarchal and hence incapable of addressing concerns of women. There is also a strong current in contemporary philosophy that is sceptical of foundationalism in any form and of universalism. And last of all the universal claims of human rights are severely limited by the practice of international politics where the particularism of both the nation and the state make any doctrine of universal human rights appear like the myth of the unicorn.

So what is the way out? Bhikhu Parekh's enlightened vision of universal human values and rights based on these values is an interesting way out. That is so because of the foundation on which this framework rests, a foundation that accepts that human beings are primarily the same by virtue of sharing membership of the human species. But they are also different as a result of their different cultural and societal affiliations. Parekh recognizes the importance of both these understandings in proceeding towards his formulation of universal human values. Thus an understanding of human rights that emerges out of pluralist universalism might just be the way out enabling a defence of human rights while being sensitive to the need to keep away from ethno-centric biases.

References

Barry, Norman P, 1992, *An Introduction to Modern Political Theory*, U K, Macmillan Education.

Beetham, David, ed, 1995, *Politics and Human Rights*, U K, Blackwell Publishers.

Bellamy, Richard, 1993, *Theories and Concepts of Politics: An Introduction*, Manchester, Manchester University Press.

Dunne, Tim and Wheeler, Nicholas J, eds, 1999, *Human Rights in Global Politics*, Cambridge, Cambridge University Press.

Heywood, Andrew, 1994, *Political Ideas and Concepts: An Introduction*, U K, Macmillan Press.

MacIntyre, A, 1981, *After Virtue*, London, Duckworth.

Menon, Nivedita, ed, 1999, *Gender and Politics in India*, New Delhi, Oxford University Press.

Plant, Raymond, 1991, *Modern Political Thought*, Oxford, Blackwell.

Ramsay, Maureen, 1997, *What's Wrong With Liberalism?* U K, Leicester University Press.

Chapter 5

MORAL RELATIVISM AND HUMAN RIGHTS

Shashi Motilal

Is morality (our sense of 'right' and 'wrong') at core relative or absolute? Few questions have engaged the attention of philosophers, anthropologists and other intellectuals so deeply and for so long as this one. The debate between Moral Relativism and Moral Absolutism (each claiming to be the true theory about morality) has thrived because of the experience of moral diversity of a multicultural society in which one sees the confrontation of diverse moral values and practices. It is true that cultural diversity expressed in diversity of lifestyles (including attire and diet), beliefs, practices, language, etc., among different ethnic groups, may not, in many cases, be moral diversity, for there could be differences of dress and diet without any moral differences. But often, cultural diversity is accompanied by moral diversity. Moral diversity simply means that there are moral beliefs held by one group of people that are not held by another, and this is obviously true. But, it is quite possible that both these groups believe in the same basic moral principles which when applied to their individual contexts yield different and sometimes opposing moral beliefs. E.g., the Inuits think it is right to kill their parents after the parents have reached a certain age – and the parents expect this – rather than have them bear the hardships of their hazardous life. This would be considered to be a totally wrong practice in most other communities where parents are venerated. But, the underlying moral principle is the same viz., the thought of protecting or keeping hardships away from parents. This kind of relativism merely describes people's moral beliefs without pronouncing them as right and therefore, preferable, or wrong and therefore, to be avoided.

Ethical or Moral Relativism as a meta-ethical theory maintains that if there are opposing moral beliefs held by members of two communities then these beliefs are both true and what makes them each true is the fact that they adhere to the moral standards adopted by each community. It goes without saying that the moral standards of one are opposed to that of the other. A strict moral relativist believes that there is no single, over arching standard of morality and that what is right and what is wrong varies from one society to another without reference to any universal moral principle. Morality includes other connected areas of concern like virtue, moral goods, moral rights and obligations. In each case, there could be forms of Moral Relativism. Moral Relativism with respect to moral rights would see the rights people have as relative to their society, state or governmental system. It would oppose any idea of a 'universal', 'transcultual concept of human right. The attempt of the moral relativist has been to deconstruct the idea of human rights; the foundationalists, on the other hand, speak of universal human rights and ground them in some universal trait possessed by all human beings irrespective of their contingent differences. In this paper, I wish to examine the claims of the 'foundationalists' and the antifoundationalist and show that there is something missing in both these approaches to the issue of human rights.

Moral Relativism takes on many forms.[1] The claims of different varieties of Moral Relativism can be stated briefly as follows:

1. Different societies have different moral codes.
2. There is no objective standard that can be used to judge one societal code better than another.
3. The moral code of our own society has no special status; it is merely one among many.
4. There is no 'universal truth' in ethics; that is, there are no moral truths that hold for all people at all times.
5. The moral code of a society determines what is right within that society; that is, if the moral code of a society says that a certain action is right, then the action is right, at least within that society.
6. It is mere arrogance for us to try to judge the conduct of other people. We should adopt an attitude of tolerance toward the practices of other cultures. (Rachels 2001: 55)

Moral Relativism is based on a certain form of argument that proceeds from facts about differences between cultural outlooks to a conclusion about the status of morality. The general argument says —

> Different cultures have different moral codes. Therefore, there is no objective 'truth' in morality. Right and wrong are only matters of opinion, and opinions vary from culture to culture.

Persuasive as it might be, the argument is not sound from the point of view of logic. The trouble is that the conclusion does not follow from the premise – that is even if the premise is assumed as true, the conclusion still might be false. The premise concerns what people believe. In some societies, people believe one thing whereas in other societies, people believe differently. The conclusion, however, concerns what really is the case. The fundamental mistake in the above argument is that it attempts to derive a substantive conclusion about a subject from the mere fact that people hold opposing views about it. But from the mere belief or non-belief in a thing no conclusion can be drawn about its existence. The thing may exist despite non-belief in it and again it may not exist despite strong believers. This is a simple point of logic, and it is important not to misunderstand it. It is not being said that the conclusion of the above argument is false only that it does not follow from the premise. The argument given by the moral relativists proves nothing.

There are some absurd consequences of taking Moral Relativism seriously. In other words, even if, in spite of the invalidity of the argument given above, Moral Relativism turns out to be the correct view, some undesirable consequences follow. These are:

1. We could no longer say that the customs of other societies are morally inferior to our own.
2. Our actions would be right or wrong merely by consulting with standards of our society.
3. The idea of moral progress would no longer make sense.

That there is a problem with each of these is not difficult to understand. There are certain practices that are wrong no matter what. For example, slavery, child abuse, rape, etc. But if we took cultural relativism seriously we would have to regard such practices, e.g. that of slavery as immune from criticism. For in a feudal society, and there have been many such societies, slavery was the norm. So, if we appeal to the notion of right or wrong in such societies, slavery was the normal and right thing to practice.

The implications of Moral Relativism are disturbing, because few of us think that our society's code is perfect. We can think of ways it might be improved, yet Moral Relativism would not only forbid us from criticizing the codes of other societies; it would stop us from criticizing our own. After all, if right and wrong are relative to culture, this must be true for our own culture just as much as for other cultures.

Lastly, if there are certain practices that are wrong no matter what then the abolition of such practices by a society does tell us that there has been moral progress in that society. But any sense of progress implies that mistakes have been acknowledged and rectified. History shows that the place of women in society (both Eastern and Western) was narrowly circumscribed. They could not own property. They could not vote or hold political office; and generally they were under the almost absolute control of their husbands. Now all this has changed and we can count it as progress. That there has been social reform implies that there is a standard of right and wrong in the light of which certain practices have been given up. So, Moral Relativism in its crude form where it states that standards of right and wrong are merely culturally determined, that there is no absolute standard of right and wrong, must itself be mistaken. Even if one is not sure of what is absolutely morally right, one can be sure of what is absolutely morally wrong. This was what Aristotle emphasized in his *Nichomachean Ethics.*

All of this points in one direction – that there is moral knowledge, i.e., knowledge about moral correctness or incorrectness which is of the nature of normative morality, i.e., has the claim of being universally and unconditionally true where exceptions are few and explainable. Of course, now the onus lies on the non-moral relativists, the moral absolutists to give examples of moral concepts and principles that are universally and unconditionally true. Further, there must be an argument that justifies belief in such concepts and principles.

Moral Relativism and Human Rights

The discourse about human rights nests in a larger philosophical context – the context which raises the question whether there are moral values or moral principles that are universally and unconditionally binding on all individual human beings irrespective of the sociocultural background to which they belong and notwithstanding the fact that this background may not recognize and accept these values. Are there common standards of 'right' and 'wrong', a shared set of moral values/virtues, a uniform idea of 'the good in life', and common notions of moral rights and obligations? To answer the above questions in the positive, will amount to espousing some form of Moral Absolutism as the true theory of morality as against Moral Relativism. It is important to note that even if there was a set of moral values that were universally accepted, this would not show, in itself, that Moral Relativism was wrong unless it could be shown that these values are shared because *there is a single true morality which is binding on all.* It must be admitted that just as differences can be explained in a non-relativist framework, so uniformities can be explained in a relativistic framework. It could be argued that peoples groups, communities share moral values and ideas not because of shared absolute moral standards but due to communication and interpersonal influences. A strong logical argument is required to prove that there is a single true morality that is obligatory on every individual human being irrespective of the societal conditions in which he finds himself.

The belief in universal, that is, 'universally accepted' moral values, is widely held. Anthropologists, moral philosophers, political scientists have often agreed on a list of values that can be considered 'universal' or 'trans culturally acceptable'. For example, prohibition against murder and stealing, the value of truth telling and treating others as one wants to be treated, compassion, love, etc. Even if one admits the wide differences between what are termed 'Western values' and 'Asian values', these may distil to a residue of shared values. However, there are staunch relativists who do believe that even the most 'inviolate' values are not universal.

Objections to the Concept of Human Rights

The moral values and principles accepted by a society are very often expressed in moral judgments couched in the language of 'rights' and 'obligations'. For example, if a society considers 'life', 'growth', 'development' as virtues then that society would accept 'right to life' as a basic right. The moral relativistic position with regard to moral rights would see the rights that people have as relative to their society, state or governmental system. Such a view might or might not equate moral and legal rights but it would certainly oppose the idea that there are universal human rights; rights that human beings have by virtue of being human. One of the first expressions of dissent on accepting universal human rights came from Melville J. Herskovits, who in 1947, drafted the Statement on Human Rights for the American Anthropological Association Executive Board and which was submitted to the United Nations. That document was directed against the idea of universal and culture-neutral human rights and it emphasized that, 'values are relative to the culture from which they derive' and 'respect for differences between cultures is validated by the scientific fact that no technique of qualitatively evaluating cultures has been discovered'.[2]

In the post-war period some anthropologists began to challenge the relativist approach by emphasizing the cross-cultural similarities in moral values. More recently there has been a change in the perspective of many anthropologists who have re-examined 'cultural relativism' in the light of claims about human rights.[3] It is not so much that Moral Relativism has been regarded as a false theory as much as a 'counter intuitive' one. Merrilee H. Salmon, in her concluding remarks in her paper, where she reviews and criticizes Moral Relativism, says, 'My arguments try to show not so much that ethical relativism is "false" but that its consequences conflict with our deepest held intuitions and that it cannot be held consistently while embracing those intuitions'. (Salmon 1997: 61)

Though the international community has adopted the language of 'rights', there is little consensus as to which rights are basic, which rights have priority and how rights conflicts are to be resolved. The United Nations Universal Declaration of Human Rights enumerates a variety of civil, political, legal, economic and welfare rights that each individual independent of sex, race, religion, social status and national origin is entitled to enjoy. Two international covenants on human rights were adopted in 1966, almost twenty years after the United Nations Universal Declaration on Human Rights. Although the covenants were a historic landmark in making international human rights standards legally binding they also planted the seeds for much dispute about priority. The debate has centred round the distinction between civil and economic rights, the usual assumption being that if there are two sets of rights, there must be a hierarchical relation ordering them. (Xiarong Li 2001) Many socialists, feminists and members of certain non-western societies have challenged the western oriented dominance of civil over economic rights. Not all philosophers have given equal status to liberty (a civil or political right) and well-being (an economic right). Although liberty/freedom has been taken to be a basic human right, the right to well-being has not been so treated. This inequality of status is based on a distinction that is central to ethics – between positive and negative duties or the distinction between commission and omission. To respect the right of freedom of another does not commit me positively to do something. I need only to be non-interfering and allow the other individual to do what he desires to do. On the other hand, I am committed to doing something if I respect the right of well-being of another individual. If people of a certain country are starving because of drought like conditions existing there, and if having enough food is 'well-being' and if well-being is a necessary condition of those people's purposive actions, then it falls on others to do something to see that that right of theirs is respected, i.e., they are provided food. The language of the covenants seems to recognize an absolute obligation to respect civil political rights but only an imperfect obligation to respect socio-economic rights since full respect for socio-economic right is largely a matter of resources, whereas full respect for civil-political rights is largely a matter of self-restraint on the part of governments.

The right to well-being, if acknowledged as a separate right, conflicts with the right to liberty of the individual. The State, which will have to bear the burden of the welfare of its citizens to some extent will pose a limitation to the right to liberty of those very same citizens in case it over exercises its powers in executing that responsibility. Nevertheless, the right to well-being which is a kind of socio-economic right has been emphasized as a distinct right from what are called civil and political rights. Both categories of rights are dependent and it is this principle of mutual dependency that is missing from the emphasis on the priority of socio-economic rights over civil-political liberties or *vice versa*.

Another aspect to the issue of human rights is its connection with what are termed as 'group rights' or 'collective rights' of a society. Some examples of group rights cited by proponents of group rights are 'right to development', 'right to humanitarian assistance', 'right to share in the exploitation of natural resources', etc. A group or collection of human beings is clearly not a human being and therefore, group rights are not human rights unless they are interpreted 'merely as the rights of individuals acting as members of social groups'. (Donnelly 1989). So, the right of people to self-determination is to be understood as the right of individuals to act collectively for self-determination. Donnelly, however, maintains that certain group rights, as for example, the right to development cannot be understood as individual human rights. Also, there are instances where group rights can come in conflict with the individual rights of members belonging to that group.

Over half a century later, one can say that there has developed an international consensus on the universal status of human rights. Governments that prevent their citizens from speaking freely, that torture prisoners, that oppress religious minorities, have been consistently criticized for violating human rights, the underlying assumption being that these rights are universal or trans cultural. The important feature of human rights is that they are entitlements we have independent of our standing in social institutions. Indeed, since social institutions should respect and/or provide human rights; human rights constitute a test of social institutions. An institution is judged to be adequate or inadequate, good or bad, in terms of its support of human rights.

If indeed there is a concept of human rights, then as A J M Milne says it must be able to meet the standard objections brought against it. He briefly states the objections as follows

> The idea of human rights as that of an ideal standard consisting of liberal-democratic and modern social-welfare rights makes many such rights irrelevant to much of humanity, including the peoples of the Third World.
>
> The idea of human rights as any kind of ideal standard ignores cultural diversity. If the ideal is to be coherent, it must be drawn from a particular tradition of culture and civilization and those who belong to other traditions have no reason to accept it.
>
> The idea of human rights as those which belong to all human beings at all times and all places, ignores not only cultural diversity but also the

> social basis of personal identity. It presupposes homogenous desocialised and deculturised human beings and there are no such beings.
>
> MacIntyre's objections, of which there are three. The first is that the notion of a right is not found in every society and is not necessary for social life as such. This is supported by the fact that in no ancient language and in no medieval language until near the close of the Middle Ages is there any expression correctly translatable by our expression "a right". The Greeks did not have a word for it! The second objection is that, if there are human rights, no one could have known that there are before the modern era. The third is that there are none, because all attempts to give good reasons for the belief in human rights have failed. Belief in them is like belief in witches or unicorns. (Milne 1986: 5)

In what follows we shall see how various attempts at justifying the notion of human rights have been successful to answer the objections stated by Milne.

Justification for Human Rights

Broadly speaking, two kinds of arguments may be adduced in support of the concept of human rights. The first are arguments based on logic and are a priori arguments where the notion of human rights is derived from the very definition of what it is to be a human being. The second kind of argument, are those that are based on human experiences or human relationships and are empirical in nature.

The concept of 'rights' is the contribution of the English Speaking world to Moral Philosophy. The Greeks had no well-developed concept of individual rights. The Stoics and the Medievals had a concept of natural law but any concept of natural right was largely undeveloped. In John Locke we find a theory of natural rights but his arguments to back up his claim that men had rights to life, liberty and property were based on theology, especially on the fact that 'all humans are God's children'. Because of its association with natural law/theology many philosophers substituted the term 'human rights' for 'natural rights'.

The Universal Declaration of Human Rights, the document that has been at the centre of all human rights discussions, does not provide much philosophical input into the justification of human rights except the reference to 'the dignity and worth of the human person'. The idea of human dignity and worth is a Kantian idea, the idea of respect for persons. But what gives human beings this superior position? Why should human beings deserve this respect? Kant's answer to this is simple. According to Kant, all things that have value have it because human beings bestow value on them. That is to say all things other than human beings have conditional value. Only human beings have unconditional value and this is because only human beings are rational and autonomous creatures. But, what gives human beings this privileged place? Is it just an accident of nature based on the fact that human beings have more power? That is not Kant's answer. For Kant, human beings because of their rational nature form an ideal rational community (a kingdom of ends). What is unique about this 'kingdom of ends' is that every member here is both subject and sovereign at the same time. They are sovereign because they formulate the moral rules that apply to all and they are subject because they should obey the rules made by themselves and others. The 'should' implied here is a logical 'should'. It is only on pain of contradicting ourselves that we can take a 'moral holiday' from obeying these rules. Hence, if human beings are rational and free beings then there cannot be separate moralities guiding human behaviour. Conversely, if there are different sets of conflicting values and principles governing human action then, these cannot be moral values and moral principles. Kant's principle, 'Treat persons as ends, never merely as means' is an example of a universally binding rational principle. Since this principle (or some version of it) is strongly entrenched in our moral consciousness, defended by strong arguments, directly or indirectly accepted by all moral theories, it can count as an absolute and fundamental moral principle. Any adequate moral theory must recognize and accept this principle (or some version of it) to be a morally consistent theory. The notion of human rights in the Universal Declaration of Human Rights is based on this idea of respect for individuals and therein rests its justification.

Many thinkers in their attempt to provide an a priori argument for human rights have echoed the same basic Kantian idea. One such argument is given by, Alan Gewirth (2000). His argument rests on the premise that action is the universal and necessary context of all moralities. All positive moralities amid their vast differences with regard to specificities of contents are concerned with action in the sense that they all are concerned with how people should act. Taking off from this point, Gewirth goes on to establish two theses. First, that 'every actual or prospective agent logically must accept that she has rights to freedom and well-being as the generic feature and necessary conditions of her action and of generally successful action'.(Gewirth, 2000: 183) Second, 'the agent logically must also accept that all other actual or prospective agents likewise have rights to freedom and well-being.' (Gewirth, 2000: 183) Gewirth calls the right to freedom and well-being for purposive action 'generic rights'. Briefly put, his argument is as follows:

1. I, as an agent, must have freedom and well-being for any purposive action of mine
2. I have a right to freedom and well-being. If this is denied then

3. others have no obligation to respect this right of mine which means that
4. they may impede my right to freedom and well-being which in turn means
5. I may not have freedom and well-being which are the generic conditions of my purposive action.

Since 5 contradicts 1, and 5 follows from denying 2, 2 must be accepted. This establishes the first thesis that I as a prospective agent have a right to freedom and well-being. The second thesis follows from the first by generalization and the Kantian criterion of 'universalizability'.

Gewirth's argument has been criticized but many others have defended it too. One of the criticisms is that there is no reason to believe that every actual or prospective agent must have freedom and well-being to perform a successful action, and simply from having freedom and well-being it does not follow that one has a right to it where this implies that others have an obligation to respect it. I think that there is reason to believe that every purposive action must be a free action since responsibility can be ascribed to an agent only if his action is free. Further, if freedom in this sense becomes a necessary condition of my purposive act then, the purpose of the act can be fulfilled only if I can make a legitimate claim to be free, i.e., if I have a right to my freedom. Once this is accepted it follows by logic that other actual and prospective agents must also enjoy this right.

The argument, which establishes 'respect for human beings' as a fundamental moral principle obligatory on all individuals, can be treated as a 'transcendental (in Kant's sense) argument' in favour of human rights. To be able to claim respect for myself as a human being is the very presupposition of my status as a human being. Gewirth's argument, similarly, is a 'transcendental argument' in favour of human rights. The generic rights to freedom and well-being are the very presuppositions of my being a purposive agent. In a sense they make my purposive action possible. Kant had identified Human Reason as that which is universally present in all human beings. Human Reason is also the fountainhead of a 'universal morality'. Proponents of the idea of human rights, taking the cue from Kant, have emphasized some one aspect of human nature, imbuing the adjective 'human' in 'human rights' with meaning and explaining the humanness underlying the idea of human rights. But in a sense such attempts are trivial for they really do not succeed in explaining what this humanness is. It functions merely as a 'posit' to explain a problem at hand. The fact of human diversity is too dominant a phenomenon and poses great impunity to attempts at finding underlying commonalities. So, to say that 'being human' automatically confers rights to individuals is in a sense to beg the question whether rights are legitimate universal attributes of human beings. Rights are normally considered to be specific claims enforceable against society or certain parts of it (in the form of institutions or the state) by persons, corporation or groups. Claims can be for recognition of certain identities, capabilities, securities, benefits, etc. This presupposes the existence of some institutional means of enforcement. The question is how 'humanity' in any form, can be taken to imply such specific claims as rights when these are dependent on non-universal social institutions like the state?

Attempts at a 'natural grounding' of rights have often been met with scepticism if not complete denial. Such efforts are debunked by deconstructivist pragmatists like Richard Rorty. (Rorty, 1993) In Rorty's view there is today, 'a growing willingness to neglect the question "What is our nature?" and to substitute the question "What can we make of our selves?" 'Pragmatist philosophy has shown 'our extraordinary malleability' the fact that we are a 'flexible protean, self shaping animal' rather than the rational animal which tradition believed us to be. In Rorty's view the 'human rights foundationalism' is simply 'outmoded' and is giving way to cultural costructivism. He is supportive of the human rights culture and even claims its superiority over other alternatives but he does so on purely ethnocentric or culture specific and not foundationalistic grounds.

Turner thinks that the foundationalistic approach does not hold ground because the Western notion of human rights has always focused on the individualistic or atomistic aspect of human nature rather than on the societal or collective aspect. (Turner, 2000) It has considered human being to be a 'social actor inhabiting an individual body' but has failed to emphasize 'the role of collective persons, and thus of humanness'. Turner says, 'the pre cultural, psychobiological constitution of human beings as individuals cannot be interpreted to confer anything as socially and culturally constituted as a "right" [...]' (Turner, 2000: 115) He believes, though, that there is a 'common aspect of the social and cultural constitution of human beings that can be identified as implying, if not conferring rights in this sense'. (Turner, 2000: 115)

Turner argues that since cultures are the products of beings of the same species, 'culture in an abstract sense can be considered a generic attribute of the species as a whole'. In his view, 'The mere existence of cultural differences does not logically preclude the possibility of cultural universals, any more than the specific differences among languages precludes the possibility of universal features of language'. (Turner, 2000: 118) He says,

> That cultures differ in specific ways thus does not in itself contravene, but rather logically presupposes, the possibility that universal properties or principles of culture might exist at a more general level. The relativist argument that to be human is to be enculturated in a specific culture

> and social system, different in many respects from all others, does not gainsay that the processes through which people produce their societies and themselves in all their cultural uniqueness might themselves share common features. Processes of social and cultural production and reproduction, rather than cultural traits, values, or norms abstracted from the social processes in which they are produced and used, might thus be considered as the matrix of general attributes of human species-being. (Turner, 2000: 119)

Turner, thus, while recognizing differences in cultures, emphasizes the universality of the processes of enculturation that can form the basis of human rights and be the common link amongst societies. He says, 'The "capacity for culture" is essentially the power to produce social existence and thus to determine its meaning and social form'. (Turner 2000: 120) Differences in cultural practices are bound to occur. But, these differences cannot form a criterion to discriminate, a basis of denying human rights. On the contrary, differences in 'encultured' human beings may 'constitute a positive, trans cultural basis of human rights'. The criterion of 'human difference' as a fundamental human right is such that it points 'not to a concept of culture in terms of inert and historical structures composed of essentialized traits or canons, but to the active historical process of creating cultural (and social and linguistic) meanings, identities and forms.' (Turner, 2000: 121)

A different kind of justification of human rights is given by Kellenberger (2001) who bases his argument for human rights on the fact of human relationships. This view looks at a human being not individualistically but as a *social* being and takes his relationships with other individuals as a basic fact about him. It is not merely a fact that individuals are related to other individuals in various relationships, but an individual *is* what he is by virtue of being so related. Relationships define the 'roles' that we assume in our lives and roles define who we are. Human beings are rational beings but rationality, however it may be construed, only forms part of our natures. What we are is, in a very significant sense, defined or determined by who we are, the different roles that we may be playing at any given time in our life. The roles we play are influenced by the sociocultural milieu in which we have our existence and this in itself is subject to change creating different 'persons' or personalities of the same person.

Kellenberger begins with a basic fact that there are a variety of interpersonal relationships that relate individual human beings like marriage, parenthood, friendship citizenship, etc. But, there is a primary relationship that each person has with each other person by virtue of nothing more than being a person. This relationship extends to people known and unknown and also to the future generation. He calls this the person/person relation. Every relationship has certain requirements that present themselves as obligations on the part of individuals who are bound in that relationship. These requirements can be met or violated. The person/person relationship also has its requirement, which is that we treat persons with the kind of respect that a person *per se* deserves. This relationship can be violated when this requirement is not met. Examples of violations of the person/person relationship are causing unnecessary harm and torture to others, having unjust/unfair dealings with persons, etc. According to Kellenberger, 'The person/person relationship explains the existence of human rights transcending cultural restrictions whereas the requirements of other relationships, themselves partially modelled by societal factors, explain the culture dependent aspect of human rights'. (Kellenberger, 2001: 140) He further says, 'the person/person relationship is a broad test for human rights and explains not only the basic human right to be treated as a person but what ever other rights there are. Thus, if there is a human right to liberty (as affirmed in Article 3 of the Universal Declaration) this is because a denial of liberty would violate the person/person relationship to those denied'. (Kellenberger, 2001: 145) The person/person relationship is truly inalienable since it exists simply by virtue of one's being a person. He clearly states that the person/person relationship does not presuppose a particular conception of a person or even that there can be a fixed definition of person in terms of some essential features. In his view, 'persons are those we meet, love, envy, sympathize with, towards whom we have duties, and with whom we have relationships of many kinds – including the person/person relationship'. The person/person relationship is compatible with the idea of a person as a social self, as also with the idea of a person as an individual with intrinsic value having a moral responsibility towards all other individuals. According to Kellenberger, the person/person relationship explains why the same values of justice, autonomy, compassion, peace, etc. have been accepted, albeit in different forms by different societies. It also explains how human rights can be recognized. Since rights derive from this basic relationship, they are not invented or created. Human rights, as the Universal Declaration says, are *recognized* and they are recognized in and through human relationships.

Both the Kantian argument and Gewirth's argument proceed on the assumption that human nature in itself, and so human purposive action also, is homogenous. The homogeneity is considered and the differences neglected. But as was seen in the views of Turner and Kellenberger, the humanness of human beings is to be sought in and through the differences that are expressed in the forms of varying cultural beliefs and practices. The humanness, whatever that may be, is the basis of human rights, but takes on different forms in differing sociocultural backgrounds. To consider only the commonness in abstraction and to make it a basis of human rights will not work. A view, which seeks to reconcile Moral Relativism with the demands of moral objectivity and moral universalism is required and Kellenberger's account seems to be an attempt in that direction.

Conclusion

The debate on the issue of the priority of human rights notwithstanding, human rights have come to be universally accepted and a great deal of effort is being made both at national and international levels to ensure that there are no gross violations of human rights while being sensitive to the cultural differences that characterize and distinguish societies and communities therein. Thus, it seems that although there are no clear solutions to human rights related problems arising out of intercultural and sometimes intracultural differences, an effort can be made to understand these differences and find ways to alleviate the problems. In such cases, the old adage – 'only the wearer knows where the shoe pinches' seems to hold true. Perhaps, what is required is the attitude of 'putting oneself in other's shoes'. Of course, it is a different question how and to what extent this is genuinely possible without facing charges of imputing meaning where there is none or a meaning that is different from the original.

Notes

1 There are many different versions and notions of Moral Relativism,, a brief account of each is given in Moser, Paul K, and Carson, Thomas L, eds, 2001, *Moral Relativism: A Reader*, New York, Oxford University Press.

2 Passage quoted in Gowans, Christopher W, 2000, ed, *Moral Disagreements: Classic and Contemporary Readings*, London, Routledge, p. 8.

3 *Journal of Anthropological Research*, Vol. 53, No. 3 (Fall 1997). This special issue has the title, 'Universal Human Rights Versus Cultural Relativity' and contains several articles by anthropologists who have re-examined 'cultural relativism' understood as a relativistic view in opposition to culture-neutral human rights.

References

Donnelly, Jack, 1989, *Universal Human Rights in Theory and Practice*, Ithaca, Cornell University Press.

Gewirth, Alan, 2000, 'Is Cultural Pluralism Relevant to Moral Knowledge' in Gowans, Christopher W, ed, 2000, *Moral Disagreements: Classic and Contemporary Reading*, London, Routledge.

Gowans, Christopher W, 2000, *Moral Disagreements: Classic and Contemporary Readings*, London, Routledge.

Kellenberger, J. 2001, *Moral Relativism, Moral Diversity and Human Relationships.* University Park, The Pennsylvania State University Press.

Milne, A J M, 1986, *Human Rights and Human Diversity*, London, Macmillan Press.

Rachels, James, 'The Challenge of Cultural Relativism' in Moser, Paul K, and Carson, Thomas L, eds, 2001, *Moral Relativism: A Reader,* New York, Oxford University Press.

Rorty, Richard, 1993, 'Human Rights, Rationality and Sentimentality' in Shute, Stephen and Hurley, Susan, eds, *On Human Rights,* New York, Basic Books.

Salmon, Merrilee H, 1997, 'Ethical Considerations in Anthropology and Archaeology or Relativism and Justice for All' in *Journal of Anthropological Research,* Vol. 53, No. 3, (Fall 1997).

Turner, Terence, 'Human Rights, Human Difference: Anthropology's Contribution to an Emancipatory Cultural Politics' in Gowans, Christopher W, ed, 2000, *Moral Disagreements: Classic and Contemporary Readings,* London, Routledge.

Xiarong Li, 'Human Rights, Development, and "Asian Values"' in Barbara MacKinnon, 2001, *Ethics: Theory and Contemporary Issues,* third edition, Stanford, Wadsworth Thomson Learning.

Chapter 6

COMPLICITY AND RESPONSIBILITY

Pratap Bhanu Mehta

Dostoyevsky's novel, *The Brothers Karamazov* is constructed around the very complex and compelling ideal that action – committing an act and thereby causing something to be – is only one and perhaps a trivial element in the moral economy of guilt and wrongdoing. In the novel, all the brothers are guilty of their father's death, although only one of them has killed him, because each recognizes that he might have done so instead. Dostoyevsky plays with a not uncommon thought: the awareness of one's actual character traits sometimes warrants feelings of guilt and responsibility, ordinarily ascribed only to wrongdoers. We are responsible in this view, *if we have the sort of character that could have done it*, even though we did not actually do it; Gunter Grass' sardonic and rueful introspections trade on this thought, and much of the literature on collective violence, during partition, derives its power from holding us responsible by asking: are you the sort of person who could have done it? Even others wrongdoing can impugn our character and our values make us feel guilty and responsible, even if we did not ourselves do anything wrong. All we need to do is counterfactually establish that we could have done it. The suspicion that one might oneself be capable of acting wrongly or monstrously is an instance of what Christopher Kutz has called counterfactual guilt. Sometimes such counterfactual guilt can help expose the deep and quotidian ways in which we are complicit in evil, whether we did or not; more often than not it explains some forms of enduring self hatred – I did not do something wrong, but I am the sort of person who could – is not an easy thought to live with.

On the other hand, and unfortunately more commonly than acceptance of counterfactual guilt or responsibility, we often witness denials of complicity, especially when our participation in evils perpetrated by large collectivities is at stake. Indeed one might argue strongly that we absolve ourselves of responsibility far too readily: we engage in what we might call counterfactual acquittal – Yes, I may have participated in bringing about evil, but anyone in my position would have done the same; or, my contribution to producing this evil is so negligible that I cannot be said to have caused it; or since so many people were involved in producing the outcome I cannot be really said to control it and am therefore not responsible – not really. Somehow individual responsibility seems to vanish under the mystifying pronoun 'we'.

Responsibility is an integral part of human relationships in its various meanings and shadings. In the interests of time I will ignore the various things we mean by responsibility: etymologically the phrase 'to be responsible' suggests the notion of giving an answer, to justify oneself or to account for action. But it also means to have caused something, and in principle one can be morally responsible without being causally responsible and vice versa. To be responsible may also be to bear the cost of something even though one is not quite either morally or causally responsible, but the cost accrues to one, in light of certain other relationships we have to a particular event. I am, in what follows, ignoring these complications and using responsibility slightly loosely. I want to focus more on a slightly different question. Individuals engage in a variety of forms of collective action and a range of questions arise about how to hold individuals responsible in contexts where the outcomes are a product of a large number of actions undertaken by other people. The most common basis for holding individuals responsible for the actions of their group is by ascribing a participatory intention to them. If a group is so structured that three conditions are met, allocation of responsibility is relatively easier. First, members are intentionally members of that group; second, the group has a collective decision-making rule and third, there is a sufficient overlap in the participatory intentions of the members of that group – they broadly share the objectives that come out of the decision making rules of that group. In such circumstances something like a complicity principle is easy to apply: I am accountable for what others do when I intentionally participate in the wrong they do or the harm they cause. I am accountable for the harm or wrong we do together independently of the actual difference I make; merely by participating and sharing the aims of the group, I am implicated.

Assigning individual responsibility in the context of collective action is thought to be problematic for a number of reasons. Most importantly it seems to violate two common sense assumptions we make in ascribing responsibility. The first is, as Christopher Kutz has named them, individual difference principle. I am accountable only if I did make a difference to the harm's occurrence. The second is what we might call the control principle. I am responsible only when I could control the occurrence of harm, by producing it or preventing it. When people act together in large numbers – and acting together can take various forms – structured collective action, as say in a corporation, joint intentional action, as say in a riot, or unconnected actions of individuals each acting in their own capacity where each individual action is morally unexceptionable, but taken together they produce great harm – say polluting the air, or the kind of thing Derek Parfit describes in the famous 'harmless torturers' example – these common sense intuitions absolve us of individual responsibility. We really could not have made a difference to the harms occurrence acting individually, nor could we have controlled the outcome, so we are not really responsible as individuals.

The temptation in such circumstances is to take recourse to some idea of collective responsibility. In principle, for the purposes of the argument here, I will assume that such collective ascriptions make sense. But even when we assign collective responsibility, the question of individual responsibility does not altogether disappear. Sometimes the group as a whole is held accountable; we simply substitute a 'we' for an 'I' as the locus of accountability. But there are two problems with collective responsibility. First, the familiar problem of why particular individuals who happen to be part of the 'we' should all indiscriminately bear the costs that come with assigning responsibility to the whole. Second, a motivational issue – forms of collective accountability often fail to provide individual motivational considerations necessary to prevent such harms from occurring in the first place. Baron Edwards' lament, that did you ever expect a corporation to have a conscience when it has no soul to be dammed and no body to be kicked, picks out a familiar worry about the metaphysics of ascriptions of collective responsibility. Where all are held responsible, it is more likely that none will feel responsible. Because individuals are ultimately the loci of normative motivation and deliberation, only forms of accountability aimed at and sensitive to what individuals can do is likely to succeed in controlling the emergence of collective harms. The fact that something is a collective responsibility does not entail that it is not an individual responsibility. In fact sometimes saying that a society as a whole is responsible is really a way of saying that nobody is responsible.

Karl Jaspers once used the term metaphysical responsibility to refer to the rather controversial idea that simply sharing an identity with perpetrators can confer a kind of responsibility or moral taint, even on non-perpetrating members of the group. So, even non-participating Germans were, on this view, morally tainted by and responsible for the monstrosities committed by fellow Germans. The idea of such ascriptions of collective responsibility is rightly held to be morally problematic. They can often themselves take the form of ethnic or racial stereotyping, they often seem to deny the link between responsibility and control, since at least some of the identities ascribed to us are beyond our control, and they violate the idea of separateness of persons – one must consider each person separately and weigh the moral accountability on the basis of their actions. But even when these objections are granted the question of complicity does not quite go away.

Let us take the following case. Imagine a person. Call him Narendra, who is a member of what we might loosely call an ethnic group that has committed atrocities against another group. If Narendra is directly involved in killing, beating, looting or worse, his responsibility is clear. But even short of that Narendra can bear responsibility. If he publicly advocated violence, he shares responsibility, if he in other words displayed the right participatory intention, he bears responsibility. If he voted for a regime that was capable of these actions and the regime then went on to perpetrate violence he is, in a certain sense responsible; even if Narendra voted in ignorance of the regimes intentions, the ignorance itself could be culpable ignorance. These attributions of responsibility are not very controversial so long as many relevant complications are admitted. For instance, the less one causally contributes to the harm, the less one is to blame for it.

Narendra might also be held responsible if he simply did nothing; for sins of omission. If he was in a position to prevent the atrocity without taking undue risk, and he knew this, failing to act would also be a form of complicity. You might argue that in acts of omission, the link between causality and responsibility is broken. I did not 'cause' this, Narendra might protest. The simplest way of responding is, simply to say that omission is a species of action as well. Narendra's omission was a choice and hence there is a causal link between what he 'did' and the outcome.

Suppose, as is often the case, Narendra cannot be held responsible for any of the reasons discussed so far. But also suppose that he is a beneficiary of the violence. These benefits can take many forms, like outright financial benefits. Violence can be part of a structure of institutionalized discrimination from which Narendra benefits simply by virtue of his membership in a group, even though he does not particularly share the group's aims. Simply belonging to that group can itself be a form of privilege – as in Narendra does not have to justify himself or his presence in this society whereas his counterparts in the oppressed group do. Some people are seen as a threat simply because of who they are; whereas members of Narendra's ethnic group face no such disability. Suppose further that there is little Narendra can do to make a difference. The circumstances are overdetermined by the actions of others. Ascriptions of responsibility in these circumstances are slightly trickier, because there is no obvious connection between Narendra's actions and his enjoyment of benefits. The connection between responsibility and making a causal difference to the world, and having choice, seems not to obtain in this instance. In what sense might Narendra be responsible?

I do not argue this point here, but if we associate responsibility with both guilt on the one hand, and causal culpability or punishment on the other, Narendra is not responsible in the usual sense of the term. But it seems to me perfectly possible that one can be responsible without being guilty. Narendra might be responsible in the sense that he owes something to the victims, perhaps simply the duty of restoring a more morally admissible texture of relations between himself and the victims of whose misfortune he is a beneficiary, even though he has not himself contributed to their misfortune, nor was he in a position to prevent it.

Of course, Narendra might be in a situation where his community and he by implication do not profit from the community's crimes. The violence leads to international condemnation, the shutting down of embassies which in turn, diminishes his prospect of employment abroad. Even if the community loses by its crimes, it is still tainted by them – we might still think that the moral position of members of this community is affected by this taint. Why might we think so?

The one easy answer is if the following circumstance obtains. Suppose Narendra is not implicated in any way other than sharing some of the beliefs and dispositions of his co-perpetrators. He himself does not kill anyone in the rival ethnic group, but harbours prejudices and fantasies about them that could sustain violence, he may even resist these prejudices but the fact remains that he has them. He could very easily say to himself: the people who did the killing were just like me; we have similar beliefs, and honesty demands that I conclude that the structure of my beliefs and dispositions are capable of producing violence. Just by possessing these beliefs and traits I am putting others in society at risk; the degree of responsibility turns on the degree of risk I pose to others. I am being held responsible based on a probabilistic calculus of causation; my shared identity makes me culpable because it is very likely that this deficiency I share with my co-groupies will give rise to violence. Now what we think of this interpretation depends in part of what we think of a larger issue. Is the difference between the racist who kills and the racist who does not simply a matter of luck – and if luck is morally arbitrary – the moral distinction between the prejudiced person who kills and the prejudiced who does not, is narrower than we might suppose. There is always a degree of indeterminacy between what one could do, what one even plans to do (imagine if Narendra had intended to join the rioting but chickenpox kept him in bed), and what one actually does. So we might still want to say that Narendra is responsible for who he is; his character and beliefs, even if he is not responsible for the crimes – other than by a process of counterfactual guilt of the sort Gunter Grass describes.

But suppose even Narendra is a genuine innocent; has never harboured ill will and has the purest of intentions, but still comes to be tainted because the group of which he is a member has committed a crime. At least, and often from the perspective of the victims, this taint lingers. For instance, you have stories coming out of the relief camps in Gujarat that victims will not talk to Hindu lawyers, even when brought in by non-governmental organizations (NGOs) with immense credibility. They would rather have no lawyer or a third-rate lawyer than a Hindu one. Of course the motives behind this boycott are complex; could be sending a signal that we do not recognize the legitimacy of state institutions. But part of it at least could be read as saying that we are all tainted by virtue of membership in a group even when we are otherwise innocent. We are tainted in this instance, not because we are guilty – in the sense that we caused something or could cause some evil, but because we become an object of fear. In other words, Narendra the innocent comes to share responsibility in so much as he now acquires a duty to respond to the legitimate fears of the victims. Even dissociation – Narendra saying I am not that kind of Hindu, or not even a Hindu at all – may not be enough. We as individuals are implicated in our groups, and acquire responsibilities which individual innocence may not absolve us of.

Since time is short let me draw out some larger philosophical implications of the story I have told above. If the line of reasoning above is plausible, notice what has happened to our conception of responsibility. First it has shifted from the question of causal attribution to a more political conception. Simply saying, I did not cause it; I could not have made a difference; I am not responsible for other people's actions – while three independently sound intuitions, do not necessarily absolve us from our responsibilities. This is because, and this is the main point I want to make, responsibility is most appropriately thought of as a political concept.

Responsibility is a political concept: what does this mean? The claim that it is political does not mean that it is best decided by the process of politics, say by democratic assemblies, nor that it is inevitably the result of partisan struggles for power. It is to claim that this account of responsibility is specific to political morality rather than a comprehensive moral or metaphysical system. Most philosophical discussions of responsibility – think of H L A Hart's for example, seem to turn on: how are acts individuated? Do we really freely perform the acts that we do? Was the person really in control of what they did? Rather I take it to be the case that questions of responsibility turn not simply upon our conception of the person, but upon a view of our relations to others. Questions of responsibility are linked to questions of what the fair terms of interaction between the parties concerned are. Take the law of torts – now slowly developing in India. In the case of accidental injury, say while driving, we can ask two sorts of questions. Could the driver really have helped it? What is the particular cause of the accident? How do we individuate that action? But whatever our answer to these questions, there is a sense in which the injured party will be left to bear the cost of the injury, if someone, the injurer or someone else in society does not pay some compensation. From the point of the victim, assignment of responsibility is in part a question of who bears the cost. Even from the point of the perpetrator, at least in the case of accidents, rather than criminal negligence, the issue will arise: is it fair to hold me responsible for the outcome by imposing costs on me to such an extent that my life is ruined? There are different ways in which societies might hold people responsible – but part of the allocation will always involve the thought that questions about responsibility in which we take an interest only have answers against the background of what the fair terms of interaction are. Allocations of responsibility are not simply a question of – did I cause it? Did I have control over what I brought about? Did my action actually make a difference to the outcome? What was my intention? These questions sever the connection between responsibility and what people owe each other. They rather focus excessively on the relation between the agent and the events that ensued. Allocation of responsibility is rather a way of addressing what people owe each other; it is a mechanism for maintaining and repairing relationships. Responsibility cannot be understood only in terms of individual capacity to act and their effects, but also needs to be refracted through moral and social relations to others and to oneself.

Suppose Narendra, the virtuous character that he comes to be, accepts his responsibility in this wider sense. But he and we might have a legitimate worry. Why is he being asked to bear the cost of actions done by others, of harms inflicted which he did not bring about and was in no position to control? Of course the burden imposed on him by way of repairing these relationships ought to be less on him than on those who perpetrated the violence, but I only want to make one point; the fact that he did not cause the harms and was not in a position to prevent them, does not automatically absolve him from bearing all costs. But the question of bearing the cost turns on in part a normative conception of the fair terms of interaction, not on attributions of causal power. In tort law we impose costs without causal liability; and we think someone ought to take responsibility – in the sense of bearing the cost, be responsible for – disabled children even though no one caused them to be such and no one could have prevented them from being such. Allocations of responsibility are part of debates over distributive justice, not simply a matter of figuring out the relation between agents and the consequences of what they do.

Think of the small functionary in a corporation about to inflict harm, or a low level police official in a riot-like situation. Mark Bovens, in his study of corporate law shows that such officials give one or more of nine excuses when accused of complicity in the harmful actions of their organizations: I was just a small cog in the machine. Other people did much more than I. If I had not done it someone else would have. Even without my contribution it would have happened. Without my contribution it would have been worse. I had nothing to do with it. I knew nothing of it. I only did what I was told to do. I had no choice. What is interesting about these excuses is that the first seven turn on the common sense intuitions of difference and control principles: again, I could not have made a difference and I could not have controlled the outcome. There are independent reasons for thinking that this form of causal dissociation does not really work. None of these excuses are adequate. The last one: I had no choice, can have some force, literally and figuratively. Most philosophers spend their time discussing what it means to 'have no choice'. If corporate whistleblowers, say the person who ratted on the big tobacco companies, said – 'my son is sick, we need health insurance, ratting will lead to lose my job and insurance. I have no choice.' We can discuss the relevant sense of no choice. What such dilemmas – the police officer afraid of losing his job – point to it the fact that our assignment of responsibility cannot be entirely independent of the question of who bears the cost for acting responsibly. This question has independent weight in the assignment of responsibility, apart from questions of causal attribution. In so far as the background social arrangements of a society are unjust, attributions of responsibility will in all likelihood impose more unfair costs on a few people. The point is not to exonerate individuals because society is unjust – we may have our duties irrespective of what others do. The point is to highlight the fact that just attributions of responsibility involve taking into account the fair distribution of costs of acting responsibly, and that too much of a focus on holding individuals causally responsible, may be a way of denying the obvious and morally compelling fact that we may not be paying our part in bearing the costs of responsibility. Responsibility is connected to justice, not just in the simple sense that he who does it must pay; but also in the more expansive sense that it is something we distribute. Whether the distribution is fair, I am arguing, does not depend only on the question of holding an individual causally responsible. It rather depends upon whether the terms on which we collectively cooperate are themselves fair.

Chapter 7

DHARMA: THE OVERRIDING PRINCIPLE OF INDIAN LIFE AND THOUGHT

S. R. Bhatt

Dharma has been one of the most dominant and pervasive concepts of Indian view and way of life. It has been the foundation of the entire life and culture of India underlying all her achievements in the fields of science, philosophy, literature, arts, morality, sociality, polity, religion and spirituality. As Prof. Cromwell Crawford has truly opined, 'To know India try grasping the myriad forms of Dharma, for in the depths of this single word lies an entire civilization'. (Crawford, 1967: XVI) *Dharma* is an extremely rich and polymorphous concept embracing diverse though not unrelated senses. In the course of several centuries it has acquired wide ramifications of meanings and has been used in different contexts–metaphysical, moral, religious, artistic, social, political, legal, etc. But its basic law-centered meaning has remained unchanged. Because of its proliferous nature no one all-inclusive definition of *dharma* can be provided and its precise meaning is to be understood from the context in which it has been used.

Indian culture is characterized by a spiritual orientation and an integral and holistic approach. Its varied and variegated fabric is interwoven with multiple ideas and ideals, thoughts and practices among which the notion of *dharma* is both pivotal and foundational. It is like a luminous jewel that not only enlightens Indian culture but also has the potentiality of illuminating the entire world culture and civilization. This claim is not atavistic but has been testified by many of the great and perceptive thinkers of the world. The Vedic seers, no doubt, stated confidently that it is a culture that is primeval and worthy of preference by the world because of its perennial significance ('*Sā prathamā sanskṛti viśva vārā*', *Yajurveda* VII.14), but all those who got its correct exposure have also so opined. Even in modern times many unbiased scholars have highlighted its contemporary need and relevance. For example, Late Prof. Charles Moore of Hawaii University writes, '[...] there are very significant ideas and concepts there–no matter how old they are–to which the rest of the world may well turn for new insights and perhaps deeper wisdom [...] India provides a basis for potential philosophical renaissance, if only the rest of the world, specially the West, will search out the new insights, the new intuitions, the new attitudes and methods which might well at least supplement if not replace or correct–and at least enlarge–the restricted perspective of the Western mind' (Moore, 1967: 8–9).

The importance and significance of *dharma,* not only in Indian context but also in the world context, can be summed up in the following verse of the *Taittiriya Āraṇyaka* (quoted by P B Tripathi in *Puruṣārtha catuṣṭaya*, p. 38)

Dharmo viśvasya jagata pratiśṭhā
Lokedharmiṣṭham prajā upasarpanti,
Dharmeṇa pāpamapanudati,
Dharme sarvam pratiṣṭhitam.
Tasmāt dharmam paramam vadanti.

i.e., '*Dharma* is the basis and sustaining power of the entire cosmic world. In this world all originated entities evolve only by following the *dharma.* Through *dharma* vices and evil get dissipated. All are situated in *dharma.* This is why *dharma* is said to be the supreme most.' If properly understood and practiced it provides meaning and significance not only to individual human life but also to the whole cosmos because it is a principle of cosmic ordering and coordination, integration and regulation, supporting and balancing and thus it is of universal welfare.

It is a hard though painful fact that cosmic life in general, and human life in particular (as human is a self-conscious ratiocinative being), is enmeshed in imperfection and consequent suffering, and therefore the quest for perfection (*amṛtatva*) and eradication of suffering constitute the *summum bonum* of life. *Dharma* has been visualized as the only effective and efficacious means to get this desired goal. Therefore, Kaṇada, the author of the *Vaiśeṣika* sutras, defines *dharma* as that from which there is realization of material prosperity and spiritual enhancement. ('*Yato' bhyudaya niḥśreyasa siddhiḥ sa dharmaḥ'*). *Dharma,* if properly practiced, is the surest means to universal welfare (*sarvabhūtahita*) that should be the goal of all cosmic processes. This goal has been variously characterized in Indian culture as *'svasti', 'śam', 'magala', 'śānti', 'kalyāna,' 'śiva',* etc. This is a goal that is not an individual's to be realized in isolation. It is a cosmic goal to be experienced collectively. Its realization is the spiritual globalization aspired for by the Vedic seer, when they wished to Aryanise the whole universe ('*Kṛṇavanto vśvamāryam.*' *Ṛgveda* IX. 63.5). Classical Indian literature is replete with innumerable expressions of intense human longings to this effect. Nowhere in any of the scriptures is it stated that this goal is an individual enterprise to be accomplished and enjoyed by a single individual. In fact, in the Indian culture there is no idea of an isolated individual as every existence is conceived as an element (*piṇḍa* or *vyaṣṭi*) in the totality (*Brahmāṇḍa* or *samaṣti*) or as one with the totality. The cosmos is to be experienced as a corporate and cooperative living (*kuṭumba* or *nīḍa*) with mutual care and share, with interdependence and interrelationship. *Dharma* is the principle that has to ensure this. This precisely is the meaning of the well-known etymology of *Dharma* as '*Dhāraṇāddharmamityāhuḥ dharmeṇa dhāryate prajāḥ.*' ('Karnṇa Parva', *Mahābhārata*, 69 58) This insurance is through the twin principles of *'yoga-kṣema'*, which along with the practices of *'asteya'* and *'aparigraha'* constitute the four pillars of the science and art of cosmic management. The *Bhagvadgītā* has very succinctly propounded this. The *jñānayoga, karmayoga* and *bhaktiyoga* propounded by it are the supreme principles of management of individual and cosmic life.

The concept of *dharma* has its genesis in the Vedic intuition of '*ṛta*' from which it has flown into and permeated every form and facet of Indian life. '*Ṛta*' conceptualizes the vision of the Vedic seers of an inexorable, unswerving and pervasive order prevailing in the Reality and the cosmos. They apprehended an immanent teleology in the Reality and 'telos-embeddedness' in the cosmic process. The very word *'viśva'* stands for the penetration and pervasiveness of order in the cosmos. '*Ṛta*' is coupled with *'satya'* (steadfastness, invariability, non-discrepancy, etc.). The Vedic seers apprehended both *ṛta'* and *'satya'* through *'tapas' ('brāhmaṇasya tapo jñanam,' Manu Samhitā* XI.236) that is a supra-conscious subliminal realization in the yogic state of existence that transcends sense-experience and intellection of mortals. ('*Ṛtam ca satyam cābhīddhāttapaso' dhyajāyata'*, *Ṛgveda*, X.190.1). *'Ṛta'* stands for order and orderly activities. This is the normal behaviour of spiritual beings. (*'ṛtasya devānuvratāḥ' Ṛgveda*, I.62.2). '*Ṛta*' is to be known and adhered to. We should have '*ṛtambharā prajñā'* and we should be *'ṛtavan'*. Any transgression, violation or deviation from it is *'anṛta'*. *'Anṛta'* is due to extraneous factors that pervert and pollute. It affects or covers up *'satya'* (*Ṛgveda*, VII. 49.3). It disturbs the steadfast adherence to *'ṛta'*. Therefore the Vedas advise and exhort us to follow the path of '*ṛta*'. *('ṛtasya panthāmanutisra'. Atharvaveda*, VIII. 8–13).

'Ṛta' and *'dharma'* are cognates and therefore later on they got conflated and the word *dharma* got currency and popular acceptance. It retained the full meaning of the word *'ṛta'* and also acquired new and additional meanings. However, its negative counterpart *'anṛta'* continued to be in use. How and why

the replacement of *'ṛta'* with *dharma* took place is an issue of *'śāstra-vinoda'* with which we are not presently concerned.

There are three close associates of the term *'ṛta'* (and *ipso facto* of *dharma*) in the Vedic literature. They are *'svadhā'* (*'svam dhārayati'* and the word *'dharma'* might have been derived from it), *'vrata'* and *'yajña'*. All the three are essential for the proper understanding and practice of *dharma*. It is unfortunate that these significant words have lost their original meanings and have been distorted much to the misunderstanding of the Vedic wisdom and with detrimental impact on Indian society. *Svadhā* stands for the inherent nature of all entities. It constitutes their *svabhāva* (nature) and sustains them in spite of mutations. *Vrata* means conduct in conformity with *'satya'* and *dharma*, which is conducive to general welfare. So '*Satyam vada. Dharmam cara*' is a *vrata*. One who follows *vrata* is *anuvrata*. As stated earlier, the *devas* are *anuvratas*. We have also been told to cultivate *devatva* (Divine Life) in us. ('*Manurbhava janayā daivyamjanam*' *Ṛgveda* X. 53.6) For this we have to be *vratadhṛta*. *Yajña* is the principle of manifestation of the multiple worlds as a corporate unity having a common source and fund. In enjoins commonality of thought, action and enjoyment. It is a principle of coexistence, harmony, cooperation and partaking. It is the *'anāsakta karma'* as enunciated in the *Bhagvadgītā*. It is the best type of karma to be performed ('*Yajño vai śreṣṭhatamam karma*', *Śatapatha*, 1.7.1.5) as it is the pivotal principle of the cosmos. ('*Yajña viśvasya bhuvanasya nābhiḥ*', *Ṛgveda*, 1,164.35). It has been defined as a collective endeavour, preserving and enhancing natural resources, and performed with the purpose of equitable and distributive sharing of the fruits. (*Sāmudāyikam yogakṣemam uddiśya samudāyangatayā kriyamānam karma yajñah*). That is why after performance of *yajña*, it is said, '*Idam na mama*'. In fact it is a transition from *'mama'* to *'sarva'*. The fruit of *yajña* is *prasāda*, i.e., to be enjoyed in distributive form (*prasārena*).

Metaphysical Dimension of *Dharma*

Dharma has two basic facets, viz., constitutive (*dhāraka*) and regulative (*niyāmaka*). Both are closely interrelated like two sides of the same coin. In its constitutive facet it is the 'Law of being', the 'deepest law of our nature', to use Sri Aurobindo's expressions. (Sri Aurobindo, 1959: 2 and 104)

It constitutes the nature of a thing (*svabhāva*) and its disposition (*guṇa*) and determines its *karma*. When Praśastapāda names his commentary as '*Padārthadharmasamgraha*' on the *Vaiśeṣika sūtras* of Kaṇāda, he is referring to this aspect of *dharma*. Every *padārtha* has its own unique *dharma* that provides it its individuality and role and function in the totality of *padārthas*. For example, it is said that *'agni'* (fire) has *'dāha dharma'* (the nature of burning) and thus contributes to the overall functioning of the cosmos. *Dharma* not only constitutes the being of things but also sustains them and the cosmos by determining their *karma* (course of action). *Dharma* causes self-preservation and evolution (*yoga-kṣema*) of every *padārtha*. *Dharma* of each *padaārtha* further contributes to the total preservation and evolution of the cosmos. Thus *dharma* serves as a means to *abhyudaya* and *niḥśreyasa* as envisaged by Kaṇāda. (*Vaiśeṣika sūtra* 1.1.2) In the *Bhagvadgītā* (IV.13) also when there is the reference to *dharma* in the context of *'cāturvarnya'* it pertains to *svabhāva, guṇa* and *karma*. When *dharma* is defined as *'Dhāraṇāddharmaḥ'* it also primarily refers to this aspect. As Sri Aurobindo puts it, 'Everything indeed has its *Dharma,* its law of life imposed on it by its nature [...]' (Sri Aurobindo, 1959: 104). Though it is distinct and specific to every individual, no individual has an isolated and independent nature. Everything partakes in the totality (*samaṣṭi*) as its member or part (*vyaṣṭi*). (Sri Aurobindo,1959: 340) When the *Majjhim Nikāya* and *Sālistambasūtra* state that *'yo bhikṣavaḥ pratityasamutpādam paśyati sa Buddham paśyati, yo Buddham paśyati saḥ dharmam paśyati'*, they are referring to this interdependence and interrelatedness of all phenomena. (Suzuki, 1963) The concepts of *brahmabhāva, sarvātmābhāva, ekātmābhāva, buddhābhāva, dharmakāya,* etc. are expressive of this truth. This is the purport of the *Avatamsakasūtra,* which while describing 'Indra's Jewel Net' as a simile for this truth says about the multiple jewels as 'One is in all and all is in one'. The point is that each entity has its own *dharma* derived from the totality, which provides it its distinct nature and sustains it.

This is the metaphysical dimension of *dharma,* which is the most basic dimension. The great Vedic seers envisioned these *dharmas* with their underlying unity long back. (*'Tāni dharmāni prathmanyāsan'*, Ṛgveda, X. 90.16) This *virāṭa darśana* (cosmic vision) and *paraspara bhāvanā* (mutuality) together make possible a natural transition from 'I' (*aham*) to 'we' (*sarvam*) as is witnessed in the *Sāmmanasya sūktas* of the Vedas, and in *śāntipāṭhas, Svastivacanas, Nāndī ślokas, Subhāṣitas,* etc. in classical literature. These are expressions of intense longings for peace, perfection and beatitude for the entire universe, to be brought about particularly by human beings as *'mānava dharma'* in a conscious, systematic and planned way, in close cooperation and with communitarian spirit. This precisely is meant when it is said that *'Dharmo viśvasya jagataḥ pratiṣṭhā'*. Only through these noble aspirations, collaborative endeavours can motivate us to act in an *'anāsakata'* manner as advocated in the *Îsopanisad* and the *Bhagvadgītā,* the manuals of cosmic management par excellence. The whole cosmos is a *yajña (Puruṣa yajña)* based on the twin principles of *'yoga-kṣema'* and regulated by the other two principles of *'asteya'* and *'aparigraha'*. These four principles constitute the pillars of every type of management, cosmic or individual. The first two pertain to the skill of performance of *karma* (*dharma*) and the other two deal with equitable and distributive enjoyment of the fruits of *karma.*

Regulatory Role of *Dharma*

The regulative facet of *dharma* is more significant from the worldly point of view. In order to sustain the cosmos *dharma* has to regulate its functioning. This regulation is needed most for the self-conscious human being (*puruṣa*) who is bestowed by nature with free will and responsibility. Thus *dharma* serves as a foundation to morality. We shall discuss this point in detail in the next section. This aspect of *dharma* comprises both virtue-ethics and duty-ethics. In fact in the holistic and integral Indian approach no dichotomies of this sort are entertained. In '*dharmic*' ethics there is symbiosis of 'fact' and 'value', 'is' and 'ought', 'what happens by nature' and 'what ought to happen', 'what happens by perversion' and 'what ought not to happen'. That is why a virtue is posited as '*artha*' (an object to be realized) and the etymology of '*artha*' is '*arthyate prārthyate iti*', but this should not be understood as 'that which is desired'.

A virtue or *dharma* is posited as a norm of conduct to be followed. It is a duty or *dharma* to be adhered to. Thus *dharma* stands both for virtue and the duty to adhere to it. Its prescription carries ought-ness or optative-ness (*codanā*) with it. That is why Jaimini defines dharma as '*Codanā lakṣaṇo'rtho dharmaḥ'*. (*Pūrva Miṃāmsā sūtra*, I.1.2) It is injunctive in nature in the sense that it ought to be pursued (*kartavyatā*). Each *dharma* is ultimately dependent upon the cosmic order for its normative power. This transcendental reference is described as '*apauruṣeyatva'* that guarantees its uncondition-ality, universalizabiltity and infallibility. This point has been elaborately discussed in the *Mīṃāmsa* literature. Knowledge of virtue generates prompting (*bhāvanā*) in the moral agent (*bhāvayitṛ*). This prompting is two-bold, viz., intention (*śābdi*) and resolve (*ārtīi*). It can again be positive (*pravartanā*) and negative (*nivartanā*). This prompting is not due to external sanctions but a result of inner motivation. As Sri Aurobindo puts it, '[…] more deeply it enjoins a spiritual or ethical purity of the mind with action as one outward index'. It is characterized by 'inwardness'. (Sri Aurobindo, 1959: 92) It is thus tripartite, consisting of knowledge, will and action. The duties enjoined are in respect to oneself, one's kith and kin, society, state, humanity and the entire cosmos. They constitute a hierarchy within an all-controlling principle of highest fulfillment of life that serves as criterion of conflict-resolution.

Dharma as a moral norm is not rigidly absolute. It admits of 'wise-relativity', as Sri Aurobindo puts it (Sri Aurobindo: 92). There may be crises-situations (situations of *dharmasaṇkaṭa* or *āpatti*) that may demand deviations, known as *āpaddharma*. Otherwise it is non-violable. These situations have been categorized and codified to eliminate arbitrariness and subjectivism. The *Mahābhārata*, the *Pūrva Miṃāṃsa* texts and the *Dharmaśāstr*a thinkers have discussed in detail such '*apavādas'* (exceptions) in the forms of '*utsarga'* (giving-up), '*atideśa'* (extension), '*samkocana'* (restriction), '*bādhā'* (obstacle), '*vikalpa'* (alternative), etc. Thus even though *dharma* is absolute, universal and eternal, its adherence depends upon the given situation. It is inexorable and mandatory in a particular type of situation, irrespective of person, time, place and circumstances. Furthermore, in a case of its violation in genuine cases there is provision of *prāyaścitta* that has both psychological and physical aspects.

Dharma is fixed and yet evolving. In the words of Sri Aurobindo, '*Dharma* is fixed in its essence, but still it develops in our consciousness and evolves and has stages; there are gradations of spiritual and ethical ascension in the search for the highest law of our nature.' (Sri Aurobindo, 1959: 104) There is evolution of moral consciousness in human society and this will continue till such time that perfection is reached. This is an ideal. Human beings do not remain contented with facts alone and aspire for the ideal. That is way there is a need for virtue-ethics. To quote Sri Aurobindo again, 'The universal embracing *Dharma* in the Indian idea is a law of ideal perfection for the developing mind and soul of man; it compels him to grow in the power and force of certain high and large universal qualities which in their harmony build a highest type of manhood. In Indian thought and life this was the ideal of the best, the law of the good or noble man, the discipline laid down for the self-perfecting individual, *ārya, śrestha, sajjana, sādhu.* This ideal was not a purely moral or ethical conception, although that element might predominate; it was also intellectual, religious, social, aesthetic, the flowering of the whole ideal man, the perfection of the total human nature.' (Sri Aurobindo, 1959: 105)

There are different *dharmas* for different individuals and also for the same individual in different situations or stations of life. So there are *svadharmas, varṇāśramadharmas, kuladharmas, yugadharmas,* etc. There is a wide variety of *dharmas.* In the words of Sri Aurobindo, 'All men cannot follow in all things one common and invariable rule. Life is too complex to admit of the arbitrary ideal simplicity which the moralizing theorists love. Natures differ; the position, the work we have to do has its own claims and standards, aim and bent; the call of life, the call of the spirit within is not the same for everyone: the degree and the turn of development and the capacity, *adhikāra,* are not equal, Man lives in society and by society, and every society has its own general *Dharma,* and the individual life must be fitted into this wider law of movement. But there too the individual's part in society, and his nature and the needs of his capacity and temperament vary and have many kinds and degrees: the social law must make some room for this variety and would by being rigidly one for all. The man of knowledge, the man of power, the productive and acquisitive man, the priest, scholar, poet, artist, ruler, fighter, trader, tiller of the soil, craftsman, labourer, servant cannot usefully have the same training, cannot be shaped in the same pattern, cannot follow the same way of living. All ought not to be put under the same tables of the law; for that would be a senseless geometric rigidity that would spoil the plastic truth of life. Each has his type of nature and there must be a rule for the perfection of that type; each has his own proper function and there must be a canon and ideal for the function. There must be in all things some wise and understanding standard of practice and idea of perfection and living rule that is the one thing needful for the *dharma*.' (Sri Aurobindo, 1959: 105)

Dharma: The Regulator of Other '*Puruṣārthas*'

The scope of *dharma* is so wide and varied that it comprehends the entire gamut of human and cosmic life. However, for the present we shall confine our treatment to a brief account of *dharma* as one of the *'puruṣārthas'* keeping the *Pūrva Mimāṃsā* context in view. There after we shall discuss *'rājadharma'* (a specific *dharma*) that provides the requisite conditions for the pursuit and realization of *puruṣārthas*. The treatment will be based on Indian cultural heritage but it will be in modern idioms with contemporary relevance.

The Quest for excellence leading to and culminating in 'perfection' has been the perennial human concern. There is an innate necessity and instinctive longing in all living beings for a good quality of life. It is not only prolongation of existence but also betterment of living that prompts all beings to carry out their day-to-day activities. The immanent teleology in the cosmic process gets reflected and expressed in human beings in a more pronounced and systematic way. All human endeavours and all pursuits of culture and civilizations have been prompted by and directed towards this existential concern. The cultivation of arts and humanities, the development of science and technology, the undertaking of material production and its trade and commerce, the organization of human conduct both individual and societal, and all manifestations of human potentialities have been stimulated by and engineered in this direction. The concept of *'puruṣārtha'* is one of the prominent formulations of this concern for realization of excellence and perfection. The scheme of four *puruṣārthas*, viz, *dharma, artha, kāma*, and *mokṣa* envelops all dimensions, aspects and stages of human existence–individual, social and cosmic. The Hindu view of life provides an integrated and coordinated schema of value-pursuits consisting of four stages (*āśramas*). Four social orders (*varṇa*) and four objects of life (*puruṣārthas*). The basic framework of this schema has perennial utility and relevance but it needs to be reformulated as per the needs of the times, places and circumstances. *Dharma* is foundational and overriding in this schema. The delineation of *dharma* by the school of *Pūrva Mimāmsā* and by the *Dharmaśāstras* has provided a foundation to morality and law in ancient India and it still continues to provide guidance to the present-day Hindu moral and legal traditions.

Human conduct is the center of all moral and legal reflections and considerations. They presuppose a particular view of human being to whom moral and legal responsibility is attributable. In the *Pūrva Miṃāmsā* system the term '*puruṣa*' is used for such an agent who is '*jñāta*' or '*vivekī*' (ratiocinative and discursive), '*svarāṭ*' (or '*svatantra kartā*' i.e., having free will and not controlled will of a *niyojya kartā*) and *bhoktā* (responsible and teleological enjoyer). The purpose of morality and law is to ensure a virtuous life through proper knowledge and righteous conduct. So the basic requirement is that virtue is to be known and the will and capability to realize it are to be cultivated. For this a three-pronged strategy is prescribed in terms of *sādhya* (end), *sādhanā* (means) and *itikartavyatā* (modalities). *Dharma* stands for virtue and virtuous conduct. It regulates human conduct and thus has instrumental value. It is a means to '*niḥśreyasa*' or '*mokṣa*', which in the ultimate analysis means 'perfection'. It also regulates a balanced and equitable realization of *artha* and *kāma*. *Artha* and *kāma* are *puruṣārthas* only if they are regulated by *dharma*. *Dharma* has to play a very vital and significant role in respect of pursuits of *artha* and *kāma*. It provides spiritual perspective to these pursuits. Legitimate acquisition of material resources is *artha* and their legitimate enjoyment is *kāma*. Both require proper management through *dharma*. Without being regulated by *dharma* they are not *puruṣārthas*. The *Mahābhārata* says, '*Dharmādarthaśca kamaśca sa kimarthaṃ na sevyate.*' (Svargārohaṇa parva 5.62). *Artha* is an economic value for the equitable distribution of which *dharma* is needed. Both the acquisition and the enjoyment of *artha* have to be in accordance with *dharma*. Likewise *kāma* also is to be regulated by dharma. *Kāma* has been given great importance in Indian culture. The *Ṛgveda* (X.129.4) declares,

'*Kāmastadagre samavartatādhi manaso retaḥ prathmam yadāīita*
Sato bandhumasati niravindan hṛdi pratṣyā kavayo manīṣa.'

In the *Bhagvadgītā* (XII.11) the Lord identifies Himself with that *kāma* which is not in contradication with *dharma ('Dharmāviruddho bhūteṣu kāmo'smi Bharatarṣabha')*. Every significant text of Indian culture emphasizes the importance of *kama* and the need to have it regulated by *dharma*.

In order to ensure norm-adherence and to check norm-violation and further to enable *dharma* to regulate *artha* and *kāma* some enforcement agency is needed. That agency is both 'an authority' (i.e. law) and 'a person (s) in authority'. Both together constitute '*rājadharma*' or '*daṇḍa nīti*'.

Whatever be the form of political governance, whether it is present-day democratic forms or possible forms 'beyond democracy' there has to be a rule of law and a system to ensure it. Without this, *artha* and *kāma* as *puruṣārthas* cannot be realized. The ultimate goal of *puruṣārthas* is attainment of all-round progress and prosperity and its equitable distribution among all aspirants without disturbing cosmic peace and harmony. This is possible if the rulers are motivated and guided by the well-known dictum of '*Sarve bhavantu sukhinaḥ, sarve santu nirāmayāḥ. Sarve bhadrāṇi paśyantu mā kaścid duḥkhabhāg bhavet.*' It is a prayer for universal peace, prosperity, health and happiness. In the present context it is important to note that this should be the guiding principle of state policies and programs and all the wings of the government, legislature, executive and judiciary, should be made to adhere to it. We do have the notion of 'public servant' for the rulers but in their actual behaviour they act as masters and lord.

The well-known proverbial statement is

> '*Nāham kāmksye rājyam na svargam nāpurbhavam,*
> *Kāmksye duhkha-tṛptāṇām prāṇīnām-ārtanāśanam.*'

There can be no better idea of a welfare state and no better ideal of a ruler than this. It is not for nothing that Mahatma Gandhi named the ideal state as '*Rāmarajya*'. The idea is that by ensuring peoples' happiness and well-being the ruler ensures his own well-being.

To shun evil and to promote good, to eliminate vices and to proliferate virtues is '*rājadharma*'. A ruler is referred to as '*dharmagoptā*'. Maintenance of law and order is known as '*daṇḍa*' and he is upholder of order (*daṇḍadhartā*). This he has to do for the peace, progress and prosperity of his people.

To conclude *Dharma* is the most pivotal and seminal concept of Indian culture. The entire cosmos is regarded as *dharma*-bound. It stands for the end and the means, the goal and the path, what is and what ought to be. It is a concept of universal and perennial significance. But it is not a theory or a doctrine. It is a view of reality and a way of life. It is something to be practiced by all, in every sphere of existence. It is an ideal, no doubt, but it is an ideal that can be actualized and has been done so in the history of humankind by some noble persons whose illustrious accounts are available to us for emulation.

References

Crawford, Cromwell, 1967, *Evolution of Hindu Ethical Ideals,* Honolulu, University of Hawai'i Press.

Moore, Charles A, 1967, *The Indian Mind: Essentials of Indian Philosophy and Culture,* Honolulu, East West Center Press.

Sri Aurobindo, 1959, *The Foundations of Indian Culture,* first edition, Pondicherry, Sri Aurobindo Ashrama Press.

Suzuki, D T, 1963, *Outlines of Mahayana Buddhism,* New York, Schocken.

Chapter 8

MORAL FOUNDATIONS OF SOCIAL ORDER AS SUGGESTED IN THE *VAIŚEṢIKASŪTRAS*

Shashi Prabha Kumar

The *Vaiśeṣika* philosophy of Kaṇāda is usually held to be a metaphysical theory. But on closer analysis it becomes clear that this stream of Indian philosophy is very rich in other aspects as well. For instance, the sixth chapter of Kaṇāda's *Vaiśeṣikasūtras* deals mainly with moral problems. This chapter is divided into two sections – the first section focuses on morality from social angle while the second is concerned chiefly with the individual ethics.[1] The aim of the present paper is to highlight some socially important moral issues emerging from the first section of the sixth chapter in *Vaiśeṣikasūtras*. But it must be admitted that the scope of this presentation is very limited in the sense that it does not discuss the *Vaiśeṣika* in its total perspective and focuses only upon the relevant portion of *sutra* text from a very specific point of view.

The word 'Moral' can etymologically be traced to the word 'Mores' (Morals) which means 'Custom' and 'Custom is some regularity of behaviour not of an individual but of a group of individuals in a society'.(Barlingay 1998:35) Therefore when we deal with morality, we have to take into account the individual conduct as in relation to others in group. In other words, morality is fundamentally concerned with social norms since moral acts generally have a bearing upon others. Society is a concept which signifies collectivity of individuals, though separate and independent, yet converging in some common goals so that order is maintained despite differences of various sorts. In other words, the social order provides a framework so that the individuals can gradually rise higher and move forward to their ultimate goals in life.

In Indian thought, the mutual relation between the individual and society and their connection to morality is best expressed by the word dharma which is literally used as a formative principle of society. ('*Dhāranāddharmamityāhur dharmo dhārayate prajāh.*' 'Karnaparva' *Mahabharata*, 69.58) The term dharma has been used in ancient India in a number of ways (Mees, 1980: 1–25), but the most importantly relevant sense here seems to be the moral means to a human end or objective. Although there are several metaphysical theories propounded by different schools of Indian Philosophy, yet there is a unity of moral outlook which pervades all of these theories and supplies a common background to all the systems of Indian thought – accordingly man is regarded here as a manifestation and expression of a deeper reality and dharma is rooted in the very function of this deeper and central reality. From this point of view, 'the basis of the concept of dharma is cosmic order. Society is an extension of this cosmic order in that its boundaries reach into the cosmic realm, and in that its regulations are designed to serve the order of the Cosmos'. (Younger, 1972: 35)

The term dharma itself is derived from the root √ *dhr*, meaning 'to support', and emphasizes the role of man in actively supporting the cosmic and moral order. Related to this metaphysical background is the idea of dharma as a norm conducive to social order and harmony. To quote Dr Radhakrishnan, 'Dharma is that which binds society together or Adharma is that which breaks society as under. Anything which makes for the consolidation of society is Dharma, anything which makes for the disintegration of society is Adharma [...] Dharma is that which makes for social coherence'. (Radhakrishnan)

It is clear from the above that in Indian view the ultimate aim of true dharma is not a self-regarding one, but an other-regarding one.[2] This provides for the ordering of human actions in such a way that they will facilitate the achievement of higher goals in life. Accordingly dharma is assigned the first place in order of preference in the four *puruşārthas* of human life. In other words, *artha* and *kāma* have to be regulated by dharma so that they could lead one to *mokşa*, the highest goal of life. These four *puruşārthas* are, so to say, psycho-moral basis of the *āśrama*-theory, the foundation of social ethics of the Hindus. As is evident from the above, dharma is the cornerstone of this philosophy.

This brings us to the point of duty versus right. The traditional Indian approach has always been a duty-centric one rather than the rights-oriented contemporary approach. That is why the welfare of the group was sought to be far greater than that of an individual's selfish motives. Hence, duty here does not only mean voluntary action but it is designated as dharma, the moral obligation of a person. Actually the special Indian texts dealing with the collective duties of human beings are the *dharmaśāstras* while Kaṇāda's delineation is only a brand of *darśana*, still it tends to explain dharma in a total perspective: social as well as individual, mundane as well as germane, material as well as spiritual, external as well as internal. In fact, the basic orientation of *Vaiśeşika*, as of all other schools of Indian Philosophy is very much holistic and integral.

The concept of dharma as expounded here does not just signify the *padārthadharma* but also *samaṣṭi-dharma vyaṣṭi-dharma*. To put it in simpler terms, dharma not merely enables man to be in harmony with his environment but also to attain his own higher goals in life both here and elsewhere. From this point of view, dharma conduces to one's own well-being as also to the good of others. In short, anything that sustains the true social order tending towards free moral development of the individual is dharma.

The significance of *Vaiśeṣika* lies in the fact that it not only talks of *moksa* or *nihśreyas* but also of worldly progress or *abhyudaya*. *Vaiśeṣikasūtras* begins with an objective of explaining the nature of dharma which is a means to both of these. According to Kaṇāda, dharma is that which is conducive to the pursuit of both, the worldly progress and personal perfection. The latter in fact presupposes the former and that, in turn, cannot be thought of without social order. Hence dharma involves both, a personal as well as a social principle, personal perfection and social order both go together. Social order is, in a way empirical, and not moral, but its foundations of course have to be moral. The purpose of these inherent foundations is to create ideal society which affords its members the facilities to develop towards perfection and liberation. Apparently 'there appears to be an irreconcilable opposition between *mokṣa* dharma and the explicitly moral social dharmas, for it seems that the dharma of *mokṣa* requires the repudiation of the moral and social aspects of human existence'. (Koller, 1972: 133) But actually it is not so in case of *Vaiśeṣika*, as is also evidenced by the following statement of a modern interpreter of *Vaiśeṣika*, 'The relativity of the well-being of society institutions is not sacrificed for the sake of spiritual well-being. On the contrary, social duty is regarded as a means to the attainment of *nihśreyas*, spiritual perfection. The way to the transcendental state of liberation is through relative duty (Dharma). Thus, after all, spiritual perfection is not opposed to material life, and is therefore to be attained through the worldly ethical behaviour of the individual.' (Sharma, 1965: 182)

In Kaṇāda's *Vaiśeṣika*, there is a synthesis of the twin aspects of life, *nihśreyas* or spirituality and *abhyudaya* or material progress. *Nihśreyas* here signifies *mokṣa* while *abhyudaya* comprises the fulfilment of *artha* and *kāma*. Dharma is the prerequisite for attainment of both *abhyudaya* as well as *nihśreyas*. ('*Yato 'bhudayanihśreyasa-siddhih sa dharmah.*' *Vaiśesikasū tra*, 1.1.2.)

As regards the question of centrality of the society or the individual, we might say that Kaṇāda's philosophy is a pluralistic realism and he seems to follow the traditional Indian ideal of a synthesis and harmony between these two, i.e. the *samaṣṭi* and the *vyaṣṭi*. 'It comprises the ethics of sociality as well as the ethics of individual capacity and is thus fuller and more comprehensive than the Platonic scheme which is the ethics of sociality only.' (Maitra, 1963: 1)

In Indian viewpoint, the two are not antagonistic to each other; in fact, they are like the whole and the part which cannot live without one another. It is an organismic approach where the well-being of one is dependent upon the well-being of the other. But still there is no denying the fact that the ultimate significance of an individual's dharma is to be sought in a social context only. 'Whoever the individual may be and whatever station he may occupy, it is only in and through society that he can realize the best that there is in him. Society is the soil in which the seed of human personality has been sown and from which it draws its nourishment so that it may bud and blossom.' (*Yamunāchārya*, 1953: 33–34) Therefore it is worth mentioning in this regard that notwithstanding some allegations about shades of individualism in the concept of liberation in Indian thought, 'Communion, mutuality and solidarity are the key-values and norms in both religion and society in India'. (Mukerjee, 1951: 11)

It is not without reason then that the first aspect of dharma in *Vaiśeşika* view has been *abhyudaya* through the stability of society, the maintenance of social order and the general welfare of mankind. It means that every individual has to strive for his own *nihśreyas* separately but *abhyudaya* has to be brought about collectively. That is why Kaṇāda deals with the moral values concerned with social harmony first and later on with the ethical ones which lead a person to *nihśreyas*, his own spiritual progress.

There is another idea of *dṛṣta* and *adṛṣtaa* in the *Vaiśesikasūtras* which can help in explaining these twin aspects of dharma in a better ways. ('*Drstādrstaprayojanānam dṛṣtābhāve prayojanamabhyudayāya.*' *Vaiśeṣikasūtra*, 6.2.1) According to that, *dṛṣta* is concerned with actions of which the motives are visible, e.g. agriculture, commerce, etc. which are collective actions. The other types of actions are envisaged as *adṛṣṭa* of which the motives are invisible, just like sacrifice, charity, *brahmacharya*, etc. which are to be performed individually. A person is motivated to perform the *adṛṣṭa* type of actions only after pursuing the *dṛṣta* ones. In other words, personal perfection can be sought in an orderly social environment only. Hence *abhyudaya* has to precede *nihśreyas* and not vice versa according to *Vaiśeşika* view.

As stated above, social order is a prerequisite for spiritual progress of the individual and has to be achieved by practising certain moral norms. But here a question arises as to what is the criterion of these moral norms and why should one be obliged to follow them? To this, Kaṇāda has explicitly stated that the same have to be observed because they have been laid out in the infallible scripture, Veda, which is the basic source of dharma since it is an intelligent creation of the divine. ('*Buddhipurvā vakyakritirvede.*' *Vaiśeṣikasūtra* 6.1.)

Dharma is theoretically rooted in, derived from and determined by the eternal Vedas. The content of dharma has been recorded in the scared texts.

(Creel 1997:12) Veda is the eternal repository of all moral actions and hence the divine sanction of social order is also affirmed in *Vaiśeṣikasūtras*.

At the same time, it is also to be noted here that the moral idea which is very deeply rooted in the scripture according to Kaṇāda, is quite logically evidenced by the belief in *karma* doctrine. In fact, this is very crucial to the proper appreciation of the moral ideal. Dharma as a moral desire and *karma* as an expression of such a desire are the two fundamental concepts upon which the whole edifice of social order has to be based according to traditional Indian thought. The doctrine of *karma* extends the principle of causation to the sphere of human conduct and 'signifies not merely that the events of our life are determined by their antecedent causes but also that there is absolute justice in the rewards and punishment that fall to our lot in life'. (Hiriyanna, 1975: 175)

This moral view of the universe is also expressed by Kaṇāda when he talks of the retributive nature of *karma* ('*Ātmātaragunānāmātmāntare Kāranatvāt.*' *Vaiśeṣikasūtra* 6.1.5.), even before dealing with moral qualities required for furtherance of social order. The implication of this statement is that the law of *karma* guarantees the relatedness of all events in an individual's life as well as in a social set-up. But the regulation of these relations has to be accomplished by dharma only. So, dharma is a regulator of human actions both social as well as individual, while *karma* is an underlying principle of the two.

In brief, it may be said that social justice is the basis of social order, and the law of *karma*, supported by dharma, paves the way for that in such a manner that one tends to fulfil his share in the scheme of society as well.

Now, coming to the specific moral foundations laid by Kaṇāda in his *Vaiśeṣikasūtras*, we find that he has classified the social groups of people according to their action and not by birth. There are three types of persons he has listed as follows:

1. *Duṣta* (wicked)
2. *Aduṣta* (non-wicked)
3. *Visiṣta* (noble)

In fact, these three types are always there in any society but what is intended here is that mixing with the first kind of persons is socially undesirable while mixing with the second and third is held desirable according to *Vaiśeṣikasūtras*. (*Vaiśeṣikasūtras*, 6.1.8.–10)

It is also to be pointed out here that the criterion of wickedness according to Kaṇāda is *himsā* (violence) ('*Duṣtam himsāyam*', *Vaiśeṣikasūtras*, 6.1.7). Those who inflict injuries of any kind upon others are evil and it is not good for the society to treat such people with equal regard. *Ahimsā* on the other hand, means a kind of tenderness or a form of benevolence to others. It is one of the formative principles of society which brings and binds people together and is present in those who are not wicked by nature. It is they who should be given preference in a social system.

Besides this objective classification based on personal qualities, Kaṇāda has also given a subjective division of the members of a society such as:

1. *Sama* (equal)
2. *Hīna* (inferior)
3. *Viruddha* (opponent)

and has suggested that interaction among the equals and with the inferiors is desirable but those who are opposed to the path of dharma have to be forsaken – even the method of forsaking them has been specified. (*Vaiśeṣikasūtras,* 6.1.11–16)

It is quite reasonable to hold that for the upkeep of social order, all sections of society must get due opportunities. No doubt the gifted ones should be elevated and treated with greater respect, but at the same time the ordinary persons should not be neglected since their cooperation and participation are equally crucial for a sound social organisation.

The next important point which Kaṇāda has made and which is morally relevant for sound social order is the virtue of *dāna.* It means sharing one's possession with his fellow beings or giving away one's wealth to society for the cause of social welfare. The concept of *dāna* is no doubt a very ancient Indian concept which emphasises generosity and compassion as important social values but what is noteworthy here is the epithet with which Kaṇāda has characterised the activity of *dāna 'Buddhipū rvo dadātih.'* (*Vaiśeṣikasūtras*, 6.1.3), i.e. it should be intelligently administered and not just ritually practised.

Although the ancient Indian tradition eulogises *dāna* just for the sake of it (*Taittiriya Upanisad,* 1.11.1–4), Kaṇāda modifies it with the qualification *buddihpurva* and provides a rational form to a hitherto ritual act. In fact, it seems as if for him '*arth-'sucitā'* (purity of wealth) is the main moral foundation for social order and *dāna* is a very significant part of it. The importance of this is highlighted by his emphatic assertion that not only *dāna* but *pratigraha* should also be practised intelligently. (*Vaiśeṣikasūtras,* 6.1) In this statement, Kaṇāda has provided a very subtle clue to social order which is remarkably poignant and has a lot of contemporary relevance as well. The clue is that one should not practise *dāna* and *pratigraha* indiscriminately just because they are moral virtues, rather one has to be very careful and cautious while following them, otherwise they might lead to corruption and social injustice.

From what has been stated above, it becomes clear that the matter of *abhyudaya* or social welfare has been dealt by Kaṇāda in the fist section of chapter six of his *Vaiśeṣikasūtras* in a very simple but striking manner. Various commentators have tried to interpret these *sūtras* in a rigid, ritualistic sense also, but the real and thorough implication of these is no doubt still called for. A modest attempt has been made here in the same direction.

To sum up, it may be said that the very first objective of *Vaiśeṣika* is the explanation of dharma which is unitive and integral by nature as is clear by the definition presented therein. Hence, the approach towards the final goal has also to be total and not partial. Accordingly not merely *tattva-jñāna* for the sake of *nihśreyas* but practise of dharma or moral duty for the sake of *abhyudaya* is also to be undertaken.

Notes

1 Here we may note that in substance, all the Hindu sages agree that any plan or scheme of social organization which aims at the best functioning of every human being as a social unit, must, in the first instance, take him into account from these two aspects. First, it must consider man as a social being with reference to his training and development in the natural and social environment in order to enable him to fulfil the final aim of his existence, and secondly this has to be coordinated with another scheme which studies man with reference to his natural endowments, dispositions and attitudes. (Prabhu 1963: 74–75)

2 '*Śruyatām dharmasarvasvam śrutvā caivāvadhāryatām*
Ātmanh pratikūlāni paresām na samācaret.' – *Mahābhārata.*

References

Barlingay, S S, 1998, *A Modern Introduction to Indian Ethics*, first edition, Delhi, Penman Publisher.

Creel, Austin B, 1997, *Dharma in Hindu Ethics*, Calcutta, Firma KLM Private Ltd.

Hiriyanna, M, 1975, *Indian Conception of Values*, Mysore, Kavyalaya Publishers.

Koller, John M, 1972, 'Dharma: An Expression of Universal Order' in *Philosophy East and West* 22, Honolulu, University of Hawai'i Press.

Maitra, Susil Kumar, 1963, *The Ethics of the Hindus*, third edition, Calcutta, University of Calcutta Publication.

Mees, G H, 1980, *Dharma and Society*, Delhi, Seema Publications.

Mukerjee, Radhakamal, 1951, *The Indian Scheme of Life*, Bombay, Hind Kitabs.

Prabhu, Pandharinath H., 1963, *Hindu Social Organisation: A study in Socio-Psychologiocal and ideological foundations*, fourth revised edition, Bombay, Popular Prakashan.

Radhakrishnan, S, *Occasional Speeches and Writings: October 1952–January 1956*, pp. 73, 218–19, 359 *et passim.*

Sharma, I C, 1965, *Ethical Philosophies of India*, London, George Allen and Unwin.

Yamunacharya, M, 1953, 'The Concept of Dharma and Its Implication to the New Society' in *Proceedings of the Twenty – Eighth Indian Philosophical Congress*, Baroda.

Younger, Paul, 1972, *Introduction to Indian Religious Thought*, London, Darton, Longman and Todd.

Chapter 9

MODERN WESTERN CONCEPTION OF JUSTICE AS EQUALITY BEFORE THE LAW AND *DHARMAŚĀSTRAS*

Saral Jhingran

While the awareness of the value of justice is quite widespread in western thought, its understanding or content has been changing with times. Plato's famous conception of justice as harmonious functioning of various parts of the individual and the society does not seem to have any place for the idea of equal dignity and rights of all human beings. This latter idea is present in Aristotle's conception of justice as lawfulness and fairness or equitability. But neither for Aristotle, nor for later medieval Christian thinkers, did the notion of justice imply the rejection of the institution of slavery.

Justice was conceived throughout the medieval period according to Greek thinker Ulpian's definition as 'giving to each what is his own (or due)'. This, as pointed out by Hans Kelsen (1957: 13) and others, leaves enough scope for any amount of social disparities and inequalities, as our understanding of what is due to someone is determined by the sociopolitical order. For example, the slaves in the ancient Greek society and the *shudras* in the Vedic-*dharmasastric* social order could claim little as their due.

It is in modern thought alone that the idea of basic equality of all human beings, especially before the law, is made central to the conception of justice. The humanism of Renaissance; the rationalism of Enlightenment and the liberalism of nineteenth century – all led to the emphasis on the dignity of the individual per se and the equality of all human beings. These ideas found eloquent expression in the writings of John Locke and Thomas Paine (1953: 80). They also interpreted the medieval concept of the natural law as endowing human individuals with innate and inalienable rights to life, liberty and equality (and in Locke's case, property also). Gradually the idea of human rights got integrated with the conception of justice 'giving everyone his due' came to mean giving everyone his rights qua his humanity.

The Declaration of the Rights of Men during the French and American Revolutions are the most impressive documents in this field. According to the French Declaration,

> Men are born, and always continue, free and equal in respect of their rights. The law is an expression of the will of the community. It should be the same to all, whether it protects or punishes; and all, being equal in its sight, are equally eligible to honours, places and employments according to their different abilities, without any other distinction than that created by their virtues and talents. (Paine, 1953: 96–97)

The idea of the basic equality of all men qua man is given a philosophical basis in Kant. Kant affirms the autonomy of the rational will which, in turn, signifies the moral worth or dignity of the moral agent or person. The equal dignity of all persons is expressed in Kant's second formulation of the categorical imperative: 'Act so that you treat humanity, whether in your own person or in that of another, always as an end, never as a means only.' In other words, a human being has an innate right to freedom (from constraint from other wills), and equality, simply by virtue of his humanity. To quote his own words,

> Every man has a rightful claim to respect from his fellow-men and is reciprocally obliged to show respect for every other man. Humanity itself is a dignity; for man cannot be used merely as a means by any other man (either by others or even by himself) but must always be treated as an end. (Kant, *The Doctrine of Virtue*: 132)

The imperative to respect every human being as an end-in-himself is derived from what for Kant is an axiomatic truth that 'rational nature exists as an end in itself'. (Kant, *Fundamental Principles of the Metaphysics of Moral:* 54 and following pages) Add to it Kant's assertion of the autonomy of will, and his third formulation of the categorical imperative regarding all rational beings together forming a kingdom of ends; and there emerges a categorical assertion of the equality, dignity, autonomy and inviolability of all persons qua rational beings. The rational nature of all human beings, just like the autonomy of will, is an axiomatic truth with Kant. The second and third formulations of the categorical imperative assert the innate, inviolable worth of every person (rational being) who cannot ever be made a means of another person's ends. This rejects in one sweep all attempts at social inequalities, coercion and exploitation.

This innate dignity of every person can be asserted either on the basis of the essential rational nature of man and autonomy of will, which are recognised as axiomatic, a priori, even in some sense transcendental, truths. Or, it can be asserted as a normative principle. The conclusion remains the same, that is, the absolute dignity and inviolability of a person (rational human being) and its concomitant principle of absolute equality of all persons.

The duty to respect every human being as a person who is an end-in-himself follows. What is more, by respecting other persons we do not obligate them, for respect as a person is every human being's due, and we are thereby only giving him what is his due. (Kant, *The Doctrine of Virtue,* p. 115 and following pages) Justice consists in giving to everyone what is her/his, i.e. respect as a person, or end-in-himself.

The basic equality of entire humanity is also well expressed in Bentham's famous formula for applying the greatest happiness principle: 'Every one is to count for one and no one is to count for more than one.'

The absolute equality of all persons also follows from the necessary requirement of all rational, including moral, judgements, as argued by Henry Sidgwick. According to him, we cannot make two different judgements in two cases which are similar in all relevant aspects. He calls it the principle of justice or impartiality, according to which,

> It cannot be right for A to treat B in a manner in which it would be wrong for B to treat A, merely on the ground that they are two different individuals, without there being any difference between the natures and circumstances of the two which can be stated as a reasonable ground for difference of treatment. (Sidgwick, 1907 : 380)

It means that our judgements, whether socio-moral or legal, must be based on some rational grounds or criteria which would make them applicable to all similar persons under similar circumstances. R M Hare calls it the 'universalizability' of all rational moral judgements. That is, when we offer any judgement regarding an action, it is implicitly accepted that it would be applicable to all acts which are similar to the given act. "We cannot give two different judgements regarding similar acts unless we can provide a rational ground for the difference in our judgements. This rational ground can only be a substantial difference in the circumstances, etc. of the two agents.' (Hare, 1968: 10 and 1972: 13)

The views of both Sidgwick and Hare have been criticized on two counts. First, C D Broad and others regard the universalizability principle as trivial or even tautologous. (Broad, 1956: 223–224) According to them, it is a basic requirement of all rational judgements, and so remains merely formal and even vacuous. Secondly, it is argued by Chaim Perelman, (1970: 481–483), Hans Kelsen (1957: 13) and others that equality of all human beings qua human beings is both irrational and impossible in view of the innumerable differences between them. They contend that equality required in justice is simply the limited equality between members of the same class. Kelsen adds his relativistic explanation that how the members of a class are defined actually depends upon the culture and sociopolitical order of a given society.

Marcus Singer has, however, strongly defended the Sidgwick-Hare criterion of justice and morality. He calls Hare's principle of 'universalizability' the'generalization principle', and explains it

> The generalization principle must be understood in the sense that what is right for one person must be right for every relevantly similar person in relevantly similar circumstances. (Singer, 1961: 19)

He explains 'relevant difference' in Sidgwick's words that it is one which can be stated 'as a reasonable ground for difference of treatment'. Singer admits that any two people may be similar to each other in one aspect, while being different in others. Which similarities and differences would be regarded relevant for a given case depends upon the context. He adds that: 'The criteria for "all similar cases" are contained in the "general grounds" or reasons on the basis of which an act is, or is said to be, right or wrong.' (Singer, 1961: 20–21)

Thus, the 'universalizability' of Hare and the 'generalization principle' of Singer mean that we cannot offer two different judgements in two relevantly similar cases; and the class of relevantly similar cases is defined in terms of a rational set of criteria or reasons. These reasons would permit only certain characteristics as relevant in a particular context, and reject all others as irrelevant. The essence of justice from our point of view consists exactly in this that the rational criteria for moral or legal judgements should apply to all human beings alike.

The same idea can be expressed through other related concepts, such as impartiality and reciprocity. Impartiality, like universalizability, is the common factor in all rational judgements. The concept of reciprocity comes very near to the concept of justice I am trying to develop here. R B Perry and Hare (1968) have developed the concept of reciprocity as integral to morality and justice. Reciprocity means that a person (or a group) cannot make an exception of himself (or itself) while applying a certain norm or rule to others. Hare has rightly understood universalizability of moral judgements in terms of reciprocity. (Hare, 1968: 95) For us, these two concepts provide the basic condition or even the meaning of justice.

P F Strawson (1970: 551) has given a very convincing elucidation of the concept of reciprocity, and rightly identified it with justice. Justice, for Strawson, as for Plato, Aristotle and many others, is a characteristic of an ideal or desirable social order. Both morality and justice consist in 'the reciprocal acknowledgement of rights and duties', or 'the necessary acceptance of the reciprocity of claims'. It means that any norm, or rule, or what Strawson calls 'socially sanctioned demand' should be applicable to all alike. A just social order is one in which the demands made on an individual by the society are complemented by the demands on others on behalf of that individual, and in which the interests of all individuals are equally safeguarded.

However, the liberals' insistence on the liberty and rights of the individual does tend to increase socio-economic inequalities to an extent that achieving socio-legal justice becomes near impossible.[1] It is in this context that John Rawls has developed his unique conception of 'justice as fairness'. Rawls starts with the axiomatic assertion of absolute equality of all persons qua their humanity:

> Each member of society is thought to have inviolability based on justice, or as some say, natural right, which even the welfare of everyone else cannot override. (Rawls, 1999: 28)

Rawls then offers his two principles of social justice:

> First: each person is to have an equal right to the most extensive basic liberty compatible with a similar liberty for others.
> Second: social and economic inequalities are to be arranged so that they are both (a) reasonably expected to be to everyone's advantage, and (b) attached to positions and offices open to all. (Rawls, 1999: 60)

Later on he modifies his second principle as follows:

> Social and economic inequalities are to be arranged so that they are both (a) to the greatest benefit of the least advantaged, and, (b) attached to offices and positions open to all under conditions of fair equality of opportunity. (Rawls, 1999: 83,302)

Justice as fairness goes beyond the concept of equality before the law. A sociopolitical order based on liberty and equality of opportunity may not be just after all, as the least advantaged sections of the society would not be able to enjoy the liberty and other rights provided for all the members of the society due to their initial socio-economic backwardness. Justice therefore consists in modifying the sociopolitical order and laws in favour of the least advantaged persons or groups.

Now, if we were to search for the conception of equality of all human beings qua their humanity, or the equal rights of all humans before the law and society, we would find a strange contradiction or tension within Hinduism. On one hand, we have the exalted Vedantic proposition of all living beings (not only humans) having the same *Ātman*; on the other hand, the *Dharmaśāstras* and even the Epics, as well as most of the *Purānas*, advocate an extremely discriminatory social system which is diametrically opposed to the conception of justice that we have presented above.

Before we try to understand the Indian (Hindu) conceptions of justice and human rights we must first know their equivalent terms (concepts) in Sanskrit, the language of ancient India. We find three or four terms used for justice; and in their turn, same terms being used for other conceptions; they are – *vyavahāra, nyāya, danda* and dharma. The term *vyavahāra* relates to law suits only, and we need not consider it here. The term *nyāya* should have been the correct equivalent of the conception of justice; and it is so used in modern India. But not so in early texts. The term *nyāya* is mostly used in the sense of natural law-called *matsya nyāya* (the law of the sea or jungle) wherein smaller fish are eaten by the big.

This cynical conception of the law of the jungle is then applied to human society. It is presumed that left to themselves people would go on the road of total anarchy; and it is only the fear of punishment *danda* that makes people follow dharma (right moral norms).[2] Thus *danda* by the king came to be not only highly prized, it also became a synonym for justice. *Danda* is the most commonly used term for justice in ancient texts, signifying that by giving punishment to the guilty or the oppressor, the king restores the earlier balance, and thus protects the weak. That could have been a good, though limited, conception of justice; but the main aim of *danda* seems to be the preservation of the status quo in the hierarchical social order. The institution of *danda* was vitiated from the beginning by the need of giving *danda*, not according to the gravity of the crime but, according to the respective castes of the oppressor and the oppressed. *Danda* or punishment, as conceived in the *Dharmaśāstras* and Kautilya's *Arthaśāstra* is very different from our modern (western) conception of justice. Here we find the main difference between the modern western conception of justice and the ancient Indian (Hindu) one. While the first aims at securing justice for, and rights of, the individual persons, the second aims at the stability and harmony of the social order. And the caste (*varna*) based social order was perceived, perhaps rightly so, as the best means (in the historical circumstance) of securing its stability and harmony.

The conception of dharma comes nearest to the concept of justice. However, it is a very profound and at the same time a nebulous concept. Various modern Indian scholars have indifferently translated the term dharma as justice, righteousness, or even law. In a famous passage of the *Brhadāranyaka*

Upanisad (1.4.14) dharma is hailed as the controller of all and the strength of the weak. Interestingly, Indian scholars have translated 'dharma' in the passage either as justice, or righteousness. For example, both Swami Nikhilananda and S Radhakrishnan have translated dharma as justice in their translation of the *Brhadāranyaka Upanisad* (1.4.14); while Swami Gambhirananda has translated it as righteousness in his translation of Śamkara's *Bhāshya* on the same. Śamkara's comments on the above passage suggest that he understands dharma as righteousness.

It is obvious that the conception of dharma cannot be taken as equivalent of the concept of justice for various reasons: it is a nebulous concept which comprehends several concepts. In the *Dharmaśāstras*, dharma is mostly used in a ritualistic context, as either Vedic-*Dharmaśāstras* rituals, or the following of large number of (ritualistic) injunctions and prohibitions of Vedas and *Smrtis*.

Śabara defines dharma as that which is enjoined by the Vedas, which assertion seems to reduce dharma to Vedic sacrifices and their various ritualistic injunctions and prohibitions. (*Mimamsa Sutra, Sabara bhasya* I.1.2) It is in this sense that Kautilya includes dharma in the four sources of justice. (*Kautilya Arthasastra*, II.7) Dharma often has metaphysical connotations also and denotes the world's moral order. In a way it is related to the idea of justice, but justice as rendered by natural moral order (*rta*), and not by human beings. As such it cannot be an equivalent of our idea of justice.

Above all, dharma means duty and/or virtue. It is in this sense that it is mostly used. Generally the moral and ritualistic duties are not kept apart and that has created quite a bit of confusion in Hindu ethical thought. (Jhingran, 1999: 55) This primary conception of dharma, as espoused in the *Dharmaśāstras* and *Bhagavadgītā*, is indirectly related to the idea of justice. It is believed that if all people followed their respective dharma*s* there would result a just and harmonious social order. It is in this sense that the *Mahābhārata* describes dharma as 'Dharma has no limits. It is that which sustains the universe'.[3]

There are four sources of dharma: Vedas, *Smrtis*, *sadācāra* and one's own conscience. (*Manu Smrti* II.6) Since Vedas do not deal with every day matters, *Smrtis* became the chief source of dharma. The dharma proposed in the *Smrtis* came to be regarded as the law that was expected to determine the entire life of Hindus. That is why A S Altekar translates the term dharma as law. (Altekar, 1984: 259–261).

Theoretically, such laws or dharma (norms) should have been the same for all members of the society. But it was not so. *Dharmaśāstras* propounds different laws for different 'classes' of persons and the grounds on the basis of which these classes were defined were varied. There was just no conception of one law for all, or of equality of all human beings before the law. To quote A S Altekar:

> Equality of all citizens before the law is one of the fundamental features of a good state according to modern notions. It has to be admitted that it did not exist in ancient India. (Altekar, 1984: 69)

Not only were these laws, as we shall see, different for different *varnas*, they were also different for different regions (*deśa*), times (*kala*), locality (*janpada*), professional guilds (*śreni*) and even larger families (*kula*). (*Manusmrti* I. 85–86; VIII.41) This could be possible because of the importance given to *sadācāra* (conduct of good people) in the ancient conception of dharma or law. Both Manu and Apastamba declare that in addition to Vedas and *Smrtis*, *sadācāra*, the conduct of those Aryans of three 'upper' classes, who are humble, have full control over their senses and are free from vices, is also the source of dharma, that is, provide standard or criteria both for emulation and judgement.[4] Apastamba distinguishes between the *rauta* or Vedic dharma (*yajña*, etc.) and *samayācarika* dharma, i.e., the dharma determined by the pronouncements or agreements of learned men of the three 'upper' *varnas*. (*Apastamba Dharma Sutra* I.1.1.1–3) Here the term used is *sadācāra*, but gradually any mode of conduct or practice that was in vogue in a particular group of people (this group being distinguished on the basis of any of the above criteria), came to be known as *ācāra* and was accepted as a criterion to judge the members of that group by.[5]

These customs were necessarily relative to place, time and other factors. The ancient Aryans were fully aware of the differences in the ways and customs of people of different regions of this vast subcontinent. Eager not to condemn anyone, they developed a very relativistic stance. They declared that the customs (norms) of a particular group, whether based on *varna*, place, time or any other factor, are to be regarded as valid for the people of that particular group in which they are in vogue, with only one condition that they should not be opposed to Vedas. (This condition was easily manipulated since Vedas do not have much to say for real life situations). But these very customs, as marriage among near relations practised among South Indians, would be invalid if practised by members of other groups among whom these customs are not recognized. (*Baudhayan Dharma Sutra*, I.1.19–26 quoted in P V Kane 1993:Vol III 858) Similarly, they contended, customs change according to the changes brought out in men's sensibilities through the passage of time. For example, the practice of *niyoga*, which was accepted in earlier times is prohibited in the modern 'degenerate age' (*kali yuga*). (Kane 1993: Vol. III 885)

> All *Dharmaśāstra* seek to protect the mores or customs of different communities, including professional guilds. They instruct the king that

> as far as possible he should take into consideration these varied customs while adjudicating cases.[6]

Now, custom or *ācāra* in this sense is very different from dharma. The first is what is practised by the people, whereas the second refers to what ought to be practised. Hindu thinkers made the mistake, common to all naturalistic thinkers, of confusing the 'is' with the 'ought', the actual with the ideal. Does it mean that what the criterion is to judge itself, is the actual? It seems so. In their attempt to be liberal, they adopted an extreme form of relativism, comparable to the postmodern relativism of Richard Rorty, Alsdair McIntyre, Charles Swoyer, Hans-George Gadamer and Paul Feyerabend.

Above all, the ethical norms and laws (dharma) were relative to one's hereditary *varna*. In the Vedic-*Dharmaśāstric* and Epic tradition, dharma is divided into two categories – *sādhārana dharma* (universal duties) and *varnāśrama dharma* (duties according to the caste or *varna* and stage of life). S K Maitra (Maitra 1963: 317*)* argues that *sādhārana dharma* is basic in this tradition, and *varna dharm*a is to be followed in accordance with the former. In actual fact, however, it is just the opposite. *Varna dharma* or duties according to one's hereditary caste are given the greatest importance, so that everywhere universal duties are to be sacrificed in order to perform one's caste duties (as in the case of Tuladhar, the saintly meat seller, who was compelled to kill animals as it was his caste duty). The ideal scheme of life was the one in which the duties were to be determined by both *varna* and *āśrama* (stage of life). In practice, however, very few people followed the scheme of *asramas*; therefore we would consider here *varna dharma* only.

Dharma*'s* core meaning is duty which is integrated with the concept of virtue. Now, this dharma is mainly conceived in terms of *svadharma* or duty according to one's hereditary caste *(varna)*, so that duties of different persons vary according to the caste to which they belong, and the place of that caste in the hierarchical social order. The social order based on hereditary castes, arranged in a strict hierarchy, has full religious sanction.

Manu Smrti, of course, gives the greatest importance to the fourfold hierarchical division of society, which is given in the very beginning. It also declares that this fourfold social older was created by God himself:

> In order to protect the universe, the most resplendent One, assigned separate duties and occupations to those who sprang from his mouth, arms, thighs and feet. (Manu Smrti I.87)

The *Bhagavadgītā* gives the exalted vision of one Self in all.[7] It also declares that the fourfold order was created by God himself who defined their respective duties according to the qualities of different *varnas*. (*Bhagvadgita* IV.13) It then goes on to describe the duties of four *varnas* in exactly the same terms as the *Manu Smrti*. (*Bhagvadgita*, XVIII. 41–44) It adds that whatever the individual or moral compulsions, one should never give up one's hereditary profession:

> Better is one's own duty (dharma), though imperfectly carried out, than the duty of another one carried out perfectly. Better is death in the fulfilment of one's own duty, for to follow another's duty (dharma) is perilous. (Bhagvadgita, XVIII.47, also Manu Smrti X.97)

It means that every one had to follow without exception the hereditary profession; and these hereditary professions or castes were neatly arranged in a hierarchical social order. The *varna* decided one's profession, status in society, the duties one was expected to perform, and one's rights vis-à-vis other *varnas*. Significantly, not only did one's hereditary *varna* decide one's place in society, it also determined a priori the moral character and personality a person was expected to develop. Thus, individuals were not only unequal as regards their duties and rights, they were also supposedly unequal as regards their personalities or moral qualities, and by implication, their moral worth. Any idea of equality of all human beings qua their humanity is totally absent from this religio-social philosophy. Rendering justice in the absence of minimum equality would be a meaningless exercise.

What is even more shocking, the virtues expected from the four *varnas* were very different. Both the *Bhagavadgītā* and *Manu Smrti* give similar list of virtues. While the virtues expected from *brāhmanas* are of high moral quality, virtues of *ksatriyas* and *vaisyas* include both professional duties and a few virtues appropriate to their professions. But not a single ethical quality is included in the list of dharma*s* of *śūdras*, their sole duty being to serve the 'upper' classes. (*Manu Smrti*, I.87; X.122–123 and *Bhagvadgita*, XVIII. 41–44) As we shall see, not only their duties but their rights as human beings also were determined by the caste (*varna*) they were accidentally born in. There was just no conception of equality of all human beings either in the society or before the law. Importantly, justice was administered and very different punishments were awarded to different *varnas* in accordance with their religio-social hierarchy. Of course, here is a very well known aspect of the *Dharmaśāstric* tradition, and any discussion thereof would be merely repetitive. Still I would like to refer to a few illustrations in support of my contention regarding the total absence of any idea of equality of all human beings before the law in the *Dharmaśāstric* tradition.

Various *Dharmaśāstras*, as also later texts, exalted *brāhmanas* as the lords of creation. They were compared to gods, and declared *avadhya* or beyond any corporal punishment. They were exempted from state tax, and were generally regarded as above law. (*Manu Smrti* I.93–96; IX. 316–319; XI. 83–84; *Gautama Dharma Sutra* VIII. 12–13) It was also contended that a *brāhmana* deserves reverence only by virtue of his birth, irrespective of his knowledge or character. A *brāhmana* boy of ten years was said to deserve the respect of a *ksatriya* of 100 years. (*Manu Smrti* II.135; *Apastamba Dharma Sutra* I.4.14.25) It was even declared that a *brāhmana* deserved the respect even if he indulged in immoral acts. (*Manu Smrti* IX. 316–319)

The degradation of *śūdras* was proportional to the exaltation of *brāhmanas*. A *śūdra* was prohibited from reciting Vedas, or even listening to them; or from performing a penance which was the right of 'upper' castes only. Even Śamkara who proclaimed one Self in all, quoted with approval *Gautama Dharma Sutra* which prescribes cruel punishments for *śūdras* who dare to challenge these prohibitions.[8] The right to property was denied to them. In fact, they had no rights as citizens, or even as human beings. Manu declares:

> A śūdra, whether bought or unbought, may be compelled to do servile work, for he was created by the Self-existent to be the slave of a brāhmana. A śūdras, though emancipated by his master, is not released from servitude [...] Since this is innate to him, who can set him free from it. (*Manu Smrti* VIII. 413–414 also 416)

Certain sub-castes of *śūdras* were declared untouchables, and were forced to live outside villages, keep dogs and donkeys, eat in broken utensils and wear clothes taken from dead bodies. (*Manu Smrti* X. 50) They were regarded so impure that they were not to be given even the leftover food of the 'higher' castes. (*Manu Smrti* IV 80; *Āpastamba Dharma Sutra* I.11.31.22) No shred of human dignity was allowed to them; and they were constantly being compared to dogs, crows and even worms. (*Manu Smrti III* .92; *Āpastamba Dharma Sutra* II.4.9.5)

The most important difference between the *śūdras* and the 'upper' classes was, however, the one before the law. While the killing of a *brāhmana* was the gravest sin (*mahā-pātaka)*, from which no redemption was possible; the killing of a *śūdra* was comparable to the killing of dogs, frogs, crows, etc. (*Manu Smrti* XI. 131–132; *Āpastamba Dharma Sutra* I.9.25.13) If a *śūdra* committed adultery with an 'upper' caste woman, his organ was to be cut off; but if an 'upper' caste male molested a 'lower' class woman, he was let off with a nominal fine. (*Manu Smrti* VIII. 359, 362, *Gautama Dharma Sutra* XII.2–3, *Āpastamba Dharma Sutra* II, 10.27, 8–9)

If a *śūdra* spoke offensively to a *brāhmana*, his tongue was to be cut off; or if he attacked him, that part of his body which was used in the attack was to be cut off. (*Manu Smrti* VIII. 270–272, 279–283; *Gautama Dharma Sutra* XII 1–14; *Āpastamba Dharma Sutra* II.10.27.14–16) On the other hand, even the murder of a 'lower' class person was only a minor sin, which required some nominal penance, or paying of a small fine. (*Manu Smrti* XI.127–131) Even interest for loan was to be higher for those who owned no property, and lower for those who were prosperous and higher in the *varna* hierarchy. (*Manu Smrti* VIII.142.) Gautama prescribes that if a *śūdra* stole something, he should be made to pay eightfold the amount of stolen goods; whereas the three 'upper' classes were to pay only double the amount. (*Gautama Dharma Sutra* XII. 15–16) It is sometimes suggested that the *Gautam Dharma Sutras* are among the oldest texts. In contrast, Manu stipulates that the *brāhmanas* should be awarded larger fines for theft than the 'lower' castes. (*Manu Smrti* VIII.338) But if *brāhmanas* were to be fined more in case of theft because they were expected to possess wisdom and high moral character which could resist temptations, then how is it that they were not awarded higher punishments for other offences, including murder, adultery and even treason? In fact, this single injunction of higher fines for theft by *brāhmanas* cannot cancel out the fact that they were mostly regarded as *avadhya* (not to be killed, or even punished).

As suggested earlier, justice is best expressed in terms of the principle of universalizability. If it is right or wrong for A to perform any act under certain circumstances, it should be right or wrong also for B, C and D under similar circumstances. It was not so in the *Dharmaśāstric* scheme. Any given act had very different meanings, and deserved very different punishments according to the *varnas* of the offender and the victim. So one and the same act was right, indifferent, wrong, or a sin according to the *varna* or caste of the agent. No account was taken of the circumstances of two persons belonging to two different *varnas* and performing one and the same act. Punishment (*danda*) was awarded not according to the nature of the crime, and the circumstances of the offender, but exclusively according to the class or *varna* of the offender and that of the victim. The process of justice presupposed and brought into focus the principle of basic inequality of all human beings. This inequality of *varnas* had nothing to do with the merits of particular cases. Legal cases were judged, not according to the relative merits of two contending parties, but according to their respective hereditary *varnas*.

It is to be remembered here that it is the individual who is the subject of justice in the modern conception of justice. It is he who seeks and is expected to get justice from the state. Not so in the *Dharmaśāstric* scheme, wherein the community or group, and not the individual, was the unit of all laws and discussion of justice. Before admitting any case, the judge was expected to know the *varnas* (and other details regarding the profession and region to which a person belonged) of the individuals involved. The individual's relations with the state and society were mediated by his caste and sub-caste. If there were any rights (as in the case of *brāhmanas*) they were vested in the group, and not in the individual. Individual's needs and circumstances were hardly ever taken into consideration. It is also to be remembered that these groups were (and still are) hereditary, and were arranged in a strict hierarchy. Some sociologists have argued that there was quite a bit of mobility among *varnas*. If so, that was only in the case of the powerful; the lives of the masses were entirely determined by the respective castes in which they happened to be born.

Interestingly, the virtue of impartiality while administering justice is very well recognized in *Dharmaśāstras*. The king, the jurors and all others involved in the judicial process were enjoined to be truthful and strictly impartial towards the friend and the enemy. (Manu Smrti VIII. 335) But unfortunately, the hierarchy of *varnas* was beyond the purview of impartiality. The judge was expected to be impartial towards friend and enemy, but not towards men belonging to different *varnas*. (*Manu Smrti* VIII. 267, 359)

I am told that this is what the idea of limited equality means. The judge was expected to be impartial or equal towards all – whether friend or foe – belonging to one *varna*. This argument does not convince me. It is true that justice does not demand absolute equality of all human beings; but the limited equality demanded by justice must be based on some significant, relevant, or essential characteristic of the person, or the act. This essential or relevant characteristic may be different in different types of cases. That is, while in some cases, merit may be the quality shared by two persons whose acts, worth, or eligibility for some job should be judged equally; in other cases, it may be the need of the two agents; or even the special circumstances, and so on. But hereditary *varna*, or the difference of race, religion, or caste can never be the relevant criterion of limited equality.

The rule of law is very well recognized in *Dharmaśāstric tradition*, and we find the exalted proposition that not even the king is beyond the law. (*Manu Smrti* VIII. 336) The king may not be beyond the law but the supremacy of *brāhmanas*, the exalted position of the king and other inequalities were built into the law itself. The *Dharmaśāstras* had a clear and sometimes quite a noble conception of justice, even though they did not use any fixed term for it. There are very reasonable and often idealistic guidelines or norms both in the *Dharmaśāstras* and the *Arthaśāstra* for awarding punishments and administering justice. But the entire discussion is vitiated by their emphasis on the principle that justice should be administered strictly according to the respective castes of the victim and the offender.

A S Altekar has observed that this inequality was not a product of Hindu polity; the king was not the promulgator of law and only administered justice according to the prevalent law. This law was derived from Vedas, *Smritis* and customs. (Altekar 1984: 247 and 259) That may be so; but what difference does it make? It only means that the sociopolitical structure was hierarchical and unequal; and this inequality was integral to Hindu thought and praxis. Above all, and as we have seen, it had its basis in the religious sanction.

Now, if this hereditary inequality and the sociopolitical system based on it are sought to be justified as 'giving every one his due', the modern mind cannot accept this. A *śūdra* could have been far superior to a *brāhmana*, and this fact is frequently recognized in Sanskrit literature. (*Mahabharata, Aranyaka Parva* 177,16; 206, 11–13) But even then the *śūdras* remained in an extremely disadvantageous position vis-à-vis the *brāhmanas*. We cannot decide what a person deserves in a given case simply on the basis of his hereditary *varna* or caste, for the obvious reason that *varna* has nothing to do with the due or deserts of a person in a given case. It means that if justice is conceived as 'giving every person his due', the *Dharmaśāstric* scheme does not offer us justice.

Alternatively, justice may be understood and practised in terms of equality of all human beings before the law, as I have tried to argue in this paper. It simply means that the different treatment of any two similar cases by a society cannot be accepted unless it can at the same time offer some 'reasonable ground' for the difference in treatment. And hereditary *varna,* caste, or sex cannot be cited as a 'reasonable ground' for any radical difference in the treatment of two persons. But this was exactly the law and practice in the *Dharmaśāstric* scheme of things. The *Dharmaśāstric* system, therefore, fails to provide for justice understood in terms of 'equal treatment of similar cases' also. The authors of *Dharmaśāstras* were mainly interested in preserving the status quo of the extremely inequitable *varna*-based social order. There was no place in it for the dignity of human beings per se, far less for any concern for the welfare of 'the least advantaged', as advocated by Rawls.

The notion of human rights is integral to the modern western conception of justice. In a way, we can say that the securing of the rights of all human beings is the goal of justice. A given socio-legal system of justice is to be judged as right or successful according as it secures the rights of all individuals – whether majority or minority, citizens or non-citizens – in a given nation state.

Apparently, the conception of rights also seems to be absent in ancient religious thought. There is no equivalent term for the concept of right in Sanskrit. The term *adhikāra* that is now being used for rights had a rather limiting meaning. The word *adhikāra* was used in conjunction with *bheda* (difference); and it meant that not all people had the *adhikāra* (right) to perform Vedic rituals, or other spiritual practices (*sādhnā*). However, it is not that human beings had no rights. Excepting *śūdras* (or rather the lowermost sub-castes of *śūdras*), all others enjoyed the usual rights of a civil society. There were even safeguards against the violation of these rights. These safeguards were in the form of obligations of individuals in particular stations of life towards others. As Altekar puts it:

> Hindu constitutional writers have approached the problem from quite a different point of views. They usually describe not the rights of the citizens but the duties of the state, the former are to be inferred from the latter. (Altekar 1984: 64)

Not only the rights of citizens vis-à-vis the state were thus safeguarded, the rights of other classes (not individuals) were also secured. Even the rights of orphans, issueless women and widows were safeguarded by promulgating that it was the duty of the king to look after their welfare. (*Manu Smrti* VIII. 27–29) Right to property seemed to be a very cherished right. It was not declared as a right, but the *Dharmaśāstras* still secure it for the three 'upper' classes by providing for extreme punishment for anyone who steals or destroys others' property.

The position of women in the *Dharmaśāstric* world was quite poor from the modernist point of view. But generally their welfare and even property rights were safeguarded by declaring it the obligation of husbands and sons to look after them well. (*Manu Smrti* III. 55–61; IX. 95) Even the welfare of *śūdra* servants was somewhat ensured by declaring it the duty of their master and mistress to eat only after feeding them. (*Manu Smrti* III. 115–118, *Apastamba Dharma Sutra* II.4.9.10–11.) Manu even advises that the maintenance of the *śūdra* servant and his family should be the responsibility of the master. (*Manu Smrti* X. 124)

The conception of *dharma* is necessarily that of duty. It is integrally related to the traditional concept of debt (*rna*). A person is supposedly born with various debts to parents, teachers and living beings, and he can hope for his emancipation only after discharging all his debts to all these sections of society. This is an exalted concept, and it has no place for rights. A person is born with debts or duties and not rights, and is not expected to be conscious of his rights. But clearly his/her rights are safeguarded or preserved by the conception of reciprocal obligations which we saw as the central feature of justice in our earlier discussion. It is brought out more clearly in the description of the relationship between husband and wife. (*Manu Smrti* II. 60, IX.45, 95) The rights of parents and younger dependents are also secured by emphasizing very clearly the duties of the householders towards them. Man's duties towards the society, state and nature are also beautifully discussed, which apparently safeguard their rights. (*Manu Smrti* III. 77–78, IX. 274) The only exception of this duty-right relationship seems to be the hierarchical social order. The *brāhmana* authors of these *Dharmaśāstras* in contravention of their own approach, managed to secure maximum rights for themselves. And of course, *śūdras* hardly had any rights.

In real life the situation would have been quite different. Neither the concept of *dharma* nor *varna* hierarchy but the power of either arms or money was supreme. There was constant struggle for supremacy between the *brāhmanas* and *ksatriyas*. Formally, *brahmanas* were given respect but the real power lay either with the king or rich traders. Real life conditions are to be gleaned from history and the Epics. But here we are only concerned with the conception or theory and not with the practice. And at that level the hierarchical social order was definitely tilted towards *brāhmanas* (and at most *ksatriyas*) and against *śūdras*. The conception of equality either in society or before the law was totally absent, thus making the achieving of a just social order impossible.

The two conceptions of justice – the modern western and ancient Indian – are different on several counts:

1. While the equality of all human beings is basic to the modern western conception of justice, it is almost absent from the *Dharmaśāstras,* and to some extent, from the Epics.
2. While the individual is mostly the locus of justice and its related issues in modern thought, it is the class, and not the individual, that is the basic unit for justice in the *Dharmaśāstras.*
3. While the conception of human rights is central to the western notion of justice, no such conception exists in *Dharmaśāstras.* (This need not have been a negative point in the world-view of *Dharmaśāstras* because their unique conception of *dharma* indirectly includes the rights of others. But even their ideal of *dharma* – duty or obligation – has been vitiated by their total rejection of the notion of human equality).

Here, I would like to acknowledge two possible and legitimate criticisms. First, it would be rightly pointed out that since I have myself acknowledged that the concept of basic equality of all human beings is more or less a product of modern thought in the West, it would be 'unjust' to condemn ancient Indian (Hindu) thought for its absence. Admittedly, the ancient Greek conception of justice, especially as expounded by Plato in his *Republic,* is almost the same as that of ancient Indian (Hindu) religious texts. Both subordinate the individual to the society. In both, the individual is seen not as an individual but as a member of this or that group. And in both, the society is conceived as a rigidly hierarchical social order. The individual came to be the focus or primary unit of social thought only in the age of Enlightenment (seventeenth-eighteenth centuries). I agree with the above observations and so have nothing to add.

Second, it may be pointed out to me that equality or even total identity of not only all human beings but also the entire sentient creation is one of the most fundamental tenets of the philosophies of *Vedanta* and *Mahayana* Buddhism.

Also, this idea was not only asserted but practised in the entire Bhakti tradition. How, then, it may be asked, could I talk of its absence in the Vedic-Hindu tradition? I would like to submit in reply that it is my belief that various religio-philosophical and religio-social-cum-moral traditions flourished in India side by side; and Hinduism itself is a complex 'religio-culture' in which it's various strands or traditions both contradict and complement each other. (Jhingran 1999: 3, 28, 211) Therefore, even though granting that the idea of essential equality of all human beings is very much there in the Indian (Hindu) thought, in the present paper my contention has been a limited one that it was almost totally absent from the *Dharmaśāstric* tradition. In as much as *Dharmaśāstras* tried to regulate the entire life and interpersonal relations of individuals in Hindu society, and their viewpoint had a determinative influence on the Hindu mind, as evidenced in popular literature such as the Epics and *Purānas*, their world view and system of values are very important for understanding and evaluating Hindu thought, culture and sociopolitical order.

Notes

1 See Webb, Sidney and Beatrice, 'Inequality and Personal Freedom', in Ebenstein, W, ed, 1970, *Modern Political Thought*, Indian edition, New Delhi, Oxford and IBH Publishing Co., p. 246.

2 See *Manu Smrti*, VII. 14, especially 20, translated by Buhler, G, 1982, *The Laws of Manu,* Sacred Books of the East Series, Delhi, Motilal Banarsidass. All references to *Manu Smrti* in the paper are to this text.

3 See, *Mahabharata*, Santi Parva 110.1; also 95, 5–14, Hindi translation, Chief editor, Satvalekar, Damodar, Swadhyaya Mandal. 1968. All references to the *Mahabharata* in the paper are to this text.

4 See *Manu Smrti* IV. 178: *Āpastamba Dharma Sutra* I.7.20. 7–8. in *The Sacred Laws of the Aryas,* Vol. 1, *Gautama and Āpastamba* translated by Buhler, Georg, 1975, Delhi, Motilal Banarsidass.

5 See Kane, P V, 1993, *History of Dharmasastras,* Vol. III, Poona, Bhandarkar Oriental Research Institute, pp. 825 ff., 856 ff.

6 *Gautama Dharma Sutra* XI.20, *The Sacred Laws of the Aryas,* Vol I, op.cit

7 *Bhagavadgītā* VI. 29–32, translated by Radhakrishnan, S, 1977, Bombay, Blackie and Sons (India) Ltd. All references to the Bhagvadgita in the paper are from this translation.

8 *Samkara, Bhasya – Brahma Sutra,* I.3. 34–38, translated by Swami Gambhirananda, 1965, Calcutta, Advaita Ashrama. Here the reference is to *Gautama Dharma Sūtra* XII. 4–6.

References

Altekar, A S, 1984, *State and Government in Ancient India,* Delhi, Motilal Banarsidass.

Artha Sastra, translated by Shama Shastry, R, 1988, Mysore, Padam Printers.

Bhagvadgita, translated by Radhakrishnan, S, 1977, Bombay, Blackie and Sons (India) Ltd.

Broad, C D, 1956, *Five Types of Ethical Theory,* London, Routledge and Kegan Paul.

Chaim, Perelman, 'Concerning Justice', in Kent, Edward Allen, ed, 1970, *Law and Philosophy: Readings in Legal Philosophy*, New York, Appleton Century Crofts.

Hare, R M, 1968, *Freedom and Reason*, London, Oxford University Press.

Jhingran, Saral, 1999, *Aspects of Hindu Morality*, Delhi, Motilal Banarsidass.

Kane, P V, 1993, *History of Dharmasastras*, Vol. III, Poona, Bhandarkar Oriental Research Institute.

Kant, Immanuel, *Fundamental Principles of the Metaphysics of Morals*, translated by Abbott, Thomas K, Indianapolis, The Library of Liberal Arts,1949.

_______, *The Metaphysics of Morals*, translated by Gregor, Mary J, 1964, New York, Harper Torchbooks.

_______, 'There is Only One Innate Right', in Kent, Edward Allen, ed, 1970, *Law and Philosophy: Readings in Legal Philosophy*, New York, Appleton Century Crofts.

Kelsen, Hans, 1957, *What is Justice: Justice, Law and Politics in the Mirror of Science: Collected Essays*, Berkeley, University of California Press.

Mahābhārata, Sānti Parva, translated by Satvalekar, Damodar, 1968, Poona, Bhandarkar Research Institure.

Maitra, S K, 1963, *The Ethics of the Hindus*, Kolkata, University of Calcutta.

Manu Smrti, translated by Buhler, G, 1982, *The Laws of Manu*, Sacred Books of the East Series, Delhi, Motilal Banarsidass.

Mīmāmsa Sūtra, Śabara bhāsya, translated by Mimamsakah, Yuddhishthhira, 1977, Ramlal Kapoor Trust. Bahalgarh, Distt. Sonepat.

Paine, Thomas, in Adkins, Nelson F, ed, 1953,*Common Sense and Other Political Writings*, New York, The Liberal Arts Press.

Hare, R M, 'Universalizability', in 1972, *Essays on the Moral Concepts*, London, Macmillan and Co.

Rawls, John, 1999, *A Theory of Justice*, Massachusetts, Harvard University Press.

Samkara, Bhasya – Brahma Sutra, translated by Swami Gambhirananda, 1965, Calcutta, Advaita Ashrama.

Sidgwick, Henry, 1907, *The Methods of Ethics*, seventh edition, London, Macmillan and Co.

Singer, Marcus George, 1961, *Generalization in Ethics: An Essay in the Logic of Ethics with the Rudiments of a System of Moral Philosophy*, New York, Alfred A Knopf.

Strawson, P F, 'Social Morality and Individual Ideal', in Pahel, Kenneth, and Schiller, Marvin, eds, 1970, *Readings in Contemporary Ethical Theory*, New Jersey, Prentice Hall.

The Sacred Laws of the Aryas, translated by Buhler, Georg, 1975, Vol. I, Delhi, Motilal Banarsidass.

Webb, Sidney and Beatrice, 'Inequality and Personal Freedom', in Ebenstein, W, ed, 1970, *Modern Political Thought*, Indian Edition, New Delhi, Oxford and IBH Publishing Co.

Part Two

HUMAN RIGHTS ISSUES

Chapter 10

FRAGILE IDENTITIES AND CONSTRUCTED RIGHTS*

Rakesh Chandra

This postmodern essay is tinged with remnants of a modern nostalgic hankering to examine whether an attempt to see how things hang together can still succeed. In this self-reflexive journey multiple narratives encrusted with the formal structure of essay writing have been replaced with an attempt at genre splicing. There is a deliberate suspension of judgement and no claim to transcendence. However, this postmodern character in certain places gives way to the modern seeking of patterns of explanation.

In the second half of the twentieth century philosophical discussions were marked by intense debates, involving Russell, Strawson, Searle, Wittgenstein, Kripke, Swinburne, Brody and many others, on the question of identity. The principle questions were: What is identity? Who is a person? What is the epistemic logical status of identity statements? And the responses, with reference to Cartesian, Kantian and Rawlsian theoretical frameworks, range from some philosophers saying that to be a person is to be a body to some maintaining that to be a person is to be a mind with others held that it is a combination of the two. Some argued that a person is a stream of consciousness and some more formally maintained only that to be a person is to be a bearer of M and P predicates. Some other philosophers have argued that a person is an animal with self-awareness and memory, endowed with the capacity to use language. For some to be a person is to be a pure ego, transcendental, if you prefer. Furthermore, it may mean to be an autonomous moral agent. In the classical Indian responses to be a person may sometimes mean to be a possessor or the conglomerate of the five sheaths, or *kosas,* and sometimes to be a pure consciousness. With each one of these characterizations there arises

*This paper is enriched by responsive dialogues with my friend Urvashi Sahni.

the additional problem of re-identification. How do we ascribe sameness to the multiple presentations of a person? Will it be a spatio-temporal continuity or a set of essential characters? Furthermore, is identity a relation or a one-place predicate? When we have an identity statement of the variety 'Hesperus is Phosphorus' where both are proper names, how do we classify them as necessary, *a priori* or empirical? Is there a difference in first person identity statements of the variety 'I am Rakesh' and 'I am a Brahman'?

Though the debates are intense, useful, deep, analytical and acutely nuanced, in an interesting sense they leave me occasionally wonderstruck. How do I walk down the street with these eminent discussants and get an answer to the very general Socratic question asked by Bernard Williams: 'How ought I to lead my life'? Specifically, when I observe the second half of the twentieth century, I find struggles for identity where the principal questions are: Is it fully human yet, to be a woman? Is it fully human yet, to be an undercaste? Is it fully human yet, to be black, poor, gay, Asian or AIDS-affected?

Is my identity as a person, as a human being belonging to a caste, class, gender, political allegiance, significant? While conflicts and confrontations within families, states and countries have raised issues of identity as they relate to my parentage, my caste, the colour of my skin, my profession, sexual preference and political ideology, philosophical mainstream response to these has to be more clearly understood.

I use the following two case studies to contextualize the questions raised above and the discussion that follows.

Sushma

Sushma is an undercaste woman, whose caste occupation was scavenging. Her father was an official sweeper. She and her brother were sent to a government school. The teacher, instead of calling her brother Mahendra, a name of an upper caste, decided to call him Ghasite – a disrespectful, nonsensical name. The teacher asked Mahendra to clear the dog's droppings from the class. The child refused. The teacher thrashed the child mercilessly. Mahendra's father came over to complain. He told the teacher that though he was a sweeper, his children, like others, had not come to school to clean and should not be asked to do so. The teacher thrashed the child again. Violated and furious, Mahendra's father hit the teacher with his broom. Sushma and Mahendra grew up with self-respect. Mahendra is now a doctor settled in the USA and Sushma is a government schoolteacher and an activist. Both use their caste name 'Valmiki'. They would like to be respected not irrespective of their caste, but with their caste identities. Sushma does not believe that her identity as a woman can be more determining than her identity as an undercaste. When academics, feminists and political activists try to convince her that women share common oppression and could be viewed as a caste, she refuses to be taken in. An international charity organization with rights-based focus on her request instituted a research consisting of 20 case studies. The findings: *dalit* women's oppression has few parallels. They are punished for caste and punished for gender, both by upper caste men and women, and by men of their own caste. This punishment gets more severe, if there is a perceived sense of upward class mobility or any sense of resistance. Sushma has no illusions about undercaste nobility. Oppressive structures leave no noble savages. There is much self-hatred, criminality and cruelty. There are many children who need to be saved from their self-hating, cruel parents. But does she want them to grow up as self-respecting *humans* or as proud *dalit* persons? Could they be both? Much to the displeasure of socialized socialists and conservative nationalists, Sushma raised the issue of caste as race in Durban. Rights-based action and the primacy of human agency are cardinal to her identity.

Qul

Qul was being lowered in his grave. We were shown his bloated pink face. Three days ago he was murdered besides the sea in Goa. My friend Qul was a dancer, a copywriter, an author and a young gay born in a Muslim family. Twenty years ago his sister was murdered by Rao. Her crime: she was the lesbian partner of Leela, Rao's daughter. At home, Qul's father was often beaten up by his stepchildren. Qul was a closet gay in a small town, an avant-garde queen in the careless Bombay and a selectively exposed invert in the double standards of Delhi. He wished to develop a gay rights lobby. The meetings degenerated into cruising rave parties. Qul stopped them. A film was made on gays. He was portrayed peeping from his house in South Extension, the upmarket part of Delhi, into the Muslim ghetto Jama Masjid (the masjid actually does not even exist in the vicinity of the area). Qul resented his portrayal as a Muslim. During the same period, he was writing an autobiographical novel, which he read to his mother. This was his indirect disclosure to his mother, herself a novelist of some repute. After the Hindu–Muslim question started coming up crassly and visibly in public spaces, Qul changed the names of his characters from Muslim to Hindu. He did not want the stereotypical gay Muslim identification. He wished to be given a legitimate space as a gay, not so much as a born Muslim. The struggles were many and so were the charades. He had his sister to protect. Who would marry a girl whose sister gets murdered for being a lesbian and whose brother is an avowed catamite? His editor might have accepted him, his colleagues may have tolerated him and his one-off partner forever used him, but Qul got killed, most probably by the drug peddling hunks on the Goan beach, where perhaps he hoped to freely celebrate his 'self'. What was he seeking? Was remaining closeted to maintain social propriety better than being penalized for disclosure? His death, whether murder or suicide, brought much dishonour to his family. His sexual preference would have messed with it further. His attempts at forming solidarity groups were botched. Identities of the disempowered can become reasons for bonding and solidarity. But this bonding may be only episodic and functional. Solidarity and belongingness cannot be arrived at on the grounds of a single feature – sexual preference in this case. But what for some may seem an incidental feature, was for Qul his central identity. His family took him to *mazars*, and he visited counselling centres. Religious leaders had spurned him, and psychiatrists had tried to cure him with electric shocks. His death was no martyr's.

What is the relevance of philosophical thought to Qul and Sushma's concerns of identity, and how do discussions in philosophy as transacted in lectures and discussions about epistemology, metaphysics and ethics inform our lives and decisions?

What are the locations of identity, and how does one straddle multiple worlds with multiple identities? Is it a self-ascription or the categorization by the other that determines Qul's and Sushma's identity? I am the emperor, a *dalit*, a woman, a black, a subaltern, a physically challenged, a *Vedantin*, a child, an Indian, a Muslim. These positions, social appellations, genetic characters and locations in power hierarchies, physical features, intellectual commitments, temporal positions, national status and religious order locate me in different spheres of identification. Philosophy debates how names refer to the objects they refer to: is it through their descriptive content and its satisfaction, or do they refer to them directly and rigidly, picking up the same individual in all possible worlds? Fascinating theories such as Saul Kripke's, extended the idea of proper names as rigid designators to include common names and natural kind terms, implying that common names like natural kind terms, e.g. gold, orange, etc., too pick up the same individuals or sets across all possible worlds. But are the names used for my identification of the same order, or is there a fundamental difference between them? How about the talk of real essences and the talk of a posteriori necessities that is metaphysical? Is an undercaste woman's identity as an undercaste woman an *a posteriori* necessity, and is her womanhood a social construct like her caste? Is her caste birth in some interesting way related to the issue of necessity of origin? How do the twentieth-century discourses in the philosophy of language intersect with the twentieth-century struggles for identity? Is there a road map that will help us to navigate from one to the other? These questions need resolution and their responses are to be put together in an intelligible form.

Many struggles of identity are struggles to throw away ascriptions, thrust on people as wretched, uncivilized, incapable of self-authentication and autonomy. Slaves and the colonized have often taken this track. In many other struggles, there is an appeal to be treated as an equal with an identity that might be different. One strand of the black struggle and some sections of the women's movement used this strategy for a while. If, for example, I'm a Muslim, Marxist and woman activist seeking legitimacy for my identity within the framework of a secular constitution, I appeal not to human rights or natural rights but to the constitutional guarantees of my country. In that, am I seeking fulfilment of rights in a post-enlightenment, power-centred framework or am I seeking belongingness in some long forgotten sense? Is identity determined in an 'I think, therefore I am' mode or an 'I think, therefore you are/you think, therefore I am' mode? On what basis do I appeal when I look from the margins and seek inclusion?

How do ethics and morality function in guiding action? Does the specificity of my position also get response from a moral theory in the form of action-guiding rules?

There has often been an appeal, with reference to human rights, by individuals and groups seeking space to express themselves as fully humane persons. What are the philosophical underpinnings of this appeal? What is the source of these rights? Many discussants argue that rights are not founded on human needs as the natural rights theorists would like to believe, nor are they based on contract. They contend that all needs theories, including the Maslow's theory of hierarchy of needs, are not borne out by facts, and even if they were, the jump from needs to rights is illegitimate. It is sometimes argued that the contract theory too is an ideation because no actual contract is actually entered into by the persons who are claiming rights. The foundation of rights that we appeal to is actually a 'construction'. This constructivist theory appeals not to the actual human nature but to the human perception of themselves. We appeal to human rights as the highest court of appeal to which we may go when other, simpler, lower contractual appeals fail us. It is interesting to note that international documents concerning human rights, including the United Nations (UN) Charter and other development policy documents, often still favour the needs theory and use Maslow as evidence. However, there does seem to be much persuasive power in grounding human rights not in a given but a posited picture of human possibility. This moral positing provides for a structure where human nature finds functioning and capabilities find fruition. Treat human beings as equal humans and you get equal humans who are not discovered but constructed.

What is the source of human rights? The international community sees this in terms of the consensus arrived at by the members of the community. This clearly is not based on an empirical investigation of human nature but on an articulated self-conception of the moral human nature. Rights then are sustained by ethos, custom or convention. This is continuous with the etymological meaning of ethics and ethical, which is: being according to ethos or custom.

How do I piece all these concerns together, and where do I think the resolutions lie? On the issue of human rights I find the constructivist picture comfortable. But this picture need not necessarily contest the needs and the contract foundationalism of human rights. Needs are natural while construction does not claim any natural foundation. However, on my own interpretation the needs and the contract can themselves be understood as posits. Their 'givenness' is historical. And their universality is founded on 'praxis' or 'phronesis' rather than on 'episteme' in some pure sense. 'What is it to be human?' is an ethical enquiry, and as Martha Nussbaum (Nussbaum and Glover 1995) puts it, it asks us to evaluate the components of our lives, which are so important that we would not call life humane without them. As contrasted with Rawls' thin theory of good, Nussbaum calls her own the thick, vague theory of good. So, is there a source of human rights in a fixed human nature? For Nussbaum, the account of what it is to be human is an especially deep, continuous sort of experiential and historical truth. It is not fixed but tentative and open ended. The inquiry, though it pays attention to biology and specificities as they shape human action, is normative. For Nussbaum, at the level one of the conception of human being, the shape of the human form of life is significant. This shape is characterized by human mortality and human fear of death. It is encrusted with the experience of body, which has hunger, thirst, need for shelter, sexual desire and mobility. Humanness is also characterized by the capacity for pleasure and pain along with the cognitive capability of perceiving, imagining and thinking. In a more embedded form humanness is identified by experiencing a sense of helplessness of infancy and childcare, of practical reason, affiliation with other human beings, relatedness to other species and to nature, humour and play, separateness and various degrees of separateness.

At the second level of the conception of human being Martha Nussbaum identifies ten functional human capabilities:

a) Being able to live to the end of a normal length human life.
b) Being able to have good health.
c) Being able to avoid unnecessary, non-beneficial pain.
d) Being able to use senses, to imagine, think and reason.
e) Being able to have attachments.
f) Being able to form a concept of good and to engage in critical reflection about the planning of one's own life.
g) Being able to live for and to others, to recognize and show concern for other human beings, to engage in various forms of social interaction, to have compassion and capability for both justice and friendship.

h) Being able to live with concern for and in relation to animals, plants and the world of nature.
i) Being able to laugh, play and enjoy recreational activities.
j) Being able to live one's own life and nobody else's. This involves non-intervention with choices that are personal and definitive of selfhood, like choices regarding marriage, childbearing, sexual expression, speech and employment.
k) Being able to live one's own life in one's own surroundings and context. This capability is, unlike personal liberty, a tool for human functioning rather than an end in itself.

She claims that a life that lacks any one of these capabilities is short of a good human life. To the charge of hegemonic homogenization or cultural insensitivity, Martha, like Sen, reminds us that since the respect for choice is itself an essential capability in the list, fear of subverting pluralism is ill founded. (Nussbaum and Sen 1993)

Will this appeal have teeth with reference to women, undercastes, blacks and others who face marginalization? Martha's answer is affirmative.

Interestingly, both Sen and Nussbaum believe that the capability and functioning discourse is an alternative to the rights-based discourse, whereas I have been mentioning their characterization of the two levels of human concept as a ground for appeal to ensure rights.

'Rights' have been seen with scepticism both by traditionalists, culture relativists and Marxists, who see in it an essential role of the state, which, according to them, is by nature oppressive and must wither away. However, I do not see that there is much sting in the two critiques, if we see rights as founded on the constructivist moral picture of human beings. I also see no irresolvable conflict between this picture and one of belongingness. There might be a suspicion that belongingness may become an excuse for the maintenance of status quo, but since belongingness is arrived at through understanding, and understanding in its very nature is creative and interpretive, this fear is unfounded. Aristotle himself spoke of practical reason inclusive of togetherness and being public. His modern interpreters too lay enough premium on dialogue discussion and inclusiveness, where inclusion does not preclude innovation and transformation.

So how do ethics help Sushma and Qul in their struggle for identity? I think it gives them a subversive tool and an appeal to moral consistency. How can you support inclusion in some spheres and reject in others, when the capabilities are the same?

Getting back where we began, we may ask about some relations between various discussions – does the talk of humanness get impacted by the discussions on the idea of person and those on identity conducted in the manner of the philosophy of language discourses, i.e., the rigid designation, the *a posteriori* necessities and the necessities of origin?

I would like to believe that though there might be a theory that holds that the moral concept of a human person and the metaphysical concept of a person have a back and forth interplay, my own inclination is to maintain that it is the decision about the moral concept first, that would determine further how the term 'person' will function linguistically: as an abbreviated descriptive class name or as a rigid designator. If my position is correct, theories of person, in terms of Cartesian ego, stream of consciousness and Lockean memory tracks, are insufficient.

Finally, let us try and summarize. What seemed to be wrong at first sight is that philosophy and particularly ethics do not provide a clear answer to a specific situation. In this case they seemed to avoid getting messed up in the cry for justice made by multiple voices in distress, which in many cases are conflicts of identity within the same person.

The other discomfort was historical – despite the claims made by a large number of influential philosophers in the twentieth century about their avowed respect for ordinary language there has been much 'technicization' and 'rarification' done in philosophical vocabulary disregarding continuities in ordinary language. For instance, most ordinary language use of the word 'moral', 'ethical' and 'good' is continuous with the etymological meaning as customary, while the ethical–metaethical divide along with the prudential–ethical divide seems to contest these continuities. Similarly, philosophic discussion on essences and identity, when focused largely on the understanding of the connective 'is', insisting that identity is a one-place self-reflexive relation and its assertion is epistemically, *a priori* and metaphysically necessary, also seems to leave cold many who use ordinary language to highlight identity struggles with reference to pluralism and universalism.

My own understanding is that the generality of philosophical theory is not an escape but an appeal to universalism. The question may be: is this universality to be understood as minimal and contentless, or as inclusive and substantial, and it pleases me that the past three decades, philosophical, ethical, political and economical divides notwithstanding, have witnessed a rich dialogue on issues of common humanity. There have been protests on the streets by people facing marginalization and recommendations to consider theoretical reconstructions in forms of feminist theory of justice, ecological humanism, etc., but despite their special focus they are best understood within the framework of non-exclusionary universalism, which at first seemed to be philosophy's undoing.

Presumptuous though it is, let me attempt to explore what this means when it comes to Sushma's life and Qul's death. Sushma lives for she continues to seek inclusion through all possible means in her resource, including international instruments conceived in the 'techne' model. She utilizes both an appeal to togetherness as well as to publicity. Qul sought belongingness too, but he hesitated to use publicity and died savagely in shade.

Should Qul be blamed or should we attempt to construct a world where all human capabilities and functioning are fully realized? The choice is evident. Philosophical discussions are a part of the armamentarium in this reconstruction and they cannot be blamed for not being the whole. A philosopher, as Rorty would say, is one of the 'conversationalist'.

On the question of connectedness in ordinary language philosophy about 'identity', however, I feel that the connections require a much more self-conscious fleshing, and I have here suggested some routes which can be negotiated. Finally to my mind – fragile identities and constructed rights hang well with philosophical universalism.

References

Coombs, Jerrold R., and Wrinkler, Earl R., eds. 1993. *Applied Ethics: A Reader.* London: Blackwell.

Donnelley, Jack. 1985. *The Concept of Human Rights.* London: Croom Helm.

Kripke, Saul, 'Naming and Necessity', in Davidson, Donald, and Harman, Gilbert, eds, 1972, Semantics of Natural Languages, Holland, Dordrecht. D. Reidel Publishing Company.

Maslow, Abraham H. 1968. *Towards A Psychology of Being.* New Jersey, Princeton: Van Nostrand Reinhold.

Nussbaum, Martha, and Glover, Jonathan. 1995. *Women, Culture and Development.* Oxford: Oxford University Press.

Nussbaum, Martha, and Sen, Amartya. 1993. *The Quality Of Life.* Oxford: Clarendon Press.

Williams, Bernard. 1985. *Ethics and the Limits of Philosophy.* London: Fontana.

Chapter 11

AFFIRMATIVE ACTION: COMPENSATION OR DISCRIMINATION?

Madhucchanda Sen

The History of the Debate

The 50s and 60s saw radical changes in the very conception of civil liberties in nations all over the world. On the one hand, there were western nations like USA, where people started recognising the injustices that have been inflicted on minorities and felt the need to make up for these years of injustice. On the other hand, there were nations like India, which were just coming out of colonial rule and were feeling the need to recast the entire social network by removing discriminatory practices from society, which proved to be real obstacles to the progress of the newly formed nation. This was done again by making up for years of oppressive practices against socially disadvantaged sections like women, backward castes and tribes, and minorities. It was felt that the country could not progress as an independent developing nation if a large section of the population still lived under social oppression. Statesmen and builders of constitutions all over the world started speaking about preferential treatment or reservation policies, or what is known as 'affirmative action'. All these involve positive steps taken by governments to increase the representation of socially discriminated sections of people like women, minorities, ethnic or racial groups or castes in areas of employment, education and business, from which they have been historically excluded. This affirmative action seemed to be at that point of history as a morally commendable effort towards rendering compensatory justice to sections of people who have for generations been subjected to abject discrimination, oppression and injustice. Today, however, this is not seen in quite the same light. It is not as though people have stopped believing in compensatory justice, but it is strongly felt by many that, in their efforts to atone past injustices, governments have actually tried to make up for one discriminatory practice by invoking another discriminatory practice. It was also felt that affirmative action, which aimed at reconciling past atrocities, was unable to wipe away the tarnished history of oppression of nations. Nor was affirmative action able to compensate the people to whom violence and discriminatory practices were perpetrated. Reconciliation of past atrocities is in a way impossible. This was felt mainly because, on the one hand, it was asked, why should some people who have never been responsible for any social injustice themselves pay for actions of their ancestors and, on the other hand, why should some people who have never been subjected to any kind of discrimination themselves enjoy extra advantage because their ancestors were deprived of their basic human rights. And so it was felt that there was something almost logically wrong with preferential affirmative action.

Policies of preferential affirmative action or reservation were discussed mostly at two levels. First of all, legislative and executive departments of governments have discussed it, and it has also been a topic of heated public debate. These two kinds of discussion have often been quite unrelated, which has caused major public unrest, as was witnessed in India in connection with the Mandal Commission Report. The unrest demonstrated precisely the lack of connection between the thoughts of the policy makers and a strong wave public opinion.

The discussion about affirmative action was not only confined to these two spheres. Soon enough this attracted the attention of philosophers. Around the 1970s they started taking part in public debates related to social liberties. It was possibly John Rawls (1971) who made philosophers aware of the fact that it is not their job to do just meta-ethics, by showing how a normative theory of justice can be formed. It is around this time that we find philosophers like Thomas Nagel (1978) and Judith Jarvis Thomson (1973) writing specifically on preferential affirmative action. Both these writers defended preferential affirmative action, though on different grounds. Thomson says that preferential affirmative action works as a kind of justice, as it compensates women, blacks and other minorities and sections of people for their past exclusion from academic institutions, jobs, business etc. This particular notion of justice has faced severe criticism, which we will discuss later. Nagel, however, makes a different point. He subscribes to the view that preferential affirmative action would bring about a kind of social good without resulting in any injustice. This again was contested by many as it was felt that preferential affirmative action tried to remove one injustice by invoking another.

The philosophical discussion about preferential affirmative action centred around two key concepts that were involved in it: justice (and along with it equality) and dessert or compensation. We shall see how philosophers have criticised the belief that preferential affirmative action is an effort towards removing inequalities in society by restoring justice. And we shall also see how philosophers have regarded as almost perverse the belief that preferential affirmative action ensures compensatory justice. These philosophers also felt that preferential affirmative action resulted in violation of several kinds of rights, e.g., "the right of an applicant to equal consideration, the right of the maximally competent to a position, the right of everyone to equal opportunity."[1] The objective of compensatory justice, that affirmative action was supposed to achieve, actually resulted in denial of merit, talent and performance. It also made people pay damages for actions of others. We find some other philosophers saying that affirmative action is nearly self-defeating in its purpose, as instead of decreasing inter racial animosity it increased it.

There are of course philosophers who came forward in defence of preferential affirmative action in the wake of all these criticisms. The main thrust of their argument was that gender, racial or caste discrimination was so entrenched in the societies, which are now adopting preferential policies, that such preferential policies would result in an overall moral improvement of the society. These philosophers also argued that such preferential treatment would neutralise the undeserved advantages that the section of the society which has been responsible for past discrimination has enjoyed. It was also felt that the individuals who are regarded to be victims of reverse discrimination and are regarded to have superior credentials for jobs, academies and business would not have such credentials unless the discriminatory practice of their forefathers had persisted this long. And consequently affirmative action was in fact restoring justice as well as giving the compensation.

Let us now discuss the criticisms that I have mentioned that preferential affirmative action faces.

Justice, Equality and Affirmative Action

As we have said before, most of those who defend preferential affirmative action claim that it manages to restore justice. The notion of justice that they are invoking is commonly known as distributive justice. There are philosophers like Robert Nozick (1977), who have been critical of this theory of justice. It is not possible to discuss his entire view about justice and equality here, but I shall try to mention the key points that are relevant in the debate about preferential affirmative action.

The notion of equality is usually tied with the notion of justice. This, however, might not be acceptable to all. First of all Nozick would say that it is not quite correct to think that if something like wealth is unequally distributed in a society then we must try to remove such inequalities right away. If the inequality results from a distribution pattern, which comes about in accordance with rules of acquisition, transfer and rectification, then there is no reason to think that such inequality is unjust. He also says that there is really no reason to suppose that the differences that we witness in our society are entirely arbitrary if they cannot be justified so to speak. In a free society distribution takes place as a result of interactions of private individuals who have the right to distribute their holdings as they wish. It is a fact that in society people engage in different kinds of exchanges in which they care very little about compensation of disadvantaged people. It is usually thought that in such a society the government has to come forward and force people to share their wealth and resources with such disadvantaged people. This is seen in the form of taxation of all sorts. Nozick has an extremely radical view about this. He even thinks that taxation is comparable with forced labour. And so he thinks it unjust to penalise people for the disadvantageous conditions of others and to make them work for their benefits.

Those who believe in preferential treatment would say that, that some people are in possession of resources is not a result of their natural talent but a result of past discriminatory practices favouring the section of the community to which they belong. Nozick says that it is not quite correct to think that one is justifiably entitled to have something only if she is also justifiably entitled to whatever she has employed in order to accumulate that resource.

The question however remains as to what a society ought to do in that case to rectify past injustices that have made sections of its population suffer discrimination for generations? Philosophers who admit the need for rectification of past injustice may still find preferential affirmative action as perverse and hence not provide us with an answer to the problem of rectification. Lisa H. Newton (Lisa Newton, "Reverse Discrimination as Unjustified", in Jan Narveson, ed., *Moral Issues*, 1983) tries to show how affirmative action goes wrong in its effort to restore justice. First of all she says that the moral ideal of equality has to be regarded as logically distinct from the 'conditions of justice in the political sense'. The moral ideal of equality is in fact dependent upon this justice. Newton says that it makes no sense to talk about equality unless we specify it with respect to something. When we speak of equality in the political context what we mean is equality of rights. Or in other words, 'equal access to the public realm, public goods and offices, equal treatment under the law — in brief, the equality of citizenship' (Newton 1983: 389). From this it follows that in a situation where citizenship is not a real possibility it makes little sense to talk about equality. If this is what justice means, then we might try to understand what injustice means.

Injustice in the political sense would mean discrimination of a section of the citizenry either favourably or unfavourably. Consequently, it would be unjust to debar citizens from privileges enjoyed by other citizens. It would be equally unjust to reserve jobs and entry to academic institutions for one particular section of the citizenry while denying that to others. And so, under this definition of justice, just as much injustice is done by affirmative action, as is done when blacks, women, lower castes were discriminated. 'Just as previous discrimination did, this reverse discrimination violates the public equality which defines citizenship and destroys the rule of law for the areas in which these favors are granted.' (Newton 1983: 390) And so, when people claim that preferential affirmative action should be adopted in order to ensure social equality, then we have to also admit that the realisation of such social equality leads to injustice. And this is paradoxical. Equality as a moral ideal, as we have already said, is parasitic on the ideal of political justice and so it is highly strange to suppose that it leads to injustice. Thus Newton concludes that if the only justification for affirmative action is that it restores social equality then it is unjust and hence also unjustified.

Newton raises two other problems. First of all, she poses the question that when we talk about minorities in connection with affirmative action, what is meant by 'minority'? In making and execution of state policies, this has to be seriously considered and clearly defined. For instance, in a vast country like India, there may be sections of the citizenry defined on racial, religious or caste lines which are majorities in one part of the country and minorities in another part of the country. It is in such cases difficult to define what constitutes a minority. And if we want to consider all sections that form a minority in some part of the country or the other, it would actually include nearly all the different sections of the citizenry defined in terms of race, caste, gender, etc. This would create enormous practical problem for governments in the enactment of preferential affirmative action. Many such programmes that are adopted by governments suffer from this problem. Since it is so difficult and in fact nearly impossible to define minority in a vast country like India or the USA, it is assumed that the racial or caste structure, and the history of discrimination thereof, is uniform all over the country and reservation policies are made accordingly. This leads to great unrest and enormous public debate. For example, it would be naïve to think the non-black American male community consists of a socially homogenous, uniform category of people. Similarly it would also be wrong to suppose that the higher caste Hindu Indians form a homogenous, uniform category.

The second problem that Newton speaks of is in fact more serious. Suppose we agree upon what we mean by minority and identify the sections of citizenry that have faced past discrimination. Even then it would be difficult to decide 'what amount of reverse discrimination wipes out the initial?' (Newton 1983: 391) There seems to be no criterion by which we might decide when we have managed to compensate a community for the past injustice done to it.

And no consensus is actually reached about how much and how long should affirmative action programmes go on till we can say that we have compensated a particular community for its past discrimination.

A Defence of Preferential Treatment

We find a defence of preferential affirmative action in Richard Wasserstrom. (Richard Wasserstrom, "A Defence of Programs of Preferential Treatment", in Jan Narveson, ed., *Moral Issues,* 1983) He says that one of the main criticisms that programmes of preferential treatment faces is that there is a kind of intellectual inconsistency involved in the very idea of such programmes. It is said that those programmes were initiated to put an end to discriminatory practices made under considerations of race, gender and caste. But these programmes of preferential treatment themselves were making preferential treatment on the basis of race, gender and caste. So there is a sort of intellectual inconsistency involved here. Wasserstrom argues that the reasons for which the initial discrimination based on race, gender and caste was regarded as wrong are different from the reasons for which preferential treatment made on the basis of race, gender and caste was regarded to be wrong. He says:

> The fundamental evil of programs that discriminated against blacks or women was that these programs were part of a larger social universe which systematically maintained a network of institutions which unjustifiably concentrated power, authority, and goods in the hands of white male individuals, and which systematically cognised blacks and women to subordinate positions in society. (Wasserstrom 1983: 394)

In a very significant sense the wrong that is claimed to be done while exercising preferential affirmative action is really not even comparable with the wrong that was done against women, blacks, low castes and minorities.

Wasserstrom also points out something very significant. He says that most of the time we criticise racial or gender discrimination because we think that discrimination based on racial or gender considerations were absolutely arbitrary and hence could never be defended. And so people who criticise preferential affirmative action come up with the same argument and say that it is equally arbitrary to take up programmes of preferential treatment based on racial or gender considerations. But the real problem with racial or gender discrimination in the first place was not this. The problem was more profound than the fact that such discrimination was based on arbitrary grounds. Wasserstrom takes the example of slavery. He says that slavery practised against blacks of the Southern states of USA in the past was horrendous not because blacks were made slaves just because they were blacks. The real reason for regarding slavery as a social evil was the practice of slavery itself. And it was inconsequential as to what criterion people used in carrying out this hideous practice. The same was true about the atrocities against women, blacks, backward castes, or minorities all over the world. Oppression is a social evil by itself and it is in a way immaterial to consider what grounds the oppressor had in mind in choosing its victim.

But isn't taking some races or castes or women as inferior an evil itself — an evil that gives rise to another evil, viz. oppression? The racist or castist or sexist psyche is developed in a society which itself takes race, caste or gender as criterion of determination of worth of human beings. And this is what is to be regarded as an evil. And so it is important to see whether a discriminatory practice demonstrated racism. But even if we grant this we cannot say that preferential affirmative action has racist, castist or sexist motives working behind it.

It is here where the question of 'intent' comes in, i.e., with what intent discrimination is made is important when we evaluate a discriminatory practice. This is a point that is made by Sara Ann Ketchum in her *Evidence, Statistics and Rights: A Reply to Simon.*[2] It would be convenient for us if we discuss this paper first.

Logical Considerations

One of the logical arguments that we find against preferential treatment is that the kind of justification that one gives in favour of preferential treatment is exactly same as the kind of argument that can be given in favour of racial or sexual discrimination. Robert Simon speaks of this in *Statistical Justification of Discrimination* (Robert Simon and Sara Ann Ketchum, "An Exchange on Preferential Treatment", in Jan Narveson, ed., *Moral Issues*, 1983). He says that a sort of statistical justification is given in favour of preferential treatment, which runs along the same line as similar statistical justification given in favour of discrimination. This kind of argument was given by James Nickel (Robert Simon, "Statistical Justification of Discrimination", in Jan Narveson, ed., *Moral Issues*, 1983). In criticising Nickel, Simon asks us to compare three arguments, which are all of the same kind:

A. 80% of candidates who score poorly on test T will fail to graduate from the university due to academic deficiencies. Therefore, the university is justified in refusing to admit any candidate who scores poorly on T.
B. 80% of women lack physical strength to perform job J. Therefore, employers are justified in refusing to consider any women as candidates for J.

C. 80% of the members of group G are victims of past injustice. Therefore compensatory programs are justified in providing benefits to all members of G.

What Simon wants to point out is that most of us who give arguments of the kind C in favour of preferential treatment are critics of arguments of the kind B which are in favour of different kinds of discrimination. He specifically mentions Sara Ann Ketchum and Christine Peirce, who accept C but reject B. Simon says that there is sort of logical inconsistency in accepting one and rejecting the other, as the arguments are the same kind of statistical argument (one given in favour of racial discrimination and the other in favour of compensatory justice). The nature of the statistical argument is such that it emphasises the strong correlation between being a member of a particular section of a community and being the victim of social injustice. And on the basis of this high correlation, governments and organisations avoid the costly and difficult procedure of evaluating possible cases of social injustice on an individual basis. Blanket reservation policies are adopted solely based on this high correlation.

We have to see if these blanket policies are to be accepted even on pragmatic and economic grounds. One could argue that many a time this results in far more expenses on the part of governments than what would be incurred in a detailed evaluation of cases on individual basis. And it might also be said that the economically disadvantaged sections of other communities are deprived of this special privilege as well. And those who support preferential treatment for those who have been subject to social injustice should also accept that those who have been subjected to social injustice for being economically underprivileged are also entitled to preferential treatment. The kinds of blanket reservation policy that are based on the high correlation statistics tend to ignore this.

Some philosophers might just say that there are serious differences between the arguments A and C on the one hand and B on the other. One might argue that the argument B in favour of discrimination against people of some particular racial or ethnic community or on grounds of gender is just unacceptable because such discrimination is so very offensive and humiliating that one cannot defend them even by showing that the argument that establishes them are of the kind that can be accepted elsewhere. They would also say that, even if the reservation policies based on statistical findings about such correlation might prove to be discriminatory to certain persons of a community which does not have a history of social depravation, we should realise that those policies never *intended* this discrimination. The reverse discrimination that results from preferential treatment is an unwanted consequence of an action or policy that had an aim of compensatory justice alone. A government can go on further and resolve to implement reservation policies made on economic grounds. But what is important for us to consider is whether there is something logically wrong in adopting a policy with the objective of removing discriminatory practices in society which itself leads to a different kind of discrimination. And in fact this is so just because it follows exactly the same kinds of arguments that would be given for the very discriminatory practices that it aims to eradicate.

In the case of A one might say that the real motive of the university is not to discriminate against previous low achievers, who could eventually perform, but just to achieve the academic goals of the university. But then one could also argue in the case of B that the company in question would say that the sole aim of the company was to maximise profit and not to discriminate on gender lines. But even then this discrimination would not be regarded as 'benign' in the way that reverse discrimination is regarded. One may also add at this point that the correlation that is specified in the case of B (the kind mentioned by racists or sexists) is spurious. And in fact the real difference between C and B is that the history of discrimination associated with the people of a particular community or gender mentioned in B is so horrendous that in their case even a 'benign' discrimination can do greater harm than other cases of benign discrimination.

Simon says that while such arguments might be valid to a very large extent and very strong in the case of societies that are sharply divided on grounds of race or caste, they would not be so strong in the case of societies in which even the historically privileged section cannot be regarded as 'monolithic and so politically powerful' community. (Simon 1983) This is true of the Indian situation as well. The high caste Hindu community does not constitute a monolithic and politically, socially and economically powerful community.

Sara Ann Ketchum in response to Simon's paper agrees that it is possibly not always quite correct to carry out programmes of preferential treatment depending just on race, caste, or gender. It is true that a real evaluation of discrimination suffered has to be made before extending preferential treatment to anyone. A son of a poor white miner from a provincial town in USA might be more deserving than a daughter of a black wealthy surgeon from New York. Ketchum says that the real problem with arguments of the kind given by Nickel is also the problem with Simon's criticism of it. Ketchum says that "they both assume that the connection between being black in a white-supremacist society and having suffered injustice is properly represented by the notion of statistical correlation, that the alternatives are requiring proof of suffering or distributing on the basis of characteristic which is merely statistically correlated with being a victim of injustice". (Sara Ann Ketchum, "Evidence, Statistics and Rights: A Reply to Simon", in Robert Simon and Sara Ann Ketchum, *An Exchange on Preferential Treatment*, in Jan Narveson, ed., *Moral Issues*, 1983)

Ketchum comes up with two examples to demonstrate that characteristics that are merely statistically correlated with being a victim of injustice might not be the true reason for such injustice. The first example is of a society, call it Society A, where there is an established pattern of white supremacy and where blacks are unjustly treated only because they are black. But in this society, by some accident, 20% of blacks have never suffered any injustice. The second example is of Society B where blacks have never been discriminated against simply because they are blacks. But however there is a practice in this society of discriminating against people over 65, members of a particular religious group (maybe Baptists) and people coming from a particular region of the country. It so happens that 80% of blacks fall in one of these three categories. So, both in Society A and Society B 80% of blacks are discriminated against. So, if we were to take into consideration statistical correlation between being black and being subject to social discrimination then Society A and Society B would be exactly the same. But surely it is not. Keeping this in mind Ketchum defines a characteristic relevant to compensatory justice:

> *C*: Being an *X* in *Y*-supremacist society, where the superiority of *Y*'s in defined in terms of the inferiority of *X*'s. (Ketchum, 1983: 363)

What is to be noted here is that there must be a conceptual connection between characteristics *C* and someone's having suffered injustice. It should not be just an empirical correlation. In the case of discrimination against blacks or women we can find such a characteristic, but in the case of preferential affirmative action no such characteristics can be found.

Ketchum further says that it is wrong to suppose, as Simon does, that preferential affirmative action robs some white males their right to jobs. Ketchum says that these policies, though they are preferential in intent, may not be so in effect. Ketchum gives an example. Suppose there is a job for which highly educated persons are required. Suppose further that if there were no policy of preferential treatment then by blind review the proportion of white males hired to blacks and women would be exactly the same as the proportion of white males and women and blacks that have applied (with adequate qualification) for the job. But if there is a policy of preferential affirmative action then, of course, the percentage of white males hired would fall. What we should note here is that, still, the proportion of white males in the profession will be several times their proportion in the population — that is, white males, who are a minority of the population, will hold a large majority of professional positions. Now, why is this so? This is so because in a society with a white-supremacist past more white males would have managed to attain the qualification required for the job than women or blacks. And, maybe, if the society had not had a history of white-supremacy then these very white males would never be able to attain the required qualification. And so, in spite of the policy of preferential affirmative action, majority of white males in America do enjoy the advantages of past discriminatory practices against blacks and women.

Now one might at this point ask that could we really blame a white male for attaining his present position due to past unjust practices of a white-supremacist society. It is true that we cannot hold a white male morally responsible for injustices from which he has benefited. But surely we could not say that he has the *right* to benefit from such injustices.

Is It a Logical Question at All?

Simon comes up with a serious objection against Ketchum. He is unconvinced about Ketchum's claim that '*all* white males have secured a *net* advantage from unjust discrimination against women and minorities'. (Robert Simon, "Rights, Groups and Discrimination", in Robert Simon and Sara Ann Ketchum, *An Exchange on Preferential Treatment*, in Jan Narveson, ed., *Moral Issues*, 1983)

This is a question worth pondering. But what I feel is that there is no easy philosophical answer to this, as this is a question empirical in nature. I also feel that in most cases where the question whether a policy of preferential affirmative action is fair or not is raised we have to really evaluate the actual situation and the society itself as well as the discriminatory practices and their actual effects on individuals. This job is not easy. And here a philosopher has little to contribute. Maybe it is wrong for us philosophers to think that we can solve or resolve this dilemma in the manner in which we are trying. These questions are to be dealt with case by case, society by society, individual by individual.

Another point that I would like to make here is that it is probably naïve on our part as philosophers to discuss this issue in isolation. What I mean to say is that we have to take into account the *politics* behind affirmative action. In each society where such policies of affirmative action have been adopted there has been a political history behind it. When we discuss and assess these policies we have to do it in their specific political context. We would not be able to make much progress in the debate itself if we are blind to the politics of affirmative action altogether.

There is yet another point that has bothered many people and me as well. The real aim of preferential affirmative action was compensation as well as the eradication of hideous social practices that viewed sections of people as inferior and hence unworthy of equal opportunities and rights. I am doubtful as to what extent these policies have managed to remove discrimination practice from the psyche of the oppressive sections of the society. In societies where preferential affirmative action is practised, whenever a person of the victim community gets a job, it is said that they could not have done it on their own. Greater divisions and alienation is created amongst communities on account of affirmative action.

The dilemma still remains and the debate lives on. Societies in which discriminatory practices were prevalent are yet to grow into societies that really acknowledge past atrocities against sections of its population. Whether affirmative action has managed to restore a moral balance in a society is doubtful. It is just as much debatable as to whether affirmative action is morally and logically defensible. But in spite of all this and in spite of arguments provided by radicals like Nozick, people do feel that there must be some way of ending social evils like castism, sexism and racism and provide compensatory justice to communities which still bear the scars of past discriminations.

Notes

1 See Robert Fullinwider, "Affirmative Action" in *The Stanford Encyclopedia of Philosophy (Spring 2002 Edition)*, Edward N. Zalta, ed. Online: http://plato.stanford.edu/archives/spr2002/entries/affirmative-action/

2 This is one of the papers in the collection of papers by Robert L. Simon and Sara Ann Ketchum, entitled "An Exchange on Preferential Treatment" in Jan Narveson, ed. *Moral Issues.* Toronto: Oxford University Press 1983.

References

Nagel, Thomas. 1973. "Equal Treatment and Compensatory Discrimination." *Philosophy & Public Affairs*, 2 (Summer): 348–363.

Naverson, Jan., ed. 1983. *Moral Issues,* Toronto: Oxford University Press.

Nozick, Robert. 1974. *Anarchy, State, and Utopia.* New York: Basic Books Inc. and Basil Blackwell.

Rawls, John. 1971. *A Theory of Justice.* Cambridge, Massachusetts: Harvard University Press.

Thomson, Judith Jarvis. 1973. "Preferential Hiring" *Philosophy & Public Affairs*, 2 (Summer): 364–484.

Chapter 12

ETHICS, HUMAN RIGHTS AND THE LGBT DISCOURSE IN INDIA

Ashley Tellis

Introduction

To be sure, sexuality is still not seen as a serious area for academic enquiry in India. The two constituencies that have taken sexuality up as a complex for research and action have been the women's movement and Women's Studies and the same-sex rights movement in India (more popularly known as the LGBT (lesbian, gay, bisexual and transgender) and, increasingly, as the 'queer' movement, another indication of how globalisation matters given the currency of this term in contexts like India despite its provenance in US academia). Both these constituencies – feminists and LGBT folk – are themselves fledgling and marginal to mainstream political and academic life in India, the two arenas in which they seek to make interventions. Consequently, their claim that sexuality needs to be focused on is also fledgling and marginal.

Both movements have used the academic and the cultural as important vehicles in the articulation of their positions and these positions have been built as much on the streets as in theoretical and academic knowledge production. Further, this articulation has borrowed heavily from the available languages of feminism and sexuality-based movements in the West (by which I mean Western Europe and North America), as the presence of both movements in the West preceded their formal formation as movements in the Third world. Both the women's movement and the LGBT one from their inception here have been accused of being imports from the West, inauthentic and inorganic to the Indian contexts. These accusations have come from the state and political parties, right and left. It does not matter if it can be pointed out that such accusations are somewhat strange, coming from where they come, given that the idea of the state and the political party as we know it come from the West as well. The fact is that such accusations still hold a lot of water in the populist imagination.[1]

Indeed, in the popular Indian imagination sex and sexuality are not issues that 'Indian society' and 'Indian culture', whatever these categories might mean, talk about. Yet, in a horrific actualisation of the discursive contradiction that Foucault points out in the first volume of his *Histoire de la Sexualite – La Volonte de Savoir* (*The Will to Power*), sex and sexuality is both taboo and everywhere in our society. One cannot open any newspaper on any day in India without seeing several pictures of semi-clad women (consider the semi-porn rags that are the supplements of *The Times of India* and *The Hindustan Times*), several reports of harassment and rape, sexualised violence in and outside the family, often carried out by agencies of the state or one community against another (the most recent in our memory here in India, for example, would include the sexualised violence against an *adivasi* woman in Guwahati, the rape of women by Communist Party of India (Marxist) (CPI(M)) *cadres* in Nandigram and Singur, the molestation of Non-resident Indian (NRI) women on New Year's Eve in Bombay and the brutal murder of two girls in Haryana late last year) and various items of gossip and articles on the sex lives of the rich and famous and on how to improve your own sex life.

Historical Background

The women's movement in India has never talked about sexuality in the way the Western women's movement did. Sexuality as pleasure was a narrative that dominated second-wave feminism in the West; here sexuality, mainly, almost exhaustively, articulated itself as violence.[2] While in the West the LGBT movement, emerging with and out of the women's movement, foregrounded the idea of pleasure, the LGBT movement here really came into existence piggybacking on the AIDS crisis and articulated itself necessarily in the languages of crisis, violence and remedial action, not pleasure. Let us look at these two moments somewhat more closely to delineate the ways in which concerns around sexuality manifested themselves in India.

The starting point of the formal women's movement in India, it is accepted by now, was the agitation against the systemic and systematic violence on women, most forcefully represented by the Mathura rape case where a tribal woman was raped in a police station by police officials. The variety of other forms of violence upon women's bodies and minds – from dowry, *sati*, the killing of the girl child and domestic violence to the violent and invasive use of ant-reproductive technologies to control women's bodies by the state and much more – the pervasive nature of violence gave Indian feminists very little scope to speak of sexuality in any other register than violence. This is not to say that sexuality was not spoken about in other ways; it is just that the dominant discourse was around violence. The academic discourse – and it was really a very rich and theoretically sophisticated body of academic work done by a certain generation of feminists, among whom can be counted Uma Chakravarti, Sudesh Vaid, Tanika Sarkar and Kumkum Sangari – showed sexuality as embedded in a variety of other discourses and contexts but was not easily understandable nor particularly acceptable to the state because acknowledging this work would also amount to the state acknowledging its own complicity with the violence upon women's sexualities and lives.

As the language of feminism became more and more co-opted by the state, the possibility of sexuality becoming a serious analytic variable in the re-organisation of society along feminist lines receded more and more into the background. Unlike in the West, where the lesbian movement emerged from the women's movement and offered a very powerful critique of heteronormativity using sexuality as its fulcrum, there was no lesbian movement here. There were lesbians, to be sure, but they chose to be silent and stay with the heterosexual confines of the Indian women's movement.[3] The LGBT movements which in the West grew alongside and as part of several other political and independent movements – like, in the US, the civil rights movement, the anti-Vietnam war movement – was never an independent political movement here. It emerged only in the 1990s as part of the anti-AIDS funding waves, as I have indicated earlier, and spoke in a political language, if it speaks in a political language at all, quite different from that of the LGBT movement in the West.

The women's movement in India today has begun to talk a language of sexuality outside of violence and, needless to say, as a result it seems contrived, borrowed as it is from the result of processes in Western feminism that have not occurred here and not emerging organically from the contexts of Indian feminist struggles.[4] In the West, by the second wave, feminists were split, especially in the US, between the sex-positive feminists and the sexuality-as-violence feminists, around that famous conference at Barnard College in 1982.[5] The sex-positive feminists saw sexuality as pleasure, supported pornography and women's sexual agency and the sexuality-as-violence feminists were completely anti-pornography, anti-complex readings of what constitutes women's pleasure, seeing most, if not all, of masculinity as violent and misogynist and had no qualms about joining hands with right-wing forces to ban pornography and advocate forms of censorship.[6]

In India, feminists have had no such battle and remained mostly silent on the question of sexuality in general and hostile on the question of lesbian sexuality in particular with a homophobia that showed that Indian feminism had little or no analytic depth or self-reflexivity on the question of sexual desire as basis for social organizing and as critique.[7] Even the rich body of academic work on feminism by scholars I named above, much richer than activist (especially in its state form) feminism, did not engage with the debate over sexual desire vs. sexual violence as the feminist subject was not ever articulated in India in terms of these two axes with sexual agency as the base.

Younger generations of feminists in India have simply adopted sex-positive feminism's language in recent theorisations of sexuality and sexual agency, which then makes it seem that Indian feminism has simply jumped over knotty problem of how to conceptualise sexuality but has not needed the necessary processual analysis that feminists from the two positions in Western feminism on sexuality did go through, but that we have not.

I am not implying that there is some teleological and evolutionary march that Indian feminism had to have taken, following the footsteps of the West, to reach full maturity. However, to merely adopt a language which is the result of a long struggle and debate in one context and place it in another, as if it had just arrived fully-formed in the latter context, does not do away with the persistence of the problem, especially if the problem has not even been posed in this latter context, let alone in the same manner. This is most evident in debates around prostitution or sex work in the contemporary Indian contexts which, instead of building on the insights of the generation of feminists to whom I have alluded and shown how sexuality or indeed prostitution has to be perceived in ways more complex than the dichotomy between pleasure and violence allows for, instead borrow the language of Western sex-positive feminists in a decontextualised manner.[8]

NGO Politics

In the realm of LGBT politics, as indicated earlier, there was no political movement. The movement, if it can be called one, came out of international funding for AIDS and is run largely by NGOs. Any analysis of the politics of global funding for sexuality coming from the North into the South or from southern governments into the social sector must take into account the larger picture of neoliberal capital and how it has made inroads into the economies of countries in the South.

Most of these NGOs, not just in India but all across the Third World, came out of similar historical processes, well-documented by now. Frederick Cooper and Randall Packard offer a useful synoptic overview in their introduction to *International Development and the Social Sciences: Essays on the History and Politics of Knowledge*, showing the processes of the emergence of the term 'development' as formed by various factors like the crisis of the colonial empires, the US need for expansion after WWII, and the convergence of US and European interests.

It is this particular conjuncture that led to the creation of international organisations in the 40s and 50s like the World Bank, the IMF and the range of UN development agencies – e.g., FAO, WHO, UNICEF, UNESCO – which led to the internationalisation of 'development.' The idea of development for all its flaws, as Cooper and Packard point out, was a liberating possibility for newly-formed African and Asian governments and gave them a sense of mission.

The ways in which this mission played out, however, were hardly even and often these newly-independent states themselves were either uncritical of the ways in which this model increased inequalities, seen in both the avid adopting and the reshaping of development discourse in Latin America[9] or were caught in the fast-moving spiral of increasing debt and sank in the irreversible processes that the 'development' – determined economy effected upon their domestic space.[10] What came to be known as 'development' gave rise to a new form of colonialism where ex-colonial powers came to define how third world nations should and should not grow.[11]

In the specific case of India Sugata Bose, among others, has shown how more complex possible routes to 'development' and conceptions of it were submerged under the articulation of what has come to be seen as a simplistic dichotomy between Nehru (Centralist/Western) and Gandhi (Localist/Indian) and, by a paradigm shift, a victory of what Bose calls 'instruments over idioms,'[12] whereby:

1) Planning, independent India's central economic process, concentrated on means enhancement, the accumulation of capital, and not on goals like the betterment of the quality of life and
2) 'An insufficiently decolonized, centralized state structure seized upon national development as a primary source of its own justification. Instead of the state being used as an instrument of development, development became an instrument of the state's legitimacy.'[13]

Critiques of this centralised state have left much to be desired. They range from neoclassical and liberal advocates of the free market, like Jagdish Bhagwati, who, of course, simply see the state as a hindrance to markets (and NGOs as simply another players in the market) to anti-science, anti-modernity, anti-development upholders of 'tradition,' 'community' and the 'fragment,' like Ashis Nandy, who romanticise away the possibility of any stringent critique of the state, predicated as their arguments are on an indigenous and unexamined nationalism.[14] Meanwhile, India's development continued apace with disastrous effects upon the economically poor and increased accumulation for the rich and the middle classes.

To take two random moments on the graph that traces Indian 'development' history to show this:

1) In the 1950s, India became heavily dependent on US wheat under the PL480 programme. There was no need for this (India was a perfectly good producer of wheat) except that India was focusing all its energies on industrialisation and, therefore, had no time for agriculture.[15] By the mid-1960s, under the auspices of United States Agency for International Development (USAID), a sisterhood programme was initiated to establish new agricultural universities in India on the model of the land grant colleges with five contracting US universities: Kansas, Ohio, Tennessee, Missouri and Illinois. Half the teachers in these Indian universities were trained at those US universities.[16] So, simultaneous with a discourse of helping with 'development' was a discourse of neo-colonial exploitation.[17]
2) It is the failure of such initiatives that led to the new-style interventions of bodies like the World Bank. As early as its 1985 Annual Aid Review, USAID took some 'major new policy orientations, including parastatal privatisation or divestiture as a major focus of USAIDs policy dialogue with developing countries.'[18] What began with bodies like the World Bank and the IMF, were openly corporate and market-run forms of exploitation of countries in the South. Consider some of the subheadings of the 1994 World Bank *World Development Report: Infrastructure for Development*: 'Running public entities on commercial principles', 'Using markets in infrastructure provision', 'Beyond markets in infrastructure', 'Financing needed investments'.[19]

Part of involving users in their own 'development' made, and continues to make, use of the nice-sounding discourses of 'decentralization', 'participation', 'going beyond the state', 'beyond the market', 'offering subsidies and budget allocations' and so on, all of which masks the basic corporate fuel of these enterprises.

I have offered this brief historical background to make two central points about NGOs:

a) there is nothing inevitable about the way in which same-sex politics is organised in countries like India or other parts of the Third World today, just as there was nothing inevitable about the course Indian nationalism took, and
b) there is inherent in my critique of 'development,' as it came to be hegemonically organised, a critique of the unthinking national acceptance of this term as well, an unthinkingness, that, I will argue, gets repeated in the arena of same-sex politics.

To graft this history on to the history of sexuality-centred NGOs is important because sexuality-based NGOs are in no way different from any other NGOs in terms of funding and practices and as sites where the dual purposes of foreign intervention I spoke of above are played out. International funding for sexuality work claims, like 'development discourse' did, to exist to help us evolutionally to the right mode of being sexual. They offer a set of tools and understandings of sexuality that we adopt, and they offer us the means to do it, arguing that we don't have the means to do it. As sexually repressed, we violate the human rights of sexual subjects, and we need help.

Beneath this, however, they have an agenda, just like the 'development' folks did. NGOs, whether working for 'development,' or on sexuality, have always been associated with moral superiority, good work for the betterment of society and, therefore, imputed a righteousness that marks them in our minds, absurdly, above capitalist processes of gain and profit. This rhetoric is often claimed by NGOs themselves, when, in fact, the telegraphic histories I have outlined show that the philanthropy of 'development' is skin-deep, and the hidden and not-so-hidden, motives are basic economic profit for the richer nations of the North.[20]

More so, in a field like sexuality where the aforementioned claims to moral superiority are even better concealed and take on an even more righteous aura. After all, one might argue, what do organisations and funders like USAID, the Ford Foundation and MacArthur Foundation or groups like Amnesty International, The International Lesbian and Gay Association (ILGA) and The International Gay and Lesbian Human Rights Commission (IGLHRC) stand to gain from sexuality-based initiatives in developing countries? They are only doing it to better conditions for sexual minorities in India, to ameliorate the conditions of people with HIV/AIDS and prevent others from getting it too, and NGOs are merely conscientised conduits for this admirable work. Such a reading would, however, be frightfully naïve.

The NGOs in 'developing' countries have practices that include seriously unaccounted for and unacknowledged forms of abuse of labour, feminism, sex, gender and sexual orientation, not to mention freedom of association, forced overtime and other labour rights violations that would be challenged were they to be found in any other sector.[21] Why does this surprise us or fill us with outrage? This is, after all, what corporate forms of organization do on a daily basis. However, our expectations for these groups are different precisely for the reasons stated above that have led to our pious conception of NGOs. The first step, then, is to disabuse NGOs of any superior aura and subject them to the same analysis as corporations that are organized around profit. Indeed, more and more NGOs are moving in the direction of corporatisation in their modes of self-organizing and operating in the world.

The next step is to answer the question: where do same-sex sexualities-based 'movements', run by such organisations, ones with the same practices as any corporation but with a chip on their shoulder, get their ideology from? As Rob Jenkins, among others, has pointed out, the problem with donor agencies like USAID is that they (a) portray civil society as sacred, moral and apolitical, and (b) portray themselves as mirror images of civil society, impartial guides without interest.[22] The facts are that there is a definite political interest on the part of NGOs and that 'civil society' (whatever that is) is not this morally superior baby of their imagination. Let us take each of these levels in turn:

(a) First, while most sexuality-based NGOs and funders do not claim to be political (indeed, as Jenkins points out, the World Bank, for example, substitutes 'politics' with 'governance' and 'political issues' with 'efficient/inefficient administration'), they do have a particular conception of 'civil society'. They want, for example, 'accountability', 'individual rights/liberties', 'autonomous centres of social and economic power', i.e. social independence that leads to free economic competitiveness and better performance, all of which is seen as democratic development.[23]

Versions of all these aims appear in the discourses of sexuality-based NGOs as well. They aim to democratise sexual space in favour of marginalised and neglected groups, fight for the rights and liberties of such groups and create an autonomous and self-sufficient space for such groups. The two other discourses that such NGOs have heavily relied upon are those of health and human rights. Health because most of these sexuality-based NGOs legitimised their existence, in the first instance, through work they claimed to be doing in HIV/AIDS prevention,[24] and human rights because there was an international human rights discourse on sexuality and sexual orientation to which they could append their own struggles and gain global legitimacy for their socially disenfranchised constituencies.

(b) At the second level, what are the donors doing when they (and this 'they' can range from charities to tax-shelter foundations like the Bill Gates one, to large organisations like the Ford Foundation) fund groups? Do we presume they are doing the great work of bettering inhuman conditions for sexual minorities in a developing country, that they are merely the impartial funders of such admirable and worthy projects that come, after all, from the native subjects themselves?

Ann Hudock has shown how northern NGOs conceive of and exploit southern ones, patronisingly seeing them, for example, as unable to lead development, lacking the capacity to plan project activities, mobilise resources and account for resources used. She has shown how the new process of 'capacity-building' has been a way for northern NGOs to disengage from direct involvement in development activities and has failed to address external factors.[25]

In the field of sexuality this is compounded by the lack of a perspective on the messy ways in which sexuality intersects with cultural anxieties about legitimacy and control in Indian, or indeed any societies. Already the Indian government and various even so-called oppositional and progressive elements have a conception of same-sex sexuality, or even sexuality per se, as foreign and not part of Indian society.

Not being very careful about how sexuality is approached in terms of intervention can have disastrous effects on a social space. The fact that these funders have an agenda, a time frame, goals to reach willy-nilly (and NGOs are tied to these, given that the next batch of funds depends on the achievements of the group in terms of its stated targets) and a certain packaged set of messages to get across means that they do not bother to listen to what the social space demands or to pay any attention to the relationship between the social space and the NGO interacting with it, given their different locations and the politics of their interfaces with one another.[26] But before I come to the problematic relation between NGOs and these groups, or indeed the people at large, aggregates of whom suddenly become 'target groups', it is important to recognise the sexual ideology of funders.[27] Indeed, it is precisely this ideology that causes many of the problems.

The Globalspeak of LGBT Rights

The internationalisation and globalisation of gay/lesbian/transgender/queer identities is, however, closely tied to economic and market processes. It is absurd to think that there are no, implicitly or otherwise, agendas of such organisations that determine the very language in which they, and donor groups like them, construct their work.[28] Moreover, it is naïve to believe that Indian NGOs are unaffected by those agendas, or indeed are unaware of them. I will come to the implications of all these sets of realities in concrete practice in a moment.[29]

Sexuality NGOs, like most other NGOs, construct themselves as the superior informers of and education-providers to the community with no engagement with how the community arranges its own information and education on these matters. While the donors have little to do with these NGOs after handing over the funds and overseeing the fact that the language of the work they do mirrors the language of their purportedly good intentions, the actual effects of this language on civil society is of little concern to them.

Since most sexuality NGO workers are usually urban and metropolitan in perspective and location, they fail to understand how lives are led even on the urban periphery (let alone the rural hinterland) and do not engage with everyday life in these spaces in any sustained way, yet take it upon themselves to speak for these 'groups'.[30] They do not help organise these groups in any self-sustaining way but only in terms of dependence (they are, after all, the NGOs' bread and butter) and in terms of constructing them as categories, which they then mistakenly represent as political categories that these groups have adopted for themselves. Sexuality is a fraught arena and such unthinking practices can only increase difficulties rather than make conditions better for already marginalised groups.

In simply taking on this language of 'LGBT' and 'Queer' and applying it undifferentiated to groups in India without bothering to learn how they understand themselves and in what languages they speak, activists and academics become willing victims in a neocolonial speaking in the coloniser's language. Rudi Bleys and Neville Hoad[31] have shown how the colonial anthropological encounter, in terms of the sexual practices the anthropologists observed, determined definitions and categories for the colonisers back home. These evolutionary conceptions were both contested by hegemonic forces that posited the West as superior and anxiously displaced such practices from their own contexts and promoted by same-sex movements in the West, which used them to form sexual categories and a nascent identity politics.

Hoad has further argued and shown how imperialism reappears in contemporary theorising of same-sex identities outside the West. Hoad speaks of the *developmental* understanding of difference, whereby the non-west is seen always as hoping to achieve the status of the advanced West, working towards its implicitly superiorised understanding of sexual identities and politics. While he indicts Western scholars for this, I argue this is equally applicable to native theorists of same-sex relations in India, for example, who simply replicate these categories without much interrogation. Instead, Hoad calls for a scrupulous historicising of colonial histories and non-western subjectivities. He writes:

> In as much as queer theory points to the underlying historical script of sexuality in the constitution of the terms of class and gender analysis, it needs to be equally sensitive to the historical conditions of the production of the category sexuality and to its contemporary global deployments and continual resignifications.[32]

To be sure, Hoad is no romantic apologist of any naïve or humanist notion of colonised subjectivity. He writes:

> I do not wish naively to assume a range of speaking subalterns, thereby subscribing to another assumption about the fullness of the agency of the *other* in an anthropological gaze, nor to pretend that the penetration

> of capital has left pure cultures, intact untainted by the west. Instead I wish to register the risks of certain dangerous, if necessary, interpretive impositions.[33]

And further on:

> ...a clear distinction between acts and identities needs to be made. Additionally, the very idea of 'sexuality' or 'pure sexual activity' (Weeks) itself as a registerable transcultural category needs to be questioned. While it is clear that acts that look homosexual to a contemporary western gaze are by and large universal, the emergence of a homosexual social identity – 'gayness' – as we know it needs to be carefully historically and geographically bracketed.[34]

I have quoted Hoad at some length because he usefully lays out the problematics of not only this type of reading of colonialism that continues to be practiced in the field of same-sex politics in India but also neocolonial deployments of the language of colonialism in contemporary same-sex politics. By buying into the globalspeak of LGBT discourse, we are unable to recuperate the richer and more complicated understandings of same-sex relations and their trajectories in India.

Human Rights as Discourse

The parallel dominant language in which LGBT groups in India construct their arguments is in the language of international human rights, and this language, once again, is at no point questioned by activists or academics in the field of same-sex rights. Gayatri Spivak has spoken with characteristically multivalent energy and persuasiveness about the need to get beyond the critique of human rights as Eurocentric and the need to 'learn with patience from below and to keep trying to suture it [a sense of responsibility] to the imagined felicitous subject of universal Human Rights'.[35] Pitting educational work among tribals in India and Bangladesh against human rights discourse, she speaks of the need to place responsibility alongside rights and understand that the possibility of such responsibility is not derived from rights. She defines the subaltern subject's culture as a torn fabric and calls for a new form of pedagogy where the teacher learns from the student below, marked by responsibility rather than rights as a 'different way into the damaged episteme'.[36]

Spivak thus points to the fundamentally flawed paradigm of human rights not because of the traditional accusations of Eurocentrism but the fact that it does not understand the subjects it seeks to coral into its discourse and that there are other, more productive ways of engaging with the violence of violated groups. Her mode is an attentive pedagogical engagement with them that requires patience and dogged learning in the process of interaction with them. LGBT activists and academics in India reproduce the violence of the language of human rights upon subjects that are epistemically situated differently by adopting it without question, and do not show this endurance and humility.[37]

Anthropologist Shannon Speed has offered a detailed account of how indigenous Mexicans in the Chiapas have 'understood, appropriated and mobilized' human rights discourses and shown how certain local appropriations and reinterpretations reconfigure the concept of human rights in fundamental ways, and that ultimately these redeployments may be challenging to neoliberal discourses and structures of power'.[38] However, unlike the indigenous Zapatistas, same-sex subjects in India are not mobilised or politicised enough to be able to engage in critiques of human rights themselves; indeed, human rights is most often invoked only on their behalf, completely uninterrogatively and in a decontextualised manner, by NGOs, both national and international.

Ethical Stumbling Blocks

What I have described above can be summarised as a series of ethical stumbling blocks that LGBT politics in India has to overcome. These can be enumerated as: the ethics of diverting HIV/AIDS funding from where it really should go (female sex workers and economically strapped mothers, injectable drug users and infected children) and offering it to marginally affected populations (MSMs and kothis, for example); the ethics of a silence on the politics of funding; the ethics of ignoring the critiques of human rights discourse and its implications; the ethics of applying identity politics of a Western kind to articulations not assimilable to this model; the ethics of speaking of behalf of others and imposing a model of the self on to others. The dangers of not facing these questions head-on, with a Spivakian sense of responsibility, will become apparent through an example from the field of same-sex politics in India.

Example

Many women marry each other across the length and breath of contemporary India, news of which is sensationally splashed across the media and then dies out. How many of us, for example, remember Babli and Geeta, the two women who married each other in Delhi in 2007? How many of us are aware that the two women lost their jobs, were ostracised by their families and were living in near-starvation conditions? (*Mid-Day*, Delhi, was the only paper to do an initial and follow-up report on them).[39] How many of us remember the three couples from Punjab – Rajwinder and Mala, Palwinder and Inderjit, Rajwinder and Baljit – who tore into our newspapers on three occasions since 2004 and left those pages just as quickly,[40] with only one returning when the media was triumphant that the couple Rajwinder and Mala had broken up with Mala, now seeing a heterosexual man?[41] Finally, who remembers the two women in Pakistan: Shahzina and Shumail, cousins who married each other and were put in jail for it by the Pakistani state in 2007?[42]

Further, where were all the great NGOs who appear to be spearheading the gay and lesbian 'movement' in this country when these couples are tormented by their families, prised apart, harassed by the state and left to fend for themselves in an incredibly hostile world?[43] Where are the women's groups who receive lavish funding to help women who are downtrodden? Where are the well-funded lesbian support groups who sticker toilets all over Delhi but are not around when same-sex identified women really need them? In Pakistan only one woman activist, Nighat Said Khan, came to Shahzina and Shumail's rescue, and she expressed horror at the complete lack of support for the women from the women's movement or indeed any group in Pakistan. Here in India, too, nobody came to the rescue of all these couples and nobody offered support. One of them slashed her wrists and almost died (Baljit), two are now starving, and the great NGO-funded gay and lesbian 'movement' does nothing about it, not even write empty emails about it as they tend to do on the *lgbt-india* LISTSERV. Surely, it is one of the terrible ironies of our globalised times that we claim to have gay bars and parties, and yet women who love women are destroyed around us. They are not even ghostly presences at these celebratory parties.

The fact is that lower class women in India (and it is mainly these women who marry so the Indian government's ruse of claiming lesbianism as a western vice will not work here) who marry each other and defy the family, the community and the nation are not good enough 'victim' candidates for foreign funding. They tend to die or break up, or not allow urban gay and lesbian subjects into their lives; they certainly do not form a long-term fundable group. They are not pliable, they do not mould their relationships and their identities to suit the globalspeak of internationally funded gay and lesbian organizations; indeed they often throw urban lesbian activists, who come to claim them, out of their houses because they understand their lives, sexualities and identities differently.[44]

The questions we need to ask are: How do these women see themselves and each other? Why do they marry? Why do they not see the sexual as the fulcrum of their identities, even as they are choosing to be with women? Why does the heterosexual Indian women's movement show no solidarity whatsoever with women who are choosing to disengage with men, with women who choose to opt out of the political economy of the giant heterosexual reproductive complex? What are the effects of this opting out of the complex? What is the critique of feminism here, in India, which remains a *status quo* heterosexual, male-identified and male-centralising project?

What we need to do is to understand their resistances to our very different conceptions of sexuality and the self and draw up new forms of politicisation that emerge not so much from what these subjects say (not only is there no need for ethnographic piety, it is also that their narratives are often hammered into moulds we want them to be in as in Maya Sharma's *Women Loving Women*) as much as what effects their ways of being in the world. As middle-class, West-identified gay and lesbian or transgender subjects (I call myself gay, for example) we also need to articulate our own particular negotiations of that term because it does not signify the same things for us across class, cultural capital and engagement with our different habitus. I do not see my gayness as manifested in a weekly gay club night, an adoption of global gayspeak, a philanthropic speaking for non-English speaking sexual minorities in urban or rural spaces, and my own formation as an ethnographic subject needs to find a voice, as legitimate a voice as any other in India, but that is the subject of a different paper.

Wild Anthropology among the Vulnerable Archaic

It is well-established by now that our particular formation as postcolonial subjects is the result of different languages and models of modernity. I want to make clear that I am not arguing from some nativist position that 'pure Indian sexuality' (whatever that might be) needs to be disinterred from under the tectonic plates of colonialism, the Western women's and LGBT movements or the language of international organisations. However, I am calling for a detailed study of all these interrelating languages to produce the most ethical and political form of critique that not just restores the place of sexuality in the web of networks that constitute the social and the political but also offers new models of engagement for feminist and LGBT subjects, whether with the state, the law or diverse social groups.

But first, let us outline the co-ordinates of what such a framework would look like. In an interview, Gayatri Chakravorty Spivak discusses the discursive makeup of society and activism's encounter with it. She states:

> There are these various ways in which you become 'involved'. But, once you do that you won't get away from textuality. 'The Text', in the sense we use it, is not just books. It refers to the possibility that every socio-political, psycho-sexual phenomenon is organized by, woven by many,

> many strands that are discontinuous, that come from way off, that carry their histories within them, and that are not within our control... If you get totally involved in political activism, you will find that you become more and more aware of the problems of the textuality of the socius.[45]

An ethical and political framework for sexuality work in India, whether in the realm of academics or activism (which are, in any case, interrelated and not in the adversarial binary in which they are often placed), will pay attention to those strands, discontinuities and histories and will not seek control but rather see where that attention takes us.

In another interview, Michel Foucault talks about how the analysis of sexuality might be the gateway to formulating new political practices:

> ...the problem is not so much that of defining a political 'position' (which is to choose from a pre-existing set of possibilities) but to imagine and to bring into being new schemas of politicisation. If 'politicisation' means falling back on ready-made choices and institutions, then the effort of analysis involved in uncovering the relations of force and mechanisms of power is not worthwhile. To the vast new techniques of power correlated with multinational economies and bureaucratic States, one must oppose a politicisation which will take new forms[46]

It is this sort of politicisation that we must seek, if we want to do ethical work on sexuality in India. Spivak's 'awareness' and Foucault's 'effort of analysis' both require a quality of attention (Simone Weil reminds us that the highest ecstasy is the attention at its fullest)[47] invoked often in the language of critics interested in building rigorously ethical and political forms of re-imagining our lives. Denise Riley, British feminist and philosopher, states that 'the challenge for feminism is to be fully attentive to every effect of gender and, by means of that close attention, also to know where gender might end'.[48] Riley adds, that such an attention would involve:

> Of how never to overlook or to mistake gender in its manifestations; but also of how *not* to bear it in mind in such a way that it must always hang like a veil to filter every glimpse of the world, as if we perceived all of it in advance; as if being women or men produced, out of that division itself, exhaustively decisive lives (emphasis hers).[49]

The conditions of possibility of such a conception came to her precisely from her reading of the Foucault of *The Archaeology of Knowledge* (which appeared in translation in England in 1972). What appealed to Riley in this book was, she says, 'the streaks of sheer obstinacy in his refusals to make reductions of discourse to history and vice versa'.[50] This method was refined for Riley in Foucault's idea of discursive formations in *The History of Sexuality Vol. 1* (1976). In understanding the nineteenth century notion of homosexuality and also the category of sex, Riley writes:

> ...as an aspect of the history of the present, it opened the way to the historicizing of any category, including that of women. And given that people understand their lives discursively, the point therefore wouldn't be to trace the history of rhetoric as if this were a layer plastered over the strata of real silent lives underneath; but to distinguish what different forms of description were active at what levels. This was surely a fully historical and indeed a materialist undertaking.[51]

It is this fully historical and materialist project that LGBT politics in India has to undertake. This is only possible through what Gayatri Spivak has called a 'learning to learn from below', and elsewhere as an 'unlearning of one's privilege as one's loss',[52] through a non-pious but rather dialogic collaboration across the thorny reality of difference. It demands being simultaneously inside and outside the object of one's inquiry, and, therefore, of oneself, in necessarily careful ways.

We know so little about these groups and 'subjects' and about ourselves. They and we might organise in ways that all of us are yet to begin to understand.

Notes

1 It is also important to note that, ironically, such claims of West vs. East also come from LGBT academics and activists who argue that India was a wonderfully gay-friendly space till the evil English happened to us, even as they fight for gay rights using the languages of the evil English systems, juridical and other. See, for an example of such an argument, Ruth Vanita's work in several books and articles. My 'Postcolonial Same-Sex Relations in India: A Theoretical Framework' in ed. Manas Ray, *Space, Sexuality, and Postcolonial Cultures* Enreca Occasional Papers 6 (Calcutta; Centre for Studies in Social Sciences, 2003), 221–231 contains a critique of Vanita and this position.

2 However, this is not to say that this work (by scholars like Tanika Sarkar, Uma Chakravarti and Kumkum Sangari among others was all about violence and sexuality only in the context of violence. Indeed, a lot of it did address sexuality in ways that were far more productive and implicitly critical of the pleasure/violence binary (about which more below). Nivedita Menon is wrong to suggest that this work has been mapped and, therefore, does not need documenting or examination, as she does in her volume *Sexualities* and is even more wrong in marking all marginalized sexualities as necessarily transgressive. Indeed, her introduction and essay in the book valorize what she calls 'the counter-heteronormative', not interrogating it sufficiently at all. See ed. Nivedita Menon *Sexualities* (New Delhi: Women Unlimited, 2007) xiv.

3 For a contradictory and problematic account of this, see Paola Bacchetta, 'Rescaling Transnational "Queerdom": Lesbian and "Lesbian" Identitary-Positionalities in Delhi in the 1980s' *Antipode* Special Issue, 'Queer Patriarchies, Queer Racisms, International' 34, no. 5, 947–97. It is republished in part in Nivedita Menon ed. *Sexualities* (New Delhi: Women Unlimited 2007). For my critique of Bacchetta, see 'Distorting Mirrors: The Global Careers of "Queerness".' Unpublished paper presented at the 'Sex, Race and Globalization' program's seminar at the University of Arizona, Tucson in 2004 and part of my manuscript *Productive Contaminations: Same-Sex Politics in Contemporary India* (forthcoming).

4 I am thinking of the work of feminists like Ratna Kapur and Shohini Ghosh and, once again, Nivedita Menon. Kapur has written on same-sex subjects and sex workers, Ghosh mainly on Hindi cinema and representations of same-sex desire but also sex work, and Menon calls for a desire that radically deconstructs and exceeds the nation. As representative examples, see Ratna Kapur, *Erotic Justice: Law and the New Politics of Postcolonalism*, (New Delhi: Permanent Black 2005), Shohini Ghosh, 'False Appearances and Mistaken Identities: The Phobic and the Erotic in Bombay Cinema's Queer Vision,' in eds Brinda Bose and Sudhabrata Bhattacharya *The Phobic and the Erotic: The Politics of Sexualities in Contemporary India* (Calcutta: Seagull Books 2007) and Nivedita Menon, 'Outing Heteronormativity: Nation, Citizen, Feminist Disruptions', in *Sexualities* ed. Nivedita Menon (New Delhi; Women Unlimited 2007).

5 For an account of it, see eds Lisa Duggan and Nan Hunter, *Sex Wars: Sexual Dissent and Political Culture* (New York: Routledge 2006).

6 These feminists included Andrea Dworkin and Catherine Mackinnon. For an account of the two positions on pornography, see Laura Kipnis, *Bound and Gagged: Pornography and the Politics of Fantasy in America* (New York: Grove Press 1996) and eds Catharine A. MacKinnon and Andrea Dworkin *In Harm's Way: The Pornography Civil Rights Hearings* (Cambridge, Massachusetts: Harvard University Press 1998).

7 A classic example of the homophobia of the women's movement was the All-India Democratic Women's Association's (AIDWA) and National Federation of Indian Women's (NFIW), the two women's groups linked to the two communist parties in India, the CPI and CPM respectively) refusal to allow Campaign For Lesbian Rights (CALERI) to march with the CALERI banner in March 8 demonstrations in New Delhi through the early 2000s. For my critique of this moment, see *Impossible Alliances?: Lesbianism and Feminism in India* paper presented at the 'Rethinking South Asian Feminism' conference at the University of San Diego, California in 2004.

8 See the work of Ratna Kapur, among others, usefully summarized in Rajeswari Sunder Rajan, *The Scandal of the State: Women, Law and Citizenship in Postcolonial India* (Delhi: Permanent Black 2005).

9 Frederick Cooper and Randall Packard, 'Introduction' in eds Cooper and Packard *International Development and the Social Sciences: Essays on the History and Politics of Knowledge* (Berkeley: University of California Press 1997), 1–41.

10 For a staggering example of this, see Stephanie Black's film *Life and Debt* and its tracing of the destruction of Jamaica along these lines, based on writer Jamaica Kincaid's *A Small Place.*

11 The standard and still highly influential account of this process remains Arturo Escobar, *Encountering Development: The Making and Unmaking of The Third World* (New Jersey: Princeton University Press 1995).

12 Bose Sugata, 'Instruments and Idioms of Colonial and National Development: India's Historical Experience in Comparative Perspective' in eds Cooper and Packard

International Development and the Social Sciences: Essays on the History and Politics of Knowledge (Berkeley: California University Press 1997), 52.

13 ibid., 53.

14 Neither of these critiques goes into how the Indian state selectively regulates flows of capital in the age of liberalization-privatization-globalization with full deference to the desires of multinational corporations to bring money in and out and very little deference to NGOs and what this means.

15 For a detailed account of this history, see Akhil Gupta, *Postcolonial Developments: Agriculture in the Making of Modern India* (Durham: Duke University Press 1998).

16 See K. C. Naik and A. Sankaram, *A History of Agricultural Universities* (Bombay: Oxford/IBH 1972) For a more detailed account of extension in India, see Bhrigupati Singh, 'The Passing of the Peasant, Or how to locate an Anthropoint?' (unpublished manuscript, Johns Hopkins University). Singh shows how the focus in all this discourse was on the peasant and his betterment and, of late, this has changed and the peasant no longer matters.

17 To ask one of many possible questions of this: how is it that many US Universities have more expansive resources on South Asia than any University in India?

18 World Bank Policy and Research Unit, *Agricultural Extension: The Next Step* (World Bank: Washington 1990), 28.

19 World Development Report 1994 *Infrastructure for Development* (NY: Oxford University Press 1994).

20 For a succinct history of the different kinds of NGOs in India, see Sangeeta Kamat, *Development Hegemony: NGOs and the State in India* (Delhi: Oxford University Press 2002).

21 See, for example, *Opening the Pandora's Box: Sexual Harassment, Corruption and Malpractice in an NGO* (New Delhi: Saheli Women's Resource Centre 2004). Lesbian employees discriminated against and ousted from Masum, another NGO in Pune, India, are also preparing a series of documents. The incidence and documentation of abuse of different kinds within NGOs is on the increase. There is also apparently no space in the NGO world for this critique. At an extremely elite retreat, organized by three sexuality funded NGOs – CREA, Sangama and TARSHI – at Manesar, a sylvan resort an hour or so from Delhi, called 'A Conversation on Sexual Rights in India', and lavishly funded by Ford in early 2007, ex-members of Masum and Vividha (the ex-Sangama hijra group) wanted to raise the issue of the discriminations against them, but were systematically not allowed to speak. Whatever the particular rights and wrongs of these cases, the fact that these people were not allowed to speak at all is inexcusable. So much for the sexual rights of activists, let alone general people! This is an example of the plain lack of democratic principles in this field, given that the organizers used the ridiculous excuse that those questions were not 'relevant' to the issues at hand.

22 Jenkins Rob, "Mistaking "Governance" for "Politics": Foreign Aid, Democracy, and the Construction of Society" in eds Sudipta Kaviraj and Sunil Khilnani *Civil Society: History and Possibilities* (Cambridge: Cambridge University Press 2001), 250–268. I am aware of what can be seen a possible conflation on my part here (and through the essay, actually), given how I define the political via the World Bank, between humanitarian funding (which is seen as non-political) and human rights funding (seen as political) as also between donor agencies, western NGOs and Indian NGOs. However, I risk these conflations for the larger points I am making about, in the first instance, sexuality, often being seen by both humanitarian and human rights groups as non-political altogether, and human rights as benignly non-political and beyond contestation (both of which are dangerous cover-ups) and, in the second, the fact that none of these donors, western

NGOs or Indian NGOs have well-worked out political ideologies about, for the first two, intervention in Third world countries vis-à-vis sexuality, and for all three, any ideologically articulated positions on understandings of sexual politics vis-à-vis funding and theoretical frameworks of conceiving of sexual orientation and sexuality.

23 ibid., 252–53.

24 The Humsafar Trust in Bombay, one of the first gay organizations in the country, was formed on the rationale that it would be an HIV/AIDS Prevention Centre. See reports by Shabnam Minawalla, 'Centre to help gays tackle health problems' *Times of India* March 16, 1996 and Saira Menezes, 'Room with a View' *Outlook* 17 April, 1996, 64.

25 Ann C. Hudock, *NGOs and Civil Society: Democracy by Proxy* (Cambridge: Polity 1999). See also excellent critiques that expose the underlying agendas of Northern NGOs, like David Williams and Tom Young, 'Governance, the World Bank and Liberal Theory', *Political Studies*, 42 (1994), 84–100 and Gerald Clarke 'From Ethnocide to Ethnodevelopment? Ethnic Minorities and Indigenous Peoples in South East Asia', *Third World Quarterly*, 22 no. 3 (2001), 413–36.

26 This leads to situations like the one in Allmora, Uttar Pradesh. For the publication of an AIDS report *Aids Aur Hum* ('AIDS and Us') in 1999, the NGO Sahayog's office on 20 April, 2000 was attacked and destroyed by unruly mobs; the activists handcuffed and publicly paraded by the police, denied bail and booked under the NSA (National Security Act); the NGO shut down. The NGO had worked in the region for years but the hurried nature of the report and the lack of thought and caution in the process led to a complete breakdown of the NGO's relationship with the community at large.

27 There is no work yet on the ideology of sexuality-based NGOs and its relation to capitalism but a good enough start is Dennis Altman, 'Rupture or Continuity: The Internationalization of Gay Identities' *Social Text* 14 no. 3 (Fall 1996), 77–94 and Alexandra Chasin, *Selling Out: The Gay and Lesbian Movement Goes to Market* (New York: Palgrave 2000).

28 For a general critique on these lines, see Antonio Negri and Michael Hardt, *Empire* (Massachusetts: Harvard University Press 2000), 35–37.

29 I distinguish the internationalization and globalization of gay/lesbian/transgender/queer identities from at least one history of the gay and lesbian movement in the US and Western Europe, delineated most painstakingly in the extraordinary work of historian John D'Emilio. A historicity of this trajectory and its difference is vital to dislocate the notion that all Western gayness or gay organizations are operating under the same imperialist malintent. The organizations I am critiquing, are those that swallow whole and regurgitate the capitalist idea of development, into which sexuality becomes interpolated as another axis of imperialist exploitation and domination. See John D' Emilio, *Sexual Politics, Sexual Communities: The Making of a Homosexual Minority in the United States 1940–1970* (Chicago: Chicago University Press, 1983, 2nd edition, with a new Preface and Afterword, 1998), – *Making Trouble: Essays on Gay History, Politic and Culture* (New York: Routledge 1992) and – *The World Turned: Essays on Gay History, Politics and Culture* (Durham: Duke University Press 2002) for an anti-imperialist history of the gay and lesbian movement.

30 Very often, it is questionable whether these are groups at all, whether 'kothis' or hijras. The former, for example, have never existed as a category before NGOization, and the latter are not really organized as a group, politically. See my critique of the category 'kothi' in 'Postcolonial Same-Sex Relations in India: a Theoretical Framework' in ed. Manas Ray, *Space, Sexuality, and Postcolonial Cultures*, Enreca Occasional Papers 6 (Calcutta: Centre for Studies in Social Sciences 2003), 221–231.

31 Rudi Bleys, *The Geography of Perversion: Male-to-Male Sexual Behaviour outside the West* (New York: New York University Press 1995) and Neville Hoad 'Arrested Development or

the Queerness of Savages: Resisting Evolutionary Narratives of Difference', *Postcolonial Studies* 3 no. 2 (2000), 133–158.
32 Hoad, 'Arrested Development', 150.
33 ibid.
34 ibid., 151.
35 Spivak, Gayatri "Righting Wrongs – 2002: Accessing Democracy Among the Aboriginals" *Other Asias* (London: Blackwell, 2007) 56.
36 ibid., 36.
37 See, for example, Arvind Narrain's chapter 'Human Rights of Queer People in a Global Context' in his book *Queer*, which does not even begin to interrogate the concept of human rights, philosophically or otherwise. Arvind Narrain, *Queer: Despised Sexuality, Law and Social Change* (Bangalore: Books for Change 2004), 14–32.
38 Shannon Speed *Rights in Rebellion: Indigenous Struggle and Human Rights in Chiapas* (Stanford: Stanford University Press 2008), 19.
39 Prawesh Lama, 'Forbidden Love Blooms', *Mid-Day*, Delhi July 12, 2007 and Prawesh Lama. 'Yeh Ishq Nahi Aasaan' *Mid-Day*, Delhi, August 25, 2007. Delhi was the only paper to do an initial and follow-up report on them.
40 For Rajwinder and Mala's story, see *The Telegraph*, 19 December, 2004. Online: http://www.telegraphindia.com/1041219/asp/look/story 4132377.asp. See *Indian Express*, 20 June, 2007, for Palwinder's and Inderjit's and Baljit's and Rajwinder's stories. Online: http://cities.expressindia.com/fullstory.php?newsid=241926
41 See *Punjab Newsline*, 19 June, 2007. Online: http://www.punjabnewsline.com/content/view/4606/38/
42 See Hamad Sindhi, 'The Oppressed Truth' *SAMAR* 26–30 June, 2007. Online: www.samarmagazine.org/archive/article.pp?id=239
43 See *DesPardes.com*, February 24, 2006. Online: http://www.despardes.com/lifestyle/feb05/lesbian-marriages.htm
44 Maya Sharma, *Loving Women: Being Lesbian in Underprivileged India* (New Delhi: Yoda Press 2006).
45 Gayatri Chakraborty Spivak, 'The Intervention Interview', in ed. Sarah Harasym *The Postcolonial Critic: Interviews, Strategies, Dialogues* (New York: Routledge 1990), 120.
46 Michel Foucault, 'The History of Sexuality' in ed. Colin Gordon *Power/Knowledge: Selected Interviews and Other Writings 1972–1977 by Michel Foucault* (New York: Pantheon Books 1980), 190.
47 Simone Weil, *Gravity and Grace* (London: Routledge 2002), 116–22.
48 Denise Riley, *War in the Nursery: Theories of the Child and Mother* (London: Virago 1983), 8.
49 ibid., 8.
50 Denise Riley, 'A Short History of Some Preoccupations', in eds Judith Butler and Joan Scott, *Feminists Theorize the Political* (New York: Routledge 1992), 122.
51 ibid., 123.
52 See Gayatri Chakraborty Spivak *The Death of a Discipline* (New York: Columbia University Press 2003), which is an extraordinary theoretical exposition of the kind of encounter I am talking about and her interview with Geert Lovink on http://www.kunstradio.at/FUTURE/DX/EVENTS/geert-spivak.html where she has a strong critique of NGOs and specifies what she means by 'learning to learn from below.' For an explicatory account of the unlearning one's privilege as one's loss, see eds. Donna Landry and Gerald McLean, *The Spivak Reader* (New York: Routledge 1996).

Chapter 13

DISTRIBUTIVE JUSTICE: LOCATING IN CONTEXT

Bhagat Oinam

One of the major problems of distributive justice is about the State providing equal opportunity to its citizens to acquire equal resources and, subsequently, attain equal welfare. Though I have used the terms and their relationships little too loosely, their theoretical and praxiological implications are problematic to a large extent. Not only are there difficulties in talking about an 'objective' conception of welfare but also in dealing between resources and welfare or between resources and opportunity. Government, providing opportunity to its citizens to enter public sectors in addition to demanding services from its citizens, aims at enabling realisation of welfare for the citizens. On the other side, the nature of welfare's definition may differ from, say, the mental states (qualitative) of the persons concerned to the measure of material wealth people could acquire. Again, measuring welfare in terms of material goods may mean bringing the equality of welfare close to the equality of resources. The problems are indeed wide beyond the purview of this particular paper. I have only tried to glean over a few problems out of the many introduced here.

In this paper I have attempted to highlight only a few problems that crop up with the State's propagation of distributive justice based on economic and social enhancement of a group depending upon certain social criteria. That is, on State's attempt to enhance opportunity to acquire 'equal' resources to some of its citizens who are socially and economically backward. Subsequent arguments in the paper will partly highlight some points of contention raised by Ronald Dworkin (1981) and partly address some concrete issues. I shall in the latter part briefly focus on India's state policies and practices, more specifically, on India's Northeast. I must also clarify that the paper in the end may look more like mapping of certain issues rather than arriving at any conclusion. This may be seen as my own limitation, for the issue I have handled demands a lot more space and deliberation. The paper may be seen as a prologue to a more intensive research, which will follow elsewhere.

Let me also state at the outset that I shall strictly confine to the developmental aspect in its narrower sense and not extend the retributive aspect into the larger fold of the development debate. However, I am aware of the unavoidability of retributive justice in the debate on welfare and utilisation of resources; it is really hard to show indifference to the questions like, how far can the State provide each citizen his/her dues as a citizen of the State. I may take up this issue, if the need arises in the course of my argumentation. The most important issue for me, at present, is to study the checks and balances in distributive justice when enhancement of well-being of an individual or a group is totally based on hereditarily determined identity structure or a politically motivated ideological construct.

My focus on the developmental issue, which largely falls under the jurisdiction and responsibility of the State, does not suggest that distributive justice is exclusively a State subject. I have confined myself only to a particular area of discourse on distributive justice so that theorisation within a specific paradigm may lead to a meaningful dialogue. The study, though ideational, focuses on the Indian social system, where caste-based politics happily mingle with democratic polity and also where the State introduces development policies with criteria on caste and tribe lines that are primarily hereditary. This State policy faces serious crisis when introduced in the North-Eastern parts of India *vis-à-vis* the issue of 'development'.

In all these marginal areas on India's development map, whether one talks of the Northeast, the tribal belts of Chattisgarh or Naxal-affected areas of Andhra Pradesh, the voices are of disenchantment of the people and the demand for justice. There are protests that injustice is done to these areas and the people, and, in specific cases, injustice is carried out by a group of people to another group within the same region. I am not going into the validity or invalidity of these voices. But the fact that they have their presence shows the seriousness of the issue, which cannot be simply brushed aside as trivial. I think that addressing these problems would bring about a better understanding of the issues of distributive justice and welfare. What ought to be studied is 'what forms of injustices are carried out' (no matter who does these) and 'what kinds of justice are demanded'. The issue is on understanding the nature of justice demanded. What form of equality, either at the individual level or the group level, as the context may demand, will amount to fulfilling distribution of justice would be one of the most complex but inevitable question that has to be dealt with. Perhaps here we ought to reflect on the ideas of 'equality of opportunity' and 'equality of resources', and subsequently 'equality of welfare'. I could substantiate the ideas through the following issues: (a) How far could equality of resources be realised when opportunity to have fair competition is not yet provided? (b) Is the thesis that job reservation policies for social groups[1] based on heredity will lead to social enhancement/welfare of the group compatible with the actual practice? (c) How is equality of resources (of individuals) achieved when customary land ownership, for instance, does not permit individual land holding? Few more policies and practices could be problematised.

Before initiating the discussion on the concept of equality, let me glean over the issue of exploring what welfare would mean to different socio-political perspectives or contexts. That is, what amounts to terming a state of affair as 'state of welfare'? The idea seems to be quite intriguing not only in political theorising but philosophically as well. Beginning with political theorising, the idea of welfare shows drastic difference or, one may say, distinctive difference in conceptual parameters between the North and the South. The observation is that in countries that are economically less affluent, i.e., either in their developing or underdeveloped stages, focus of the people is on highlighting spiritual heritage, religious and cultural resurgence, etc. These highlights project a sort of identity of the community or the nation which shows *their* heritage or religious *weltanschaung* as uniquely owned by them, not present in other cultures. These adjuncts can serve as a criteria for distinguishing 'we' from 'they', the 'sacred' from the 'profane'. Interestingly, what is being considered as welfare is attainment of certain spiritual state or cultural forms largely valued as a common goal for those people considered a constituent part of the society or nation. It is this value that is supposed to be provided by the society or culture (collectivity) to the individuals for realisation. And its realisation is largely seen as a realisation of individual wellbeing and welfare of the society at large. Such forms of valuing have been seen by a few scholars as signs of protest and resurgence due to failure to cope up with the current trend of the dominant model, say, capitalism. The examples are the resurgence of *hindutva* in India or Islamic *jehadis* in the Middle East, extending up to South East Asia (Ahmad 2001). For those who oppose such a formulation the alternative is the 'clash of civilizations'[2] and not necessarily that of Huntington and his thesis. I am open to both views. Keeping the debate aside, what is intended through this highlight is the 'plurality of contentions'. Or one may use the term 'multiplicity of models'. The models, as highlighted above, are primarily on defining the nature of welfare that one visualises or ought to visualise. And I have intended to see this visualisation less on the individual and more on the collective domain. Even though these political models are quite general and not free from criticism, it more or less shows the difficulties in talking about equality of welfare when there isn't just one idea of the welfare itself. At least it has been debated in the developing countries that the idea of welfare, as propounded by the liberal tradition in the West, cannot be applied with the same yardstick in Oriental civilisations, for their civilisational values are different. The generally projected image is that while Western civilization has been more material in nature, Oriental civilizations are spiritual. I am not so much bothered with the validity of these claims as with the *differences* in political theorisation.

Coming to philosophical discourses, much has been discussed by Ronald Dworkin on this subject. He explains the problem of 'equality of welfare' in detail; that there are subjective and objective natures of the term. Right now, I do not necessarily pursue the idea that for a possible formulation of equality of welfare (even as a mental state) to be objective, equality of resources (largely material) of some sorts ought to be prevailing as a basis for the fulfilment of the former (Dworkin 1981, 224–226). The argument is that it is through materialisation of the idea of 'equal distribution of resources' as a just form of distribution that will give a near total realisation of equality of welfare. A lot more discussions are being shared at present on this issue,[3] which I would not like to look into detail here. I would rather position myself with the thesis that what has been stated in Dworkin's (Dworkin 1981, 187–196) initial illustration of several generic theories such as 'success theories of welfare', 'conscious state theories', and 'objective theories', suggests plurality of models in explaining the nature of welfare. I cannot, as has been done by Dworkin, favour the third. I see all three as alternate theories that, in all possibilities, are able to explain (even with limitations) the concept of equality of welfare in some way or another. Let us cast some doubt for the time being on the overarching conception of objectivity. Interestingly, Dworkin suggests plurality in the much-projected 'objective' theories/conceptions.

To stretch a bit this plurality thesis, whether in the lines of Dworkin or otherwise, we could explore the relative character of the general theories of welfare. Happiness as a state of welfare will be different from 'order' as welfare. A communitarian ethics at times may highlight certain *order* or organic continuity as the highest form of ideal that an individual should aim at. Attainment of such an *order* in the society (or State) would be considered as achieving the welfare state. Even if happiness is taken as a generally accepted ideal of welfare, happiness of an artist may be different from that of a beggar.[4] Let me bring back my earlier illustration that conception of happiness in a traditional Oriental society may be drastically different from that of a western society. Relativism in political theorising of distributive justice could be brought here as a manifest of a deeper philosophical debate.

Having shown the open-endedness of the welfare theory, let me now come closer to what Dworkin would call 'objective *conceptions*' where some form of measurability has been shown as a criteria to arrive at a possible understanding of welfare. This approach of mine may sound little confusing, if not contradictory, as though I am eating up what I have been so far pleading for. My intention is to show the complexity in talking about distributive justice. The effort is to highlight the stereotyping of our welfare policies introduced by the State. It is to counter both the unitarists as well as the cultural relativists. It is the time for theorising the possibility of *limited* objectivity and order.

The theoretical need for *limited* objectivity is this: if welfare is a relative concept and it's various conceptions do not seem to have any common attribute or mode of operation, then how can we talk about distributive justice? Is there any wisdom in talking about the concept if it is so open-ended that there is no sense in talking about welfare and, subsequently, distribution? It is here that some sort of working 'objective' conception of welfare needs to be formulated. We might partly take recourse to Wittgenstein's *family resemblance*,[5] but I think it does not fully explain the difficulty we are faced with. The reason, perhaps, is because the paradigm of Wittgenstein's study is not into defining social issues which are primarily praxiological. Taking due note of *family resemblance*, let me call this 'limited objectivity'. This idea will not only highlight the necessity of an objective character of welfare, but also take cognisance of the relative nature of the concept.

Objectivity in welfare can be best brought out when its realisation is linked with material achievement. This is possible through distribution or sharing of resources. Accordingly, Dworkin explains distributive equality under 'equality of welfare' and 'equality of resources'. The distinction, though not new, highlights the importance of the traditional utilitarian categories of wealth and happiness. Distributive justice aims at attainment of equality of the people/citizens. Equality can be further seen as follows: (a) equality of welfare as a state (of mind) to be attained based on possession of certain values (economic or otherwise), and (b) equality of resources on equal possession wealth, mental and physical capabilities, etc. Justice can be said to be given when the State provides its citizens equal opportunities to achieve welfare by enabling to possess equal resources. By going on this line, I would abstain from the general impression of distributive justice as 'equality of opportunity' alone.

What Dworkin calls 'equality of welfare' is not free from difficulties. If attainment of welfare is a state of mind, it is doubly problematic to talk about the objectivity of welfare. The utilitarian goal of wellbeing is happiness, pleasure or enjoyment. Happiness or enjoyment is a psychological state. Unless these are quantifiable, objectivity in its strict sense cannot be realised. Psychological study of these states on a group of people can be, at most, provided through a generalised statement but not as objective in the empirical sense. Even a psychologist in order to arrive at a generalised statement uses certain data to justify generality. These data are visible responses in a person or a group of persons to establish correlates with the non-visible mental state. Validity of such an exercise to explain a totally open-ended and abstract mental state is a difficult task, the result still being questionable.

Dworkin's claim to objectivity is that by measuring the control of resources in similar traits/fields one can come out with an objective result of the 'state of welfare'. Welfare is not measurable, but resources are. The further argument is that a person's welfare consists in the resources available to him/her, broadly conceived to include mental and physical competence, education and opportunities as well as material resources. This means that two persons attain/can attain same level of welfare if both of them are healthy, mentally sound, educated and equally wealthy, and, over and above, fall under a similar trait (Dworkin 1981). Malcontent in one of them, say, due to emotional stress, will not/cannot be considered as a criterion for differentiation. If we accept such a criterion of differentiation as that of malcontent, welfare issue will become a totally subjective affair ever impossible to be made objective. But what seems to follow from these arguments is that objectivity of such mental states as happiness and enjoyment is extremely open-ended and loose. It still makes sense when we talk about it in the individual level. But once attempts are made to extend it to a collective level, things seem to go out of hand. It is extremely difficult to formulate welfare for a community as a psychological state of mind. No doubt such exercises are carried out by social scientists. But I have projected above the necessity of such an objective status to be conferred on welfare. It is out of necessity rather than anything *essentialistic* that we talk of the *objectivity* of welfare.

Pursuing this line of thought, equality of welfare and equality of resources are distinguishable but not separable. The inalienable relationship between the two is that the state of welfare is both inconceivable and unrealisable without the availability of the resources. It is only when individuals have near equal access over the resources in and around them and he/she utilises the same for the enhancement of his/her livelihood that the state of welfare can be said to be achieved. Though the two are conceptually distinguishable, one cannot be separated from the other; at least attainment of welfare makes no sense without availability of resources.

Let me also briefly remind (not to be ignored from our current discussion) that distributive justice aims at providing one his or her dues. Egalitarianism, in the literal sense, say, of providing equal salary to all, irrespective of efficiency possessed by different persons, cannot be said to be a just act. To be just in providing wealth and happiness to everyone is quite different from the one mentioned above. 'To be just' also means making everyone equal according to capabilities, aspirations and needs. Applying conditions does not mean that we are proposing a meritorious theory of justice. Each has his/her own needs and priorities, not merely talking from psychological perspective, but because of stark material conditions (socio-political and geographical factors, for instance). Equality is to be based on need and potential together.

Let me now focus on the utilisation and management of the resources. It is anthropologically studied that the human development enhanced considerably with the emergence of private property. The sign of human development from the tribal mode of production to the agrarian system is marked mainly by the introduction of private property. Freedom to accumulate wealth and will to generate it further has lead to the state of civilisation we are in today. We have also learnt from our history that attempts have been made by nations to abolish private property and make all the resources and wealth state-owned. This exercise has not, however, succeeded. The communist countries have now enhanced wealth-accumulating capacity of the individual citizens. This clearly shows the importance of private property. Steps are bound to be taken up as compromising method where State in the face of stark competition has to enhance its wealth generating capacity. This has been experienced in the developing countries like India, where public sectors by and large have failed miserably compared to the private sectors. This does not mean that the state-owned sectors should be completely closed down. Sectors such as education, health and home affairs require intensive government intervention. On the other hand, wealth generating sectors call for further privatisation to give satisfactory results. However, we ought to be cautious of the faceless and senseless nature of the market economy. I am not siding with any of the extreme positions, i.e., being a blatant follower of market economy or a firm believer of public sector.

The dual standard of the government comes when, on the one hand, it realises the inalienability of the private property and necessity to give individuals their dues; and on the other, government-owned employment generating sectors are flooded with group-based programmes. Also, we practise adult franchise based on 'one man one vote' as a symbol of democratic principle of representational governance, but State still encourages collective land ownership in many parts of the Northeast, discouraging individual entrepreneurship and development through banking. There are some serious flaws in all of these policies.

What has been witnessed in the fifty years of India's history of distributive justice is the large-scale introduction of group-based (hereditary) reservation policy. This policy is primarily aimed at providing equal resources to the socially deprived groups. The theoretical formulation of the policy is this: 'The country has witnessed a long history of social exploitation through caste hierarchy. Because of this, the communities in the lower strata of the caste hierarchy and those tribal populations in the periphery of the nation's mainstream culture should be given privileges to have equal opportunity to hold government offices and equal participation in nation building. Subsequent economic security will lead to equal or near equal share of possessing resources (and consequently welfare).' What is expected through the policy is individual emancipation, but the criterion is collective (social identity). Where the aim is economic self-sufficiency of the individual the criterion is non-economic. It is not the economic status of the individual but the social identity which will qualify one to be an economic beneficiary. It seems that the policy axiomatically presumes that individual upliftment within a caste will naturally lead to collective upliftment of the entire caste, without, perhaps, visualising in the process a possible emergence of a class within the caste.

The introduction of reservation policy is through a group-based model of economic distribution. With the group-based model of distribution (keeping the term 'economic' aside for the time being) I mean groups that are politically motivated or based on heredity. A development scheme of a particular government, say, based on the position below poverty line is not a group-based economic model of distribution. Though under the scheme a makeshift group is formed, it is only functional. Any individual, irrespective of his or her caste, religion or domicile, is entitled to fall in that makeshift group. In fact, it is not a group but a functional cluster. On the other hand, a government scheme on development meant only for the Dalits disallows people who are not Dalits, even though they also deserve benefits from such schemes. The criteria of enrolling in such a scheme is based on a structure not directly and immediately related to the development philosophy. Interestingly, on the other hand, a rich Dalit has the right to avail, by the criteria of the scheme, the benefits that morally he or she does not deserve. To be more precise, my problem is with the State policies that aim at enabling vertical social mobility of the group rather than of individuals. Ultimately it is the individual and not the group who gains the benefit. Instead of categorising a citizen by the criteria of measuring the resources possessed by him/her, it is the social identity of the individual that serves as the criteria.

Let me illustrate another contradiction with the issue of land ownership. In the tribal areas of the Northeast individuals cannot own any private property. In the case of the Kuki tribes, the land belongs to the village head, whereas in the case of the Nagas, the village council have authority over the land. Furthermore, in the hill areas land mapping is not properly done, which results in loose mapping of the area of operation/possession. A clear-cut boundary in between the reserved forest and tribal inhabited areas is also not clearly mapped out. The problem is that the idea of ownership, which prevails in the village, gets unrestrictedly extended to the entire hill areas. The need is for individual entrepreneurship and possession. In these underdeveloped areas it is land as resource (capital) and not multinational or government sectors that has to be exploited for development. Given the present state of affair, taking note of the level of education, awareness, and social mobility, individual entrepreneurship and ownership seems a better option. Of course, individual entrepreneurship should take place under a wider canvas of social structure and relationship, as has been the case in some areas of Rajasthan, where water-harvesting programmes are initiated successfully.

The above argument may sound unacceptable on the ground that the tribals should be allowed to lead their own ways of living, not to be disturbed from their natural habitat. This, of course, is not possible with the pace of development taking place all over the globe. World has indeed become a global village. The impression of changes has already been witnessed in the tribal areas, particularly visibly in the Northeast. The role of the State is to intervene and channelise the mode of development rather than converting the tribal inhabiting areas into an open sanctuary of primitive people. That would be repeating what Americans have done to the native Indians. In fact, developing the standard of living of these people will help them from being marginalized and left out.

The argument that tribals should lead their traditional mode of living and their internal organic relationships should not be disturbed holds ground so far as the argument confines to respecting the traditional mode of living of the tribes. There are two pertinent counter arguments to the above thesis. Firstly, if tribals should not be exposed to modern ways of living, which are certainly more pleasurable than the traditional form of living, are we not depriving them of the 'new' forms of pleasure and, consequently, some form of happiness or welfare? While the rest of the world enjoys the fruits of modern science and technology, is it ethical on the part of those already enjoying the fruit to deprive these people of the benefit? Secondly, anthropological findings have already proved that every form of society has emerged out of tribal ways of life. The difference has been that, while many have evolved to more organic forms, for a few it has been a slow, mechanical way of life.[6] To presume that tribals will be happier in their traditional ways of life is to propound a thesis that social evolution is *not* possible.

Dworkin's 'equality of resources' becomes relevant here. All resources, both natural and human, must be made available to all the citizens. The type of resources necessary for an individual will be determined by the state of mind, capability and need of the individual concerned. But it should also be kept in mind that amiable ground should be provided where individuals are *equipped* to possess 'near' equal capabilities and state of mind, if not needs. Time for the the State comes when citizens are provided equal infrastructure and opportunity to compete fairly and possess equal resources. Availability of both the targets and infrastructure as well as resources (in regulated form) is what is expected. The time has come now for treating the tribals as individuals as much as the rest of the humanity (Indian in our case) is, and not highlight them as segregated segments. This may create more backlashes in the long run. Already the country has started witnessing the politics of identity based on religion, ethnicity, caste, etc. with hints of looking for overhaul at development policies. For the time being, the problem is too complex to side with any hardened position.

Let me present only this. The unfortunate story about the country is its unclear mixing up of individual and collective/community identities in formulation of development policies. Indian State has not recognised the primacy of individual(s) and egalitarianism in spirit, though 'primacy of the individual' is enshrined in the Fundamental Rights of the constitution. Instead of seeing the citizens as individuals, each one of them has been seen along with one or more identities based on religion, caste, language or community. Each one of the identities is a social construct. We, no doubt, live with these identities. But difficulty arises when development programmes (providing opportunity) meant for individual citizens are converted into those for groups. Criteria based on heredity and ideologically tinted categories only lead to exclusivity and isolation rather than encompassment.

The very fact that the political participation of the citizens in the exercise of adult franchise is counted on the individual citizenship and not on representational votes of a community shows that the country exercises a democratic pattern of the representational system, that election of the representatives is based, in principle, on individual citizen's single non-transferable votes. This shows that spirit of the political democracy is the individual and not groups. The irony is that *this* individual is pushed back to the fringes when utilisation of resources comes to count. In the development model application is based on the presumption that individual's existence and his/her identity is seen as a part of a particular group identity to which the individual belongs. Plurality of identity is an undeniable fact. Difficulty, however, lies on the priority given to one type of identity over another.

To conclude, since the idea of 'limited objective welfare' has to be worked out to have a just distributive system in/of the State, we must also see that the idea is possible only by relating with equality of resources. Equality of resources (again limited)[7] among the citizens can be made possible only when individuals are provided equal infrastructure and opportunity to have access over the resources. And what is required in our state policies is to give cognisance of this fact while formulating development models so that each needy receives benefit of the available resources under his individual identity and not under any determined social constructs.

Notes

1 Groups here refer to a caste, tribe, ethnic community, or religious community.
2 There are several writings on the subject, the most appropriate of which I would trace to the writings of Sri Aurobindo. I have chosen Sri Aurobindo for his formulation that Indian culture and that of the West are different and distinct, each having their own uniqueness. One is not to be subsumed under the other. See, Sri Aurobindo's *The Foundations of Indian Culture.*
3 A lot more discussion has been initiated on Dworkin's theory of equality and sovereign virtue. See, *Ethics*, Volume 113, No. 1.
4 Dworkin, though, has shown limitation of this argument to bring about the idea of objectivity in its fold. See his 'What is Equality? Equality of Welfare.'
5 I am referring to the minimal possibility of Wittgensteinian family resemblance.
6 I am referring to the Durkheim's distinction of 'organic' and 'mechanical' forms of society. See Raymond Aron's *Main Currents of Sociological Thought.*
7 Possessing equality of resources, as mentioned earlier, must be determined by mental and physical competence, opportunity, education, wealth, etc.

References

Ahmad, Aijaz. 2001/2002. 'Politics of the Far Right', *Lineages of the Present.* Chicago: Verso.

Aron, Raymond. 1965/1967. *Main Currents of Sociological Thought – 2.* London: Penguin Books.

Aurobindo, Sri. 1968. *Foundations of Indian Culture.* Pondicherry: Sri Aurobindo Ashram Press.

Dworkin, Ronald. 1981. 'What is Equality? Equality of Welfare', *Philosophy and Public Affairs*, 10, no. 3. Princeton: Princeton University Press.

Symposium on Ronald Dworkin's 'Sovereign Virtue', *Ethics*, 113, no. 1. October 2002. Chicago: University of Chicago Press.

Wittgenstein, Ludwig. 1953. *Philosophical Investigations*, trans. G.E.M. Anscombe. Oxford: Basil Blackwell.

Chapter 14

PUNISHMENT AND HUMAN RIGHTS

Ruplekha Khullar

The application of the philosophical theories of right and wrong in the moral rhetoric that surrounds many a burning issue today has become a raging fashion, at least in the West. Unfortunately this fact clouds the very real and significant contribution that a rigorous and systematic training in philosophical analysis can make towards a balanced and even-handed approach to questions such as abortion, euthanasia, cloning, animal rights, suicide and human rights. Philosophy needs not only to lend techniques of reasoning to a moral debate. It actually helps us to take sides while appreciating the strengths of opposing arguments.

There is much moral rhetoric that one finds in magazine articles and lobbyist pamphlets on the issue of human rights. But strangely not much public debate goes into the question of punishment and what is befitting treatment for a transgressor who has sinned against society. What, if any, consideration is given to the protection of human rights of the sinner, the criminal. One aspect of the whole subject of punishment, however, has received a sizeable amount of attention and that is the question of capital punishment. Anyone and everyone has something to say about it but the interesting questions are raised by the philosophers. There is the question of whether the capital punishment is another form of killing that lobbyists or philosophers have to justify. There are utilitarian arguments for and against it. There is the claim that execution is wrong because it is a cruel and unusually violent form of punishment. And then there is the question of the justification for the death penalty.

Punishment in general can involve a vast array of questions and intricacies. Punishment involves the taking away of rights.

One may in a broad sweep agree with H. L. A. Hart's standard definition of punishment in terms of the following five features:

a. It must involve pain or other unpleasant consequences.
b. It must be for an offense against legal rules.
c. It must be for an actual or supposed offender for his offense.

d. It must be intentionally administered by human beings other then the offender.
e. It must be imposed and administered by an authority constituted by legal system against which the offense is committed. (Hart 1959, 160)

Anthony Flew (1954), J.D. Mabbot (1939), S.I. Benn (1958) and A.C. Ewing (1929) among contemporary writers echo the main idea with a slight variation in terminology. Anthony Flew proposes that punishment must be an 'evil', an unpleasantness to the victim. J.D. Mabbot holds that most punishments are not direct afflictions of suffering but the deprivation of a good. And A.C. Ewing defines punishment as a kind of negative wage adding further that punishment properly means pain inflicted by an external agent as a mark of disapproval for the wrong done.

But this is only the so-called central case of punishment. Hart also lists other cases as he believes that important issues like moral justifications, rationality and severity of punishment etc. cannot be made to turn around an exact definition. (Hart 1959) And it is precisely these issues that impact on the question of human rights and fundamental freedoms that are an inalienable part of a person or people. The peaceful citizen, the common criminal, the conscience objector, the political outcast and even the terrorist all have human rights. For violation of national and international law they must be tried and punished according to the law of the land. Quintessentially, it is a set of valid regulative principles that must resonate in the lives of those who are governed by it. What must be endorsed is that the law of any land must not make a specious appeal to its own indigenous brand of governance. The relativistic view, that a country's political system is its own business and above criticism from other nations, is unacceptable in an increasingly interdependent world. The principles of good governance must be genuinely universal in their scope and content. This applies to the system of punishment adhered to by any nation. No system of punishment can claim legitimacy unless it corresponds to cross-cultural convictions about the inviolability of the human person and accepts without arguments the spirit of the Preamble to the Universal Declaration of Human Rights:

> Whereas recognition of the inherent dignity and of the equal and inalienable rights of all members of the human family is the foundation of freedom, justice and peace in the world[1]

The effect of the cultural variance on universal human rights invariably highlights the fact that culture is at the root of human rights abuses everywhere (especially in South Asia). Very often the philosophical and political question at stake is 'who defines human rights' with the tacit understanding that we set our own standards.

Is the western notion of universal human rights applicable in Asia or is it the product of western ethnocentrism and cultural hegemony? The West has watched with horror attempts by Asian Nations (Singapore's Lee Kuan Yew and Malaysia's Mahathir Mohammed in particular) to curtail Western style human rights in the name of social harmony and economic development. Such ethical relativism is used very often as a justification for the curtailment of rights. The question is: does a human right have intrinsic value or is it tied to economic, social and political considerations endemic to a particular state? There are many aspects to the issue of punishment in this context. For one, there is the question, by whom and how punishment is to be meted to states that are found guilty of human rights violations. Human rights are the rights demanded and recognized by the society, which is represented by the government and its civil servants. And they are promoted through international agreements.

The international instruments of human rights provide a vast array of measures available for the formal implementation of these rights and of international forums and conventions where nations agree to hold each other accountable in maintaining certain standards of protection of these rights.

Complaints systems and redressal procedures are built into the international organisations, and these seek to supervise human rights and attempt to forestall or rectify their violations.

Complaints systems such as the International Labour Organization, UNESCO, UN, The Council of Europe, the Organisation of African Unity, Amnesty International, (an NGO) and the International Commission of Jurists carry out a periodic review and report at the international forums about administrative and legislative amendments and the status of human rights in various countries. Individuals can complain directly to an international organisation for the redress of alleged violations. Under the European Convention ten states have accepted the Optional Protocol, which gives the right of individual complaints. The European Human Rights Commission represents the individual in court.

The nature of punishment, if a State or person is convicted, is usually in terms of granting damages. The words 'punitive measures' or 'penalty' are more appropriate and suggestive than the broad term 'punishment'. The penal action takes the shape of reparation or economic sanctions or social and political isolation in extreme cases.

Does this mean that the rights of the weak and the oppressed are defended? Rarely! There are general factors that inhibit the implementation of these rights in International organizations such as:

a) Member states inhibit each other ideologically and otherwise.
b) There are vast differences in the mind-sets of, say, the Western world on the one hand and the Socialist Bloc and the Third World on the other.

Compounding this is the abysmal absence of empowering provisions in the constitutions of the states for the vulnerable sections of society. When the violator is the state it usually goes scot-free. E.g., Narendra Modi's Gujarat!

But a more interesting question is in the arena of criminal justice about punishment meted out to the individual transgressor and how, if at all, his human rights are not breached in the receiving of such punishment.

Hindu law by and large reflects the spirit of ancient Indian theories of punishment as propounded in such great detail in the *Manu Smrti* or the *Mānavadharma śāstras* of Manu. Punishment in the ancient Indian Society had three main aims:

a) Retribution, which meant repayment or adequate response, which the community feels the offender deserves to get.
b) Protection of society against the crime and potential criminals, including the aim of deterrence as a corollary.
c) Expiation or penance for the crime committed by the offender. This last was such a prominent response to crime in ancient Indian society that it either overlapped punishment or substituted or even modified it. It appears that the reformative aim of punishment or rehabilitation of the offender, so prominent a driving theme in western thought, is an aspect of expiation as understood in olden times.[2]

The laws of Manu are echoed in all the *dharmaśāstras* and the epics when it comes to retribution. The prescription is simple – the guilty ought to be punished! And, adding to this, 'A criminal shall be punished in proportion to his crime' (*Yathā-aparādha, yukta-danda*). (See the Śatapatha Brāhmana, II.6. 1.1–13)

The idea is almost identical to the classic case of retributivism as propounded in the West, most notably by Kant. In *The Metaphysics of Morals* he defines a crime as an infringement of the public law, which renders the guilty person incapable of citizenship. He is then deserving of just punishment according to the law of retribution – like is to be exchanged for like in matters of offence and penalty. Thus, according to Kant, the criminal pays for his crime by experiencing the pain he inflicted or a semblance of it. Kant suggests that, imposing specific punishments for specific crimes courts, should be guided by the law of retribution, but he does not give many examples of the way in which this law pairs crimes with appropriate punishments. However, one of the few offences for which an exact match is given without compromise is murder; for that crime the fitting punishment is death. (Kant, *1991*: 155–156)

But in general Kant supported the Talio principle or the principle of Lex Talionis: 'An eye for an eye and a tooth for a tooth'. It required the punishment of a responsible offender by inflicting on him an evil similar in quality and quantity to the crime he had committed. Thus, if a man committed murder, he must die. If he killed the son of another man, his own son shall be put to death. If a man destroyed an eye of another man, his own eye was to be gouged out!

Notwithstanding the obvious difficulty with calculating proportionality according to Talio, the principle was in general applied until, in the course of history, it began to be considered as too barbarous, and a more modified Talio replaced it. Yet the quantitative principle remained 'equal amount of injury for injury'.

The interesting point is that on the principle of retribution most penalties targeted the 'body'. Punishment was physical in nature and included amputation, the gauntlet, flogging, fettering, etc. Other punishment also attacked the body but indirectly, in the form of imprisonment, deportation, solitary confinement and even starving. And more often than not the motive was revenge on the perpetrator and not just punishment. The fact that the 'body' is owned by a human being capable of suffering pain is almost obliterated.

The first human right to be jettisoned in this case is dignity. Not a shred of it remains once the mechanism of arrest, conviction and punishment is set in motion. Retribution aims to wound not just the body but mind as well. Infliction of pain, often debilitating and mutilating, becomes a social good.

The horror of retributive measures has, however, propelled humanity to move away from corporal punishment towards more subtle methods.

Foucault in his *Discipline and Punish: The Birth of the Prison* documents this receding movement, evidenced in eighteenth-century Europe with the emergence of a new theory of law and crime, as a new moral and political justification for punishment. He notes the following:

a) Torture of the criminal as a public spectacle disappeared in the late eighteenth century.
b) Penalty or punishment began to be viewed as essentially corrective.
c) From the nineteenth century onwards punishment begins to be seen as adaptive to the individual offender.
d) The 'body' as the major target of penal repression disappeared and so did the idea of punishment as a spectacle. Punishment ceased to be a ceremony and became more a legal or administrative practice.
e) More and more, policy veered towards using prisoners for public work and menial tasks.
f) Somehow the thinking surfaced that punishment, which concluded the crime, was itself in some way linked with the crime. Punishment equalled if not exceeded in savagery the crime itself and made the spectator accustomed and insensitive to a ferocity from which it was essential to divert them.

g) Thus punishment tended to become more effective in its inevitability and not in its visible intensity. 'It is the certainty of being punished and not the horrifying spectacle of public punishment that must discourage crime... The exemplary mechanics of punishment changes its mechanisms (Foucault, 77: 9)
h) The publicity shifted from the penalty to the trial that ended in conviction. The process of justice ceased to associate itself with the shame of inflicting punishment, leaving this act to others under the seal of secrecy.
i) In the punitive practices today the body is no longer the recipient of physical punishment, at least not directly. Imprisonment, handcuffs, forced labour, solitary confinement, etc. are physical penalties because unlike fines, suspension from work, etc., they directly affect the body. But the body here serves only as an instrument. It is used only as means of depriving the individual of a liberty. Physical pain is no longer a constituent element of the penalty. Not even in the death penalty is the death brought about with the accompaniment of pain.[3]

This shift away from pain and indignity to the body was resoundingly dictated by a growing awareness of human rights issues and discourse.

We are being increasingly reminded that the ends of the criminal law is the maintenance of certain values, such as the protection of the life of human beings, physical and mental non-violability of the person and the maintenance of order and peace in society. This subjects punishment, including retributive punishment, to serve the higher end of a good social purpose.

From Foucault's observations one also notes a tendency to vindicate moral eclecticism. As H. L. A. Hart claims, any morally tolerable account of the institution of punishment must exhibit it as a compromise between distinct and partly conflicting principles. But the over arching and guiding principle must be some venerable social ethical goal, such as the solemn reaffirmation of the right for all men to have liberty and dignity in life. (Hart 1959: 160)

A principle of punishment that historically is claimed to surface next to retributivism is the deterrence theory. This theory assumes that fear of reprisal works as an effective psychological preventive to limit crime. The core of deterrence as a moral theory refers to the fear of punishment as a motive for law-abiding conduct.

Records of a deterrent metaphysical punishment are abundant in Indian Pauranic and epic literature. According to Manu, the slayer of a Brahmin enters the womb of an animal or a very low caste person. In the case of Manu, an effective intimidation may indeed be produced by combining both metaphysical and legal means but in contemporary society deterrence can only work, if it works at all, on the strength of a legal penalty.

If deterrence is seen as arising from the very idea of the punishment so that there is a preventive effect on people from any form of punishment, then deterrence may be considered as a sound moral justification. But the motive of deterrence may and often does take a very menacing form. Sometimes severe punishments are inflicted for even culpable negligence. And it seems intrinsically wrong to punish a man in a disproportionately harsh manner in order to influence the behaviour of others.

Furthermore, with regard to the criminal conduct, the law-abiding people, who would not commit a crime even if there were no punishment, are not deterred. Nor are hardened criminals and repeaters on whom deterrence doesn't quite work. In these two cases therefore deterrent punishment is unprofitable and vain and unjustifiable. It also easily leads to the hardening of punitive violence. But the more serious question is whether deterrence works even on potential offenders or the criminally inclined. Enough research has gone into showing that the simple formula that the prospect of punishment deters potential offenders from committing other punishable acts can no longer be held as true in an unqualified form. The issue becomes very urgent when one debates the deterrence effect of capital punishment.

As sociologists have tried to affirm, it is the social isolation process which keeps most people law-abiding, not the police. The function of punishment as example has and will exist at least as justification, but the difference that has been noted in recent times is the insistence on economy – one must punish exactly enough to prevent repetition. Excess has given way to economy and this is a result of heightened awareness of the need to protect the rights of men.

Talking about generalized punishment, Foucault leads the discussion into the most recent view of moral justification of punishment, that is, reform and rehabilitation. According to him, the injury that a crime inflicts upon society is the disorder that it introduces: the scandal that it gives rise to, the example that it sets, the incitement to repeat it, if not punished, and the possibility that it sets in motion possibility of the crime becoming widespread. Therefore, in order to be useful, punishment must have as its objective the consequences not only of the crime but the consequences of itself. Further he says that there is a scarcity of great crimes; on the other hand, there is the danger of everyday offenses multiplying. So, one must seek a qualitative relation between the crime and its punishment. One must calculate a penalty in terms not of the crime, but of its possible repetition. (Foucault 1977, 78)

The best example to set, that may have a good chance of having a salutary effect, is a reformed or re-socialized criminal. Reformation aims at the removal of a criminal disposition of mind by improving the offender. Since it aims not only negatively to remove the criminal disposition, but also positively to improve the man, it is the soft option in penal theory. In principle at least, it is the most humane option and seeks to recognize the intrinsic value of a human being. To acknowledge the possibility of redemption through expiation (*prayaschitta*) and reintegration into social life, is to accept that a man's nature is fallible, that crime does not have to blight the core of a man and that it is possible to restore order and health to society without sacrificing its members.

Regarding crime as a kind of social disease, Gandhi talked of the need for society itself to cleanse the evil within it. His repeated question is, does the society have a moral right to punish anyone opposing it? To put his ideas in context, however, one has to remember that, as an ideal anarchist, Gandhi made a distinction between a basically non-violent society and a violent colonial state. Thus, while a state based on structural and ideological violence has hardly the required moral status to punish those who break its rules, a non-violent society has the justification in its righteousness to treat offenders.

Consider the following words by Gandhi as epitomizing the most spirited defence of human rights:

> Even the hoodlums are part of us and, therefore, they must be handled gently and sympathetically. It is not only right but also profitable to wish well to the wrong-doer in spite of his wrongs, however grievous these may be... Ahimsa teaches us to take even an erring hooligan into our warm embrace.[4]

Hegel seems to think that punishment itself tends to reform a criminal. Punishment is the negation of a negation, and pain is administered to improve the wrongdoer.

It is interesting to note then that the prisons, which represented in the past not the punishment itself but the beginning of the process, and were used to detain individuals awaiting trial or for the infliction of corporal punishment such as the death penalty, etc., have now become the most representative form of punishment and a vast institution with innumerable enforcement personnel, wardens, social workers and other correctional officers.

There is of course a well-entrenched debate on whether prisons, even reformed prisons, do actually correct? Or more generally, does enforced correction reform an offender? Bentham, true to his utilitarian upbringing, held that there are punishments which have a tendency to render those who undergo them still more vicious. Punishments which involve incarceration can be extremely dangerous, particularly when applied for slight offences and to juvenile offenders. Prisons, he claimed, instead of being places of reform are schools of crime.[5]

One psychotherapist, Benjamin Karpman, writes that reformatories do not reform. Everything in prison tends to harden criminality into a fixed form of behaviour. (Karpman, vol. 47: 17)

The question is, if rehabilitation is the purpose, are prisons not actually obstacles to it? It begins to look like reform cannot be carried out in prisons. Many minds are now attempting to search for methods that may help society to deal with its erring and recalcitrant members through education and counselling.

The regularly utilized techniques are casework and individual counselling, not occurring in an institutional setting. The aim is integration, reduced recidivism and increased community and vocational adjustment.

Penal reforms are being debated and, wherever possible, implemented. The thinking is changing. But what is true at ground level, is for all to see.

Notes

1 As documented in the chapter on the Universal Declaration of Human Rights in Ian Brownlie, ed. *Basic Documents on Human Rights*. Oxford: Clarendon Press 1971: 106–107.

2 All references to the excerpts from *Manusmrti* are from P. V. Kane, trans. *The History of Dharmasashtra* vol. 5. Poona: Poona Press 1977.

3 The first four chapters deal with the subject at great length.

4 Mahatma Gandhi. *To the Hindus and Muslims*, as reproduced in the Revised New Edition of *The Collected Works of Mahatma Gandhi*, vol. 25, Ahmadabad: Navjivan Trust 1963: 349. Gandhi gave this speech in Karachi in 1942.

5 Jeremy Bentham. *Principles of Penal Law*. See *The Works of Jeremy Bentham*, vol. 1, John Bowring, ed. Edinburgh: William Tait 1983: 383. Also see Bentham's *Introduction to Principles of Morals and Legislation*, Wilfrid Harrison ed. Oxford: Basil Blackwell 1948: Chapter 13 where Bentham defines crime as doing wilfully that which law forbids.

References

Benn, S. I. 1958. 'An Approach to the Problems of Punishment', in *Philosophy*, Vol. 33: 325.

Ewing, A. C. 1929. *The Morality of Punishment*, London: Kegan, Paul, Trench, Trubner & Co. Ltd.

Flew, Anthony. 1954. 'The Justification of Punishment' in *Philosophy*, Vol. 29: 291–307

Foucault, Michael. 1977. *Discipline and Punish: The Birth of the Prison*, Alan Sheridan trans. Middlesex, England : Penguin Books.

Hart, H. L. A. 1959–1960. 'Prolegomenon to The Principles of Punishment', in *Proceedings of the Aristotelian Society*, Vol. 60: 160.

Kant, Immanuel. 1991. *The Metaphysics of Morals*, M.J. Gregor, trans. Cambridge; Cambridge University Press.

Karpman, Benjamin. 'Criminal Psychodynamics', in *Journal of Criminal Law, Criminology and Police Science*, Vol. 47: 17.

Mabbot, J. D. 1939. 'Punishment', in *Mind* 48 (190): 152–167.

Chapter 15

RIGHTS OF THE 'MAD' IN MENTAL HEALTH SCIENCES

Ranjita Biswas and Anup Dhar

aapnara shudhu monke bandhte jaanen, monke bujhte paren na
(all you psychiatrists know is how to *rein in* minds;
you don't *understand* the mind)

The above is a statement made by a 'patient' in a psychiatric hospital. The 'patient', whom we cannot name due to a certain code of confidentiality, had been under a long period of treatment in the same psychiatric hospital. Every time the 'patient' was called for an interview with the psychiatrist, he came with a small notebook. The notebook contained pages of 'incoherent' ramblings from which he would try to read out excerpts (*only* excerpts) for us. Each time the 'patient' made a demonstration of his 'psychosis' in an *explicit* manner, the number and dose of medicines increased. In the subsequent sessions the 'patient' appeared more groggy and slurred. But every time the 'patient' looked capable of continuing his (broken) dialogue with the psychiatrist ... continue the dialogue in the hope of establishing his sanity. Until, finally, somewhat in exasperation the 'patient' made the above statement.

What would the psychiatrist do? How would s/he respond to the charge? The doctor-patient relation (here the relation between the 'psychiatrist' and the 'mentally ill' or the more fashionable 'mentally challenged') has been an area of intense debate. The doctor has been described as the *expert,* godlike or godsend, who bestows health or life. The patient is said to be a *layperson,* who entrusts faith, belief and the authority in the doctor to make decisions and judgments on his/her behalf.

It is the patient's right to expect reasonable skill and care from the doctor in an effort to give relief. This entails unconditional attention to the patient's welfare as well as judicious use of the doctor's knowledge and expertise.

The patient is also entitled to all information pertaining to the illness, its nature, course, prognosis, treatment undertaken, its consequences and hazards, and he also reserves the right to refuse treatment at any point of time. Assuming the doctor to be the expert, the autonomy of the patient is just as important.

The doctor is bound by the Hippocratic Oath and not only bears the moral responsibility to do no harm but also to provide health benefits to the patient. The medical profession itself is said to be self regulatory, bound by a code of medical ethics that defines the duties of the doctor towards the patient, duties that bear an intimate relation to the patient's rights and expectations. In this respect, medical ethics is not merely a moral parameter; it is also a legally sanctioned code of conduct. Medical ethics, as they are commonly understood, could be derived from two different understandings of the doctor-patient relationship (Kaplan, Sadock and Grebb, 1994: 1189–90):

1. Medical paternalism
2. Autonomy theory

Medical paternalism is the traditional model for the physician-patient relationship, in which the doctor is supposed to treat the patient as a caring parent would treat a young child. The physician is presumed to know what is best for the patient just as a parent would for the child and has no obligation to explain each decision or to ask permission to perform actions that are done to benefit the patient. The physician is presumed to have knowledge that the patient may be almost incapable of understanding or, in the physician's judgment, is better off not knowing. On the other hand the autonomy theory conceives the relationship between the doctor and the adult patient as that between two responsible persons – responsible for their own and separate selves. A normal patient is presumed to have the ability and the right to make rational and responsible life decisions. The patient is autonomous (self-governing) and has the right to self-determination that must be respected, even if the best-intended decisions are thought to be against the patient's best interests. But the autonomy theory also holds that paternalistic treatment may be justified when those persons lack the capacity to be autonomous – for example, children, profoundly retarded persons and sometimes persons branded psychotic.

Because of the unique nature of the disorders suffered by the mentally ill, the principles of beneficence and autonomy may be interpreted in many conflicting ways, giving rise to conflicts on the value of and belief in the most appropriate care[1]. While many proponents of informed consent feel this is a moral condition underscoring all doctor-patient relationships, it obviously poses significant problems when applied to the mentally ill. The notion of consent is a much debated virtue when it concerns the mentally ill, who could also be considered purportedly irrational, sub-human, a theme that keeps recurring in all areas of their lives and not just in their treatment. The basic question is thought to be whether a 'mentally ill' person is capable of giving an informed consent, given the state of impaired reasoning and suspended ability to make rational choices.

Critics of the school of informed consent argue that mentally ill patients are not always capable of giving informed consent for the appropriate mode of treatment. They maintain that making the informed consent a right by statute, while desirable in an ethical sense, would only hinder the ability of patients to receive the treatment they need. Many psychiatrists argue strongly for compulsive treatment on the grounds that a patient's right to treatment necessitates a reciprocal obligation by psychiatrists to provide the most effective and humane treatment possible, even against the patient's expressed wishes. They argue that the psychiatrist is in a much better position than either the patient or the courts to assess the treatment needs and decide what is best for a particular patient. Furthermore, they contend that the excessive legal regulation of treatment procedures clearly subordinates the treatment of mental illness to 'a never-ending series of adversarial confrontations' between patient and doctor. This intrusion of the legal system into therapy was seen as unnecessary and causing cracks in the therapeutic relationship. Another dimension to the issue of consent is whether an involuntarily confined person (a number of psychiatric 'cases' need institutional treatment at some time or other, during the course of their illness), whose overriding concern is to leave the institution, can give 'free and voluntary' consent to treatment. In most cases, the subtle and not so subtle pressures of the attending psychiatrists, given their virtue of knowing what is 'wrong' with the patients and what is 'right' for them, the family and/or the community, given their overtly altruistic concerns, render the 'consent' less voluntary — and in some cases involuntary. This is particularly important if a patient is led to believe that his or her release is contingent upon cooperation with treatment which in most cases boils down to complying with the orders without questioning and therefore making a show of 'good behaviour'. 'Parole' is a system, which allows patients, who are well after a period of institutional treatment, to go home for a short visit. Their behaviour during this short stay at home then becomes the basis for further discharge plans. The question that often arises in this context: is involuntary confinement a way to protect individuals from the potential consequences of their illness, or is it a form of social control?

It appears from such arguments that the basic conditions for informed consent — adequate access to information, ability to receive, understand and interpret information, freedom from both overt and covert coercion in making and executing decisions (say, in giving consent) — perhaps do not apply to those individuals designated 'mentally ill'. One line of contention that could follow from this: the psychiatric institution is the best refuge for the mentally ill and the psychiatrist is the best arbiter of what is good and what is bad for the patient. The other related line of contention could be that if these people are thought to be incapable of informed consent, if they are thought to be incapable of making 'rational' and 'autonomous' choices, if they lack in capabilities, can we make an argument at all for the 'rights of the mentally ill'? While one could make an argument for the rights of all 'sane' individuals, of all 'conscious', rational, choosing subjects, of all 'normal' minds, one could not make an argument for the rights of the 'insane', the 'mad', the 'non-conscious', the 'abnormal' among minds. The argument for the rights of the 'mad human' (the *mad* human is perhaps less than human) appears furthermore thin in the case of the 'mad woman'. It is thinner still in the case of the 'mad non-white woman', the 'woman' and the 'colonial' being further repositories of unreason, unreason understood as madness. The somewhat converse argument could be that this distinction (a distinction, or difference, that borders on a certain dualism) between the normal, ordered mind and the abnormal, deranged mind flows out of a certain hegemony of Reason over the others of reason which, in turn, flows perhaps from our allegiance to Aristotle's 'laws of thought' or from our belief in 'classical two-valued logic'.

From the rather simple question of 'institutional access' – access of the 'mentally ill' to cure-care (which in actuality is a question of health related infrastructures, say, the number of beds, the number of medical and paramedical staff per patient, etc.) – from the question of the humane treatment of the 'mentally ill' (which in actuality is a question of not the quantity but the *quality* of health care available) we move over to the question of epistemology, to a certain violence of knowing and the ethics of knowing. This brings us to the question of the relation of reason to unreason; the pathologization of unreason *vis a vis* Cartesian Reason; the re-writing of unreason as madness would therefore come up for discussion in this paper. We would have to ask whether reason's relation to unreason takes off first from a particular knowledge of the mind or the knowledge of the mind in general? Does it then find itself refracted into a certain knowledge of the normal mind, and thereafter into a knowledge of the abnormal mind, the abnormal mind being the mind of unreason, or, for that matter, of the mind of madness, it being very nearly no mind at all? Is it then also a question of the mind knowing the no-mind, the non-mind? Is it then a question of the reason knowing unreason, science knowing madness? Is it then also a question of the Western science knowing savage unreason, male reason knowing woman's madness? Does the knowledge of unreason, unreason understood as madness, find itself refracted further into a knowledge of the colonial woman's madness or, for that matter, into a certain knowledge of the mad colonial woman, the 'colonial' and the 'woman' being further repositories of unreason?

The paper would thus have to contend with the following moments:

the mind
the normal mind (or the mind of reason)
the abnormal mind
the mind of unreason
the mind of madness where unreason is understood as madness
the no-mind (or non-mind), where the mind of madness is considered nearly no mind at all
knowledge of the no-mind, knowledge of the mad colonial woman by Western reason and science

We thus find the world of mental health science breaking down into two:

mind/non-mind
normal mind/abnormal mind
(white male) reason/(native colonial woman's) unreason
sanity/madness
order/breakdown
etc.,

Actually, it never really is two but *one* which actually is the logic of the One and the Same. This is because unreason, or for that matter, unreason understood as madness, is not another, but is simply the negative, the dark, the derogatory, the lacking underside of Reason. This perhaps follows from the modern[2] forms of thought where the world is divided into two clear divisions: 'p' (here, Reason) and '~p' (here, unreason/madness), where 'p' is valued and the other (~p) is devalued (Irigaray, 1985a, 1985b; Plumwood, 1993; Moitra, 2002). Thus '~p' is interpreted as the universe without 'p'. '~p' then cannot be independent or positively identified but is entirely dependent on 'p' for its specification. This way of defining '~p' has several detrimental consequences (Plumwood, 1993):

(a) '~p' becomes the *background* at times
(b) '~p' becomes the *dependent other* at times
(c) '~p' is *homogenized* at times
(d) at times there is a *radical exclusion* of '~p' (Moitra, 2002: 66 – italics mine)

> In such a system of thought, difference [between reason and unreason] is always understood in hierarchical terms, the distinction between difference and discrimination is overlooked. … To emphasize the difference between a value-neutral difference and a value-loaded difference it would be useful to respectively use the terms 'dichotomy' and 'dualism'. When two domains [reason and unreason] are attributed contrasting values [Reason and madness] then as a corollary there is a difference in dispensation. The merging of a logical distinction with an ethical distinction is caused by the play of power … Power inferiorizes the 'other'. … 'A dualism then is more than a relation of dichotomy, difference or non-identity, and more than a simple hierarchical relationship'. Dualism is a kind of rational practice … dualism employs the concept of difference or dichotomy in a way that deepens discrimination, it also deepens the power over power relation … In dualistic practice the other [here, unreason] is the complementary [~p], the underside of the Top or the margin of the Centre. As a result, the other is defined in relation to the master as a lack, a negativity.[3] (Moitra, 2002: 73)

The relation of reason to unreason, the hegemonic understanding of reason and the supplementary understanding of unreason as only and nothing but madness has been put to severe criticism by the anti-psychiatrists (Laing, Szasz), by the post-structuralist French philosophers (Lacan, Foucault, Deleuze, Derrida) and by the feminist philosophers (Irigaray, Cixous, Grosz).

Critiques of the 'Mainstream' Psychiatry

This section tries to make sense of the theoretical critiques that have come up against 'mainstream' psychiatry (which are in fact critiques against hegemonic Reason both at the level of institutional operations as well as epistemology). The anti-psychiatry movement was an anti-authoritarian, even romantic attack on psychiatry's use of psychiatric diagnosis, its use of psychotherapeutic drugs and electroconvulsive therapy (ECT) for treatment and cure and its reliance on involuntary hospitalization – hospitalization not by the will of the patient, not as a contractual arrangement between doctor and patient or between the 'service provider' and the 'client', but as an operation considered necessary by others, say, the doctor and the relatives/friends of the patient.

Thomas Szasz, through an exposition of mental illness as a myth, helped precipitate a crisis in the field of dominant biomedical, institutional psychiatry. His critiques of diagnosis and therapy make polemical use of historical instances – for example, the presumed similarity between labelling a person 'witch' in the

Renaissance and labelling a person 'insane' in the present century. In the 1960's, existentialist themes were taken up by R. D. Laing to mount a critique on the organized psychiatry. Laing gave madness a 'ringing endorsement' and described schizophrenia as a meaningful response to family and social relations. In Laing's view, mental illnesses were existential predicaments often characterized by insights and perceptual realms unavailable to those judged 'sane': the 'mad' are inarticulate *poets*; psychiatrists are articulate know-nothing. For Laing, mad persons are victims of a corrupt upbringing: 'Behaviour that gets labelled schizophrenic is a *special strategy that a person invented in order to live in an unlivable situation*'.

> What's wrong is not 'in the patient,' but in his family and society. The problem is also in the psychiatrist who diagnoses and treats the patient, thereby increasing his or her confusion and self-doubt. If guided with kindness and understanding the schizophrenic experience could become a transcendental journey of death and rebirth toward a new, more positive meaning in life: 'Madness need not be all breakdown. It may also be breakthrough …' (Breggin, 1991: 37)

Michel Foucault (1988) through his work on the 'ship of fools', 'the great confinement', the Salpetriere under Pinel, or the York Retreat under the Tukes,[4] sees psychiatric practice as linked with a whole range of institutions: economic, social, and political. He tries to grasp with greater certainty, through a 'science as dubious as psychiatry', the interweaving of the effects of power and knowledge. In the history of psychiatry Foucault reads the history of how 'silence was imposed on madness', how madness was interned, made into an object of knowledge and of the gaze, the eye that governs. He also shows, how the exclusion and the internment of madness found a sort of structural niche prepared for it by the history of another exclusion – the exclusion of leprosy.[5] Foucault (1988) moves from the 'free trade' of the Middle Ages to the 'determinations' of the 'classical age' – a logos that permitted purportedly a dialogue between reason and madness, that permitted their free exchange up to a point (a point Foucault calls the Decision) where the dialogue was broken off, where reason and madness were divided into two soliloquies, where madness was 'dismissed, excluded, and ostracized from the circle of philosophical dignity … ordered away from the bench as soon as summoned to it by Descartes … this last tribunal of the Cogito'.

Feminists, too, have contributed to the critique of the mainstream psychiatry. Some have emphasised the disruptive dimension and the defiant note of dissent inherent in women's multiple expressions of unreason/ madness. Others have interpreted this as the subversion of the linear logic of male rationality. Transposing the hysteric's malady to the realm of politics Grosz emphasizes:

> ... hers is a mode of defiance of patriarchy, not the site of ... frustration. In this sense, the hysteric is a *proto-feminist*, or at least an isolated individual who, if she had access to the experiences of other women, may locate the problem in cultural explanations of femininity rather in femininity itself. The hysteric's defiance through excess, through overcompliance, is a parody of the expected. (Grosz, 1989: 135)

Elaine Showalter emphasizes the constitutive element in the hysteric's stance by suggesting that an expression of unreason/madness can also be read as a failed rebellion, as a symbol of the desperate communication of the powerless. Back home Jayasree Kalathil warns us that romanticising women's madness as dissent could well undermine her pain and suffering and serve to strengthen binaries of man-woman, reason-unreason, mind-body.

The spirit of the above critiques of psychiatry – a spirit that at the same time is a spirit, a character, a will, an ethical binder and a specter – haunts perpetually the institution of psychiatry. The critiques started off by positing the pertinent question: is there any such natural object as madness at all? But it also stretched the question to adopt the constructivist logic and establish madness as a mere construction, a sociolinguistic phenomenon. Most of the arguments within schools of anti-psychiatry were founded on the assumption that illnesses were simply myths dreamed up by experts to control the non-conformists. Processes of 'knowing' and 'labelling' (which are usually one-way causal processes) practised in dominant psychiatry, no doubt, offer little choice or agency to those labelled mad and culminate in a violent reduction of their experiences to clinical syndromes. Schools of critiques of psychiatry, on the other hand, while stressing the culturally constructed nature of discourses on madness, read and impute too much agency in the corporeal manifestations of the hysteric. But critical narratives emphasizing the social and linguistic dimension of mental disorder could well overlook the pain and suffering of persons deemed mad. Mental health professionals and care-givers living in close proximity with those diagnosed mentally ill have criticised the rather naïve celebration of insanity as dissent. They express quite understandably a certain disdain for those who glorify, romanticize and almost sanctify pathological states.

The biology vs. society, nature vs. culture and illness vs. myth logic remains central to the most debates surrounding the origin, evolution and phenomenology of mental illness. Perhaps the point would be to move beyond these binaries in order to make sense of how specific clusters of 'pathological' conduct become intelligible as symbols of historical rupture and social struggle. This is not to deny the role of physiological and intra-psychic processes in distressing/pathological experiences. Locating mental illness within the realm of history, culture and politics would perhaps show up the multi-dimensional relationship between knowledge, structural oppression and the phenomenological being. (Fee, 2000: 9)

Perhaps the time is ripe now to occupy a space that could be named, for the sake of discussion, *(post)psychiatry*. This naming would not serve to define or give concrete form and content to the (post)psychiatry. The 'post' of this psychiatry would indicate sequentiality as much as a going beyond to another goal, to a conceptual beyond. Anti-psychiatrists have in their own way somewhat unsettled our firm belief in the concepts and practices of psychiatry. Post-modern philosophers, on the other hand, have hinted at the limits of modernism – at thinking the world in terms of binaries, impenetrable hierarchical doubles: reason/madness, normal/pathological, health/disease, doctor/patient and analyst/analysed. Psychiatry can take either of the two directions from here. It can erase all dissidence by embarking on a path of rigorous research, infiltrating every hitherto unknown corner of the chromosomes, untying all the knots of every receptor in the brain and finally mapping and reducing all the complexities of thought, behaviour and emotion to one universal, to one readily available and easily modifiable 'master molecule'. Or else psychiatry could abandon the race to certainty and truth. Uncertainty and half-truths could well become its constitutive features. Perhaps psychiatry would do well to work softly towards an imagination that is beyond both the present day psychiatry (dominated by the biomedical) and the anti-psychiatry – beyond both an obstinate holding on to the citadel of the biomedical and a simple dismembering of it. Radical Psychology, Critical Psychiatry and the Material-Discursive-Intrapsychic Approach are perhaps modest beginnings in that direction. But for that to begin we need to shed our obstinate and near arrogant belief in our sciences, in the Truth of our sciences, a belief that sometimes assumes fundamentalist proportions.

Rights as Democratic Sureties

Amita Dhanda discusses madness, lunacy, mental illness and mental disorder – this 'progressive' array of terms – as representing a trajectory of subtle ideological differences and also an exercise in de-stigmatisation. According to Dhanda, the first two terms, 'madness' and 'lunacy', designate issues related to ethico-legal and psycho-social infringements, while the notion of mental illness stresses bio-medical aetiologies. In contrast to these Dhanda advocates the use of the term 'mental disorder'. For her, the term represents the interests of the insane the best;

the concept of disorder, she argues, underscores both the bio-medical and ethico-psycho-social underpinnings of expressions of unreason and serves to secure a representation of whom/what in the eyes of the legal system and the rights discourse (Dhanda, 2000: 22). Here it would not be out of place to note that a different rendition of 'disorder' could perhaps be achieved through the use of the terms 'disease' or 'distress'; both of these terms represent nor the abnormality (i.e., the deviation from the norm/normal), nor the pathology, but, in turn, the subjective pain and suffering of the multiple expressions of unreason.

Dhanda (2000) shows how and why the question of the rights of the mentally ill became a necessity: misconceptions about mental illness in the society at large, stigmatisation and discrimination of people suffering from mental disease/distress often caused a denial of their civil, political, economic, social and cultural rights as well as impede their access to care and integration into society. The fact that mental disorders can affect a person's ability to defend his or her own rights and interests further aggravates the situation. The legal framework is said to have manifold functions. On one hand, it protects society from the more dangerous/harmful manifestations of mental disorder, on the other hand, it seeks to protect persons with mental illness from exploitation and decides the extent to which mental disorder negates legal capacity. (Dhanda, 2000: 20) The rights of the mentally ill have been the subject of discussion and public policy at different levels. International recognition of the basic human rights for persons with mental illness came as late as 1991 with the adoption of the *Principles for the Protection of Persons with Mental Illness and for the Improvement of Mental Health Care* by the General Assembly of the United Nations.

The most striking mental health care initiatives of the last two decades in our country have been the Mental Health Act (1987) and the National Mental Health Program (1982). The Mental Health Act is a major legislation in the field of mental health and it became operational in 1994 in all Indian states. This act replaces the Indian Lunacy Act of 1912. It lays down regulations regarding the admission and discharge of patients, about judicial inquisition of the alleged mentally ill, about rights in matters of property and contracts, including marriage and its legal dissolution.

The National Mental Health Program in India is based on the concept of community psychiatry. It sought to redefine the concept of psychiatric treatment by giving up custodial care and the method of segregating patients from the community. Instead, it stressed the de-institutionalisation and de-centralization It promotes community participation in the development of mental health services. The National Mental Health Programme vows to ensure easy availability and accessibility of minimum mental health care through a diffusion of mental health skills to the periphery of the Health Service System and through the equitable and balanced distribution of resources.

The Mental Health Act and the National Mental Health Program have been described as a definite and positive contribution in the field of mental health. It is said to have served to de-mystify mental illness, and it also emphasizes the protection of the interests of patients and a promotion of their well being through a judicial safeguard of their rights. Concretisation of the rights rhetoric in the form of health policies and legislations has been shown to be bifocal. It promotes the care and treatment rights of the mentally ill as well as facilitates their community living.

Community psychiatry[6] provided a way to address the problems produced by the de-institutionalisation by ensuring comprehensive treatment of the severely ill in the community at large – from hospitalisation, case management and crisis intervention to day treatment and supportive living arrangements.

There was a time when mental asylums were built outside the cities and functioned primarily to protect the community and not to treat the insane. Today we seem to have come a full circle when we talk of setting up community mental health centres to cater to the needs of such people. In India we find coexisting all three forms of psychiatric service: mental hospitals, general hospital psychiatric units and the community mental health program. The latest phase in the development of mental health services in India – the community care approach and the involvement of the primary health care physicians – has seen the birth of the National Mental Health Program. From custodial care to community care new concepts and knowledge has emerged in the mental health field. This new knowledge has also influenced the treatment methodology. But all such concepts have revolved around the biomedical model. The national mental health program for instance has been seen as concentrating only on the diagnosis and care of the chronic and the severe mental disorders. These are described as the 'difficult cases', creating problems in management in the community milieu and largely treated by giving moderate to heavy doses of psychiatric drugs. The illnesses prioritised by the program easily fit into the bio-medical model and can be easily identified and brought under control by the primary health care staff through drug dispensing. This way the state can also maintain its surveillance over the aberrant behaviour of the 'mad' with the community now a willing partner. Though the present day mental health program professes to be different, it overlooks the community concepts of mind, the local concerns and the local practices while framing a new community care and support system. The National Mental Health Program has been criticized as a policy that remains constrained by the existing structure of the health delivery system, occupying only a peripheral position in the same. It retains all the paraphernalia as well as the loopholes of the public health sector, except that it focuses on more stringent case identification and foolproof administration. Moreover, the program serves to shift the state's responsibility for care of the mentally ill to the communities, thereby enhancing the disinvestments process that is holding sway over the country's health policies. (Davar 1999, 242–249)

Rights vs. Ethics

...ethics cannot be put into words...

Wittgenstein, 1961: 6.421

In spite of the four 'revolutions' in the history of mental health science, one can never ignore the question of the obvious coercion of the 'normal' (be it the coercion of the more distant and more detached mental health professional or the coercion of the more involved community' over the 'mad'. Whether the 'mad' are treated in the mental health institution or in the community, one will have to look at the hegemony of Reason (p) over unreason (non-p/lacking p) – at the very reduction of unreason to madness – to its being pathological by virtue of its being unreason, i.e. by virtue of its being not-reason (non-p). There can perhaps be no question of the rights of the 'mad' without the concomitant question of an ethical relation (notwithstanding the impossibility that haunts any such relation) of reason/science/doctor to unreason/madness/patient. An ethical relation between doctor and patient is not just a question of a humane or sensitive handling of the patient by the doctor. It is also a question of the presuppositions of the conceptual apparatus that drives the mental health professional to engage with the patient in the way he or she engages now. In other words, it is a question on the needs to look at the structures of knowledge/reasoning that inform the response of the 'courier of scientific knowledge' (Achuthan, 2004) in the mental health clinic. An ethical relation in the mental health clinic thus relates to the ethics of knowing as well; it relates to the way one knows, what one knows, how one knows, what results from such knowing. Is there a certain objectification of the known in the process of knowing? Is the process in one way or another somewhat reductionist? Does the knower homogenise the known in the process? Does knowing in any way reduce the known to silence; is there a certain exclusion – a *foreclosure*?

The other, more fundamental problem regarding any knowledge/science discourse concerning 'madness', or for that matter, concerning any history of madness, is that the whole field is fraught with a few nearly insurmountable epistemological difficulties: Is there any witnessing to madness? Who can witness or rather who can lay claim to witnessing madness, to witnessing the singular and irreducible alterity of *the* (singular) Other? The very same difficulties would perhaps haunt the possibility of any knowledge of the mind. Who knows? Who knows whom? How do we know? Do we know through our minds? How then does one mind know another? What are the bases of our claims to knowledge? Are our claims tied in one way or the other to history/culture? Here we are 'echoing and engaging with Kant's "what can I know?" and his probing of the limits of reason and reason as a limit' (Didur and Heffernan, 2003: 2).

Foucault writes a history of unreason (as well as reason). He shows through his history (or in other words, his story) how the history of unreason (as well as reason) is in reality the history of the hegemony of Reason over unreason. Foucault writes a *history of knowing* – history of reason knowing unreason (Davidson names Foucault's project 'historical epistemology'). Foucault shows how in the process of knowing there is a certain play of power, how a history of knowing is in reality a history of the exclusion of unreason and the exclusion of madness from thought itself. Foucault wants therefore to re-write a history of unreason-madness itself, before being captured 'and paralysed in the nets of classical reason' (Foucault, 1988). He wants unreason/madness to be the subject of his book in every sense of the word: its theme and its first-person narrator, its author, madness speaking about itself – madness speaking on the basis of its own experience and under its own authority, not from within the language of reason. Foucault names his project as 'archaeology of silence'.

Derrida [1978] points at the very impossibility of such a project: '[I]s there a history of silence? [I]s not archaeology, even of silence, a logic, that is, an organized language, a project, an order, a syntax, a work?' Derrida asks: Do we not access madness with the language of the very reason we denounce? Does not our verdict unceasingly reiterate the crime?

Foucault, of course, is not unaware of the near unconscious complicity with the language of reason that haunts his project of accessing madness before the *Decision.* Then again, Foucault pursues a project that is impossible. It is as an ethico-politics of the (im)possible – WHERE ethics IS AN 'experience of the impossible'. Otherwise we would only be continuing the Cartesian exclusion of the 'mad' by Reason.

Derrida, instead, stresses the *moment* of unreason that inheres inalienably in reason – unreason as a possible menace at the very heart of the intelligible. Derrida prefers the term 'dissension' instead of 'Decision' as the single act that separates reason and madness. Dissension underlines 'a self-dividing action, a cleavage and torment interior to meaning *in general*, a division within the very act … *dissension* is internal. The exterior (is) the interior …' (Derrida, 1978).

Derrida (1978), while never subscribing to the Foucauldian notion of the Decision, reads in the history of mental health science[7] the history of a return (Derrida, 1994) to the self-dividing action, to the cleavage and torment interior to the meaning in general, which, in other words, is also the symptomatic return of the repressed.

Descartes is alleged by Foucault (1988) to have executed the 'summary expulsion of the possibility of madness from thought itself' in the first of the *Meditations*, which, in other words, is a turning away of the Cogito from madness.

Hence the possibility of a *return* – a return of Freud, a return to 'madness' at the level of its language. For Freud, too, madness would be unreason, but this time one would resume a dialogue with unreason and as if lift the Cartesian interdiction. And lift it as if to reopen for a moment a dialogue that was broken off once in the classical age and that would be broken off again by the language of psychological positivism. Psychology breaks off from madness, from a certain truth of unreason. Psychoanalysis breaks off from psychology by speaking with the unreason that speaks within madness. But that, too, is possible only for a moment, operating as if only a hinge (Derrida, 1994) in this nearly unsuspended history of suspended dialogue.

Freud returns to the madness, to unreason (Derrida, 1994). Lacan (1977a, 1977b) and Derrida (1978, 1987, 1994), albeit contradictory, return to Freud.

This return of a certain Freud or of a certain strain (even if marginal) of psychoanalysis to unreason at the level of language; this setting up of a dialogue with unreason, a certain standing face to face (face to face not in the Hegelian but in the Levinasian sense) with unreason is fundamental to any ethical relation, to any relation based on responsibility[8] in the mental health clinic. We explore the possibilities inhering in such a possible return to unreason in the last section of this paper – the section that brings up and discusses the clinical contours of Lacanian psychoanalysis. We, along with Lacan, try to delineate in that section the contours of an ethical engagement with unreason – an engagement that is also an engagement with the phenomenology of mental disease/distress – an engagement that tries at the same time to be epistemologically less violent.

The question that further haunts this work of writing: how could we then set up a dialogue with unreason and yet not be Hegelian? Do we need, on the one hand, a different structural metaphor of/for the mind, if we need metaphors at all to represent the mind in all its complexities, considering all the while the question of the unconscious? Do we need, on the other hand, a different understanding of epistemological encounters? In fact, we do not need encounters any more. In our search for a different structure of mind and simultaneously a different structure of knowledge we come across Freud's notion of the mystic writing pad. Freud, through this notion, works on and around the brink of a radically different philosophy of mind. 'If there were only perception, pure permeability to breaching, there would be no breaches. We would be written, but nothing would be recorded; no writing would be produced, retained, repeated as legibility. But pure perception does not exist: we are written only as we write, by the legacy within us which always already keeps watch over perception, be it internal or external. The "subject" of writing does not exist if we mean by that some sovereign solitude of the author. The subject of writing is a *system* of relations between strata: the Mystic Pad, the psyche, society, the world. Within that scene, on that stage, the punctual simplicity of the classical subject is not to be found' (Derrida, 1978).

In this paper, we have thus moved from the question of the rights of the mentally ill/challenged to the question of an ethical relation with unreason, to a certain ethics of knowing, a knowing that is at the same time less violent.

W(h)ither then, Epistemology?

We need therefore a foray into the (im)possibilities of limits of knowing – a critique, on the one hand, of classical epistemology, a breakdown of the strictly dichotomous understanding of cognitive rationality and sociality, whereby the context of discovery is seen to bleed into the context of justification and, on the other, of the full-blown relativism of 'anything goes'. In their efforts to climb the greased pole, leading to a tolerable yet meaningful doctrine of objectivity, feminist philosophers or philosopher feminists have alternatively held on to the both ends of the dichotomy of radical constructionism and spontaneous feminist empiricism. Others, while working through such binarisms, have looked for standpoint theories, for feminist contextual empiricism, for partial perspectives[9] or epistemologies of location, critical positioning and situating. Instead of a view from above or nowhere, they argue for a view from the perspective of a complex and contradictory embodiment. Instead of disembodied vision, instead of clear distinct scientific truths about the 'mad colonial woman' we *re-turn,* therefore, to a more robust conception of the epistemological subject, to a certain 'speaking with' (Moitra, 2002) rather than a 'speaking to' the analysand, and also to a certain splitting of the senses, a (con)fusion of (limited) voice, (partial) sight, (empathetic) hearing and (responsible) touch.

Splitting as the condition of another epistemology – an *other* epistemology? Splitting as the companion of the Cartesian Cogito?

Freud, the master and the analyst, looks for the real meaning in woman's madness. Bose (1980) looks for the scientific meaning behind the colonial woman's madness. Irigaray and Grosz (1989) look for the disruptive meaning in hysteria-anorexia. Perhaps it is time now to look instead for a possible *re*-turn of madness in the production of meaning, which in other words, is a possible *re*-turn of the multiple others: unreason as the other, woman as the other and coloniality as the other within the white masculine western Reason.

The return of the multiple *others* in the white masculine western Reason would perhaps necessitate a certain questioning of dualisms – e.g., reason/unreason, mind/body, sane/mad, normal/abnormal – dualisms that, in turn, give way to the hegemonic monism of the thinking/Reason over its multiple others (being, body, unreason).

From the Ethics of the Impossible to the Ethics of the Real

In the final section this paper moves from the prevailing ethical ideology to a certain 'ethics of the real' that relates, in turn, with the 'ethic of truths' (Badiou, 2001).

> The prevailing 'ethical ideology' has two 'philosophical poles'. First, a (vaguely Kantian) universalizing pole which, indifferent to the particularity of any given situation, proscribes in any advance any possibility of an organized ... *situated* intervention in the name of collective 'Good': ethics here is grounded in the abstract universality of general 'human' attributes or rights. And second, a (vaguely Levinasian) differential pole, attuned to the irreducible alterity of the Other: ethics here is expressed in an equally abstract respect for mainly cultural differences.
>
> Neither *this* universality nor *this* alterity [Badiou suggests] can be rigorously founded without tacit reference to theology, either way, the [prevailing] ethical ideology conceives of 'man' as a fundamentally passive, fragile and *mortal* entity – as a potential victim to be protected (most often, as a 'marginalized', 'excluded' or 'Third World' victim, to be protected by a dutiful, efficient, and invariably 'Western' benefactor/exploiter.[10]
>
> By contrast, ... [Badiou's] *ethic of* [subjective[11]] *truths* presumes that every individual can be active and 'immortal', is indifferent to established or state-sanctioned differences, operates in the realm of practical division (for or against the event[12]), and situates its affirmation precisely there where the stay of the situation can see only the non-known and the non-obvious. (Badiou, 2001: italics mine)

This journey from the prevailing/hegemonic ethical ideology to Badiou is also a (although not too explicit) journey from classical philosophy to a psychoanalytically informed philosophy. One could ask: why do we need to make this journey from philosophy (epistemology as the encounter with knowledge) to psychoanalysis (analysis as an encounter with unreason, madness and the real or the truth)? Is it because 'psychoanalysis renders visible the constitutive madness of modern philosophy' (Zizek, 1998)? Is it because psychoanalysis brings to the foreground what was foreclosed in the Cartesian theatre? And this is precisely 'what Lacan was doing all the time: reading hysteria or obsessional neurosis as a philosophical "attitude of thought towards reality" (the obsessional compulsion to think because "if I stop thinking, I will cease to exist" as the truth of the Cartesian *cogito ergo sum*) …' (Zizek, 1998: 2).

> … the whole of modern philosophy, from Descartes onward, involves an inherent reference to the threat of madness, and is thus a desperate attempt to draw a clear line that separates the transcendental philosopher from the madman (Descartes: how do I know I'm not hallucinating reality?; Kant: how to delimit metaphysical speculation from Swedenborgian hallucinatory rambling?). (Zizek, 1998: 2)

The question that we wish to ask in this section is: can psychoanalysis set up a meaningful engagement with madness? Or more precisely, can the (Lacanian) analytic setting offer a possible conceptual space to explore questions of 'othering', which flows not from the violence of the mental health institution but also from a certain knowing, as well as explore questions related to the other heading (Derrida, 1992) – the other heading of classical epistemology – the other heading of the classical clinical encounter, *so* that there is an engagement with madness, so that there is no turning away from madness? It is in answer to this question that we try to bring in the somewhat symbolic example of Lacanian psychoanalysis and the notion of the Lacanian Real that resides inalienably within Lacanian psychoanalysis. This is, of course, not to say that we propose to turn every mentally distressed person to Lacanian psychoanalysis. We wish Lacanian psychoanalytic setting (with special reference to the Real and to certain ethics of the real) to be an ethical bind on all clinical settings in the mental health situation. The setting of Lacanian psychoanalysis is therefore used and reiterated to bring up and highlight the idea/ideal of a clinical engagement we wish to imagine: how, while not giving up on an engagement with the irreducible phenomenology of mental disease/distress, one could still think through the possibility of a clinical engagement – how one could still listen to and speak with unreason (Moitra, 2002) – how one could still think of a possible relationship with unreason (and even with madness) that could be ethical not just at the institutional level but even at the level of knowledge/truth production.

In an earlier section we have already discussed Descartes' turning away from unreason and Freud's subsequent return to unreason. In this section we will discuss Lacan's return to Freud. For Lacan '[t]he meaning of a return to Freud is a return to the meaning of Freud'. It is also a return to psychoanalysis as (essentially) an analysis of 'lack', of a certain lack in being and also as the traversing of the lack in being and the lack of analysis – where analysis lacks (the beyond of analysis, the beyond of the pleasure principle to the encounter with the insurmountable discontents in civilisation).

Lacan asks: are we not 'ourselves ... made of the same clay as those we mould'? (Lacan, 1977a) and thus puts into doubt the secure binaries (reason/unreason, mind/body, thought/affect, normal/abnormal) that inform the clinical setting. He adds: psychoanalysis (PA) has nearly nothing to do with 'an emotional re-education of the analysand'. What is psychoanalysis then? PA has nothing to do with confession. It has nearly nothing to do with the rehabilitation of the analysand's disheveled ego in a secure and normative environ. That is the job of either the priest[13] or the American ego-psychologist. PA is all about the unconscious[14] (or maybe more about the Lacanian Real), though Lacan never makes an agency of the unconscious – the unconscious remains as the other discourse. The final authority in the analytic setting thus resides in the analysand's unconscious not in the analyst as some master of knowledge. But the unconscious within the analysand is rejected by the analysands themselves and projected onto the analyst. The analyst must therefore occupy the space of the unconscious in the analytic setting.

It has become a commonplace to say that psychoanalytic free association is marked by the person of the analysand. Where then do we situate the analyst – the person of the analyst? Who analyses? It is not just from the angle of the analysand that Lacan approaches the subject of psychoanalysis. The person of the analyst – the analyst as 'other' – must disappear, if he or she is to stand in for the unconscious of the analysand. He or she must become that abstract Other – radically foreign, strange, *not me* – that speaks inadvertently in the slips and cracks of the analysand's discourse. The Lacanian analyst thus occupies at least three moments in the clinical setting:

1. Initially, the analyst as a person or the person of the analyst occupies the position of the Imaginary other: the analyst is an 'other', an imaginary object (*autre*) for the analysand.
2. The depersonalised analyst occupies thereafter the position of a symbolic other: the analyst is the Other, a symbolic object [*autre*] for the analysand.
3. The analyst finally occupies the position of the cause of the analysand's unconscious formation: the analyst is an object, a Real object [object *a*] for the analysand.

"Certainly, the psychoanalyst directs the treatment. The first principle of this treatment, the one that is spelt out to him before all else, and which he meets throughout his training, to the extent that he becomes utterly imbued with it, is that he must not direct the patient. The direction of conscience, in the sense of the moral guidance that a [Brahmin] might find in it, is radically excluded here. ... The direction of the treatment is something quite different. ... The analyst's discourse ... must be opposed to any will, to master." (Seminar XVII: 79) Just as the analyst must abdicate the role into which he or she is often cast by contemporary psychology and psychiatry – as the master of reality, as the judge of what is real and what is not real – so too must the analyst abdicate the master's discourse in all its forms. For it makes the analyst hard of hearing.

And yet the Lacanian analyst can never be detached or distant. This is because in the Lacanian understanding of the clinical setting the analysand does not really want to change – he or she does not want to get better. If 'symptoms' have developed, it is because a great deal of energy/enjoyment/*jouissance* has become tied up in those symptoms. The patient has a great deal invested in keeping things the way they are, for he or she obtains what Freud referred to as a 'substitute satisfaction' from symptoms, a certain *sinthome*,[15] and cannot be easily induced to give it up. It is as if the patient is secretly committed to *not* rocking his/her boat, as if the patient *enjoys* his or her symptoms.

Hence the analyst cannot rely on some sort of 'will to get better' on the analysand's part, on some genuine desire to change or even a genuine desire for self-knowledge. Analysands have perhaps a more deeply rooted wish not to know what went wrong – a passion not to know. Once analysands are on the verge of realizing exactly what it is they have done or are doing to sabotage their lives, what their deeper motives are, wherein lies their *satisfaction*, they very often resist going any further and flee therapy. It is a certain moving away from the truth.

Thus, the desire to continue therapy, the desire to undergo therapy, the desire in therapy, desire that serve as the motor force of therapy is the analyst's not the analysand's. In the majority of cases the analysand is looking as if for an excuse to leave, to discontinue therapy. Analysands tend to break off therapy when they sense that they are being asked to give up (*sinthome*) something they are not prepared to give up. Thus the analysand's desire to continue therapy *must*, at certain times, wane or disappear altogether – otherwise the analysand's essential conflicts tied up in his or her symptoms are not being affected.

It is the analyst's desire and not their own flagging desire that allows them to continue. Desire finds language in the analyst's, 'I'll see you tomorrow'. Hence, the analyst must maintain a position of desire (not of a desiring being) he or she must act out – must play a part of pure desirousness.

The analyst's desire refers not to the analyst's counter-transferential feelings – his position as desiring subject – but rather to some kind of 'purified desire' – desire or pure desiring as a function, as a role, a part to be played – an enigmatic desire that does not tell the analysand what the analyst wants. It is never the desire of a subject that lights the analysand as object. It is desire disembodied.

The analyst's desire is a desire that emphasizes, through non-verbal interventions, punctuation and scansion in the variable-length session and/or verbal intervention, oracular speech as every manifestation of the unconscious[16]– every unconscious manifestation of the unconscious. And since the 'unconscious is structured like language'[17], analysis looks for the 'purloined letters' of the analysand that determine the lives of the analysand – snatches of the analysand's conversation that surface from their being set aside. Analysands bring up their purloined letters into the analytic setting, and analyst attempts to render them, make them somewhat legible to the analysand, which in other words, is all about uncovering hitherto hidden/ unacknowledged/disavowed determinants of desire.

Psychoanalysis aims not at the intended meaning, not at what analysand means to say but at what he or she actually said: at the letters *per se* of what analysands say and the strange but relevant associations they make with other letters or other somewhat less obvious or obscurely intended meanings. Lacan insists on the apparently nonsensical concatenation of letters – on verbal bridges. Hence: 'stick to the letter of the text'. 'The analyst should rather proceed by attending closely to the logic of the signifier, to those detours and swerves in the discourse of the patient which mark the irruption of unconscious desire.' (Norris, 1987: 115)

Psychoanalysis is about opening up the space of the analysand's desire, setting the analysand's desire in motion. Is then the goal of analysis an opening up, a dialectisation of the analysand's desire and then an attempt to free it from the deadly grip of the Other's desire? That is, retrieving the desire of the analysand from the domain and control of the Other, i.e. making one's own desire *that* desire of the Other – the Other's desire that brought us into being.

In the 1960s Lacan viewed the dialectisation of the subject's desire as an untying of the knots in the analysand's desire, as bringing up to the light of day the manifestations of the subject's unconscious desire. Is psychoanalysis then a thing of giving subjective language to desire that was hitherto trapped in the Other? Does analysis then come to a successful end via the Symbolic? Is the end of the analysis reached through the development of a decided desire or a determined desire: desire that does not allow itself to be swayed or dictated by the Other, a once unconscious desire that is no longer subject to inhibition? Can desire therefore take us where we want to go: beyond the analytic setting, beyond neurosis, hence towards cure? Is not the desire endowed with a utopian edge in this method of analysis?

Desire comes from the Other, and *jouissance* is on the side of the Thing. Later Lacan comes to see that unconscious desire is not the radical, revolutionary force he once believed it to be. Desire is also subservient to the law, language and the Other, however abstract the Other may be. What the Law prohibits, desire seeks. Desire can never free itself of the Other as the Other and the Other's prohibition is responsible for the desire's very being. Desire is inscribed within the Other.

The subject is some*thing* else. The subject is no longer conceptualized as a pure lack that gives rise to desire. The subject, for later Lacan, is that which exists outside the Other.

Outside the Other? Outside language? What is it that exists outside the Other, outside language? This outside is not the Freudian *id* – the seat or locus of the drives before the father's 'no', before language, the law and the prohibition. This outside is produced in and through analysis. Analysis *produces* an outside related to the lost object (object *a*) which produces *jouissance*. Lacan in his later years shifts from identifying the subject with an unconscious desire to identifying the subject with the drive. Analysis aims at the reconstitution of the analysand not in relation to the Other's demands or the Other's desires but in relation to the partial object that brings satisfaction: object *a*.

Lacan's aim in the psychoanalytic setting would now be the separation of the analysand from the Other, from the inhibitions and influences of the concrete others that surround the subject and also from the internalized Other's values and judgements.

In the analytic situation or setting Lacan moves thus:

1. From the Imaginary to the Symbolic and then to the Real[18]. The subject would have an Imaginary, a Symbolic and a Real face, each of which predominates at a certain point in analysis. The aim of the analysis would be to bring the analysand through these different moments to the point where interpretation hits the Real, where the subject as a drive, the subject as Real comes to the fore.
2. From the Other's demand to the Other's desire to the subject as drive[19]. As a demand the subject is stuck in the imaginary register; as a desire the subject is essentially a stance with respect to the symbolic order; as a drive it is a 'subject in the real'.
3. From alienation in the Other to separation from the Other *and* a traversing of the fundamental fantasy.

The three Lacanian moments constitutive of subjectivity can be schematized as three substitutions or substitutional metaphors. In alienation the Other dominates or takes the place of the subject, in separation object *a* as the Other's desire comes to the fore and takes precedence over or subjugates the subject, and in the traversing of fantasy the subject subjectifies the *cause* of his or her existence (the Other's desire: object *a*) and is characterized by a kind of pure desiring without an object: desirousness.

Thus, analysis moves from the Other as demand, to the Other as desire (object *a*) and finally to the Other as *jouissance*.

Does analysis end here? Do we thereby find health, cure and care? Do we find *the* truth?

This last section of the paper started with Kant (categorical imperative) and Levinas (ethics of the impossible) as the two 'philosophical poles' of the prevailing/hegemonic 'ethical ideology'. It had then somewhat parted company with Kant and Levinas (although one can never deny the importance and import of their respective understanding of ethics) and moved over to Badiou and his ethic of (subjective) truths. This it had done to set up an engagement instead with ethics of the real, that this paper wishes to propose as an alternative to the prevailing/hegemonic 'ethical ideology' – a radical ethical imaginary that draws heavily from Lacan and links up rather explicitly Badiou and Lacan; that links up, on the one hand, ethic of truths and, on the other, ethics of the real.

Ethics of the real is an articulation of the ethical question from the point of view of the location of the (sexed/gendered, coloured/raced, exploited/classed) human with respect and in relation to the real [*reel*] – the real as foreclosed, as that which is disavowed doubly in the normal conscious life of psychological status quo. The real, rejected from any stable assignation of place within the symbolic, is what seems empty or void or the 'dark continent' from the perspective of those who represent or dominate/hegemonize the situation. Access to the real is achieved through an essential encounter (Badiou would call this enduring encounter an event – an event that as if tries to escape all structuring normality).

But then, having hit the real, 'in order to "keep going" the subject of truth must resist the temptation to impose an absolute definitive order of truth … Such an imposition would effectively objectify the truth … A truth compiles, step by step, everything that affirms the strict generic universality of all members of the situation. The point is that any such generic affirmation cannot be made"in theory" or *a priori*, as the basis for an established consensus. It can take place only through an "evental [*evenementiel*] break with the status quo [break with the *sinthome* that holds the Borromean knot – a radical repudiation of all merely consensual social norms], a break sparked by an event that eludes classification in the situation … "The" ethic of truth, then, is fully subordinate to the particularity of *a* truth. There can be no "ethics in general", no general principle of *human* rights, for the simple reason that what is *universally* human is always rooted in particular truths …' (Badiou, 2001: xii–xiv).

There is thus no end to analysis, there is no end to our engagement with the real, with truth – one needs to 'keep going' …

Notes

1 A principle that is especially relevant to the ethics of mental health policy is *justice*; justice (as distinguished from *law*) is understood in this context as a fair distribution and fair application of psychiatric services, as well as fairness in procedures of involuntary hospitalization and treatment of people considered dangerous to themselves or to others.

2 'Modernism ... denotes a mindset, a way of thinking. ... The overarching natural conditions for rational thought are commonly held to be the laws of thought ... [that are] fixed and inviolable ... [and have an] universal essence. Aristotle spoke of three laws of thought – they are the law of contradiction, the law of excluded middle and the law of identity. During the enlightenment and the post-Enlightenment modern period these laws were accepted as common heritage, they were preserved and passed down through the generation of thinkers. ... The predominant trend has been to treat Aristotle's discovery that "man is a rational animal" as an indubitable truth. For all men to be rational all men must have the same thought structure, thought must always be guided by reason, which implies being guided by the three laws of thought. ... Postmodern philosophy is ... critical of the"classical law of thought".' (Moitra, 2002: 66–69).

3 'Genevieve Lloyd [Lloyd, G. 'Reason, Science and the Domination of Matter' in *Feminism and Science*, eds Evelyn Fox Keller and Helen E. Longino. Oxford: 1996] suggests that rationality has been conceptualised as the transcendence of what is feminine. ... reason ... has always been developed as a disavowal of what has been taken as characteristic of women. Women are seen as having a lesser presence of reason and a different type of intellectual character – they always think in concrete terms whereas "the man of reason" think in abstract terms'. (Moitra, 2002: 73) Nearly the same argument could be made for the 'native' or the 'colonial'. Hegemonic understandings of Reason see reason as also the transcendence of what is 'native' or what is 'colonial'. Does hegemonic Reason and the hegemony of Reason then evolve out of a certain repression-foreclosure of not just the madness, but also of woman and the colonial? Does 'unreason' then become a convenient trope for the ready cohabitation of the 'mad', the 'colonial' and the 'woman'? Does the projection of 'unreason' on the primitive other, on the 'colonial space/subject' construct in turn the category of the 'na(t)ive (wo)man'? Does the notion of the 'woman of unreason' or the 'naturally mad woman' come to construct coloniality and the colonial stereotypes? Does the image imputed to the 'colonial (wo)man' come to engender western European ideas of madness?

4 According to Foucault, the much trumpeted moral therapy of Pinel or Tuke should be seen not, as customarily, the freeing of the insane from the obscene terrors of whips, chains but rather as the imposition of more subtly terrifying 'mind-forged manacles' of guilt and self-control.

5 Foucault shows how leprosy vanished from the Western world at the end of the Middle Ages while the sanatoria, the structures that housed the lepers, remained. The Ship of Fools, or *Narrenschiff*, appeared as leprosy disappeared. Foucault shows how in the classical age the ship of fools became moored and became a hospital. Madness was thus tamed. Foucault sees the physical disappearance of leprosy and leper houses as just as important as the cultural changes he charts. A space opens up as leprosy vanishes. It is almost as if a permanent space exists in which certain people can be defined and excluded; when leprosy no longer fills this space, madness appears to occupy it. Madness did not exactly replace leprosy, but the shift between the two conditions represented a

move from a concern with diseased bodies to a concern with abnormal behaviour and diseased minds.

6 The official history of psychiatry is said to be a history of revolutions or turning points. Some speak of the removal of chains in the asylum at end of the eighteenth century (by Phillipe Pinel of France, in 1792 in La Bicetre, William Tuke in England and Dorothea Dix in the United States) as the first revolution, the outcome of enlightenment after a period of 'dark ages' when mental illness was thought to be a consequence of sin and witchcraft. The second revolution is said to be the introduction of Freud's psychoanalysis, which offered an alternative to mental institutions. The therapist worked in the community and the patient was a member living in the community. The third was the birth of psychopharmacology in the 1950's. The various pathways in the brain and its neurotransmitters like norepinephrine, serotonin, and dopamine were studied intensively in the 1950's and 60s. This revolution also brought about a corresponding revolution in the standards of diagnosis (DSM-I to DSM-IV). Community psychiatry with its growing emphasis on deinstitutionalisation has been understood as the fourth revolution.

7 A history of mental health science does not necessarily coincide with a history of psychiatry. This research would try to resist the passing off of Western schools of 'mental health science' (Freudian, Skinnerian, Pavlovian, etc.) or colonial traditions of 'healing of the mind' (Ayurvedic, Yoga, Tantric, Shamanic, Folk, etc.) as dead tributaries of a more majestic stream of modern knowledge, Psychiatry. I use the broader term mental health science to designate a vast collection of heterogenous western disciplines concerned with the 'mind', its pathological expressions and the subsequent methods of healing or cure.

8 'In her paper "Righting Wrongs" – delivered at Oxford University as part of the Amnesty International series of lectures "Human Rights and Human Wrongs" – Spivak describes two forms of culture: responsibility based (subaltern) and rights based (Northern), arguing that both need supplementation, one by the other ...' (Didur and Heffernan, 2003: 7)

9 Haraway, D. 1996. 'Situated Knowledges: The Science Question in Feminism and the Privilege of Partial Perspective' in *Feminism and Science* (eds. Evelyn Fox Keller and Helen E. Longino) – Oxford University Press.

10 Badiou 'rejects the almost universally accepted argument that ethics should essentially concern the Other as such (as potential victim of violence or misrecognition) ... Perhaps nothing is more orthodox today than a generalized reverence for the other *qua* other [the other (every other) is indeed *other*, absolutely other: "*Tout autre est tout autre*", the other as alterity] ... the alterity of the other ... Couched most notably in terms of the logic of the *gift*, Derrida's ethical reflections circle obsessively around notions of inaccessibility and secrecy, around that which is beyond [re]presentation or identification, around subjective impossibility, around "madness" and "forgetting".' (Badiou, 2001: xv–xxiv) Badiou tries to provide an 'inspiring, rigorously argued alternative to the tired moralizing truisms of neo-Kantian universalism on the one hand [along with its more American offshoot: liberal analytic jurisprudence] and a more or less tolerant liberal communitarianism on the other'. (Badiou, 2001: xxx)

11 'Access to the realm of truth ... is wholly subjective: it is founded only on the subjects who "bear" its trajectory'. (Badiou, 2001: ix)

12 '... a truth procedure can begin only with some sort of break with the *ordinary situation* in which it takes place – what [Badiou calls] an *event*. An event has no objective or

verifiable content. Its "happening" cannot be proved, only affirmed and proclaimed'. (Badiou, 2001: ix)

13 Lacanian psychoanalytic therapy cannot be characterized as a contract, and the widespread use of the term 'client' to qualify patients seems misguided in a Lacanian setting. To be a client suggests that one is a consumer and that one knows exactly what one is asking for and what one will receive – something which is certainly not true of any kind of Lacanian therapy. The notion of contract suggests that the parties enter into an agreement at least as apparent equals. But in Lacanian therapy the analyst sidesteps the patient's demands, frustrates them and ultimately tries to direct the patient to something he or she never asked for. While 'client' may be preferable in certain respects to 'patient', which tends to pathologize or stigmatize the person in therapy, Lacan proposes a different term: *analysand.* The *–and* ending of analys*and* is a gerund form (like *–ing* at the end of a word in English), which implies that it is the person (of the analysand) in therapy who does the work of analyzing, not the analyst.

14 Lacan emphasized the evident lack of continuity in the conscious psychic life. His psychoanalysis concerns itself with the gaps, splits, ruptures that result from the apparent discontinuity because these gaps constitute a system that is entirely different from that of consciousness: the unconscious. Lacan repeatedly posits the importance of Freud's decentering of the Cartesian subject of consciousness *vis a vis* the retention of the subject in the American ego psychology. The existential subject of autonomous individuality and free choice is also shown to be *constructed* libidinally, socially and linguistically. In his lecture, titled 'The mirror stage as *formative* of the function of the I as revealed in psychoanalytic experience' [italics mine], Lacan laid the grounds for opposing 'any philosophy directly issuing from the Cogito'. He "teaches us not to regard the ego as centred on the perception-consciousness system, or as organized by the "reality principle" ... [but to] start instead from the function of *meconnaissance* that characterizes the ego in *all* its structures". [italics mine]

15 '*Sinthome* comes to be placed in the centre of the three circles of the Borromean knot, that which actually keeps them together in order to form a knot'. (Dolar, 1998: 36)

16 Lacan in his earlier works emphasizes the unconscious. In his later works Lacan emphasizes the irruptions of the Real in analytic discourse.

17 '[T]he Freudian unconscious is situated at that point, where between cause and that which it affects, there is always something wrong', 'there remains essentially in the function of cause a certain *gap*', 'what the unconscious does is to show us the gap'. 'In this gap something happens ...' (Lacan, 'The Four Fundamental Concepts of Psycho-analysis', *The Freudian Unconscious and Ours,* 22).

18 Something anomalous always shows up in language, something unaccountable, unexplainable: an aporia; aporias point to the presence within the Symbolic of the Real; Real as kinks in the symbolic order – where drive is an activity related to the lost object which produces *jouissance.*

References

Achuthan, A. 2004. "Women and Midwifery in the Indian Context: Between the Practical and the Propositional" in *Women's Education and the Politics of Gender* – Bethune College, Kolkata.

Badiou, A. 2001. *Ethics: An Essay on the Understanding of Evil,* translated and introduced by Hallward P. London: Verso.

Bose, G. 1980. *Svapna.* Calcutta: Bangyia Sahitya Parishad.

Boyers, R. 1971. *Laing and Anti-Psychiatry,* Harmondsworth: Penguin.

Breggin, P. 1993. *Toxic Psychiatry.* London: Harper Collins.

Brown, P. 1973. *Radical Psychology,* London: Tavistock.

Cooper, D. 1970. *Psychiatry and Anti-Psychiatry.* London: Paladin.

Davar, B. V. 1999. *Mental health of Indian women: A feminist agenda.* New Delhi: Sage.

Davidson, A. I. 2001. *The Emergence of Sexuality: Historical Epistemology and the Formation of Concepts.* Harvard: Harvard University Press.

Derrida, J. 1978. *Writing and Difference.* London: Routledge and Kegan Paul.

_______ 1987. *The Post Card: From Socrates to Freud and Beyond,* trans. Bass, A. Chicago: University of Chicago Press.

_______ 1992. *The Other Heading: Reflections on Today's Europe.* Bloomington: Indiana University Press.

_______ 1994. '"To Do Justice to Freud": The History of Madness in the Age of Psychoanalysis' in *Critical Inquiry* 20 (Winter 1994).

Dhanda, A. 2000. *Legal Order and Mental Disorder,* New Delhi: Sage.

Didur, J. and Heffernan, T. 2003. "Revisiting the subaltern in the new empire" in *Cultural Studies,* Volume 17, Issue 1 January, pages 1–15.

Dolar, 1998. "Cogito as the Subject of the Unconscious" in Zizek, Slavoj & SalecI,.\Renata (eds.), *Cogito and the Unconscious* – Durham: Duke University Press.

Fee, D. (ed.) 2000. *Pathology And The postmodern: Mental Illness As Discourse And Experience.* New Delhi: Sage.

Foucault, M. 1988. *Madness And Civnilization: A History of Insanity in the Age of reason.* New York: Vintage.

Grosz, E. 1989. *Sexual Subversions: Three French Feminists.* Sydney: Allen & Unwin.

Irigaray, L. 1985a. *Speculum of the Other Woman.* Ithaca: Cornell University Press.

_______ 1985b. *This Sex Which is Not One.* Ithaca: Cornell University Press.

Kaplan, H. I., Sadock, B. J., Grebb, J. A. (eds) 1994. *Synopsis Of Psychiatry* – 7th edition. New Delhi: B.I. Waverly Pvt. Ltd.

Kendell, R. E., Zealley, A. K. 1993. *Companion to psychiatric studies* – 5th edition. Edinburgh: Churchill Livingstone.

Lacan, J. 1977a. *Ecrits.* London: Tavistock.

_______ 1977b. *The Four Fundamental Concepts of Psychoanalysis.* London: Hogarth Press.

_______ 1997a. *The Psychoses (1955–1956),* trans. Grigg, R., book III of *The Seminar of Jacques Lacan,* ed. Jacques-Alain Miller. New York: W. W. Norton & Company.

_______ 1997b. *The Ethics of Psychoanalysis (1959–1960),* transl. Porter D., book VII of *The Seminar of Jacques Lacan,* ed. Miller J.-A.. New York: W. W. Norton & Company.

_______ 2007. *The Other Side of Psychoanalysis.* trans. Grigg, R., Book XVII of *The Seminar of Jacques Lacan,* ed. Jacques-Alain Miller. New York: W. W. Norton & Company.

Lacan, J. 1985. *Feminine Sexuality,* eds Mitchell, J. & Rose, J., trans. Rose, J.). New York: W. W. Norton & Company.

Moitra, S. 2002. *Feminist Thought: Androcentrism, Communication and Objectivity.* New Delhi: Munshiram Manoharlal.

Norris, C. 1987. *Derrida.* Cambridge, Massachusetts: Harvard University Press.

Plumwood, V. 1993. *Feminism and the Mastery of Nature.* London: Routledge.

Zizek, S. 1998. "Introduction: Cogito as a Shibboleth" in *Cogito and the Unconscious* (ed.) Zizek, S. – Duke University Press – Durham.

Chapter 16

CHOICE, LIFE AND THE (M)OTHER: TOWARDS ETHICS IN/OF ABORTION

Anirban Das

> '... it is always in a dilemma and a certain non-knowledge ... as to what it would be best to do, it is at the moment when two contradictory imperatives are in competition, that a responsible freedom can be exercised as such.'
>
> Derrida (2002 b)

After Foucault with the too well known intertwining of knowledge and power and after Said with his indictments of the colonizing impulse of knowledge it might be easy to point at the exclusions and the latent coerciveness of 'universal rights'. At the level of its working, to show the dominance of the international financing organizations based on the northern countries and the diverse overt and covert ways in which these dictate the terms of understanding, control and day to day activities in the nation states of the south. In this transfer/ translation of knowledge, power and economy, the roles of the various non-governmental organizations (NGOs), of well-meaning individuals and globalized functionaries of the state and techno scientific institutions along with certain 'local' level initiatives are gradually becoming clearer. Detailed analyses and critical descriptions of the dynamics of these efforts are crucial, yet do not exhaust the problem. The conceptual issues involved must be unravelled (I do not propose this as an easy and self-congratulatory positivist gesture but in the deconstructive spirit of attempting the (im)possible yet unavoidable task of unwinding the ever-tangled loop of thinking, being and doing, of taking the risk of decisions, however contingent, where it is impossible to decide). Writing this essay on rights, I as a brown male intellectual from India, remain inscribed in and written over indelibly by the presuppositions of the modern gendered individual (marked by caste, class and colony) and the notions of individual rights as they have appeared in the last few centuries in the small promontory of land called Europe. The writing of rights also involves, to extend a little more, the righting of wrongs – to stand for what is right, *pause*, might.

In this paper, I try to look at the notion of universal rights as bearing within it, along with the idea of 'having or claiming a right or set of rights', something different, a certain 'kind of social Darwinism' about 'righting wrongs' (Spivak 2002) – a presupposition of one's *self* always being in the right and of dispensing of rights to the others. This is not to discard the concept of rights in its entirety but to point at the limitations that inalienably mark its existence and working – '[t]he enablement must be used even as the violation is re-negotiated' (Spivak 2002). Looking at the rights question in this light enables one to re-configure the arguments surrounding abortion. As Shefali Moitra in a short yet incisive piece (1999, 12) asserts, we become aware that 'an overarching principle for conflict resolution' is not always available whenever there is a 'moral conflict'. An acknowledgement of 'experiences which are not conducive to formalization and other traditional modes of explanation' becomes imperative in this context. As the notion of *rights* becomes problematic with the implications of the *might* and the *wrongs*, the formal and universalisable principles of *personhood* and *morality* that involve the 'abortion issue' get shot through with the lineaments of the *body*, the *contexts* and the *otherness* of the woman, the colonized and non-capital.

The prevailing debates around the question of abortion revolve round two contending positions. The *pro-choice* argument asserts the rights of the woman over her body and life. As an individual, she has to have the freedom to choose whether to go on with her pregnancy, and whether she wants the changes in her ways of living that being a mother entails. The *pro-life* position argues for the rights of the foetus to life. As the foetus is regarded as a human being and a prospective or (in some arguments) even a real person, an abortion is an act of murder. In this very simplified rendering of the arguments, the latter seems to have an edge, slight but definitive. For, put in these terms, it seems to be a question of inconveniences (however dreadful or agonizing) of one person (the 'mother') versus the killing of another (the foetus/'baby'). That this is not so obvious is borne out by the amount of debate it has produced. The literature on the issue is huge and would need at least a monograph to sum up the contending positions. I take up two/three of the debates to point out certain presuppositions that persist over divides of opinion, and for me at least, seem questionable.

The debates on the question of *personhood* have traditionally been argued with respect to the status of the foetus. As if an '... answer to these questions guarantees a resolution of the entire abortion issue ... if the fetus is human, it must not be aborted except when the mother's life is endangered (and, for some, not even then); but if it is not human it may be aborted under any circumstances' (Weiss 1978, 66). There have been efforts to demarcate the exact point in time from when the foetus acquires personhood: from the time of conception to the formation of the vital organs, the time when 'it' becomes *viable* (that is, able to live on its own with supports other than the mother's womb), and so on. 'At what stage of fetal development, if any, and for what reasons, if any, is abortion justifiable?' – Weirtheimer (1982, 43) puts the question in a succinct manner.

His essay goes on to show the futility of such a query as the various shades of the liberal and the conservative positions restate each other's positions turned inside out. As the liberal ('pro-choicer') tries to define a distinctive trait that differentiates some one stage in the life of the foetus from the previous ones, so that abortion may be justified before that stage, the conservative ('pro-lifer') points at the continuity of consecutive stages and the impossibility of such a definition and extends this notion of continuity to that between the foetus and the child so that foeticide and infanticide becomes the same. Now the liberal might extend this argument to the indefinability of the boundary between the human and the non-human. S/he may stress the aggressive anthropocentrism in the conservative's reverence for the 'potential' human at the cost of all other pains and violence involved. As we will shortly see, the 'other half' of the (hu)man is the closest and most obvious object of this violence of forgetting. The conservative points out the inability of the liberal to specify the properties that mark out the 'person' from the 'non-person' so that s/he can morally assert the right to abort before the attainment of those qualities. He himself is 'equally unable to say what properties something must have if it is to have a right to life' (Tooley 1972).[1] The arguments for continuity and/or discontinuity per se do not lead to a pro-life or pro-choice position: '[I]f you are led in one direction rather than the other, that is not because of logic, but because you respond in a certain way to certain facts' (Weirtheimer 1982, 52–53).

To bring in the question of the subjectivity of the observer/questioner is not to evade the urgency of the ethical dilemma in the problem of abortion. It is to move on to a newer terrain in search of answers that seem unattainable in the familiar field of reasoning based on universal principles of rights and individual persons as discrete entities. We now have to deal with the contexts in which the question is raised, pay attention to the changes and continuities in the perceptions of the foetus (especially with the ubiquitous use of visual technical aids to 'reach into' the womb of the woman, like the ultrasonogram), to the multiple levels of ideologies, powers and interests acting in the viewing of abortion in a specific setting. But before all these, let us shift our focus to the other 'person', the *other*[2] (not the self of the Hegelian diad) person, whom the debates on 'personhood' forgets to mention, as if personhood involves the foetus alone. We are speaking of the 'mother', the woman who bears the child.

In 1971, a pregnant single woman (Jane Roe) in America brought a lawsuit challenging the constitutionality of the Texas criminal abortion laws, which proscribed procuring or attempting an abortion, except on medical advice for the purpose of saving the mother's life. Argued on December 13, 1971, reargued October 11, 1972 and decided January 22, 1973, this was the famous Roe vs. Wade (District Attorney of Dallas County) case.[3] The judgment deals in detail with the 'history of abortion' – in the sense of a narrative of the prevalent attitudes of the society, popular thinking and the American medical establishment to abortion, – along with the questions of rights of a person, definitions of *personhood* ('the word "person," as used in the Fourteenth Amendment, does not include the unborn'), rights to privacy, and the specificity of the pregnant woman as a claimant to personal choice. It leaves open the question regarding the time when life begins in the mother's womb, 'When those trained in the respective disciplines of medicine, philosophy, and theology are unable to arrive at any consensus, the judiciary, at this point in the development of man's knowledge, is not in a position to speculate as to the answer.' [410 U.S. 113, 160] Here it again narrates a history of the different opinions in religious and popular knowledge regarding the issue.

The verdict, however, recognizes 'that the State does have an important and legitimate interest in preserving and protecting the health of the pregnant woman, ... and that it has still another *important and legitimate interest in protecting the potentiality of human life*' (emphasis added). Bordo (1993, 312) points at the 'many frequent misapplications' of this clause in favour of forced caesarian section operations on unwilling and/or unable-to-give-consent (for example, comatose) 'mothers'. 'The slippage from state interest in foetal life (which Roe grants) to the elevation of that interest above the preservation of maternal health ... converts the protection of foetal life into a doctrine of maternal self-sacrifice', she rightfully asserts. But before going on to this question of the ignoring of the mother-woman in a bid to protect the rights of the foetus, we return to the Roe case for a short while.

The judgment recognizes and endorses the right of 'personal privacy' that endows the woman with the right to decide her abortion, but not in an absolute and unqualified sense. It claims that at some point of time in pregnancy the interests of the state in safeguarding health, in maintaining medical standards, and in protecting potential life 'become sufficiently compelling' to retain its regulatory power over the abortion decision. The relevant portion of a summary of its decision runs as follows:

1. A state criminal abortion statute of the current Texas type, that excepts from criminality only a life-saving procedure on behalf of the mother, without regard to pregnancy stage and without recognition of

the other interests involved, is violative of the Due Process Clause of the Fourteenth Amendment.

(a) For the stage prior to approximately the end of the first trimester, the abortion decision and its effectuation must be left to the medical judgment of the pregnant woman's attending physician.

(b) For the stage subsequent to approximately the end of the first trimester, the State, in promoting its interest in the health of the mother, may, if it chooses, regulate the abortion procedure in ways that are reasonably related to maternal health.

(c) For the stage subsequent to viability, the State in promoting its interest in the potentiality of human life [410 U.S. 113, 165] may, if it chooses, regulate, and even proscribe, abortion except where it is necessary, in appropriate medical judgment, for the preservation of the life or health of the mother.

2. The State may define the term "physician," as it has been employed in the preceding paragraphs of this Part XI of this opinion, to mean only a physician currently licensed by the State, and may proscribe any abortion by a person who is not a physician as so defined.

We have dealt with a single case and its decision in detail to bring out an initial moment (so late, in the 1970s!) of the woman's fight for her rights to choose abortion.[4] Note that the rights thus gained are not absolute but with modifications that often render themselves liable to be misused. And there is little likelihood to find in these rights the absolute and aggressive swallowing of the foetal wellbeing that later pro-lifers would try to impute on them. Instead, the judiciary has meticulously worked out the stakes of the state and the physician ('a medical responsibility') that tightly delineates the rights of the woman. Yet how this woman, so carefully circumscribed by the state and the medical establishment, vanishes from the discourses of pro-life arguments and popular institutional thinking is the enigma that we now address. For that we look into a slightly different category of women than the demoniac aborting mothers, yet not an iota less vilified or maligned.

'Cocaine Mothers' and 'Crack Babies' were the leading legal problems to get the attention of foetal rights discourse in the 1980s USA.[5] Balsamo (1999, 238) speaks of *Melaine Green*, twenty-four year old woman, who was charged in Illinois 'with involuntary manslaughter and the delivery of a controlled substance to a minor for allegedly taking cocaine shortly before her daughter was born'. This was a typical case of a 'monster' woman who, for her own questionable pleasures, exposes her own unborn child to risks of disablements and death. In her extremely well-argued essay, Susan Bordo (1993) has cited cases where the mother is charged with criminal neglect of the child for failing to follow medical advice in pregnancy (Pamela Rae Stuart case in 1985), a woman making an automobile accident while intoxicated being prosecuted for 'vehicular homicide' of her foetus that was aborted (in Massachusetts), and a woman being prosecuted for 'felony child abuse' with the 'crime' of drinking while pregnant. Speaking of popular perception, she tells the story of a case where a woman in late pregnancy (the third trimester), was referred to in the media and by the participants of a talk show as well as the anchor as having acted selfishly when she went for a drink. This, despite the risk of a drink at that stage being minimal. The reasoning was, 'that pregnant women who engage in *any* activities that have even the *slightest* risk are behaving "selfishly" ' (82, emphasis in the text). And remember, the importance of routine clinical care and social services to the pregnant women is far from satisfactory even in the United States (Bordo cites a government task force report to this effect). A society that hardly and grudgingly (do not forget the numerous complaints about wastage of public funds to support 'undeserving' mothers) makes any attempt to minimize the risks imparted on the mother through bad working conditions, pollutions, marital maltreatments and abuses, et cetera, passes on the accusation of selfishness to the mother. This society that:

> '... forces a woman to bear a child when she does not wish to have one, offers her little or no support when she does, and punishes her when it decides she is acting irresponsibly, is itself guilty of foetal abuse' (Hubbard 1994).

The positing of the foetus in opposition to the mother remains at the heart of the abortion debates. In a curious turn of logic, as the focus of attention concentrates on the foetus, the mother-woman gets reduced to a receptacle – almost passive, if not aggressively dangerous and harmful – for the foetus.

Valerie Hartouni (1999) in her 'study in reproductive technologies' talks about a 1993 U. S. Supreme Court ruling in the *Bray v. Alexandria Health Clinic* case. It involved the 'rescue' demonstrations by anti-abortion activists at abortion clinics to disrupt the functioning of the clinics. The question was whether this was an infringement over the rights of the women seeking abortion in making their destination inaccessible for them. The Court ruled that this was not the case. Hartouni rightly highlights the reasoning of the Court as interesting and suggestive of prevalent beliefs and thought-systems:

> '[A]ntiabortion demonstrations do not deprive women of having or exercising any constitutionally secure right or privilege because such demonstrations are conducted for the sole purpose of protecting the abortion's "innocent victims" and *thus have nothing to do with women.*' (257)

The 'obviously' laudable efforts to rescue 'innocent human lives' do not involve the women just because these efforts declare their 'targets' to be the foetus instead of the woman. That this foetus is *situated* in the womb (the *body*) of a woman and the activities cause very effective and real hazards to the women concerned are not to be taken into account. These do not matter as relevant. The concerns of the women are irrelevant. The woman is as if obliterated, except for being the unavoidable abode of the future citizen of the state, whose only claim to well-being is in the form of a healthy incubator. The expressions of care, affection and regard for the mother is suffused with this sense of silent (as completely unnoticed) effacement of the woman. Bordo (1993), who raises the question 'Are mothers persons?' in the title of her piece with a sub-heading 'reproductive rights and the politics of subject-ivity', succinctly remarks,

> '... the disturbing fact remains that increased *empathy for the fetus* has often gone hand in hand with decreased respect for the *autonomy of the mother.*' (86, emphasis added)

Just note that here the feminist position speaks in the language of individual 'autonomy', and the purported conservative argument invokes 'empathy', a familiar trope in feminist ethical thinking. This points at a paradox in the feminist thinking of the issue of abortion and reproductive rights that borders on an *aporia* in the Derridean sense. But more of that later.

Does the woman thus entirely vanish? Or parts of her remain? A single part? Part that stands for the whole? A metonym ... of the woman ... that once was?

The swollen belly of the pregnant woman has replaced the woman as a being in a significant member of the body of citizens, someone might assert. The belly for the woman is like the head for the man. Creating metonyms socially is never an innocent act. We briefly look into the contexts of the technological wonder called the US nation state that situates this woman-belly.

The foetus versus the mother/woman. If it is the standard version of the narrative, then this story has a number of sub-plots. These intertwine and form patterns. One of these is the well-known inter-weaving of the woman, the nation and the mother:

> '... the pregnant woman is the main legitimate space in which the category *female* converts into a national category and changes the meaning of citizenship ...' (Berlant 1994)

Obviously, citizenship is treated here not only as a judicial category but also as a key moment of the social imaginaire. If to be a member of the community of citizens of a nation is to be a part of a common heritage *and* a lineage of descent, the role of reproduction as re-production of the commonness is vital. The family remains the all-important link in the perpetuation and the immortality of the nation. Being part of the family, every individual mortal member of the nation shares the taste of immortality. The same transcending of finitude purportedly marks the woman in her role of mothering. Let us be careful. We do not want to assert that the meanings associated with the phenomenon of the woman's bearing of a child is exhausted by this dynamic of the reproductive family and the state and nation.[6] Nevertheless, this 'uterine economy' continues to be a dominant and repressive apparatus that mould the subjectivity of the woman and reduces her to the synecdoche of the womb.

The discourses of science and technology are very much participants in the objectivisation of the woman to her reproductive parts. Note the relative yet almost complete occlusion of the component of non-productive pleasures (the 'clitoral economy' as Spivak 1993 names it) that are associated with these same anatomical structures – significantly named 'reproductive' – and the forgetting of the multiple possibilities of the economy of pleasure of the woman (Irigaray 1985 – this is only a contextually relevant reduced element of her rich and detailed argument), which the reproductive economy entails. There have been numerous studies, both essays and monographs on a general plane and in specific settings, on how the techno-science establishment has dealt with the body of the woman and has reduced the woman to the womb (Balsamo 1999, Berlant 1994, Hartouni 1999, Hubbard 1994, Martin 1987, 1990, 1996, Treichler 1990). Berlant's meticulous and trenchant critique of the science-representation-nation nexus points at the implicit analogy of the nation and nature that works to valorize the 'natural' development of the woman to mother and the foetus to the child. This normalized development is then projected on to the 'progress' of the nation as if the latter depends on the former. The foetus, as legitimately as the nation, has the right to normal development. However, here, as Berlant shows with ingenuity, the purported subjects are themselves objectified:

> 'The movement for fetal rights is ... also a development in the history of national sentimentality, where complex political conditions are reduced or refined into the discourses of dignity and of the authority of feeling.' (154)

The nation, as also the foetus, remain objects of honour and 'feeling', devoid of the diverse dynamics of material and ideational processes that go on to make them up. The immediate location of the foetus in the tissues and organs of the woman, and its intimate relations with the mother are glossed over to present it as a disembodied self-contained entity in the image of the atomized individual, a citizen of the modern nation-state. Paradoxically, the figures of the minority and the disenfranchised induce a sentiment of imagined marginality in the face of an invented hegemonic centre. The minority, as the foetus is figured in this discourse, remains a stereotype, lacking the real dynamics of beings and becomings.

The irony of the situation is, as the foetus – open to the technical gaze of medical investigations (amniocentesis, ultrasonogram, electronic foetal heart monitoring, and so on) – begins to be visualized as a 'real' entity, its reality gets reduced to personhood. As if, to be real, the *foetus* has to be a real, whole *person.* The specific dynamics of its existence, as distinct from the 'baby' at birth, has to be effaced to establish its continuity with the person, which is the *telos* of the fetal existence. Even *within* the progressivist narrative of the sciences, the technological innovations might be seen to produce a body of knowledge that pointed at the disjunctures, and not only the continuities, of the foetus with the 'person', going well beyond the 'earlier' notions of *homunculus* and the likes.[7] Those discourses that go beyond such a one-dimensional view of the authority of science to faithfully represent truths of nature think of nature-(wo)man-machine in a co-constitutive continuum. Nature (as also the 'human' and the machine) is not just *natural*, self-present and unmediated. It is *also* constructed through material and ideational activities of (wo)men and machines and the non-human organisms. On the other hand, machines are not *only* constructions through the ingenuity of the inventors. They are material and natural in senses that include the imperative to be in accordance to the 'natural' laws. Not to forget, these laws, in their turn, are also 'material-semiotic actors', both material and semiotic entities.

The cyborg[8] is the term that would probably denote the mode of existence in such a view. Here, matter and meaning constitute each other in continuously shifting and contingent processes. The foetus, in such a theory, is a cyborg in that it is both material and a creation of ideational processes that we have so far been discussing. For Donna Haraway, the cyborgs are 'illegitimate offsprings of militarism and patriarchal capitalism' – illegitimate, as they are 'exceedingly *unfaithful* to their origins'. This implies that though the foetus are *created* as much by the union of the sperm and the ovum in a specific bio-chemical environment as by the ideological and political environment of today's global US capital-centric patriarchal-racial system, it *exceeds* and does not conform fully to the conditions and intentionalities of its material-ideational origins.[9] Carol Mason (1995) has rightly drawn our attention to the danger of a facile celebration of the possibility of non-conformism implied by this excess. In the abortion debate, the cyborg (the foetus) *may* very well replicate its originary purposes faithfully. One should not play down the task of facing such a predicament.

The positing of a mother versus foetus situation – the outcome of a dense and often impenetrable array of situations consisting of religious sentiments and technoscientific inventions, of stereotypes of minorities and the universal language of rights, of global capital and household relations of power – is an instance of the devious ways in which the Self-Other relationships may be invented. The foetus is the prospective self, the Subject with capital S, created to be in a continuum with the citizen-subject of the state of America. The other is not one. The woman-mother is the container for the foetus, an aggressive threat, effaced from the dominant discourse of rights, reduced to the synecdoche of the womb. This has dire real consequences for the woman:

i) criminal prosecutions for endangering the foetus within their bodies,
ii) caesarean sections without consent through mandates of the courts,
iii) exclusion from jobs and benefits, to which women had recently been gaining access, on the grounds of fetal protection.

Ruth Hubbard (1994) goes on to elaborate on each of these predicaments and points at the undoing of reproductive rights discourse at the cost of the woman. We move on to a different terrain of a third world state, India, to look into how similar notions have different itineraries, though remaining identifiably similar, in different spaces.

The Medical Termination of Pregnancy Act was passed by both houses of the parliament, the Government of India, in 1971 and it came to force on the 1st of April 1972. One might rightfully think that the debate over the rights of the women (mothers) to choose abortion pitted against the rights of the unborn (persons?) to life, that rocks law-courts, public communications and the feminist academia in America, has questionable relevance for India where abortion is legally sanctioned with little controversy around it. Remember that the Roe vs. Wade case, which was not a parliamentary act, came to be decided in 1973. Still today, many states in the US are reluctant to provide rights that women in India have been enjoying for more than three decades. Not that social taboos, personal emotional responses or scriptural injunctions were conducive on any account in India. The key to the anomaly, where the so-called developing and the under-developed have overtaken the 'developed' in the race for progress, is the readiness of the Indian state to step-up its measures of development that, for India at least, seemed to involve a scrupulous control of the increasing trend in population growth. Family planning and population control were the twin targets that prompted the government rather than the assertion of the rights of the woman over her body. The concerns of women, that were taken into account, were that of health, in the sense of goods to be provided rather than rights to be recognized, 'in relative isolation from the women's movement' (Phadke 1998). But are we being too spiteful and unnecessarily discriminating in putting the issue thus?

Shilpa Phadke (1998) tries to find an answer to the question, whether the initiative of the government of India in bringing about the MTP Act was prompted by pro-choice concerns or its population control policies. Her essay deals with contemporary statements of government officials and documents to bring out that the act was simultaneously promoted by two different anxieties. One was the potential effect of the act to a lowering of birth rate and thence to family planning and population control. The other was about the hazards to the health of the women caused by abortions being done by non-qualified, untrained and ill-equipped practitioners under unhygienic conditions. The *doctors* and the *demographers* were the chief driving forces behind the act. This was reflected in the domineering role that was accorded to the medical and the population control institutions in the carrying out and the rhetoric of enunciation of the act. As Phadke (1998) notes,

> '[t]he MTP Act, which in law offers women greater control over their bodies, ... becomes an instrument of control when it is interpreted by the state as a means of family planning'.

The thrust in the family control programs in India has always been, and still is, on population management.[10] This presupposes a journey to modernity for the nation. Yet, this modernity that the Indian nation aspires for, is a 'different' modernity, based on 'indigenous traditions'. The women as the bearers of this tradition in their ascribed role of *responsible* mothers and efficient homemakers nurture the future of the nation, the children. This is evident in the rhetoric of the official and semi-official (pedagogic) documents and materials of the *family welfare planning* (Chatterjee and Riley 2001, 837).

In India, does the language of development override the pro-life arguments? In view of the rhetoric and the logistics of planning (again a hallmark of modernity), our answer would be yes. Also keep in mind, the fascination in the doctors and the health establishment with high technology devices of contraception *vis-à-vis* the perceived passive role of the concerned women. The women, as in case of the poor and the underdeveloped in slightly different contexts, are held responsible for their own predicaments. The emphasis of the programs remains on female contraception (during emergency the strong resentment against forced 'male' sterilization was perfectly legitimate in its democratic content, yet was also symptomatic of a lack of awareness regarding the male component of contraceptive practices). The language of *choice* – of rational, free individuals – in contraception is hollowed out of its content. To abort no longer remains a choice. It becomes an imperative of development (through international agencies, science establishment, plans, modernising impulse, etc.). Choice becomes the only choice. The question of control over the woman's (own) body becomes relevant. Contraception puts up the question of the woman's body. Against not the traditional patriarchy but the modern patriarchy that 'liberates' women. Yet, the element of 'liberation' is also unmistakable. This is gendering, not overt patriarchy. It works not only at the level of overt power, but also at that of meanings and economy. This does not make the dichotomy of 'choice' and 'life' irrelevant, but points at the situatedness of its working. What could be more poignant about the marks of location than the strange and macabre twist the pro-choice legislation takes, by which thousands of girl children are selectively aborted through connections of techno-science, family and the state.[11] Sex selective abortion is the 'neutral' term that tries to bring this paradox of a phenomenon into the discourse of international civility.

So, where is the woman? Again, a blank space in the rhetoric of abortion and family planning. Is it her 'fate' to be so? Is that fate linked to the language in which she remains inserted? The language of rights and the individual? Does the woman have an *other* language? *Other* to the rules of the same? What should be a feminist position in the abortion debate?

A *pro-life* argument, notwithstanding its feminist rhetoric (if at all it deems necessary to use that language), renders the woman invisible. A ready answer for the *pro-choice* argument obviously remains within a discourse of the rights of the individual. Tooley's (1972) rigorous exercise of the logistics of this narrative leads to the scary proposition of a defence of infanticide on certain occasions (the infant, like the foetus, does not possess 'the concept of a continuing self' and thus lacks 'a serious right to life'). As is already evident from our discussion, pace Tooley, we want to respect this subjective scare in the face of an abstract and value-neutral objectivity of reason.

So far, we have been discussing the multiple ways in which the woman – her stakes in a given situation, her body, her presence – continues to be discriminated against in particular contexts and sites of thinking and action. Sometimes she is demonized, sometimes effaced, at other spaces reduced to a synecdoche or even forgotten doubly (in the sense that the act of forgetting the woman is itself forgotten, as if nothing has happened).

To speak thus of the woman, to point out the discriminations being heaped upon her is a feminist task. That does not exhaust the work. There are problems, which still need to be addressed. Beyond the *rights talk* of the 'choice'. We will hurriedly go through these before coming to a close.

Our brief review of the debate on the abortion issue in an earlier section reveals a veritable 'narrative collapse' in the juridical statements involved. As Myrsiades (2002) has ably worked out in her long and detailed discussion, the 'story lines' of the foetus and the pregnant woman occupy 'conceptually incommensurable premises'. The judicial apparatus that faces the task of mediating between the two is bound to a collapse of the resolution and has to exert its authority in certain ways to feign a temporary solution. In a way, this becomes a classical case of a differend:

> 'As distinguished from a litigation, a differend would be a case of conflict, between (at least) two parties, that cannot be equitably resolved for lack of a rule of judgement applicable to both arguments. One side's legitimacy does not imply the other's lack of legitimacy.' (Lyotard 1983)

Myrsiades sees this as a chance to keep the conversation open without coming to a neat closure of the debate. As this essay hopes to make clear, we do take a certain 'side' in this play of incommensurables. A differend that works endlessly in a purportedly value-neutral abstract field of reason might be brought to sudden halts in specific situations – in the fraught field of sexual difference and discrimination, you ought to take the side of the 'other' woman, the side of choice. Within the space of rights, one takes the *moment*ary decision. Yet, one has to think beyond the choice of rights. Do not forget that the choice has been taken over a rugged terrain of incomprehension. A responsibility to the 'other' of this divide, to 'life', informs this decision.

Maybe this is something akin to what Moitra (1999) calls the 'split position' that the woman has to take with regard to the abortion issue? In her insightful and rigorous dealing of the issue of rape, Nivedita Menon (2000) had urged us to see the feminist project as 'not one of "justice" but of "emancipation"' (104). In the context of the abortion debate, even this call for emancipation is not sufficient. The call of the self of the foetus for emancipation from its bodily debts to the mother could equally be in the offing. Moreover, here emancipation is fraught with the destruction of another, an 'other' who is, more often than not, tied with bonds of love and responsibility to the woman. To try to free the selfhood of the woman from the 'sexually defined body of woman', as Menon suggests while dealing with rape, is to forget the embodied selves of human and non-human actors like the woman, the foetus, the instruments of biomedical techno-science and the law that go on to constitute each other and call for responsibilities of each for all others.

Menon's bold attempt to question the universality and the 'impossibility' of justice has a rare analytic clarity. Paradoxically, this clarity sets the limits of her argument. In a detailed and insightful discussion on the question of abortion (1996), she brings out how the concerns confronting the feminist in India are quite different from the feminist in the West/America. While the latter, working in the context of efforts to criminalize abortion, has to put stress on 'retaining women's access to safe and legal abortions, and ensuring that the state intervenes positively through laws and administrative measures', the former works in a site where amniocentesis is being used to determine the sex of foetuses and to selectively abort the female foetus. As such, she has to tackle the dilemma of working for safer access to abortions on conditions of more autonomy for the woman along with a cautious attempt to curb the abortions done by women to get rid of prospective female children. Menon offers no simple solution to this problem. Instead, she points at the impossibility of a universal justice and the contrary assumption implicit in the 'discourse of law' – an assumption 'that justice can be attained once and for all by the fixing of identity and meaning'. '[R]ights are constituted by particular discourses', she asserts, a mode of constitution to which the 'discourse of rights' remains blind.

Nuanced and theoretically aware, this position nevertheless works within a too neat binary of justice/law. The Derridean thematic, she refers to, would point at the *simultaneous* working of a possibility and an impossibility in the process. Impossibility does not preclude possibility. Regarding justice, Derrida, in the piece Menon refers to (Derrida 2002 b-1990), remains obsessively engaged in the intertwining of the meanings of justice, law (as *droit* and as *loi*) and right (also in both the senses of 'being right' and 'having a certain right') and constantly points at both an implication as well as a disjuncture of justice and law. Though he speaks of a 'deconstructibility of law' and an 'undeconstructibility of justice', thus implying a 'non-passage' between the two, as Spivak (1999, 427) points out: 'Justice is disclosed in law, even as its own effacement'. For a deconstructionist, the reference to the 'experience' of disclosure and effacement in simultaneity is important. Otherwise, as has been with Menon, the responsibility to the other that inalienably informs the experience of justice would look like an eclectic move to be added on pragmatically to a well-defined (though contingent,) category called justice. Here, as is evident with Menon, justice remains historically contingent – 'constituted by specific moral visions' – keeping the question of the necessity to engage with its *general* undeconstructibility at bay in a celebration of epistemic relativism (albeit with a pragmatic nod to an ethics of 'responsibility'). Cautiously, we try to explicate the nature of this responsibility. For a blanket ethic of responsibility for all constitutive others may amount to a non-response to each – it becomes just a naming of a relationship that blurs all specificity in the obligation for any one. The relationship to each 'other' is a singularity. The alterity of each is unique, as is the singularity of the ethical subject.

The question of abortion is intimately linked with the question of sexual reproduction by men and women. A somewhat radical move might point at the marks of 'the ideology of motherhood' and the 'uterine economy' of the family built into the call of *responsibility*. Yet it is not easy to disentangle the implications of this purported complicity. Whether motherhood can so easily be dissipated in the celebration of 'other sexualities', sexualities that themselves may very well be reproducing oppressive and hierarchical systems, is still open to much feminist debate, even within the radical space. The ethicality in the call of the other (wholly and intimate at the same moment) may work across that contested terrain. Moreover, Donna Haraway (1990) reminds us that (hetero)sexual economy need not necessarily flow into the familial circulation, that instead sexual difference is a potential scandal for the liberal conception of the individual and internally sufficient Western 'self'. For sexual reproduction always takes two. And neither parent is *continued* in the child, which is a 'randomly reassembled genetic package',

> '... where there is sex, literal reproduction is a contradiction in terms. The issue from the self is always an(other).' (143).

Sexual difference and reproduction, even when they perpetuate the continued production of the Western Man, perennially belie the project of generational continuity. They always produce difference, as they are out to (re)produce the same. In a way, the foetus is the ultimate metaphor for this difference in sameness. The woman has thus to split when she asserts her rights and emancipations for 'choice' as she, at the same time, perceives the call of the other within, with responsibility.

Is it really so difficult to think simultaneously of a sexuate difference in rights and a call of the wholly other that presents itself as *this* intimate embodied other? Maybe we can give another reckoning.[12]

Notes

1 Later in the essay, we will discuss the problem with Tooley's extreme rationalism. The abortion and related debates on the human embryo continues in a number of directions (Campbell and McKay 1978, Hursthouse 1991, Kirejczik 1999, McMahan 1993, Sofia 1984 are a few examples of this variegated space). We choose a specific line, which to us seems to reflect some of the principal concerns.

2 The profound and deeply rooted sense in which the 'mother' is the *other* in lay and technoscientific, juridical and religious discourses will be borne out by our following discussion. See especially Bordo (1993) for a philosophically aware and detailed handling of the issue.

3 The whole text of the judgment with concurring and dissenting opinions of the judges are available online at the website of 'Priests for Life' hosted by 'Catholic online' and has been extensively used in the following discussion on the topic.

4 Remember that the government of India had passed the 'medical termination of pregnancy' (MTP) act in 1971. The multiple implications of this 'progressive' gesture are dealt with later in this paper.

5 See Balsamo (1999) for a detailed argument.
6 See especially Haraway (1990) for a possible different reading of 'sexual reproduction' and its ultimate transgressive potentialities, though she is well aware of the problems and coercive implications that we are speaking of.
7 See Weir (1998) for an interaction of the 'foetus' and the 'baby' in medical and lay usage respectively to denote the *foetus*. Medical usages self-consciously maintain the differentiation between the two.
8 Unlike most of the conceptual tools in today's theoretical world, this category may surely be adduced to Donna Haraway.
9 Rapp (1999) and Traweek (1999) are two of the many studies dealing sensitively with the reception and perception of medical reproductive technologies in diverse communities and individuals. These definitely show how people negotiate, while trying to come to terms with, these technologies and concepts and 'exceed' the meanings and roles allotted to them by the discourse of science.
10 Not that the US fares any better in this respect. Mason (1995) tells how abortion services and female sterilization have been combined in certain government systems. In 1972, between 100000 and 200000 sterilizations were funded by the federal government. A strong racial bias (the number of black and Chicana women being disproportionately high) marked these efforts. The liberal feminist movement had also been complicit to some extent. An instance of internal colonization!
11 See Balakrishnan (1994) and Weiss (1995), and especially, Menon 1996.
12 As the reader must have understood by now, this last section of the essay relies heavily on the thinking of Emmanuel Levinas (especially as he had been read by Jacques Derrida and Gayatri Chakravorty Spivak) in an unusual and counterintuitive conjunction to Luce Irigaray. I propose to deal with the relevant texts responsibly in a different paper. Here, I trace the arguments in their first tentative steps to writing.

References

Balakrishnan, R. 1994. 'The social context of sex selection and the politics of abortion in India' in *Power and decision: the social control of reproduction*. Cambridge: Harvard school of Public Health.

Balsamo, A. 1999. 'Public pregnancies and cultural narratives of surveillance' in *Revisioning women, health and healing: feminist, cultural, and technoscience perspectives* eds, Adele E. Clarke and Virginia L. Olesen. New York and London: Routledge.

Berlant, L. 1994. 'America, "fat", the foetus' in *Boundary 2* 21(3), Autumn 1994, 145–195.

Bordo, S. 1993. 'Are mothers persons? Reproductive rights and the politics of subject-ivity' in *Unbearable weight: feminism, western culture and the body*. Berkeley, Los Angeles, London: University of California Press.

Bronfen, E. 2000. 'The body and its discontents' in *Body matters: feminism, textuality, corporeality* eds, Avril Horner and Angela Keane.

Campbell, T. D. and Mckay, A. J. M. 1978. 'Antenatal injury and the rights of the fetus' in *The philosophical quarterly*, 28(1), 17–30.

Chatterjee, N. and Riley, N. E. 2001. 'Planning an *Indian* modernity: the gendered politics of fertility control' in *Signs: journal of women in culture and society* 26 (3).

Derrida, J. 1976 (1994). *Of grammatology*, trans. G. C. Spivak, Baltimore, Maryland : Johns Hopkins Press.

_______ 1981. *Dissemination*, trans. Johnson, B. Chicago: The University of Chicago Press.

_______ 2002 (1990) a. 'Force of law: the "Mystical Foundation of Authority" ' in *Acts of religion* by Derrida, J., ed. Anidjar, G., New York and London: Routledge.

_______ 2002 b. 'The aforementioned so-called human genome' in *Negotiations: interventions and interviews, 1971–2001*, ed. Derrida, J., trans. Rottenberg, E.. Stanford, California: Stanford University Press.

Ettore, E. 2002. *Reproductive genetics, gender and the body*. London and New York: Routledge.

Haraway, D. 1990. 'Investment strategies for the evolving portfolio of primate females' in *Body/Politics: women and the discourses of science* eds, Jacobus, M., Keller, E. F., Shuttleworth, S. New York and London: Routledge.

Hartouni, V. 1999. 'A study in reproductive technologies' in *Revisioning women, health and healing: feminist, cultural, and technoscience perspectives* eds, Clarke A. E., and Olesen, V. L. New York and London: Routledge.

Hubbard, R. 1994. 'The politics of fetal/maternal conflict' in *Power and decision: the social control of reproduction*, Ed. by Gita Sen and Rachel C. Snow, Cambridge, Massachusetts: Harvard University, Center for Population and Development Studies.

Hursthouse, R. 1991. 'Virtue theory and abortion' in *Philosophy and public affairs* 20 (3).

Kant, E. 1970 (1785). *Kant on the foundation of morality* translated with commentary by Liddell, B. E. A. Bloomington and London: Indiana University Press.

Kirejczik, M. 1999. 'Parliamentary cultures and human embryos: the Dutch and British debates compared' in *Social studies of science* 29 (6).

Kumar, R. 2002. 'Gender in reproductive and child health policy' in *Economic and political weekly* August 10, 2002.

Lyotard, J-F. 1985. *The differend:* phrases in dispute, trans. Abbeele, G. V. D. Minneapolis: University of Minnesota Press.

Martin, E. 1987. *The woman in the body: a cultural analysis of reproduction*. Boston: Beacon Press.

_______ 1990. 'Science and women's bodies: forms of anthropological knowledge' in *Body/Politics: women and the discourses of science* eds, Jacobus, M., Keller, E. F., Shuttleworth, S. New York and London: Routledge.

_______ 1996. 'The egg and the sperm: how science has constructed a romance based on stereotypical male-female roles' in *Feminism and science* eds, Keller E. F. and Longino, H. E.. Oxford, New York: Oxford University Press.

Mason, C. 1995. 'Terminating bodies: toward a cyborg history of abortion' in *Posthuman bodies* eds, Halberstam, J. and Livingston, I. Bloomington and Indianapolis: Indiana University Press.

Mcmahan, J. 1993. The right to choose an abortion' in *Philosophy and public affairs* 22 (4).

Menon, N. 1996. 'The impossibility of 'justice': female foeticide and feminist discourse on abortion' in *Social reform, sexuality and the state* ed. Uberoi, P.

_______ 2000. 'Embodying the self: feminism, sexual violence and the law' in *Subaltern studies XI: community, gender and violence* eds Chatterjee, P. and Jeganathan, P. Delhi: Permanent Black and Ravi Dayal Publisher.

Moitra, S. 1999. 'The abortion issue: the male female gender divide and duplicity of theory and practice' in *Margins: of knowledge body and gender* August 1999.

Myrsiades, L. 2002. 'Split at the root: narrative collapse in abortion jurisprudence' in *Cultural studies* 16(3), 365–400.

Phadke, S. 1998. 'Pro-choice or population control: a study of the medical termination of pregnancy act, Government of India, 1971' in *re/productions* issue 1.

Rapp, R. 1999. 'One new reproductive technology, multiple sites: how feminist methodology bleeds into everyday life' in *Revisioning women, health and healing: feminist, cultural, and technoscience perspectives* eds, Clarke, A. E. and Olesen, V. L.. New York and London: Routledge.

Sofia, Z. 1984. 'Exterminating fetuses: abortion, disarmament, and the sexo-semiotics of extraterrestrialism' in *Diacritics* 14 (2).

Spivak, G. C. 1993. *Outside in the teaching machine.* New York and London: Routledge.

_______ 1999. *A critique of postcolonial reason.* Seagull: Calcutta.

_______ 2003. 'Righting wrongs' in *Human rights, human wrongs: Oxford Amnesty lectures 2001*, ed., Owen, N. Oxford: Oxford University Press.

Squier, S. M. 1995. 'Reproducing the posthuman body: ectogenic fetus, surrogate mother, pregnant man' in *Posthuman bodies* eds, Halberstam, J. and Livingston, I. Bloomington and Indianapolis: Indiana University Press.

Treichler, P. A. 1990. 'Feminism, medicine, and the meaning of childbirth' in *Body/Politics: women and the discourses of science* eds, Jacobus, M., Keller, E. F., Shuttleworth, S. New York and London: Routledge.

Tooley, M. 1972. 'Abortion and infanticide' in *Philosophy and public affairs* 2(1).

Traweek, S. 1999. 'Warning signs: acting on images' in *Revisioning women, health and healing: feminist, cultural, and technoscience perspectives* eds, Clarke A. E. and Olesen, V. L. New York and London: Routledge.

U.S. Supreme Court abortion decision Roe v. Wade, 410 U.S. 113 (1973).

Weir, L. 1998. 'Cultural intertexts and scientific rationality: the case of pregnancy ultrasound' in *Economy and society* 27(2&3), May 1998.

Weirtheimer, R. 1982. 'Understanding the abortion argument' in *The problem of abortion* ed. Feinberg, J.

Weiss, G. 1995. 'Sex selective abortion: a relational approach' in *Hypatia* 10 (1).

Weiss, R. 1978. 'The perils of personhood' in *Ethics* 89(1), October 1978 (66–75).

Chapter 17

THE NATIONALIST PROJECT AND THE WOMEN'S QUESTION: A READING OF *THE HOME AND THE WORLD* AND *NATIONALISM*

Rekha Basu

In this paper I propose to examine two texts by Rabindranath Tagore, *The Home and the World*, (hitherto abbreviated *HW*), a novel, and an essay, or more precisely, a set of four lectures published under the rubric *Nationalism*. *HW* was published serially in a journal called *Sabuj Patra* (*The Green Leaves*), edited by Pramatha Choudhury, in 1915–16 and translated into English by Surendranath Tagore in 1919. The four lectures on *Nationalism*[1] were delivered around the same time. Rabindranath's critique of the nationalist ideology in these two texts, one a non-fictional narrative and the other a fictional narrative, hinges upon his conviction that nationalism ignores the claims of both individuals and communities who supposedly go into the forging of a nation-state.

In *HW*, Rabindranath foregrounds the question of women's identity to interrogate the discourse of nationalism. In his recent book, P. K. Datta (2003) has pointed out that the *Sabuj Patra* 'phase' in Rabindranath's literary/intellectual trajectory raises the gender question. Between 1914 and 1917, at least three stories in *Sabuj Patra*, viz. *The Wife's Letter (Strir Patra), Women Unknown (Aparichita)* and *House Number one (Poila Number)* center around women who seek self fulfillment by moving out of Procrustean roles which subordinate them. I believe *HW* shares more than an incidental literary/intellectual affiliation with these stories.[2]

Bimala in the novel emerges as an indispensable factor to the contrary reformist agendas formulated by her husband Nikhil and his friend Sandip. An important question, to which I shall address myself, is: how much is the autonomy of Bimala sustained through each of the Nikhilesh's and Sandip's projects, the former inspired by tender love, the latter by an unabashed narcissism.

In this context, I have found a simultaneous reading of *HW* and *Nationalism* enormously rewarding. The novel reads like a tract in political philosophy with the protagonists engaged in a polemical exchange over concepts such as *swadeshi* and *stree-swadhinata*. The essays, on the other hand, greatly lyrical in tone and sometimes repetitive and tedious in argument, nevertheless appear to anchor these debates in a metaphysic which is emotionally charged but consistent with Rabindranath's subsequent views. The novelist and the philosopher get amalgamated.

HW, a novel set on a Bengal *zamindar's* estate in 1908, unfolds before the reader in the context of the partition of Bengal in 1905. The *Swadeshi* movement, cutting across religion, class and caste divergences, was an impromptu response. Sumit Sarkar (2002) informs us that Rabindranath initially provided an animating force[3] for the movement. He organised *raksha bandhan* on the day of the proclamation of the partition. The thread-tying, however, was conducted between Hindus and Muslims as a gesture of religious fraternity to thus ally themselves against the British design to undermine their unity. However, as Rabindranath was to gather later, the reigns of the movement were gradually appropriated by the upper caste Hindu *bhadralok* who employed overtly Hindu imagery and metaphors to get a mass base for the movement. This resulted in the alienation of the non-*bhadralok* sections of the population, including Muslims. The movement turned communal, and Rabindranath, completely disillusioned, withdrew from his leadership role within the movement. *HW* and *Nationalism* are an outcome of a meticulous reflection on the antinomies that had crept into the *Swadeshi* movement primarily because of the manipulations of the Hindu elites.

HW is a love story that is simultaneously an engagement with the discourse of the *Swadeshi* movement and the variegated responses it elicits from different characters in the story. Nikhilesh, a *zamindar*, and Sandip, his friend, represent two contesting interpretations of *swadeshi*. Their contrary views become divulged on the person of Bimala, Nikhilesh's wife. Within the novel, both men have endeavoured to pull Bimala out of the confining interiors of the 'home'. As Ashish Nandy (1994) has observed, 'Bimala... is the link between the two forms of patriotism the men represent. Not only is she the symbol for which Sandip and Nikhil fight, but her personality incorporates the contesting selves of the two protagonists and becomes the battlefield on which the two forms of patriotism fight for supremacy.' (Nandy 1994: 14)

In *HW*, Bimala is introduced to the readers as a self-aware and self conscious woman, as someone who remains on the whole unperturbed by the intrigues that go on in a joint family. All of this has been made possible because of Nikhilesh, who earnestly persists in liberating his wife from the narrow confines of domesticity.

Going beyond Nikhilesh's nurture is Sandip's aggressive courting of Bimala. He succeeds in bringing her out of the inner recesses of the house into the living room, a physical space earmarked for male confabulations. Bimala succumbs to Sandip's erotic/patriotic appeal to help serve the nation's cause, by assuming its inspirational instigation. Reflecting on her easy capitulation, she says, 'Sandip's hungry eyes burnt like the lamps of worship before my shrine. All his gaze proclaimed that I was a wonder in beauty and power... I who before was plain had become suddenly beautiful. I who before had been of no account now felt in myself all the splendours of Bengal itself... For Sandip Babu was not a mere individual. In him was the confluence of millions of minds of the country. When he called me the Queen Bee of the hive, I was acclaimed with a chorus of praise by all our patriotic workers.' (Tagore, *HW*: 50)

Tanika Sarkar (2001) attributes this endowment of divinity on Bimala to the Bengali literature of 1880s, which, she reports, was very woman centric. In response to the historical charge perpetuated by Macaulay that the Bengalis were effeminate and a race of cowards, '...Bengali nationalism, as an oppositional ideology, – therefore, defiantly worshipped and glorified in the female principle. For Bengalis, accustomed to the worship of a variety of female cults, emotional resonances connected with an enslaved mother figure tended to be particularly powerful.' (Sarkar, T. 2001: 251)

This '...image of woman as a goddess or mother served to erase her sexuality in the world outside the home.' (Chaterjee 1989: 249) Resisting Bimala's/ Sandip's personification/divination of the country as a person, mother and goddess, Nikhilesh observes that it is wrong to transfer the aberrations of a person to one's country, 'I dare not permit the evil which is in me to be exaggerated into an image of my country – never, never.' (Tagore, *HW*: 38) Further, Nikhilesh asserts, 'I would know my country in its frank reality, and for this I am both afraid and ashamed to make use of a hypnotic text of patriotism.' (*Bande Mataram*) (Tagore, *HW*: 36). This view is reiterated in *Nationalism* where Rabindranath writes, 'Neither the colorless vagueness of cosmopolitanism, nor the fierce self-idolatory of nation-worship is the goal of human history' (Tagore, *Nationalism*: 2).

It is interesting to look at the contrary patriotism in *HW* as embodied in the person of Sandip. He is clear that '...my country does not become mine simply because it is the country of my birth. It becomes mine on the day when I am able to win it by force' (Tagore, *HW*: 45). Sandip is clearly unaware of his use of circular logic that legitimises the British imperialism. Re-endorsing this philosophy of the brute force he asserts, 'Nature surrenders herself, but only to the robber' (Tagore, HW: 45). He believes that he exercises a powerful impact on women because of this '... masterful passion – not a passion dried thin with the heat of asceticism, not a passion with its face turned back at every step in doubt and debate, but a full-blooded passion.' (Tagore, *HW*: 48) As Datta comments, 'By attracting women, Sandip proves to himself that as a man he possesses the force and intensity of desire, with which he can master reality and make the nation' (Datta 2003: 13). Sandip symbolises the power of mighty men, which is brutally exercised in its career over Nature and women alike and which allows for a Promethean exploitation of both.

The ideological basis for Sandip's position is reproduced by Rabindranath in *Nationalism*. About the ideology of the nation Rabindranath writes, 'A nation, in the sense of the political and economic union of a people, is that aspect which a whole population assumes when organised for a mechanical purpose... when with the help of science and the perfecting of organisation this power begins to grow and brings in harvests of wealth, then it crosses its boundaries with amazing rapidity. For then it goads all its neighbouring societies with greed of material prosperity, and consequently mutual jealousy, and by the fear of each others' growth into powerfulness.' (Tagore, *Nationalism*: 5)

Sandip's nation-rhetoric is chauvinistic and one of political expediency. His lack of moral scruples once the goal is sighted and his deliberate espousal of injustice – 'Whenever an individual or nation becomes incapable of perpetrating injustice it is swept into the dust-bin of the world' (Tagore, *HW*: 79) – are all ingredients in the 'nation' that he constructs. And in *Nationalism* power has been defined as 'a scientific product made in the political laboratory of the Nation, through the dissolution of personal humanity' (Tagore, *Nationalism*: 6).

Nikhilesh, by contrast, resisted the fetishization of the Nation undertaken by Sandip and his student followers. The glorification of Bimala at the hands of Sandip, far from being an emancipatory project, is actually a reiteration of his masculinity. Nikhilesh, clearly the authorial ideologue, visualizes his nation in androgynous terms. Mark his observation: 'My wife – Does that amount to an argument, much less the truth? Can one imprison a whole personality within that name?' (Tagore, *HW*: 64) Engaging in self-criticism he concluded that hitherto he had taken Bimala's love for granted. 'But the thing I forgot to calculate was that one must give up all claims based on conventional rights, if one would find a person fully revealed in truth.' (Tagore, *HW*: 41) Nikhilesh's well-intended move to modernise Bimala had been deficient because it had superseded Bimala's volitional agency. In a somewhat dramatic scene, which is strange considering his otherwise quiet, inconspicuous demeanour, Nikhilesh sets Bimala 'free': 'I had simply come to understand that never would I be free until I could set free. To try to keep Bimala as a garland round my neck, would have meant keeping a weight hanging over my heart.' (Tagore, *HW*: 134)

One can understand Nikhilesh's attitude towards the *Swadeshi* movement if one tries to understand Rabindranath's own reservations about nationalist movements. According to Amartya Sen (2002), Rabindranath was suspicious about such patriotism which limits both the freedom to engage ideas from outside 'narrow domestic walls' and the freedom also to support the causes of people in other countries. Rabindranath was hostile to communal sectarianism, such as an exclusivist Hindu orthodoxy that was closed to Islamic, Christian or Sikh perspectives. Andrew Robinson (2002) reports that Rabindranath and his family were among the earliest Bengalis to experiment with *swadeshi* businesses. Rabindranath believed that, rather than concentrate our energies in throwing the British out, we should strengthen indigenous industries and become self-sufficient. In *HW* Nikhilesh tried to invent an apparatus for extracting juice from the dates. He also started a rural bank. Tragically, both the ventures nearly rendered him bankrupt.

Nikhilesh's specific problem with Sandip's brand of *swadeshi* was that it was coercive. Both in the context of the relation with his wife as well as in the context of the *Swadeshi* movement, Nikhilesh did not believe in compelling acquiescence. Here Ashish Nandy's remarks are very insightful. He says, '*Ghare-Baire* offers a critique of nationalism but also a perspective on the form anti-imperialism should take in a multi-ethnic, multi-religious society where a colonial political economy encourages the growth of a complex set of dependencies. In such a society, the politically and economically weak and the culturally less westernized might be sometimes more dependent on the colonial system than the privileged and the enculturated. The novel suggests that a nationalism which steam-rollers society into making a uniform stand against colonialism, ignoring the unequal sacrifices imposed thereby on the poorer and the weaker, will tear apart the social fabric of the country, even if it helps to formally decolonize the country.' (Nandy 1994: 19)

The *Bande Mataram* variant of nationalism, embodied in the person of Sandip, is likewise desensitised to gender, caste and class. Commenting that the same proclivity is to be found in the nation, Rabindranath wrote in *Nationalism*,

> 'This abstract being, the Nation, is ruling India. We have seen in our country some brand of tinned food advertised as entirely made and packed without being touched by hand. This description applies to the governing of India, which is as little touched by the human hand as possible. The governors need not know our language, need not come into personal touch with us except as officials.... But, we, who are governed, are not a mere abstraction. We, on our side, are individuals with living sensibilities.' (Tagore, *Nationalism*: 7–8)

And further, 'The truth is that the spirit of conflict and conquest is at the origin and in the centre of Western nationalism; its basis is not social co-operation'.

(Tagore, *Nationalism*: 12) This is well brought out by Rabindranath in an essay *Sadupay*. He refers to the hostility of a large number of Muslims and subordinate caste Namasudra peasants to boycott in the East Bengal countryside. Rabindranath observes there, 'We have demanded closeness from them without ever having tried to be close to them earlier... We imagine that the Mother has become real for the whole country through songs and emotional ecstasy alone.' (Sarkar 2002: 123)

In *HW*, Sandip joins forces with Harish Kundu, a ruthless *zamindar*. They decide to organise a Durga Puja. The expenses for the same are being extracted from Kundu's lower-caste and Muslim peasants. This leads to a Muslim backlash. Mohammedan preachers are being sent from Dacca to incite trouble. The novel ends in a communal outbreak and one of its victims, ironically, is Nikhilesh. Sumit Sarkar records, 'It led him (Rabindranath)... to perceive a basic incompleteness in the *swadeshi* concept of freedom. It is this notion of freedom, of individual human rights affirmed, if need be against community discipline, that lay at the heart of Rabindranath's more general critique of nationalism – and it would also provide the basis for a widening of his horizons concerning gender in the post - *swadeshi* era.' (Sarkar 2002: 122–123)

Within *HW*, Sandip's nationalist project has been eliminatory and overwhelmingly masculine. Women are not consulted at the level of the 'metaphysical' planning of the movement – when the goals of the movement would have been envisaged, strategies formulated, cadre-leaders appointed, etc. They are requisitioned when icons, symbols and imagery are required to enlarge the amplitude of the movement.

Nikhilesh believed in *atmasakti* – a continual and empathetic interaction with all the peasants working on his estates.[4] Sandip and his band of young nationalists became impatient with this initiative at the local level. They began to call for an armed struggle to achieve *swaraj*. A distinct version of 'devotional nationalism' began to evolve which utilised the icons of Kali and Durga. (Datta 2003: 12) As Radha Kumar puts it,

> '...their popularity can be seen as an expression of the crisis in established orders of power and dominance, largely engendered by the British encounter, in which elites sought, and were forced to redefine themselves. It should perhaps be noted here that in worshipping Durga and Kali an emphasis was being laid on energy, nature and action: ***prkrti*** and the material aspects of ***Shakti***, which can be both protective, as in Durga, and erotically destructive, as in Kali.' (Kumar 1999:45)

The opportunistic manipulation of women was central to the nationalist project. As Sumit Sarkar has observed in his essay *Nationalism and Stri-Swadhinata*,

> 'Sandip's conquest of Bimala takes the form of lavish, excessive praise and apparent adulation, placing her on a pedestal as virtual symbol of motherland and religion, calling her *mokshirani*, queen-bee of the entire patriotic hive. She does not really come into any public arena... but is repeatedly assured by her lover that everything in the movement is happening because she is its inspiration. The strong erotic note displacing the mother-figure with would be mistress and sheer crudity of the manoeuvre is Sandip's alone, but otherwise there remains an affinity with the ways by which *Swadeshi* nationalism simultaneously exalted and subordinated women.' (Sarkar 2002: 132)

The women's question was pivotal to public debates in early and mid-nineteenth century Bengal. Then, towards the close of the century, there was a sudden diminution of women's issues from such debates. (Chaterjee 1989: 233) There has been an attempt to attribute this decline to the politics of nationalism which, it was felt, was fundamentally conservative. Now Partha Chatterjee believes that the nineteenth century debates about social reform generally, and the women's question in particular, were intensely ideological. (Chaterjee 1989: 236) The prototype for those debates was western liberalism. In order to understand the progressive whittling away of the women's question we have to scrutinise the nationalist ideology. And there we find, observes Chatterjee, that far from a decentering of the women's question in favour of the political struggle, there is, in fact, a resolution of the women's question in complete accord with its (nationalism's) preferred goals. (Chaterjee 1989: 237)

The resolution was built around a division of culture into two spheres – the material and the spiritual. It was believed that Europeans had acquired mastery over the non-Europeans in the material domain, which comprised of science technology and rational forms of economic organisation. Further, the nationalists perceived that in the spiritual domain the East was superior to the West. This material-spiritual distinction could be stretched to an analogous dichotomy – between the outer and the inner. The 'inner' (home) anchors spirituality and its sovereignty is guarded by women. The world 'outside' then would represent the male-pursued domain of material interests. The nationalist agenda was to concede colonization of the material and the outer world but conserve the spiritual and the inner domain. As Chatterjee has analysed, 'The new patriarchy advocated by nationalism conferred upon women the honour of a new social responsibility, and by associating the task of "female emancipation" with the historical goal of sovereign nationhood, bound them to a new and yet entirely legitimate subordination.' (Chaterjee 1989: 248)

Is this the fate of the women in *HW*? Rabindranath displays a startling clarity about this question in his construction of the character of Bara Rani,

Nikhilesh's elder brother's widow. Nikhilesh and Bara Rani have shared memories of a happy childhood, separated as they are by an age gap of just three years. Bara Rani had entered the house at the age of nine. In the face of Nikhilesh's nostalgia for the fun-filled, carefree days of their childhood, Bara Rani's lament is really heart wrenching: 'No, brother dear, I would not live my life again – not as a woman! Let what I have had to bear end with this one birth. I could not bear it over again.' (Tagore, *HW*: 190)

For Bimala, the loss is on three fronts: as a wife (Nikhilesh has a bullet through the head), as a mother (Amulya, who had aroused 'maternal affection' in her, is slain) and as a goddess (Bimala is able to understand Sandip for his self-covetousness). I believe, Bimala has evolved as a political subject even as she deciphers Sandip's politics for its opportunism. Bimala's survival is more than physical - she provides the retrospective on all the lives that impacted on her own. It is difficult to visualize for Bimala the role of a conventional widow *simpliciter*.

The 'new patriarchy', which Chatterjee talked about, does not seem to apply to the protagonists of the three stories that I mentioned in the introduction (Tagore, *Selected Short Stories*). Mrinal in *The Wife's Letter* after fifteen years discovers her autonomy *outside* marriage. Her description of the anonymity that encompasses an ordinary housewife is deeply penetrating. Her winding up of the letter with, 'I too shall live. At last, I live. Bereft of the shelter of your family's feet, *Mrinal*' (Tagore, *Selected Short Stories*: 218) is resounding in its courage and its celebration of freedom, which is unencumbered by a patriarchal husband and his family. Similarly, Kalyani in *The Woman Unknown* chooses to stay single after the mishap that her marriage has turned out to be. She has dedicated her life to educating girls. Anila in *House Number One* walks out of her marriage and the lover. All are women who have declined to tread the weather-beaten path that most would embrace because the landmarks are familiar.

Bimala of *HW*, on the other hand, has hardly the transgressive subjectivity of the heroines of the *Sabuj Patra* phase. But the importance of the narrative lies in its interrogation of contrasting yet common patriarchies represented by the discourses of Sandip and Nikhilesh respectively. And this the *HW* surely succeeds in achieving. The stories then carry this movement forward and provide more explicit resolutions for women entrapped in patriarchies.

Notes

1 Macmillan published them in a consolidated form in 1950.

2 The stories and *The Home and the World* are written in *Chalitbhasha* instead of the Sanskritized *Sadhubhasha*.

3 He composed the stirring song *Bangalar mati Banglar Jal* (Bengal's Soil, Bengal's Water), in P. K. Datta, ed. 2003. *Rabindranath Tagore's The Home and the World: A Critical Companion.* Delhi: Permanent Black. p. 4.

4 P. K. Datta reports that Rabindranath made a series of trips to his estates in Selaidaha and Patisar in East Bengal when he was writing *HW.* He became aware of the dire condition of the peasantry. In fact he utilised his Nobel Prize money in the local Patisar Cooperative Bank in order to ease their burden.

References

Chatterjee, Partha. 1989. 'The Nationalist Resolution of the Women's Question' in Sangari, Kumkum and Vaid, Sudesh, eds, *Recasting Women: Essays in Colonial History,* Delhi: Kali for Women.

Datta, P. K., ed. 2003. *Rabindranath Tagore's The Home and the World: A Critical Companion.* Delhi: Permanent Black.

Kumar, Radha. 1999. *The History of Doing, An Illustrated History of Movements for Women's Rights and Feminism in India 1800–1990.* Delhi: Kali.

Nandy, Ashish. 1994. *The Illegitimacy of Nationalism.* Oxford: Oxford University Press.

Robinson, Andrew. 2002. 'The Home and the World' in Dutt, Ajanta, ed., *The Home and the World.* Delhi: Doaba House.

Sarkar, Sumit. 2002. *Beyond Nationalist Frames: Relocating Postmodernism, Hindutva, History.* Delhi: Permanent Black.

Sarkar, Tanika. 2001. *Hindu Wife, Hindu Nation.* Delhi: Permanent Black.

Sen, Amartya. 2002. 'Tagore and His India' in Dutt, Ajanta, ed., *The Home and the World.* Delhi: Doaba House.

Tagore, Rabindranath. 2002. 'Selected Short Stories' in Chaudhuri, Sukanta, ed. *The Oxford Tagore Translations.* Oxford: Oxford University Press.

——— *The Home and the World,* Tagore, Surendranath, trans. 1985. London: Penguin Books.

Chapter 18

ON THE IDEA OF OBLIGATION TO FUTURE GENERATIONS

Nirmalya Narayan Chakraborty

Until the first quarter of the twentieth century it looked obvious that mankind would continue to exist for all time to come. Development of nuclear weapons compelled man to get worried about the possibility of extinction of the human race. Increase in the population, resulting in environmental pollution and accompanied by limited resources, has been the major cause of the worries human are faced today. Naturally in this context, the question arises whether the present generation has an obligation to future generations so that our sacrifice could ensure the continued existence of the human race, preventing it from future extinction. People have started pondering over this question since there are events that could threaten human survival. Since the existence of future generations in many ways depend on what we do now, the question whether or not we should try to prevent the extinction of mankind is an important issue, not only of pure academic interest but with direct consequences on many contemporary problems as well.

The central question in this discourse seems to be whether we, as the present generation, have any moral obligation and to what extent we have the duty, if we have any duty at all, to the future generation, so that it would be morally incumbent for us to make sacrifices now to bring happy people in the world or to avoid them from being brought to the world.[1]

Admittedly, this issue has several facets worth discussing. In the present discussion I would like to sharpen the two questions just mentioned, without trying to defend any thesis falling on either side of the debate. Also, any discussion on the ethical issues is generally done in the background of some overarching general conception of morality. At present, I am not particularly keen on defending any such conception of morality. My approach is a bottom-up one, i.e., from a common sense analysis of the issue of obligation to future generation I would like to arrive at a general theory of morality, if there is such a theory at all. Understanding the intricacies and nuances involved in the question is my main aim here. Answers to the question whether we have any obligation to future generation extend from one extreme to another. If morality is a matter of agreement or a contract between free rational agents, then future people, simply by virtue of being future people, cannot be a party in the contract or enter into an agreement with us. So we are not morally bound to do anything for the future generation. If, on the other hand, morality is about maximizing happiness, then, assuming that our sacrifices now would benefit the future people where the number of generations to come is an infinite one, the total amount of happiness summed over all those generations would far outweigh the sacrifices of present people, and consequently we owe everything to future people. I believe that in practical life as well as in philosophy extreme positions are always fraught with many difficulties. The trouble in both the academic pursuits and everyday life is that it is difficult to improve intelligibility while retaining the excitement. So the middle way seems to be the correct way, or at least that is what I tend to believe.

What is so special or unique about the question of our obligation to future generations? If morality eschews duties among human beings, then even the future people *qua* human beings would be included in that arena. Future people differ from present people only in terms of placement in a future *time*, as many people are placed in a far bigger *space* from us right now. Future people are not less real than, say, Nigerians or Mexicans. But there are features of future people that make the handling of the question of our obligation to future generations different and difficult to handle. First of all, the relation or interaction between future people and us is one-way. Our decisions or actions affect the future people, but there is no way the future people would affect us. Secondly, future people will luckily inherit our stock of *knowledge*, if not food, water, etc. This is an important thing that the present bequeaths to the future. Thirdly, the population of future generation is infinitely large. There is no theoretical limit to the number of people to come. Even if the world comes to an end at a particular point in time, the number of people in future generations would be hopelessly large. Fourthly, and this is an interesting point, the existence of future people depends on us. If we, the present people, decide to stop procreating, then the future would cease to come into being. So, how many people there will be in future depends on our decision now.

A close look at these features reveals how difficult it is to bring the future people in moral discourse. Not only we can determine and distribute the good and evil over an infinite number of people without any fear of retaliation or hope of reward, we can even determine their existence. Considering the result of massive growth of knowledge that took place in the last century, who knows the exact nature and the kind of developments that might take place in the human cognitive realm in times to come? Since knowledge makes huge differences in human life, we are virtually in the dark about the result of growth of knowledge in future generations. In practice, though, we can confine our plans to near future, say, next hundred years or so. But, nonetheless, the issue regarding remote future remains.

The fourth feature poses special problems. If the existence of future people depends on us, then we have to decide the number of future people. Also, we have to decide, how we should distribute the resources between present and future people. Obviously, these two questions are related. If we do not have any obligation to the future generations, then it really does not matter how many future people there would be, and consequently we do not think of distribution of resources at all. But if we accept our obligation to future people, then of course we have to think of the number of future people, for distribution of resources would vary depending on the number of future people, and so we have to think of the principle that would determine the distribution. Even conceptually speaking, first we have to decide, whether we should produce somebody or not, and then we can decide the nature of our moral dealing with them, if that is at all possible.

The problem, that the first feature gives rise to, manifests itself once we consider the possible ground of the population principle. By 'population principle' I mean an answer to the question how many people there ought to be in future. One could argue that, while formulating population principle, one should take into account the 'interests' of everyone concerned, where interests roughly mean the goal of life, quality of life, etc. The crucial question for our purpose is: Who is 'everyone'? That could be, 1) all the people presently alive; 2) all people, including the future generations; and 3) all people, including *possible* people, people who could be born or conceived, whether they actually are or not. One should note the difference between 2) and 3), a difference that would be explained in the course of this discussion.

The main idea behind our talk of 'the duty to future generations' is that we owe something to somebody and here somebody is the future person. If we generalize this then we must acknowledge that duties must always be to someone. If there is no 'someone', then we cannot talk of the consequences of my action or inaction. If no one is affected by my action or non-performance of it, then that action or inaction could hardly be treated as a violation of duty. Needless to say, this approach comes very close to our common sense.

But once we start thinking of future people, the problem starts raising its head. One commonly held view is that we have a duty to sustain human race. But can we have a duty to human race? Human race obviously is not a person; at best it is a set of persons. It is not obvious that we owe something to such a set or to some such similar idea of mankind as a whole. At best one could propose that we owe this duty to perpetuate human race to future persons. So here we are talking of our duty not to any group or any idea but to individual persons. The problem creeps in at the moment we find that these persons are future persons. If we fail in this duty, there is none to whom we can be said to have done injustice. If we do not perform the duty of perpetuating future people, then they simply won't exist. And so there would not be anybody to whom we might have been said to have failed in our duty. If the person to whom the obligation is directed does not exist, then can I have an obligation at all? Thus it seems that this obligation can exist only insofar as it can be fulfilled. I can have a duty to procreate a future person only if the future person exists, but then my duty to future person is parasitic on my procreating the future person. Unless the future person exists, I cannot be said to have a procreating or any other duty to that future person. So the obligation to the future person is an obligation that cannot be violated. For here I have a duty to procreate somebody only if that somebody is there and that somebody will be there only because of my procreation. One could, of course, talk of duty to procreate future people, saying that otherwise the present generation would be worse off or, say, because all the people (present and future) would be better off. Notice these matters of being 'better off' or 'worse off' are matters of empirical study of social, economic conditions prevalent in a society. The blanket claim that there is a duty to sustain human race is difficult to make sense of, philosophically speaking. Unless, of course, one promises someone to procreate a child with him/her, for there one does have a duty to procreate the future person, but this duty to procreate actually rests on the duty to keep ones promise. Most people, I suppose, would still procreate children simply because of their instinct or because they like children and so on. But these are hardly the things that justify our obligation to procreate future people. It is difficult to make sense, philosophically speaking, of the claim that I have failed to perform my duty to the future person simply by refusing to make that possibility happen. What sense would one make of the claim that by refusing to actualize the possible, one violates the rights of the possible? Possible persons are not persons with any specific features like blond, black, etc. Possible persons simply are not persons.

If we go by utilitarianism, that won't help. Utilitarianism says that an agent should perform the act that would maximize the utility of all persons. Now, if we ask, with regard to the present case, whether the promotion of utility by procreating new people would be counted on all four kinds mentioned above, the answer hinges on whether we take future people and possible people into our consideration. If one denies the entry of future people in the utilitarian purview, then one could very well argue that by not producing a person we cannot be said to do any disutility to her, for there is no 'her' to whom one could have done the disutility. But if one takes the future people into account, then, of course, one could argue that if the child would have had marginal utility, which is well above average, then it would be one's duty to have that child. The obvious question here would be, how much does 'well above average' means? Apart from this calculative aspect of utility, would it not be unintuitive to claim that in the present case it is one's duty to be a parent, failing which, one's action would be regarded as an immoral act?

The main question behind this discussion is this: does the creation of a new life, i.e. conception, result in conferring some benefit on the person who is born? Even if the resulting person turns out to be a happy one, conception does not happen to someone who is already there, and so we cannot say that the resulting person would be better off or worse off than she would have been if conception did not take place. One could, of course, set the utility-state of the future person at zero, if she is not conceived, and then her utility-state increases when she is conceived and so on. But this way of looking at the problem seems to equate a person who is neither happy nor unhappy with a person who was never born in the first place. This seems counter intuitive.

The thorny issue, it seems to me, is that whether existence is a necessary prerequisite to be an object of duty. Can I talk of having a duty but not to anyone, for that 'anyone' is not there, she does not exist? Of course, I can bring her to existence and then talk of my duty to her. But do I have a duty to bring her to existence? Once again the problem here is that it is not obvious that by not conceiving I have done harm to a future person, for it is notoriously difficult to make sense of the claim that the future person would be worse off, if I did not conceive her, than if she was conceived. One could argue that, since life in itself is so valuable, it is our duty to create life whenever possible. Here, one needs to clarify the idea of life being valuable in and of itself. Should we value the life of the killer bacterial germs and let them kill people? Why should we put more value on human life than other life forms? Moreover, if I find out that the child I am going to conceive will have a miserable life if born, would I still be duty bound to procreate that child simply because life itself is valuable? A positive answer to this question sounds repugnant. Quantifying 'how miserable' would be a difficult job. But apart from that, repugnancy is often defended by saying that the child, if born, would be so miserable that it would be better off dead. In fact, termination of pregnancy on medical grounds is often backed up by this argument. Notice the expression 'better off dead'. Does it imply that we calculate the dead person as having utility-level zero and then the utility-level increasing as her journey to the world begins with the birth? Not necessarily. We must remember that death happens to someone. Non-existence is not an event that happens to someone. There is nobody for whom the question would arise, whether she would be better off dead or better off born. Death might maximize ones utility, but not so with non-conception.

Problems crop up when we think of the principle that would decide whether the contemplated child would have a sufficiently good life to justify me in procreating it. If we think of the utility of all the people and not only of the child, then all the people can again be divided into all the present and future people and myself. Among these present and future people again there may be some people who especially care about the prospective child and those who do not. In the prospect of my procreation of a child, obviously my parents would be affected the most because of their emotional attachment, proximity, etc. The vice chancellor of my university would not be that affected. How far shall we go in calculating the utility of other people is again a difficult issue to handle.

One could perhaps guess that the underlying idea behind this discussion is that duty is a relational term and unless the relata exists, any talk of duty seems to be spurious. And this relational nature of duty could perhaps rest on the contract humans have made to have a better and secure life. Given the fact that natural resources are exhaustible, it is perhaps time to ponder, taking the utility of all present and future people into consideration, whether asserting our duty to future people stands philosophical scrutiny.

Note

1 I take this opportunity to express gratitude to my teacher Jan Narveson who got me interested in ethics. While writing this paper I heavily draw on Jan Narveson's paper 'Future People and Us' in *Obligations to Future Generations*, R. I. Sikora and Brian Barry eds. Philadelphia: Temple University Press 1978.

References

Govier, Trudy. 'What Should We Do about Future People' in *Moral Issues*, Narveson, Jan, ed. Toronto: Oxford University Press 1983.

Parfit, Derek. 'Future Generations' in *Moral Issues*, Narveson, Jan, ed. Toronto: Oxford University Press 1983.

Patridge, Ernest, ed. *Responsibilities to Future Generations*. New York: Prometheus Books 1981

Sikora, R. I. and Barry, Brian, eds. *Obligations to Future Generations*. Philadelphia: Temple University Press 1978.

Chapter 19

MORALITY IN CYBERSPACE: INTELLECTUAL PROPERTY AND THE RIGHT TO INFORMATION

Maushumi Guha and Amita Chatterjee

The emergence of the Internet as a popular means of creation and dispersal of intellectual goods has caused ripples of dissent among experts in intellectual property rights. The quarrel is between those who think that the Internet upholds the right to information and those who see it as a representative of the right to profit from intellectual goods. Those who value the Internet for its potential to encourage a free flow of information across geographical and political boundaries recognise the right to information as a basic human right. Those who value the Internet only for its commercial potential violate that right and impede the free flow of information across the Net. Information is power. The right to information must, therefore, be recognised as a basic human right and must be respected in order to make sure that individuals across the world stand at an equal footing. With this in view, we give moral support to those who uphold the free flow of information across the Internet and voice our protest against those who have *only* profit-making in mind, heedless of the needs and rights of many.

Information technology has progressed in leaps and bounds in the past few decades. Not only have IT-related advances been fast, the public has been quick to adopt them in real life. But just as in other technological spheres, the growing use of computers, predominantly the Internet, has given rise to a fresh set of moral issues. In this paper, we shall be concerned with one such issue – the clash between the right to information and the right to profit from intellectual property – and suggest that the Internet is best seen as a means of free communication and exchange of intellectual goods. Hence, there should be no *undue* control of this information network.

The right to intellectual property is a broad theme and we have chosen to restrict our inquiry in several ways. As mentioned, our immediate concern will be the conflict between the right to information and *the right to profit* from intellectual property *over the Internet* and we shall adopt *a moral approach* to the problem. There are some specific legal, economic and political considerations (apart from the technological ones) that form part of any comprehensive study of the issue at hand. We shall not concern ourselves with them directly. All the same, morality being an elementary social concern, our paper will have broad implications for experts working in other areas of social inquiry. Also, any pronouncement on the admissibility of the right to profit from intellectual goods over the Internet is likely to have an impact on the admissibility of such rights in general. This is partly due to the fact that the Internet is such a vastly adopted tool and partly due to the desire to have uniform laws on any subject. We might imagine a time when the Internet has crept into every household and become the standard tool for the creation and dissemination of intellectual property. Law-making bodies might then consider having a uniform system of laws for intellectual property in general, using the Internet-based laws as model. In short, despite the restrictions on the scope of this paper, its implications outstrip its immediate concerns.

The Metamorphosis of Cyberspace

In this section, we give a brief introduction to the Cyberspace and our changing impressions of it. The term 'Cyberspace' is used interchangeably with the term 'Internet'. It was introduced by William Gibson in his novel, *Neuromancer* (1984). Internet technology was developed in the U.S. in the 1970s, primarily for military purposes. By the late nineties, however, the Internet had acquired users who had nothing to do with any defence institution or any institution whatsoever. It had made its way into individual homes and offices, connecting people all over the world.

Considering its unprecedented capacity to connect and inform, the Internet may be looked upon as the perfect solution to our communication problems and to a number of other problems as well. It can act as a school, a letterbox, an encyclopaedia, a publishing venture, a business house, a conference room, a telephone, a television set, a cinema, a radio, a newspaper and a canvas. Given the variety of tasks it can accomplish, it is no wonder that people nurture utopian dreams about Cyberspace. Some look upon it as a shared domain, free from national and geographic boundaries, which encourages *unhindered* interactions between individuals and communities from far-flung areas of the world. They give far greater importance to the social implications of Cyberspace than its commercial ones.

This encouraging picture, however, gets blurred when one considers the significant rise in Internet 'crimes' and other problems associated with its use.

For one, not everyone *has* access to the Internet, which is undoubtedly the most powerful tool for disseminating information in the current age. A society that is already fractured into power groups can do without yet another power-divide – a divide between those who have and those who do not have access to the Net.

Those who do have access to the Net, however, face the danger of infringement upon their civil and privacy rights – hackers abound the Internet and anything from e-mail to credit card number can be tracked by them. Also, thriving on the Internet are pornographic websites that would horrify even adult sensibilities. Children and teenagers are often the targets and victims of these websites. One must also not forget vested interest groups like terrorist organisations that use an apparently innocent medium to serve vile ends.

These problems get multiplied because people look upon Cyberspace as something magical and mysterious, almost as though it were a separate realm of existence, unaffected by and detached from the 'real' world (Agre 1998). There are some (hackers and their likes), who even consider Internet crimes (like hacking and creation of computer viruses) to be a sign of computer wizardry (Rogerson 1995)! Given such notions, people often believe that a crime in the 'real' world is not a crime over the Internet. Even the normally law-abiding citizen may falter when it comes to the Internet. One who finds it unimaginable to steal money from a colleague's drawer may download a poem from the Internet and pass it off as one's own in a gathering.

Predictably, international bodies as well as individual countries are adopting measures to curb Internet crimes. In particular, they are devising ways to discourage the violation of intellectual property rights like the copyright. As a consequence, what was proclaimed to be a 'harbinger' of the free flow of information is now all set to become another controlled network, ultimately to be exploited by unscrupulous business houses and individuals for their money-making dreams.

A Clash of Rights

We have been talking about the clash between two rights – the right to information and the right to profit from intellectual property. We need to know clearly what these rights are about. In other words, we need to lay down what we shall understand by 'information' and 'intellectual property'. We shall understand these expressions loosely or broadly. The word 'information' may be taken to mean anything that may appear before us in any form: a map, a mouse, a cat, a tree, a lock, a book, a directory, a programme, a coding, graphics, a poem, an academic article, a journal, collected data or even email. In this broad sense, an intellectual good can easily be seen as a package of information.[1] So, anything that hinders the free sharing of intellectual goods will clash with the right to information. As the copyright situation stands today, our right to information is, indeed, greatly curbed. Access to information protected by copyright laws is mostly determined by monetary capacity. Obviously, there are individuals and states that can afford to 'buy' information at any cost. But there are others who cannot. To them, the Internet epitomizes the right to information. One can look for information on almost any subject on the Net and hardly have to pay for it. One can send electronic messages (e-mail and instant messaging) to one's loved (and not-so-loved!) ones anywhere in the world. One can accomplish a number of other tasks over the Internet that one couldn't have imagined doing even a few years ago.

However, the laws of the land have not spared the Internet (or shall not spare the Internet for long) and web hosts, realising the immense commercial potential of the Net, are putting a price on things that were earlier 'free'. Even the most popular sites, which had nothing to do with anything commercial, are being forced by large commercial houses and courts to abandon their free sharing practices. An example is the popular music-exchange site, Napster. Even three years ago, music-lovers could obtain free membership and exchange popular Western songs from their own collections. Commercial houses, which had sole proprietary rights over these songs, saw Napster as a potential threat to their businesses and went to court. The court gave its ruling in their favour and Napster was compelled to stop the free exchange of music that it was famed for.[2] This is one of several examples. Many electronic-greeting websites, which used to give free access to members (and even the occasional visitor), have now become paid-sites. The trend seems to be setting in even as far as the 'free' e-mail services are concerned. Mailbox sizes are being greatly reduced and the day is, perhaps, not far when Yahoo or Hotmail will charge all its members a fee for its services.[3]

The picture that emerges from the above account is a clear indication of the clash of rights we have been talking about all this while. The conflict between the two rights is a conflict in more ways than one. It is a conflict between *freedom* and *control*. The right to information stands for some very fundamental principles like freedom and equality. The right to profit from intellectual goods (like the copyright) may be seen as opposing those principles, for example, by imposing restrictions on the freedom to be informed. Considered carefully, the conflict between the right to information and the right to profit from intellectual property is also a conflict between *two* individual *freedoms* – the freedom to be informed and the freedom to own property. The owner of a copyright can claim total freedom with regard to the intellectual good he owns; he can claim that he is free to make use of it in any manner he deems fit, to demand a price for it or even to prevent others from using it for the simple reason that he *owns it*. The problem is, therefore, not only of deciding, which should win: freedom or control, but also of deciding *which freedom* should win.

Arguments in Favour of Intellectual Property Rights

It is not as though the right to information gets threatened *only* by intellectual property rights. A variety of attitudes may lie behind the rejection of the right to information, ranging from the paternalistic to the liberal, to the downright conservative. There are people who reject the right to information, or at least refuse to attach much significance to it on the ground that certain kinds of information (say, defence information or medical information) cannot be and *should not be* shared by all. They mostly argue from the premise that the security of the country or even the individual may be at stake if information does not fall into the right hands. But the *principal* cause behind the rejection of the right to information is the near glorification of the right to profit from the ownership of intellectual creations.

The arguments stated in this section support intellectual property rights in general. Intellectual property rights include the right to profit from the ownership of intellectual goods, like the copyright. But they also include the moral rights of the creator of an intellectual good, like the right of proper attribution. Unfortunately, a majority of the arguments favouring intellectual property rights are, in truth, arguments supporting the right to profit from intellectual goods.

An intellectual property right, like the copyright, is usually defined as follows:

> a protection that covers published and unpublished literary, scientific and artistic works, whatever the form of expression, provided such works are fixed in a tangible or material form. This means that if you can see it, hear it and/or touch it, it may be protected. If it is an essay, if it is a play, if it is a song, if it is a funky original dance move, if it is a photograph, HTML coding or a computer graphic that can be set on paper, recorded on tape or saved to a hard drive, it may be protected. Copyright laws grant the creator the exclusive right to reproduce, prepare derivative works, distribute, perform and display the work publicly. Exclusive means only the creator of such work, not anybody who has access to it and decides to grab it. (Rebeca Delgado-Martinez V. 1998)

Let us now take a look at some concrete arguments presented in favour of intellectual property rights:

1. The creators of an intellectual good must garner the rewards for it. That will be possible only if they are recognised as the *owner* of their creation. If they become the legal owners of their intellectual creation they will

have the right to use it for any purpose and exclude others from using it in any manner. Most importantly, they will have the right to profit from the commercial use of their creation. No one else must have the right to enjoy it in any manner, certainly not commercially (unless, of course, the owner gives consent, in which case there probably would be a sharing of profits).

2. If the innovators are not given such rights or if they are not sufficiently compensated or rewarded for their merit, then they will not feel encouraged for further creation. To encourage innovation, there must be an incentive and this incentive must come in the form of actual benefits.
3. In a very important way, the creators identify themselves with their creations. They also expect others to do the same. The moral rights of the creator must, therefore, be recognised. These include citing and acknowledging created works properly.

These arguments are extended to intellectual goods created and transferred electronically so as to make intellectual property rights apply to such things as websites, software applications, etc. It is argued further that the Internet provides greater scope to flout intellectual property laws, so such laws should be enforced strictly in Cyberspace.

Two Types of Rights and Two Types of Goods

Let us distinguish between two types of rights of intellectual property after Andrew Alexander (1995). Alexander differentiates between *commodity* rights and *moral* rights of intellectual goods. Intellectual property rights are, for the most part, *commodity* rights. Commodity rights give owners of intellectual property, complete commercial control over them. In other words, they ascribe commercial worth to intellectual property. The owner can, therefore, profit from the use or sale of such property and also (legally) prevent others from its use or sale. *Moral* rights, on the other hand, do not (necessarily) ascribe commercial value to intellectual property. They are expressions of the creator's moral claim over his or her creation(s). Our having a moral right over this article simply means that we should (would expect to) be acknowledged if anyone uses it for any purpose. So moral rights of intellectual property include such privileges as proper attribution (the creator of an intellectual good must be formally recognised as its creator) and integrity (someone's intellectual creation should not be disfigured, distorted or used in any way unacceptable to the creator).[4]

Like Alexander, we shall also distinguish between two types of goods, *joint* goods and *non-joint* goods. An example of a non-joint good is an apple. An apple is a thing that cannot be shared indefinitely. At some point of time, someone or the other must be deprived of its use or consumption. A non-joint good is, therefore, one whose availability is restricted or scant and which cannot be shared beyond a limit. On the other hand, take a poem or the piece of information that there is water on Mars. What kind of good is it? Certainly not non-joint, since, the poem or the information, that there is water on Mars can be shared indefinitely. Sharing it does not diminish its value – qualitatively or quantitatively – nor does it take anything away from the poet or the scientist. It is, therefore, a joint good.

The important question is how do the two types of rights stand in relation to the two types of goods? There are four possibilities: we can have commodity rights over joint goods, commodity rights over non-joint goods, moral rights over joint goods and moral rights over non-joint goods. We are interested in the first and the third categories. The first two arguments stated in the previous section are in favour of commodity rights over joint goods, particularly, intellectual goods. The third argument is in support of moral rights over intellectual goods.

Arguments Against the Right to Profit from Intellectual Goods

We shall begin this section by countering the first two arguments given in favour of the intellectual property rights in section 3. In this context, let us go back to the definition of an intellectual property right as stated in that very section. The definition says, 'Copyright laws grant the *creator* the exclusive right to reproduce, prepare derivative works, distribute, perform and display the work publicly. Exclusive means only the *creator* of such work, not anybody who has access to it and decides to grab it.' (Rebeca Delgado-Martinez V 1998, emphasis ours). *Firstly*, we would like to draw your attention to the distinction between the *creator* and the *owner* of an intellectual good and point out that in the case of an intellectual creation, it is often the case that the owner of the good is different from its creator. A commodity right like the copyright gives the *owner* of the copyright and *not the creator*, sole proprietary rights over an intellectual item. In most cases, a few commercial houses and big businesses that own the copyrights, control the flow of information. Neither the creator nor the user benefits in any real sense from the exercise of commodity rights.

Secondly, a close look at the basic argument in favour of intellectual property rights will show that it does not stand, for there is no necessary connection between intellectual creativity and market gain. Teachers do not share innovations and ideas with any hope of material achievements. Artists, musicians, writers and creators in general do not create only with the hope that they will gain monetarily from their creations. They create because creation is an urge, a talent, a natural disposition. Some of the greatest works of art and literature were created outside the constraints of copyright, for copyright is a modern notion, which was unknown before the Statute of Anne (1710). Reward is not necessarily monetary. Intellectual creativity is in itself, a rewarding engagement. Rewards may also come in the form of recognition or in the form of intellectual debates and exchanges over created goods. Most importantly, all innovations or creations do not deserve to be rewarded. Surely, a terrorist's malice-ridden parody does not deserve any reward?

Above, we tried to show why arguments in favour of the right to profit from intellectual goods (ownership rights or commodity rights over intellectual goods) do not stand. These arguments appear even weaker when they are applied to the Internet. We shall explain why when we give some independent arguments (below) to show why the right to profit from intellectual goods should not win against the right to information, particularly in Cyberspace. Let us take a look at those arguments.

1. If the conflict between the right to information and the right to intellectual property is seen as one between freedom and control, then we shall argue after Mill (1869) that, freedom being of greater value than control, having free access to information and ideas is a natural, ethical right that everyone must enjoy. Abridgement of freedom in any specific case needs to be justified, but whether the right to profit from ownership of intellectual goods can be a satisfactory justification for the curtailment of the right to information may be seriously doubted.[5] Commodity rights over intellectual goods are one of the causes of the imbalance of power that exists between the developed and the under-developed countries of the world.[6] Information is another name for power. Whoever has (free or easy) access to it is powerful (and more often than not, manipulative). Most of the control that affluent states exercise over their lesser cousins is owing to the fact that the latter are less *informed*. There is a vicious circle – information comes at a cost, so it cannot be accessed by all; those who have access to it are far from willing to make it available to those who cannot afford it; so those who have no access to it are made worse off day by day. Commodity rights over intellectual goods should be derecognised over the Internet because it is the only channel that has the potential for worldwide use by developed as well as third-world nations, enabling one and all to have access to information that otherwise comes at a cost.
2. If the conflict between the right to information and the right to profit from the ownership of intellectual goods is seen as one between two individual rights, then also we shall vote in favour of the former. We have already mentioned that we must distinguish between the owner and the creator of an intellectual good. We have also pointed out that it is the *owner* of the copyright that benefits, neither the creator nor the user. So, how can we

justify the right of the owner, who is not the creator, to earn profit from the use or sale of an intellectual good that he or she has not created? The individual's right to earn profit from an intellectual good cannot override another individual's right to be informed.

3. Indian culture, too, has emphasised the value of knowledge as opposed to riches. It is no wonder that since time immemorial, rich texts have been passed down from generation to generation without any mention of any author. For the aim was to share and to encourage a common good, to bring about upliftment of character. The Preamble to the Indian Constitution declares India to be a socialist republic. The right to property, which was earlier listed among the fundamental rights, is no longer recognised as one. On the other hand, cultural and educational rights, the right to equality and the right to particular freedoms are recognised as fundamental rights under the Indian Constitution. The right to information may be regarded as a right to a particular freedom – the freedom of information. It may also be regarded as an auxiliary of the right to equality. We may also think of the right to information as being part of cultural and educational rights. It may not be wrong to conclude, therefore, that the Constitution of the largest democracy in the world provides greater support to the right to information.
4. Excessive control over the movement of information across the Internet will encourage the development of technology that will violate the privacy of 'netizens', for large organisations and governments who are in the business of protecting intellectual property rights will try to make sure that no violation goes unnoticed. Such organisations will develop new ways of encrypting data and of detecting information from user machines. Also, there would be cause for great concern if such technology fell into unscrupulous hands. Moreover, the greater the control, the greater will be the tendency to break away from it. External impositions tend to test the patience of the people on the receiving end of those impositions. With every technological progress to control the flow of information, new technology will emerge to counter it. Hacking, spamming, virus development and other things, considered 'crimes' in Cyberspace, will get further boost.
5. Intellectual property being a joint good, there is no reason why its creator must feel threatened if others have access to it or make use of it. A joint good, as we have seen, can be shared indefinitely without causing any harm to the creator or to the good itself. On the other hand, if commodity rights are claimed over intellectual goods, people might be deprived of its benefits in some predicted or unpredicted manner.
6. Very importantly, a free sharing of ideas and information is most likely to encourage innovation and greater creativity. Why must we always begin at the beginning when we are starting on a new venture? Wouldn't it be

much simpler if we built upon foundations already laid? Why must we be 'constantly forced to reinvent the wheel' (Samudrala 2001) rather than move from wooden tyres to steel radials? In fact, we must seriously ask, whether it is at all possible to invent or innovate in vacuum! All that we can think of today is a result of what we received from some source or the other – whether directly or indirectly. Our article is a clear example. Nothing we've said in it is something that someone somewhere has not already thought or spoken about. So the real question is, *can we* possibly *reinvent* the wheel? In fact, commodity rights disrespect the contribution of innumerable persons whose efforts go into the creation or enhancement of an intellectual good.

7. An open system, in which intellectual property is shared freely, is a system that promotes creativity and innovation. Much time is saved in the process, since innovators are not required to start from scratch. At the same time, there is a flow of ideas from several directions, enriching the original work. Most importantly, snags or lacunae can be identified and rectified with much greater ease.[6]

Intellectual Property and Moral Rights

We have listed several reasons why we think that intellectual property rights that grant ownership of intellectual goods are unjustified. Cyberspace should be freed from constrains of commodity rights, since they hamper the free flow of information, which is the original idea that encouraged the growth of the Internet. Also, commodity rights disrespect the contribution of the innumerable sources that enhance intellectual creations and grant ownership privileges to a few, sometimes to people who have not created the goods. This takes us to one argument we have not yet considered – the third argument stated in favour of intellectual property rights in section 3. In that argument, it is emphasised that the moral rights of the creators of intellectual goods should be recognised. We fully endorse this view and believe that 'netizens' should be made aware of the moral rights of those behind intellectual creations so that they appreciate and acknowledge the skills and efforts of the latter. Moral rights include, among others, the right to proper attribution. Sometimes even educators fail to cite references and web addresses, believing (falsely) that one doesn't need to do so in case of the material downloaded from the Net. The notion of 'free' information is, in this case, somewhat twisted. 'Free' does not mean 'to be used without citation'. 'Free' simply means 'need not be paid for' or 'can be used without formal permission from the writer/creator'.

Whether moral rights should be legally enforced by a professional body or not is an issue we leave to legal experts. Empirical considerations of all kinds – technological, legal, economic and political – would be required to give shape to our conceptualisations. But such considerations are beyond our expertise and also the scope of this paper. At the same time, we believe that these are important beginnings.

In the end, we would like to point out that we are not in the business of doing away with intellectual property rights from our social and legal framework altogether. Our intention is to do away with such rights over the Internet, that too, only one variety of intellectual property rights, namely, commodity rights.

The good news is that the outlook on intellectual property seems to be changing. There is a clear indication of this change of attitude in the 1996 World Intellectual Property Organization's (WIPO) Diplomatic Conference where the WIPO Copyright Treaty and the WIPO Performances and Phonograms Treaty were adopted.[8] In spite of the fact that the two treaties were adopted, some of the issues raised by the scholars and professionals from forty five countries show that the UNESCO objective is to develop a scale of values in Cyberspace, to reinforce the free flow of information and to head off any over-reaction that might lead to excessive regulation of the communication networks' (United Nations Chronicle 1997).

Notes

1 Luciano Floridi, 'Information Ethics: On the Philosophical Foundation of Computer Ethics' in *Ethics and Information Technology*, 1:37–56,1999.

2 Visit http://www.findlaw.com for details of the Court proceedings. Also, visit http://www.wired.com for interesting perspectives on Napster. There is, of course, Napster's own website, http://www.napster.com

3 'New technologies, backed by new legal doctrines, have the potential to transform all or part of the network environment into a "pay-per-use Panopticon," in which every use of every work available on-line could be licensed, monitored, and billed by electronic means.' (Jaszi 1997)

4 There are several websites, which provide information on moral rights over intellectual creations, for example http://www.caslon.com.au/ipguide16.htm and http://www.finlaysons.com.au/ipt/moral.htm

5 However, we are aware that there may be strong paternalistic grounds to withhold information from Internet users. Examples of such information have already been cited in the paper (military information being an instance). Under usual circumstances, such information would not appear on the Internet. However, there is a very thin line between information that can be and information that cannot be found on the Net. So, one very important question that has not been addressed in this paper is whether paternalistic grounds can be acceptable justification for denying the right to information. That question will raise further issues. One important question that will demand attention is whether all kinds of information can be dumped under the common head 'joint good'. For if certain kinds of information (like military information) cannot be shared, they cannot fall under the broad category of joint goods. One thing, however, needs to be made clear: the question of an intellectual property right or any opposition to it arises only with respect to information *actually available* in some form or the other (information

in some tangible form), not with respect to *potential* information. So, even if paternalistic reasons force our policy makers to keep away certain kinds of information from us, that will not have any direct bearing on our paper.

6 'There is a strong case for opposing intellectual property. Among other things... it exploits third world peoples.' (Martin 1995)

7 See Raymond (2000). Also, visit the website of the Free Software Movement started by Richard Stallman in the 1980s, for further insights.
http://www.gnu.org/home.html
http://www.gnu.org/philosophy/why-free.html

8 Visit http://www.wipo.org for the text of the treaties.

References

Agre, Philip E. 1998. 'Yesterday's tomorrow' in *The Times Literary Supplement*, July 3, 1998 Available Online at http://dlis.gseis.ucla.edu/people/pagre/tls.html

Alexander, Andrew. 1995. 'Intellectual property: The impact of the web', *Proceedings: AUGG'95 and Asia Pacific World Wide Web'95 Conference.*

Delgado-Martinez V., Rebeca. 1998. *What is copyright?* Online: http://www.whatiscopyright.org/

Gibson, William. 1984. *Neuromancer*. New York: Ace Books.

Jaszi, Peter. 1998. 'Is this the end of copyright as we know it?' in *Nordisk Forum för biblioteckschefer.*

Martin, Brian. 1995. 'Against intellectual property' in *Philosophy and Social Action*, Vol. 21, No. 3. Online: http://www.uow.edu.au/arts/sts/bmartin/pubs/95psa.html

Mill, J. S. 1869. *On Liberty*, Ed. by Edward Alexander, 1999, Broadview Press, Canada.

Raymond, Eric Steven. '*The Cathedral and the Bazaar*' in *Knowledge, Technology and Policy*, Fall 1999, Vol. 12, No. 3, pp. 23–49.

Rogerson, Simon & Terrer, Ward Bynum. 1995. 'Cyberspace: The Ethical Frontier' in *The Times Higher Education Supplement.*

Samudrala, Ram. 2001. *A primer on the ethics of 'intellectual property'*. Online: United Nations Chronicle. 1997. 'WIPO addresses Internet copyright'.

Chapter 20

VIOLENCE – A RIGHT TO THE SURVIVAL OF THE SELF?

Anup Dhar[1]

Philia begins with the possibility of survival.
Surviving – that is the other name of a mourning
whose possibility is never to be awaited.

— Derrida, *Politics of Friendship*

Mr. & Mrs. Iyer

A bus full of passengers makes its way through the hilly tracts of the southern part of India. As the bus makes its way through the hills, a riot breaks out somewhere on the route the bus is to follow. The bus is invaded by a group of Hindu fanatics. They are in search of Muslims. They undress one by one the male passengers of the bus to find out who among them are Muslims. As they go about doing this, one passenger, presumably in a bid to save all the passengers of the bus, cries out: '*Hum sab Hindu hain.*' ('We are all Hindus.') It is at this moment that a male passenger (named Cohen), seated at the rear end of the bus, interjects: 'No, not all are Hindus – *they* are not Hindus.' And he points at an old couple seated in the left hand corner of the bus: '*They* are Muslims – they are not Hindus.' The old couple is dragged out of the bus, never to be seen again. When asked later why he did such a thing, the visibly dejected and crestfallen Cohen answers: 'They would have caught me. I am a Jew. I do not have a foreskin.'

It was as though he was saying: 'I did not wish to do such a thing, but there was no way I could have saved my own life. My survival depended

> solely on the non-survival of the old Muslim couple. I would have to single them out as Muslims; I would have to hand them over to the Hindu fanatics, if I were to prevent their examining my private anatomy.'

The above narration tries to follow somewhat faithfully a scene depicted in the film *Mr. & Mrs. Iyer*, directed by Aparna Sen. The film is the story of a certain Mrs. Iyer, a 'conservative' Hindu woman and a certain Jahangir Chaudhury, an 'enlightened' yet sensitive Muslim man named (re-christened) Mr. Iyer by Mrs. Iyer herself in a bid to save his life, save him from being dragged similarly out of the bus and killed. Mrs. Iyer, along with her child and Jahangir Chaudhury, happen to be co-travellers in the same bus. In the scene depicted above, they are seated side by side as they watch with bewilderment the dragging out of the old Muslim couple. A few minutes back, Mrs. Iyer had come to know that Jahangir Chaudhury was a Muslim. She had not taken too kindly to his being a Muslim.[2] The fact of her being a Hindu and his being a Muslim was about to produce a certain rift, a divide in their emerging association. But the overt violence on the old Muslim couple had perhaps redrawn boundaries once again. A few minutes back Mrs. Iyer and Jahangir Chaudhury were on opposite sides of the 'religious divide' – now they were both on the same side of another divide – the divide of those on the side of violence and those on the side of non-violence.

In the same scene, as the fanatics are about to approach Jahangir Chaudhury, Mrs. Iyer, seated just beside him, places her child on his lap and cries out, as if to declare their common identity: 'Mr. and Mrs. Iyer!'

This singular act of naming – naming in the reverse because in Hindu communities it is the man who (re)names the woman, and the woman is made to take up the (sur)name of her husband after marriage – by a conservative Hindu woman ensures the survival (at least for the time being) of the Muslim man. I wish to sharply distinguish between Mrs. Iyer's and Cohen's approach to the question of survival. Cohen ensures his survival at the cost of the survival of two others while Mrs. Iyer ensures the survival of another – an Other – by putting at risk her own survival. The very fact that Mrs. Iyer was lying to the Hindu fanatics could well have jeopardised her own survival had the Hindu fanatics come to know of the 'original' identity of Jahangir Chaudhury. This distinction between the two approaches is not to make a moral comment on one (here Cohen) but to bring up somewhat metaphorically the question of the ethics of survival. While one can never deny one's right to survive or right to live (here, Cohen's right to live), one could, in one's self-survival, still be unselfconsciously sensitive (without being abrasively ennobling) to the question of the Other, to certain ethics of survival where one does not just ensure one's self-survival, does not just lay and pursue a claim to the *right* to one's own survival – but remains at the same time sensitive to the question of the simultaneous survival of the Other.[3] In other words, one attaches, one links up one's own survival to the concomitant survival of another – survival of the Other – something which Mrs. Iyer had done with a certain risk-taking. This is important not just because our survival is sometimes too intimately and too substantively tied to the survival of the Other – say the survival of the human species on the one hand, and the survival of nature on the Other – but because this relates to a more general question of ethics: would the self survive, at least metaphorically, to the exclusion of the Other or would the self survive in critical yet firm embrace with the Other?

Trying to move (not altogether) beyond a simple rights paradigm, this work of writing tries to explore the question of survival also at a more ethical level. This is important because the question of violence is related in ways more than one to the question of survival – the 'simple' desire to live – Cohen's violence on the old Muslim couple is not borne out of the wish to be violent *per se* – in fact, he could well have been an extremely non-violent person – but is borne out of his 'simple' desire to live, a desire that cannot be put to question, but which somewhat paradoxically puts two others to death. Who can deny Cohen his right to live? At the same time, who can deny the right of the old Muslim couple to live? What if the rights of one appear to infringe upon the rights of another? What resolutions can one expect within the rights paradigm, within a discourse of rights? Or does one need to move beyond the question of rights and move instead to the question of an ethics of survival?

Ethics of Surviving Selves

This is an essay on the possible ethics of survival, the ethics of surviving selves – on *life*. This is also because the dead, as a rule, do not write.[4] They are written about. The dead do not 'know' their own death. Although only the dead may, yet, have an experience of death – a somewhat singular experience that is nearly inaccessible to all others – there is, perhaps, never enough time to 'know'[5] death. It is the living we who try to make sense of death. We write on death. We cheer, condemn, co-opt or cash in on death.

This is not much of a writing on death. This is not much of a *writing*. It is more an act of *mourning* or *melancholia* (Freud, 1957: 237–58), perhaps, in the most perpetual sense.

But then, how do we mourn the dead? How do we mourn the loss of the Other? Mourning is both a Statist and a Brahminical affair. Keeping flags half-mast for seven days and then ritual service every year, year after year, which in actuality is perhaps an act of forgetting. We remain instead in a perpetual melancholia, in mourning that is forever suspended, deferred, that is never complete – the letter that never reaches its destination. The lost Other remains encrypted within us. The Other is not engulfed.

En*crypt*ment… not interiorisation. The 'crypt' perhaps is an apt metaphor, because the ego comes to contain and keep alive within itself the 'cadaver' of the Other. Instead of the cadaver being consigned to a legal burial place, his or her memory is entombed in a fast and secure place ... (through) the setting up within the ego of a closed-off space, a *crypt*, ... a kind of anti-introjection, comparable to the formation of a cocoon around the chrysalis. In the encryptment there is an enveloping within one's boundaries of an Other that remains undigested.

This is much less a writing on death than a writing on life[6], on survival, on survivors, who have put the Other to death in order to secure their survival.[7] It is a writing on their *perceived* threat to survival and on the violence of their survival. It is also a writing on the possible 'ethics of survival'. It is a search for ethics where the Other is not cannibalised.

The cannibal survives by eating the Other. His survival – his continued existence – depended on the non-existence of the Other.

We look instead for an ethics of survival where the desire of the 'self' to survive neither devours nor annihilates the Other. But that would also necessitate an engagement with the moment of the Hegelian 'trial by death' (Hegel 1998: 114) and the resolution of the trial by death in relations of lordship and bondage – in relations that are not explicitly coercive but hegemonic.

Our journey, our search for the ethics of survival – a search that remains crucial in our cherished escape from violence starts from Ahmedabad, passes through Auschwitz, passes through nineteenth century Bengali writings on the imagined extinction of the Hindu community, passes through masculine Hindu self-assertion in *Suddhi* and *Sangathan* movements, passes through Godse's assassination of Gandhi and arrives once again at Ahmedabad.

Ahmedabad: *Meta-name* of Violence or *Meto-nym* of Violence, or Both?

> … henceforth, growing old will not bring (them, the survivors) closer to death, but quite on the contrary carry (them) away from it. (Semprun 1998, 15)

Somewhat without respite – without a break, breather, lull, relief or let up we move – move from one killing field to another … until we find ourselves engulfed, swallowed up by killing fields … swallowed up by the somewhat curious odour of killing fields … 'sweetish, cloying, with a bitter and truly nauseating edge to it' … a haunting smell that somewhat tenaciously follows us. The slightest distraction of a memory brimful of trifles, of petty joys would be enough to summon the smell. 'Distraction from the shimmering opacity of life's offerings ... distraction from oneself, from the existence that inhabits and possesses us, stubbornly, obtusely: the obscure desire to go on living, to persevere in this obstinacy for whatever reason, or unreason. It would take only a single instance of distraction from oneself and the strange smell would always return ... at random, out of the blue, at point blank range' (Semprun, 1998).

The *smell* from the killing fields... estuaries of death... crematory ovens...

Killing fields – from insignificant ones to some more catastrophic ones that take up Auschwitz-like proportions. Why name Auschwitz as the reference point any more? Ahmedabad may well be considered the more clandestine re-incarnation of Auschwitz. Ahmedabad with 'Sabarmati' – a worn out inspiration, perhaps only a few miles away. Now they are light years apart. They lost each other at the moment Godse fired the first shot from his gun. Ahmedabad now becomes a fitting reply of the harassed children of midnight to the Father who failed to protect his daughters at Noakhali. And Sabarmati flows... a solitary soul, head bowed – 'crimson to this day with the blood of dead deer'.

Our steps remain marked by two apparently contradictory moves. As a first move, we zoom onto the killing field, onto the acts and facts of violence that Ahmedabad so cruelly symbolizes. Unparalleled[8] in magnitude by all other forms of violence – as practically the most grotesque face of violence Ahmedabad becomes the *meta-name* of all forms of violence. And then, as a second and subsequent move, a somewhat paradoxical move, we, however impossible it may seem, try to move out of the particularity of the killing fields. We have to, because Ahmedabad is just one. Here Ahmedabad is nothing more than a *metonym* of all the violence that goes on around us. Reading Ahmedabad as a metonym, we try to move out – albeit for a while – out of particular acts of violence, acts which are nevertheless gruesome, acts which are nevertheless to be condemned, to a maybe more *robust* reading of violence. We move, or at least try to move, to a possible space where violence is conceptualised more as a pervasive phenomenon – hence the need of a more robust analysis - and less as simply the organized (i.e. pogrom-like) or mad (i.e. riot-like) act of individuals or groups of people. This is not to, in any way, trivialize, downplay, dilute, distort or distance ourselves (into the insulation of a theoretical cocoon) from the concrete pain and suffering that Ahmedabad was and still is.

Ahmedabad, therefore, for the span of this writing, or maybe not even for the entire span of it, is '(o)ne name for another, a part for the whole' (Derrida 1994). The historic violence of Ahmedabad is treated here as a metonymy. 'By diverse paths (condensation, displacement, expression or representation)' we try to decipher through the singularity that Ahmedabad is 'so many other kinds of violence going on in the world. At once part, cause, effect, example, what is happening there translates what takes place here, always here, wherever one is and wherever one looks, closest to home' (Derrida 1994). We take a close look at what takes place here, always here, wherever one is and wherever one looks. And we do this, we try to get near violence, nearly at the violence in order 'to get as far away as possible' (Theweleit 1987) from violence. Such an approach to violence necessitates, in turn, the abandoning of secure oppositions of Us and Them; where Us and Them represent the opposing arms of a binary. Instead, one needs to see how *we* and *our selves*, how the very secure and untouched repository of the *Us* remain implicated in violence.

> … Us/Them, Secular/Rioter, Human/Animal, Tolerant/Bigot, Sage/Savage, Modern/Feudal, Enlightened/Superstitious, Rational/Emotional, Scientist/ Follower of Faith, Non-violent/Violent …

The binary of Us/Them operates through a maximizing of the difference between the two arms of the binary; a certain absolute impenetrability of forms of *self* and the Other. The subsequent impulse at correcting this difference and gap would be an erasure of difference through the hegemony of the secular and enlightened Us over Them, which, in other words, is a homogenizing impulse, a Statist impulse, an impulse at reducing all the differences, all unassimilated *others* to the logic of the One and the Same through law and legality – either the sameness of nationhood and/or citizenship.

Here, the Other is not (an)other but (my)self – the Other *is* my self.

A more complicated understanding of the binaries Us/Them would entail an appreciation of the complicity of Us, even if implicit, in structures of violence closest to home. Maybe not overt acts of violence. But complicity in the somewhat covert[9] flow of violence – the silent, almost surreptitious survival of violence; violence sustained in the 'rule of order', violence sustained in everyday life, which, in other words, *is* the everyday life of violence: violence in the family, home, workplace and school – violence in the individual, in peers and groups, in communities and institutions, in the state, judiciary and army – violence in our very survival. A certain imperialism of violence – violence that colonizes – violence that is associated inalienably with the order of things, with governance, with the operations of power – power that produces.

Violence that is there, *within us.*

Violence is what *we* desire, somewhat unconsciously, which gives violence its unconscious psychic life. Some violence is considered legitimate: violence of the state, the police, the army, the judiciary over the errant, the deviant; 'legitimate' violence of colonialism, of the sponsored development of the 'Third World'. Some violence is considered necessary: violence of the party, of a large organization getting out at the 'others', at the 'deviation' of the others; of a certain elimination of the opposition, of dissent, of a non-conformist. Some violence is considered normal: violence of the parent over the child, the teacher over the student, the doctor over the patient, the nurse over the psychotic.[10]

Does the violence of everyday life – everyday violence, which is legitimate, necessary and normal – in some way prepare and secure the ground for a much larger violence? Do they serve as nurturing nursery beds for a more grotesque form of violence? Surely, one cannot think of just one cause that produces the 'Ahmedabad effect'? Economic, political and cultural processes (Resnick & Wolff 1987), processes related to class, race, gender, sexuality – they all play a mutually constitutive part in the production of the 'Ahmedabad effect'.

A Further Question...

But then a further question haunts the 'act of speculation' that is this work of writing – a question that can perhaps be asked only to the self that is surviving at the cost of the Other. Or perhaps, are we not all surviving at the cost of others? Is not Israel surviving at the cost of Palestine? But then, what is so natural about the survival of self, survival at any cost – at the cost of the Other? Is survival then always already violent, something that intrinsically impinges on the survival of the Other? Is there anything *natural* about the violence of survival – is there anything *natural* about the annihilation of the Other for the survival of 'self'? Is the survival of the 'self' – both survival and the survival of the 'self' to the exclusion of the Other – nothing but natural? Or is it made to look natural, naturalized discursively – the naturalness of the natural produced and reproduced through reiterative performative gestures that, in turn, make us used to the violence, to the violent ways of *be-ing*?

This is not to question survival *per se*. That would be too counterproductive a gesture after the Gujarat carnage.[11] This is to question the obsessive rhetoric of the survival of 'self' in the face of a threat to survival that fuels, or is invoked to fuel, acts of violence on the Other. This is to question the obvious *fact* of survival made obvious by the *science* of survival. This is to question a science premised somewhat teleologically on a founding threat to survival, a subsequent struggle for survival, a natural selection thereafter and, finally, a survival of the fittest. This is not to produce opposing facts/truths that demonstrate the imaginary nature of a perceived threat to survival, that describe the threat as more imagined than real – though such a move remains quite necessary. Rather, this is a move towards an ethics of survival, taking into consideration the fact that even if the threat is at times *not* real in a very realist sense, it is nevertheless productive of subjectivities – of structures and layers of identity that guide us in our actions, that exert gravitational pull in the way we organize our lives. Interpellated, as we are, by this threat of 'a dying race' – this threat, however much imagined, however phantasmatic it is, produces effects/affects.[12]

A Dying Race

Dwarakanath Bidyabhusan, echoing the anxiety of 'a dying race', wrote in *Nababarsiki* in the year 1880 an article titled 'Banglar Loksonkhya' ('Census in Bengal'):

> ...another subject/cause for worry is that the number of Muslims have increased and have slowly become equal to that of the Hindus. The Hindus outnumber Muslims by only five lakhs.[13] For a number of reasons the regeneration/reproduction of Muslims families is being greater than Hindus. *Who can say, India would not become the land of the Muslims some day?*[14] (translation mine)

C. A. O'Donnell, census commissioner for 1891, on the basis of the slower growth rates of Hindus as observed in and from the figures of the census, 'leapfrogged across simple logic to deduce the number of years for Hindus to disappear altogether'.[15] 'H. H. Risley, Home Secretary of the Government of India, who had proposed the partition of Bengal in 1903, speculated: "Can the figures of the last census be regarded in any sense the forerunner of an Islamic or Christian revival which will threaten the citadel of Hinduism or will Hinduism hold its own in the future as it has done through the long ages of the past?"'.[16] U. N. Mukherjee's *Hindus – A Dying Race* 'was serialized in *The Bengalee* during the month of June in 1909 ... It was published twice as a book in 1910 and sold at four annas, which was an easily affordable price for its English language readership. The author followed this up by writing the *Coming Census*, a Bengali translation of which he distributed 25,000 copies free of cost. Another 25,000 copies of a modified Bengali version of (*Hindus – A Dying Race*) called *Hindu Samaj* were also distributed free. ... [T]he debate on the census was acquiring a nation-wide importance. ... the appearance of Lala Lajpat Rai's "The Depressed Classes" in *The Modern Review* in July 1909 – barely a month after the publication of (*Hindus – A Dying Race*) – provided a sense of shared concern'. (Datta 1999: 27) Seventy years later, a Hindu Mahasabha publication is seen to echo nearly the same anxiety. The Hindu Mahasabha publication carries the title *They Count Their Gains – We Calculate Our Losses* (Indra Prakash, New Delhi, 1979) drawn from the concluding lines of one of U. N. Mukherjee's texts. (Datta 1999: 22)

How would *Hindus – A Dying Race* respond to its own imminent death? The *imagination* of the nation named 'India' was not just driven by hegemonic Hindu ideals – ideals perpetuated by *Shuddhi* and *Sangathan* movements in the 1920s. The imagination was somewhat premised on violent ways of *be-ing*, on forms of Hindu virile manhood[17], perhaps from the very beginning.

One could see somewhat from the very beginning a clash of imaginations – idea(l)s – idols.

> Hindus, rise, why are you bearing pain. What are you worrying for and so getting defeated? To *live* without courage is useless. (Gupta 1998)

In the face of the threat of extinction, threat of being wiped out by the castrating Other, threat of vivisection the only way to survival, was retaliation – retaliation to the extent that one now cannibalises the threatening *other*. It could be a day of mindless, mad outrage/outburst as in Chauri Chaura.[18] Or it could be a day of willed, conscious, cognizant, planned assassination.

I reproduce below an excerpt from *Why I Assassinated Mahatma Gandhi (And the Events, the Accused, and the Epilogue)* to delineate the trajectories and contours of an emerging Hindu self. I reproduce thereafter excerpts from pamphlets circulated in Gujarat before and during the *pogrom* to demonstrate how the 'emerging Hindu self' found fruition on the very banks of the Sabarmati.[19]

> I, Nathuram Vinayak Godse, the first accused above named respectfully beg to state ... that the teachings of absolute 'Ahimsa' as advocated by Gandhiji would ultimately result in the emasculation of the Hindu Community and thus make the community incapable of resisting the aggression or inroads of other communities especially the Muslims. To counteract this evil ... Apte and myself ... started a daily newspaper *Agrani*. ... I always strongly criticized Gandhiji's views and his methods such as 'fast' for achieving his object, and after Gandhiji started holding prayer meetings, we ... decided to stage peaceful demonstrations showing opposition. ... There was a *wide gulf between the two ideologies* and it became wider and wider as concessions after concessions were being made to the Muslims, ... culminating in the partition of the country....
>
> Having reached Delhi in great despair, I visited the refugee camps at Delhi. While moving in the camps my thoughts took a definite and final turn.... I spent the night of the 29th thinking and re-thinking about my resolve to end the ... further destruction of the Hindus....
>
> In 1946 or thereabout the Muslim atrocities perpetrated on the Hindus ... in Noakhali, made our blood boil. Our shame and indignation knew no bounds ... I (was) determined to prove to Gandhiji that the Hindu too could be intolerant when his honour was insulted.
>
> ... Gandhiji is being referred to as the Father of the Nation .... But if so, he has failed in his *paternal* duty in as much as he has acted very *treacherously* to the nation by his consenting to the partitioning of it .... It was for this reason alone that I as a *dutiful son of Mother India* thought it my

> duty to put an end to the *so-called* Father of the Nation, who had played a very prominent part in bringing about the *vivisection* of the country – *Our Motherland* .... I .... believe .... non-violence .... will lead the nation to ruin ... Indian politics in the absence of Gandhiji would surely be *practical, able to retaliate, and would be powerful with armed forces* .... the nation would be free to follow the course founded on *reason*, which I consider to be necessary for sound nation building. (Answer to Charge Sheet by Nathuram Vinayak Godse on 8.11.1948, italics mine)

In Gandhi Godse was looking for a somewhat menacing abstraction of the paternal role as the possessor-protector of the mother and the place of the Law. Instead, Gandhi happened to be the effeminate internal Other of the nationalist Hindu self. One had to do away with the internal Other – the perpetual *spur* in the somewhat virile re-construction of the nationalist Hindu self. One had to do away with competing signifiers that somehow skewed the quilting and the sedimentation of virile Hindu 'identity'.[20] And this foreclosure[21] of the inassimilable internal Other could be done only in the name of the survival of a dying race. The concessions the internal Other were making to the threatening *other* – the *other* that was a threat to the survival of the Hindu – could be cited as justification for the doing away of the *internal* Other. Hence an *assassination* that in turn sets up possibilities for a more violent encounter with the threatening *other* – the *other* as a foreigner, as an outsider, as the *external other*[22] of the hegemonic Hindu identity.

To demonstrate how a more virile Hindu self sets up the grounds for a more violent encounter with the threatening *other* – the *other* as an outsider, as the *external* Other of hegemonic Hindu identity, I reproduce below an excerpt from a pamphlet published by the C. G. Road Shop Owner's Association in Ahmedabad. The pamphlet contains in print the speech of Chinubhai N. Patel, Vishwa Hindu Parishad state leader, delivered on April 4, 2002 (italics mine).

> Dearest soul *brothers*,
>
> *Namaste*! … I want to talk to you about something very important … You are a very important and responsible person of this country and *your life is valuable. There is a great danger to your life and that of your family.* I have come to warn you. In the secure and safe Hindu localities in spite of security guards outside how safe are you in your bungalows? The traitorous Muslims will come in truckloads kill the guards and then enter the bungalows. They will kill you in your bedrooms and drawing rooms. Today lakhs of Hindus are afraid of this happening and those living in *mohallas* stay up all night in groups to guard us … In 1947, first in Sindh province, then in Punjab and Bengal, they attacked Hindu bungalows and killed about 15 lakh Hindus cruelly and without any pity. This is a *historic fact* and it

> can be repeated today. *Then how safe are you and I in our own homes.* … At the time of partition … they … while carrying sticks, swords, knives, and lighted torches, raped lakhs of our Hindu mothers, sisters and daughters and then killed them. … About 15 lakh Hindus were killed cruelly and Hindus were wiped out in their own country. The land tuned red with the blood of Hindus… If a nation forgets its history it is doomed to live it again. 'History repeats itself.' After breaking up the nation … the Muslim population in the country has again reached 16 crores. They are plotting to kill crores of Hindus… The Godhra incident is just one symptom of the cancer… Godhra is only the trailer…in the last thousand years of Muslim rule in India two crore Hindus were murdered ...
>
> Hindus have now woken up … to combat the atrocities that the Muslims have handed down to us. … If we are attacked we will attack right back. … we will not be able to survive if we do not unite. … [T]o give monetary help to Hindus is an investment for our safety and security. … Hindus have no option but to unite – otherwise they will not survive … the country that learns its lessons from history and plans its future accordingly always survives, while others are destroyed – etch this truth in your heart.

Another excerpt from a pamphlet published by 'An Indian':

> *Reply to bricks with stones*[23]
> When India got her independence, there were 3 crore Muslims in India. Now … there are 35 crores … My Hindu brethren, unite and form a free Indian army … annihilate the enemy … take Ram's name and attack,
>
> We will kill Muslims …
> We will burn Jamalpur and empty Dariapur …
>
> We Hindustanis swear we will seek you out and kill you,
> This is the tradition of Raghukul …
> We will cut them and their blood will flow like rivers.

Gujarat followed Godse. Godse followed the impulse of *Suddhi* and *Sangathan* movements. U. N. Mukherjee followed Dwarakanath Bidyabhusan. Inder Prakash followed U. N. Mukherjee. H. H. Risley followed C. A. O'Donnell. And all of them in their respective philosophies seem to follow a nearly commonsensical understanding of a 'tooth and claw' struggle for survival – a natural selection among the ones engaged in struggle – and ultimately *only* the survival of the fittest. What feeds, nourishes this understanding of 'life'?

Is it nurtured by science? Is it nurtured by *the* science of survival – the way *nature* is described in and by science – the way (human) nature *is*?

The Science of Survival: What *Is*

> Without an *ultimate goal* or end, there can be no lesser goals or means: a series of means going off into an infinite progression towards a non-existent end is a metaphysical and epistemological impossibility. It is only an ultimate goal, an *end in itself* that makes the existence of values possible. Metaphysically, *life* is the only phenomenon that is an *end in itself*: a value gained and kept by a constant process of action. Epistemologically, the concept "value" is genetically dependent upon and derived from the antecedent concept of "life".
>
> — Ayn Rand

Would ethical 'value' be then derived from the antecedent concept of 'life' as the only phenomenon that is an end in itself? Perhaps in estuaries of death, amidst the arid door of crematory ovens, one can only fall back on 'life' and draw rather intuitively upon an ethical responsibility to 'life'. But when we find ourselves trapped in an obsessive rhetoric of survival (the unreservedly over-valued survival of just the Americans as against all others) derived from a rather overwrought notion of a threatening *other* (the *Taliban*) – something that provides theoretical ground to and justification for an annihilation – exclusion of the threatening Other for the sole survival of the *self*, for certain metaphysics of self-survival (as in the war of America against Afghanistan) over all others in a posited war of all against all, one finds it quite difficult to pursue an ethical value derived *solely* from the antecedent concept of life. The questions that keep coming up somewhat without respite: Is 'nature', in Tennyson's redolent metaphor, 'red in tooth and claw'? Is our very survival, our *existence*, the very fact that we *are*, that we are to discuss violence, borne on a certain foundational and fundamental violence? Is the very survival of *self* predicated on a certain, violence on the Other … on *others* … on *others* that provide the 'material'–'discursive' substratum for the survival of *self*? Or perhaps, it is the very question and possibility of survival that makes the *self* and the *others*. The possibility of the survival of an individual, the survival of species that by far bypasses the survival of an individual, and ultimately the survival of genes that carry within them the potential to survive well beyond the extinction of a certain species … survival as the sole metaphysics of presence.

> On the one hand we have the beguiling image of independent DNA replicators, skipping like chamois[24], free and untrammelled down the generations, temporarily brought together in throwaway survival machines, immortal coils shuffling off an endless succession of mortal ones as they forge towards their separate eternities. On the other hand

> we look at the individual bodies themselves and each one is obviously a coherent, integrated, immensely complicated machine, with a conspicuous unity of purpose. A body doesn't look like the product of a loose and temporary federation of warring genetic agents who hardly have time to get acquainted before embarking in sperm or egg for the next leg of the great genetic Diaspora. (Dawkins, 1989: 234)

Richard Dawkins' *The Selfish Gene*, originally published in 1976, makes some startling assertions with respect to the question of survival. 'We are born selfish,' says Dawkins. Although he says at places that 'genes have no foresight' and 'they do not plan ahead' Dawkins imbues genes with a 'consciousness' that transcend bodies and the limits of bodies – limits in both space and time. Through an almost natural and in-built selfishness genes strive to replicate themselves beyond mortal bodies and the mortality of bodies, as if they are consciously planning how best their survival could be achieved:

> Certainly in principle, and also in fact, the gene reaches out through the individual body wall and manipulates objects in the world outside, some of them inanimate, some of them other living beings, some of them a long way away. With only a little imagination we can see the gene as sitting at the centre of a radiating web of extended phenotypic power. And an object in the world is the centre of a converging web of influences from many genes sitting in many organisms. *The long reach of the gene knows no obvious boundaries*. (Dawkins, 1989: 86)

Because for Dawkins individual organisms do not survive from one generation to another, while genes do, it follows that 'natural selection' acts on what survives, namely, the genes. Therefore, all natural selection acts ultimately at the level of DNA. At the same time, each gene is in competition with each other to reproduce themselves in the next generation. What, after all, is so special about genes? The answer is that they are *replicators* – surviving machines – that somewhat mechanically reproduce survival.

In this view, the replicator of life is the gene; thus the organism is simply the vehicle for the genes ('survival machines—robot vehicles blindly programmed to preserve the selfish molecules known as genes … they swarm in huge colonies, safe inside gigantic lumbering robots'). It is a recasting of a famous aphorism that a hen is simply the egg's way of making another egg. An animal, for Dawkins, is only the DNA's way of making more DNA to the extent that the DNA molecule might *desire* the demise of the harbouring animal if it suits the survival statistics of the said DNA. It is, as if a somewhat instrumental Reason and a disinterested

'DNADESIRE' is doing away with every hindrance in the path of its propagation – even if that hindrance is the 'harbouring other'. Dawkins imbues genes with certain mystical qualities for survival – qualities that are essentially teleological.[25] Qualities that somewhat explain what *is* – what nature and human nature is. The question of what *ought* remains entirely subservient to what *is*. What *is* would in a unidirectional cause-effect relation determine what *would*, what look nature and human nature would take. So any innovation in the realm of what we *ought* to do/be is bound to fail as it runs counter to what *is*. For instance, he would say: 'Contraception is sometimes attacked as "unnatural". So it is, very unnatural. The trouble is, so is the welfare state. I think that most of us believe the welfare state is highly desirable. But you cannot have an *unnatural* welfare state, unless you also have *unnatural* birth control, otherwise the end result will be misery even greater than that which obtains in nature.' He continues, 'the welfare state is perhaps the greatest altruistic system the animal kingdom has ever known. But any altruistic system is inherently *unstable*, because it is open to abuse by selfish individuals, ready to exploit it. Individual humans who have more children than they are capable of rearing are probably too ignorant in most cases to be accused of conscious malevolent exploitation.' According to Dawkins, child adoption is against the instincts and interests of our 'selfish genes'. 'In most cases we should probably regard adoption, however touching it may seem, as a misfiring of an in-built rule,' says Dawkins. 'This is because the generous female is doing her own genes no good by caring for the orphan. She is wasting time and energy, which she could be investing in the lives of her own kin, particularly future children of her own. It is presumably a mistake which happens too seldom for natural selection to have "bothered" to change the rule by making the maternal instinct more selective.'

Here, one encounters two questions. One, will the theory of evolution (the *what is* of human nature) be the ground for/of ethics (the *what ought* of the human culture) at all? Two: if so, will it necessarily flow from Dawkins' theory of evolution? Stephen J. Gould and Donna Haraway[26] have offered alternative readings of evolution that could also be the ground for a conceptualisation of ethics. In more ways than one, Darwin himself laid the theoretical foundation for what later came to be called evolutionary ethics. One of his contributions was a more sophisticated understanding of natural selection and its behavioural implications than is found in many Social Darwinist (and neo-Darwinist) caricatures. His most famous slogan – 'the struggle for existence' – was, as Darwin himself pointed out, somewhat hyperbolic. The problem of survival and reproduction in fact encompasses a great variety of specific circumstances, from plentiful resources and easy living to extreme scarcity, from mutual symbioses to literal cases of 'nature, red in tooth and claw'. As Darwin wrote in *The Origin of Species*:

> Animals of many kinds are social; we find even distinct species living together; for example, some American monkeys; and united flocks of rooks, jackdaws and starlings ... The most common mutual service in the higher animals is to warn one another of danger by the united senses of all ... Social animals perform many little services for each other; horses nibble and cows lick each other for external parasites ... Animals also render more important services to one another; thus wolves and some other beasts of prey hunt in packs, and aid one another in attacking their victims. Pelicans fish in concert. The Hamadryas baboons turn over stones to find insects, etc.; and when they come to a large one, as many as can stand around, turn it over together and share the booty. Social animals mutually defend each other. Bull bisons in North America, when there is danger, drive the cows and calves into the middle of the herd, while they defend the outside...

In fact, in *The Origin of Species* Darwin explicitly theorized that co-operative behaviours, including the division of labour and even altruism, could well have evolved via natural selection. In *The Descent of Man*, Darwin carried his reasoning about natural selection and sociality two significant steps further. Seeking to account for the emergence of 'social and moral faculties' in evolving hominids, Darwin proposed that three distinct evolutionary mechanisms were involved: (1) 'family selection' (kin selection), (2) mutualistic co-operation, which modern theorists have variously labelled 'intraspecific mutualism' (West Eberhard), 'tit-for-tat' (Axelrod and Hamilton), 'reciprocant selection' (Hamilton), 'reciprocity selection' (Boorman and Levitt), 'synergistic selection' (Maynard Smith) and 'egoistic co-operation' (Corning), and (3) group selection, or the differential survival of groups of co-operators. Darwin emphasized that these mechanisms were not necessarily antagonistic but could well have been complementary and mutually reinforcing. (Peter A. Corning, 'Evolution and Ethics: An Idea Whose Time Has Come?' (Part I) in *Journal of Social and Evolutionary Systems* 19(3): 277–285)

On the other hand, in Dawkins' scheme, societies are broken down into organisms, organisms into cells, cells into molecules, and molecules into atoms. For Dawkins, human nature is to be understood by analysing human DNA. In his highly atomised worldview, he leaves little room for the existence of either multiple levels of analysis or complex modes of (over)determination. He ignores relations or connections between cells and organisms, between parts and wholes and between selves and others.

Do we then need to work further on the importance of an ethical reflection in one's organization of 'self'? (The 'self' is understood here as *cannibal* – as naturally cannibal, as that which can continue to survive *only* through devouring of the Other, an eating of the Other, a thorough digestion, an appropriation and internalisation of the Other – in a war of all against all.)

An excerpt once again from a pamphlet circulated by the VHP and the Bajrang Dal just before the carnage at Ahmedabad reiterates:

Your life is in danger. You might be killed any time.
Lord Sri Krishna told Arjuna – 'Lift your weapons and kill the non-religious'.
The Lord wants to tell us something also …

The Lord wants to tell us something also. The Lord – religious or scientific – tells us perhaps: your survival depends on the non-survival of a few 'others' – on the extermination of some 'others' – on the termination of the continued survival of some.

The Ethics of Survival: What *Ought*

We look for an ethics of survival that is not cannibalistic[27], that is not merely appropriative – an ethics where the Other is not transformed into 'my property, my object', where s/he is not reduced to 'what is mine, into mine, meaning what is already a part of my field of existential or material properties', and yet, the Other is not put to neglect.

We need 'to learn to live finally'. Learn to live. Can one learn to live by itself – all by itself, out of context? To learn to live, 'to learn it *from oneself and by oneself*, all alone, to teach oneself to live … is that not impossible for a living being? Is it not what logic itself forbids? To live, by definition, is not something one learns. Not from oneself, it is not learned from life, taught by life' (Derrida, 1994: xvii–xx). It is learnt perhaps from the Other, perhaps by and from, and through death; at least from the other at the edge of life. 'At the internal border or the external border, [perhaps] it is [more] a heterodidactics between life and death. … [and] nothing is more necessary than this wisdom. It is ethics itself: to learn to live … does one ever do anything else but learn to live … This is, therefore, a strange commitment, both impossible and necessary … It has no sense and cannot be *just* unless it comes to terms with death. Mine as [well as] that of the other. Between life and death, then, this is indeed the place of a sententious injunction that always feigns to speak like the *just*' (Derrida, 1994: xvii–xx).

What follows then? What happens between the two – between life and death or maybe between all such similar 'two's', between the *fort/da* (gone-far away/returned; there/here) of the Freudian spool, between what the child disperses and what the child reassembles, between disappearances and re-turns, between lack and re-presentation, between absence and presence? Does it not follow from here that if 'learning to live' remains to be done, it can happen only between life and death – in-between life and death, neither in life nor in death *alone*, neither in the pure ecstasy of living nor in the pure anguish of death, neither in the pure principle of pleasure nor in the drive of death. But perhaps, in that which limits the full presence of both life and death in the spectral, in the living on beyond death, in the mark of the deadly finitude of death – death as finitude beyond life, beyond the pure pursuit of the pleasures of living – as the *beyond* of *the pleasure principle.* (Derrida, 1987: 292–337)

Beyond **the Pleasure Principle:** ***Beyond*** **Survival**

In *Beyond the Pleasure Principle* (1920) Freud replaced the pairing of drives – the 'libidinal' and the 'egoistic' – that had served him for more than a decade of psychoanalytic theorizing with a new and more dramatic pair of contestants: life against death. Or maybe he was not in any way positing another pair, metaphysical and secure in their binarisms. This was more of an encounter of the theorist of the 'pleasure principle' with the *beyond* of the 'pleasure principle', with what limits the infinite play of the 'pleasure principle', what produces a certain finitude, what cracks, splits, ruptures the secure organization and teleology of pleasure – pleasure and the pursuit of pleasure with, as if, a life of its own... desire seeking out of its own desire objects of desire. This encounter of Freud with finitude, with the traumatic knowledge of vulnerability-mutability in the face of a desire for immortality and the subsequent detour in psychoanalytic theorizing that follows thereafter, sets in motion the Freudian *fort/da* – the somewhat alluring Freudian engagement with absence/presence, with an 'inscription' and an 'erasure' that is never comprehensive, never total, never full.

Freud's inattention to death is particularly striking in his early case studies, on which he is said to have based his theories about the 'pleasure principle'. In these cases studies the causes/factors precipitating 'hysterical symptoms' in his three main patients – Anna O., Emmy von N., and Elisabeth von R. – quite markedly involved an encounter with death – an encounter with not just the truth of the human mortality, but also the fallibility of symbolic codes. Yet Freud, in his interpretation of each case, either overlooks the connection between hysterical symptoms/trauma and human mortality or translates it into issues of sexually coded loss: castration (loss of the phallus) or abandonment (loss of love). It is in *Beyond the Pleasure Principle* that Freud shifts critical attention from the *phallus* to the *omphalos*[28] – from an explicit phallocentrism driven by desire *to* death – death as the metaphorical *navel* of all feelings of finitude (Bronfen, 1998: 16).

But this is not, in any way, metaphysics of death. Neither is it metaphysics of survival. It is survival as the site of an ethical relationship of self, of survival itself, of self-survival to that which is an Other of survival and of self – a non-violent relationship to the infinite as infinitely other, to the Other.

Beyond Mere Cannibalism

We remain in search for a survival that is not cannibalistic, that is not secured at the expense/extinction of the other. And hence we arrive at a further question: what if the war of all against all does not result in the survival of one and the death of the other – what if the 'trial by death' does not automatically resolve in the survival of one and the death of the other – in the natural selection of one survivor and one non-survivor in the Hegelian duel? What if there is something other than the duel of the Hegelian double, and what if Darwinian 'natural selection' is not the obvious endpoint, the obvious resolution of the duel? What if the self does not cannibalise the Other – does not manage to cannibalise the Other? What if both live, but perhaps one is driven by the 'pleasure principle' and the other by the 'reality principle'? [29] What resolutions can one expect in the silence of the cemetery that has now descended on Ahmedabad? What would and could be the relations after the carnival of cannibalism is over? In the silence when all difference has been silenced? In the trial of death[30] between the Self and the Other, survival of the fittest has remained the organizing principle in the self's organization of self – in the organization of relations of 'lordship and bondage' (Hegel, 1998: 111–119). But then, what happens between the 'lord' and the 'bondsman', who are never the lord and the bondsman before their struggle unto death – in fact, before the resolution of their struggle unto death? It is the very resolution of their struggle that produces the relations of 'lord' and 'bondsman', produces relations of the self and other who would hitherto be lord and bondsman. That the 'lord' does not kill (or cannot kill), cannibalise (or cannot cannibalise) the other, that the lord allows (or is forced to allow) the other to survive, that the lord terminates (or is made to terminate) the struggle, when he perhaps could have carried it to his victory, his complete mastery over the other where the other is no more, where the other is all but dead, and that the other, when faced with death, considers the principle of survival worthwhile produces relations far more complex than relations of just the Self and the Other – produces, perhaps, the logical dawn of hegemony, or maybe the gloom, the nightfall that hegemony was and is.

> ...one is the independent consciousness whose essential nature is to be for itself, the other is the dependent consciousness whose essential nature is simply to live or to be for another. The former is lord, the other is bondsman. ...The lord puts himself into relation with both ... to a thing

as such, the object of desire, and to the consciousness for which thinghood is the essential characteristic. (Hegel, 1998: 111–119)

In the Hegelian dialectic between lord and bondsman, one can now shift focus to the hidden contract between the two: the imperative to the bondsman consists in the following formulation: you be my body for me, but do not let me know that the body that you are *is* my body. The disavowal on the part of the lord is thus doubled: first, the lord disavows his own body, he poses as a disembodied desire and compels the bondsman to act as his body; secondly, the bondsman has to disavow the fact that he acts merely as the lord's body and act as an autonomous agent, as if the bondsman bodily labouring for the lord is not imposed on him but is his autonomous activity: "*a freedom … enmeshed in servitude*" (Hegel, 1998: 119). This structure of double (and thereby self-effacing) disavowal is precisely the moment of *hegemony*[31], the more crucial moment in our somewhat long and tenuous journey (Butler, 1997; Butler, Laclau and Zizek, 2000; Chaudhury, 1994; Chaudhury, Das and Chakrabarti, 2000). This also takes us further to multiple forms of othering as possible expressions of hegemonic operations – thereafter, to multiple layers of violence – 'legitimate', 'necessary', 'normal' – and hence to the need for a more robust reading of violence.

Forms of *Othering*: Forms of Violence

At the beginning there is perhaps neither the Self nor the Other. The Self and the Other are perhaps retroactive constructions that we get in the end. But then, let us begin from the end, from the Self and the Other – the different possible relations of the Self with the Other.

1. Encounter with the Other:
    - To begin with, one may be *unaware* of the Other. One may not know of the existence of the Other. The Other is *unknown*, it is beyond cognition.[32]
    - One may all of a sudden *discover* the Other. Columbus discovers the Other and names it *America*.
    - One may thereafter *forget* the Other, this being the first act of forgetting.
    - One may not forget the Other. One may *acknowledge* the Other … stand face to face with it and embark on a life and death struggle with the Other … a battle until the death of one of the fighters.
2. Repression of the Other:
    - One may have with the acknowledged Other a relation of *lordship* and *bondage*.
    - One may thereafter try to *know* the Other, 'penetrate' with available epistemological tools the innermost recesses of the *unknown*. In the process one may *objectify* the Other. One may *reduce* it to mere/bare essentials. One

may *homogenize* the other. Reduce the Other to stereotypes. Differences among and in the other are thus disregarded. 'Homo-hegemonisation' (Derrida, 2002: 371–386) of both arms of binaries produces *dualisms*.
- One may *banish* the Other to the margins.
- One can make the Other an *untouchable*. One can relegate the Other to the ghetto of the untouchable. The hegemony of the Hindu could only be organized through recognition, through consent of the untouchable to its infinite un-touchability, it being infinitely un-touchable, where the Self *never* 'touches' the Other.

3. Forgetting the Other:
    - One can *forget* the Other that was once acknowledged; which in other words is a backgrounding, a denial of the Other, a dependence that is denied, a disavowal. One may forget the fact that one has forgotten the Other – a double disavowal. The other vanishes: a radical exclusion, a hyper separation, a *foreclosure*.

We arrive at multiple forms of othering as productive of multiple forms of violence, multiple forms of violence as productive of multiple forms of othering and multiple forms of othering as a possible expression for hegemonic operations. This in turn necessitates a search for violence beyond mere cannibalism – a search into the more subtle and pervasive operations of hegemony. This also necessitates a search for an ethics beyond *both* cannibalism and hegemony.

I separate the moments of cannibalism and hegemony as logical others, as logically other to the Other. Perhaps the two inhere – one in the other – and produce overdetermined effects/affects. Primitive accumulation remains as the more rugged, more savage edge of the rule of capital. Physical cannibalism as the uncouth underside, the grubby substratum of a more civil, more nuanced rule of law – the law of the patronymic, the law of the High Hindu Hegemonic, the hegemonic rule of the Hindu 'lord' over the culturally 'other' – the Other who is now also the 'bondsman', who is held tightly leashed to a 'civil' form of bondage – a servitude masquerading as 'freedom'. No wonder, the High Hindu Hegemonic called for elections, called for the more civil moment of representative democracy once the carnival of carnal cannibalism was over.

Ethics Beyond Cannibalism and Hegemony

> Love of *One* is a barbarism; for it is exercise at the expense of all others. The Love of God, too.
>
> — Nietzsche

What, then, are the ethics of survival, the ethics beyond both cannibalism and hegemony? An ethics where the Self and the Other are linked inalienably in a certain deconstructive embrace, where life is lived as the call of the wholly other, lived by and through a responsibility to the other, lived while being bound by accountable reason. Is an ethics of the Self – an ethics of the survival of self – the Self as responsive to the call of the Other – an 'experience of the impossible', an impossible experience between 'self-interest' (the self-interest of Cohen in *Mr. & Mrs. Iyer*) and 'responsibility' (the responsibility to and of Jahangir Chaudhury as taken up by Mrs. Iyer), an experience that would menace any calculus of interested action?

> What will return ... not in order to contradict the Pleasure Principle (PP), not to oppose itself to the PP but to mind the PP as its proper stranger, to hollow it into an abyss from a vantage point of an origin more original than it and independent of it, older than it within it, will not be, under the name of the death drive or the repetition compulsion, an other master or a counter master, *but something other than mastery, something completely other.* In order to be something completely other, it will have to not oppose itself, will have to not enter into a dialectical relation with the master (life, the PP as life, the living PP, the PP alive) ... (Derrida, 1987: 317–18)

What is this something that is other than mastery ... that is something completely other? Can one call it the *auto-bio-thanato*[33]*-hetero-graphic* writing of ethics? (Derrida, 1987: 336) *Auto-bio-graphic* writing of ethics ...[34] *Bio-thanato-graphic* writing of ethics ... *Hetero-graphic* writing of ethics ... Writing ethics? Writing of ethics? But then, what is writing without repression?

What is repression without a return of the repressed? This act of writing is addressed somewhat to the cannibalistic and the hegemonic – to the Self who, in the face of a real or imagined threat to survival, organizes its own survival but in the process either devours or dominates the Other. What happens if the treat to survival is not imagined but real... as in the case of the Other the Self devours or dominates? Would not the terms of the address get severely skewed when one has in mind the survivors of Ahmedabad? Would this writing of ethics become a prescription for a feminine passivity in the face of the devouring-dominating Other? Although we would like to somewhat stubbornly resist violence, we remain in search of an ethico-politics beyond both virile masculinity and feminine passivity, beyond both making the other the object of the Self's desire and the Other *being* the object of the Self's desire.

Notes

1 This act of writing can begin only with a *confession*: this writing comes more as an *appeal* – an appeal to the hegemonic community. It is written as if from within the hegemonic community, as if a member of the hegemonic community is making an appeal, an appeal that is made at least with the acute awareness that the author of this paper belongs in pen and paper to the hegemonic community, however much he may deny his identity as such. This paper thus tries to come up with an ethics for the hegemonic with the belief that a re-thinking of the ethics of the hegemonic relates in one or the other way to the 'more difficult task of counter-hegemonic ideological production' (Spivak, 1988). It looks for an ethics of the hegemonic with the concomitant understanding that the same standard of ethics may not apply for the non-hegemonic community. It thus fails to propose a universal standard for all to follow. Its search for an ethics remains refracted by perspectives of power – who occupies which position in the hierarchy of positions. It also remains refracted by perspectives of class, race, gender, sexuality, etc.

2 It was actually his being a Muslim in her association that Mrs. Iyer had not taken too kindly to, where the onus is on the other as untouchable to *not cross the path* of the Brahmin as Self.

3 One remains painfully aware, of course, that such an unselfconscious sensitivity is not available to Cohen – he carries the anatomical mark of difference that places him in near-inseparability from *that Muslim couple*.

4 The dead *do* write. They may write, as when death comes not inevitable not as a fate, but as a *choice* – say in suicide, in suicide squads, in a situation of a fast to death (Chaudhury, 1994; Chaudhury, Das, Chakrabarti, 2000). Here the dead do write. They do get themselves inscribed – inscribed through death within the Symbolic. But the question that would still remain important: in what ink do the dead get themselves inscribed? Do they write in white ink? Do they speak the language the White speak? Do they speak the same language of violence or the language of the same violence?

5 One of the *aporetic* experiences touched upon by Derrida (1993) is the experience that 'my death' can never be subject to an experience that would be properly *mine*, that I can *have* and account for, yet that there is, at the same time, nothing closer to me and nothing properly *mine* than 'my death'. 'Aporias are distinguished from logical categories such as dilemmas or paradoxes, as experience is from presupposition. Aporias are known in the experience of being passed through, although they are non-passages; they are thus disclosed in effacement, thus experience of the impossible.' (Spivak, 1999: 427).

6 The shadow of death – of the innumerable people who died in Ahmedabad - looms large over this writing. And yet, this writing tries somewhat paradoxically to focus on 'life', on the way we 'live', on possible ethics of living. In a milieu where living for one means death for the other, where survival of 'self' can only be secured at the cost of the other one perhaps needs to focus on life, on reconfigured ethics of living.

7 This is much less a writing on surviving others who have somehow managed to escape the cannibalism of surviving Selves, who have not been put to death by surviving Selves. They remain as the *repressed* Other of this act of writing and two questions that relate somewhat immediately to them haunt this writing. One, does the fact that they have *not* been put to death in any way spare them the violence perpetrated on their less fortunate associates. Would the fact that they have survived the carnage reduce them to being bondswomen to the Lordship of the high Hindu hegemonic? Two, what could be the ethico-politics of their subsequent survival – a survival over which looms large the somewhat real and relentless threat of extinction – both physical and symbolic.

8 Unparalleled by what? By the extent/span/nature of violence? By the number killed? But then, why should it matter how many were killed? What number of the killed would satisfactorily, statistically constitute genocide? At what number does genocide begins – genocide *per se*? And why should the question of number persist at the centre of all reflections on violence? Is it not enough to know that they *are* all killing fields – whatever the number of the victims? Ahmedabad is one killing field. Gujarat is another. India is the Other killing field that is devouring day in and day out its unassimilated others; 'India' as an imagination produced and reproduced through reiterative gestures, an imagination that is studded with killing fields that from the day of its naming is killing unnamed others. Ahmedabad, Gujarat, India – could they then be one name for another? Could they be different incarnations of the same virile violence that secures our being – our being within our Nation-State and the very *be-ing* of our Nation-State.

9 The distinction between 'overt' and 'covert' is conceptual. Overt and covert are in no way empirical categories – categories that describe the two substantive faces/facets of violence. One can also discern in this distinction perhaps a move between the Marxist understanding of power tied principally to the State *and* the Foucauldian understanding of the seamless web of power tied to no subject/agent in particular, which, in other words, is also a move between the repressive state apparatus and the ideological state apparatus or maybe between coercion and hegemony.

10 This somewhat tentative categorization of violence into 'legitimate', 'necessary' and 'normal' is only for conceptual convenience. One can surely think of forms outside the three mentioned above. One can also see clearly how one form of violence necessarily bleeds into the other form. In fact, I remain undecided about the category that could accommodate and describe the violence of the *huMAN* over the *woman*. It could at one and the same time be considered 'legitimate', 'necessary' and 'normal' by the *huMAN*.

11 In fact, living in a virtual estuary of death, the survivors of Gujarat can ask a completely different question: what is so natural about death?

12 What happens when the threat is real as in the case of the Muslims in Gujarat or maybe in the case of the peasants of Chauri Chaura? Can we still think of ethico-politics in the face of a real threat to survival? Setting aside for a moment the enormous and necessary weight of facts and truths, can we think a politics of justice – a justice that remains menaced by the ethical. Can we still form collectives, organize ourselves in 'mobs' that seek justice – justice divorced from Law – but does not necessarily cannibalise the other? But for that one will perhaps have to move beyond the standard interpretation of collectives as brotherhoods, as brotherhood among men.

13 The census figures, to which Dwarakanath Bidyabhusan refers, give the following figures: Hindus – 18100438; Muslims – 17609135; Kaibartadas – 2064394; Chandal – 1620545; Kayastha – 1160478; Brahmins – 1100105; men – 3 crores 34 lakhs; women – 3 crores 35 lakhs; The sub-division of the Hindu population according to caste does not add up to make a number that is even remotely close to that of the total Hindu population cited in this text. The number cited for men and women if added up far outnumbers the number of Hindus and Muslims. The author of course builds up a very strong argument in favour of polygamy *for* men based on the number of men and women, where women outnumber men by one lakh. According to the author, left to a monogamous arrangement, one lakh women would remain unmarried.

14 Dwarakanath Bidyabhusan, 'Banglar Loksonkhya' in *Nababarsiki* (ed. Dwarakanath Bidyabhusan). Calcutta 1880: 75–77 (CSSSC/BSP Record No. 53; BSP Catalogue No. 236; Acc. No. 1112) A number of articles at around the same time could be seen

echoing nearly the same concerns and the same anxieties. Articles titled 'Bharate Mussalman' ('Muslims in India') (*Bandhab (Nabaparyya)*), ed. Kaliprasanna Ghosh. Dacca 1875: 187 (CSSSC/BSP Record No: 35, BSP Catalogue No: 447/448); 'Bharat Rodan' ('India Crying') (*Bandhab*. 1875: 307), 'Bharatbarsha Ebong Onanya British Upanibesh' ('India and the Other British Colonies') (*Bandhab* 1876), 'Bharater Projaniti' ('The Subject Policy in India') (*Bandhab* 1878), 'Yavan' (*Bandhab* 1878), 'Hindu Bhugol' ('Hindu Geography') (*Bandhab* 1878), 'Shibaji' (*Bandhab* 1878), 'Bharate Aryajati' ('The Aryan Race in India') (*Bandhab* 1878), 'Muhammader Uttaradhikari' ('The Descendents of Muhammad') (*Bandhab* 1878: 519) all in one way or another, in metaphorical or in real terms, talk of a dying race and a decline-demise of the Hindu in the hands of the more aggressive Yavan as against the phenomenal rise of the Mussalman since 622 AD, the year of the death of Muhammad. This rise of the Mussalman is attributed to their rather single-minded pursuit of the Kafir in the name of religious crusade.

15 *Census of India, 1891, Vol. III, Bengal,* C. A. O'Donnell (ed.). Calcutta 1893, as cited in Pradip Kumar Datta. *Carving Blocs: Communal Ideology in Early Twentieth-century Bengal.* OUP 1999: 24.

16 Cited in Pradip Kumar Datta, *Carving Blocs: Communal Ideology in Early Twentieth-century Bengal.* OUP 1999: 24.

17 A related question that immediately comes to mind and that is extremely important to any understanding of non-violence: if violence is masculine aggressivity what would be an ethics of non-violence that is not correspondingly feminine passivity? Gandhi and Godse would represent two responses to the death – real or imagined – of the Hindus. We remain somewhat divided, somewhat lost between the virile masculinity of Godse's response and the *apparent* feminine passivity of Gandhi's response.

18 Amin (1995) shows how the nationalist rendition of this outburst could instead be related to some sense of retributive justice. 'Chauri Chaura ... is not the work of culpable individuals; it is caused by reflex action. ... paradoxically, this extreme reflex action is seen to stem from the *swayam sevaks* disciplined disposition. The extreme consequence ... i.e., the murder of twenty-three policemen, is preceded in time, both immediate and historical, by police repression ... exceptionally fierce *lathi* and cavalry charge, and the firing which the disciplined *satyagrahis* withstood for a long time. ... *It was because they were disciplined for a long time that they finally lost their heads.* ... The assent of the Indian reader is sought by portraying an insufferable scenario ... *On that day, even a saint would have lost his head.*' (Amin 1995, 51–55)

19 *Why I Assassinated Mahatma Gandhi (And the Events the Accused, and the Epilogue)* is the title of a book written by Gopal Godse (Surya Bharati Parkashan, New Delhi, 1993). The book contains the statement of Nathuram Godse originally published under the title 'May it Please Your Honour'.

20 We understand identity not as given, not as an *a priori*, but as a contingent articulation, a hegemonic articulation organized along certain nodal points – nodal points as 'privileged discursive points of ... partial fixation' (Laclau 1990). Nodal points, anchor floating signifiers through metonymic surplus meanings and fix a signifying chain, the process of fixation being always contingent upon a complex process of overdetermination. A *single identity* – the hegemonic Hindu identity – is thus organized through surplus meanings flowing from nodal points. But what would qualify as a nodal point? This of course would be a matter of constant contestation and would not be only a cultural fact. The moment of the emergence of a certain nodal point remains constituted by economic, political and cultural processes.

21 The hegemonic principle tries to reject the incompatible idea together with the affect, this being the first act of disavowal, and then behave as if the idea had never occurred to the ego at all, this being the act of the subsequent disavowal, the act of double disavowal. This act of double disavowal - one can also name it *foreclosure* – would embody two complementary or perhaps simultaneous operations: (1) production of the hegemonic Subject through (2) expulsion from this Subject of the traumatic bone of contention, an expulsion that, in turn, reproduces the subject as Subject. This in turn produces the apparent sedimentation and stabilisation of the three Lacanian registers: the Symbolic, the Imaginary and the Real. Gandhi refuses the apparent sedimentation and stabilization of the three registers. He remains as the traumatic bone of contention within phallogocentric closure, as if as the Real that refuses to be foreclosed, that refuses to be disavowed – disavowed doubly – that remains within, tenaciously within, as the outside that is all too constitutive, as the outside that as if refuses to remain outside, as the *constitutive outside* of the Symbolic that hinders/rocks the *becoming* of the hegemonic, that keeps the high Hindu hegemonic somewhat in a state of suspension. (Lacan 1977a, 1977b; Spivak 1999)

22 The external other could be given the accommodation and the status of a secondary citizen, if it obliged the hegemonic Hindu by paying obeisance to the desire, culture and national imagination of the hegemonic. If it did not play the part of 'bondswoman', it would have to face the wrath of the Lord. If it happens to threaten the Lord, i.e. the survival of the Lord, it would have to pay with its 'life'.

23 This is an excerpt from another pamphlet published by 'An Indian' and received by *Communalism Combat* on 28.03.2002.

24 The 'chamois' is an extremely agile goat antelope (*Rupicapra rupicapra*) of mountainous regions of Europe, having upright horns with backward-hooked tips.

25 Dawkins was, of course, later forced to backtrack to some extent, modifying his arguments in the later editions of *The Selfish Gene* (1989) and in *The Extended Phenotype* (1982). He says his flamboyant language left him open to misrepresentation and misunderstanding: 'It is all too easy to get carried away, and allow hypothetical genes cognitive wisdom and foresight in planning their "strategy".' He nevertheless defends his fundamental argument and views life 'in terms of genetic replicators preserving themselves by means of their extended phenotypes'. And that 'natural selection is differential survival of genes'. Dawkins now says, 'genes may modify the effects of other genes, and may modify the effects of the environment. Environmental events, both internal and external, may modify the effects of genes, and may modify the effects of other environmental events'. But this concession aside, Dawkins' main thesis remains.

26 Stephen Jay Gould explains: 'Organisms are much more than amalgamations of genes. They have a history that matters; their parts interact in complex ways. Organisms are built by genes acting in concert, influenced by environments, translated into parts that selection sees and parts invisible to selection. Molecules that determine the properties of water are poor analogues for genes and bodies.' Donna Haraway is equally critical of the impulse that drives Dawkins and his colleagues at the human genome project: 'Most fundamentally … the human genome projects produce entities of a different ontological kind than flesh-and-blood organisms, "natural races", or any other sort of "normal" organic being. … the human genome projects produce ontologically specific things called databases as objects of knowledge and practice. The human to be represented, then, has a particular kind of totality, or species being, as well as a specific kind of individuality. … In other words, this data structure is a *construct of abstract human-ness,*

without a body, without a gender, without a history, and without personal and collective narratives. It does not have a culture, and it does not have a voice. This electronically configured human is an a-cultural program. And in this very construction it is deeply culturally determined – we find ourselves confronted with a "universal human", *constructed by science as practiced in North America at the close of the 20th century.* This version of 'human unity in diversity' is not liberatory but deeply oppressive. To achieve such a vision in a positive sense, *culture* cannot be separated from *biology.* Moving toward this vision requires the respect and protection of all human diversity that is to be found in the cultures and narratives of different peoples, and not in their DNA. *All versions of the human story, all human meaning-making, would need to be heard in all their different voices.*'

27. *Cultural cannibalism*, to use Luce Irigaray's metaphor, is the unethical reduction of the other to the status of 'me' or 'mine', rather than s/he to whom I make the address, s/he who addresses me.

    Derrida, on the other hand, tries to articulate an ethics on the failure or lack that haunts the site/structure of any cannibalism. The other resists my knowledge and memory of him or her. Derridean ethics allows us to ask if Irigaray's concern that ours is a culture of successful cannibalisms concedes too much to hegemonic articulations. One can then ask, what are the comparative ethics and politics of these articulations, of both the success of cannibalism and somewhat necessary failure of cannibalism? Faced with imminent death the only hope of the Other perhaps lies in the fact/belief that cannibalism also has its limits. But then we do not wish to stretch this argument too far nor do we wish to quieten our disturbed selves with the belief that cannibalism has its limits. Instead we see and discern in a cannibalism that is *limited – lacking* – the possibility of *hegemony*, the possibility of a subtler yet more pervasive rule of the hegemonic (Deutscher, internet article, http://muse.jhu.edu/journals/differences/v010/10.3deutscher.html). The other critic to cannibalism has come from ecofeminist circles, where ecofeminists have shown, even at substantive levels, that the Self cannot continue to survive in complete exclusion of the Other.

28 'By shifting the emphasis in my reading of the Oedipal story from incest and patricide to failed matricide, and by interpreting the ensuing self-castration as the metonymic substitute for a desire to eradicate the site of one's origin – the mother's womb and the child's remnant of this connection via the navel – I am moving away from the sexual coding of castration. I want to suggest instead that at the epicentre of all traumatic knowledge … lays a recognition of mortality. … The field of mythopoetics has seen the navel as a symbol for the site not only of origin but also of termination. …Christian mythology sees the altar as an *umbilicus terrae*, and stories of antiquity have always drawn on the connection between the navel and the grave, vault, or tomb, this anatomical mark signifying the mortal wound that taints all human life from birth.' (Bronfen, 1998: 16)

29 In an early formulation, Freud makes a theoretical distinction between the pleasure and the reality principles. The pleasure principle aims for immediate gratification. The reality principle involves the internalisation of a deferring mechanism that gradually lessens the need. The reality principle is a kind of survival mechanism. What Freud calls the *primary processes* produce a kind of discharge that is dangerous if unchecked, and so *secondary processes*, like repression, detour/delay and deferral, put obstacles in its way.

30 One could obviously inquire into the very justification, historical or otherwise, of any such 'trial of death'. The justification, in the first place, for any such trial and further,

for a trial by death as being the founding, the organizing principle of relations of the Self and the Other. One could ask: why does Hegel propose the 'trial of death' as being the originary impulse in his thought experiment? Why would there be at all some originary moment, a moment that is so intensely decisive, that decides once and for all the future, the teleology of the Self and the Other? Could there not be some more mundane, and in a way, a somewhat less spectacular origin or maybe *origins*? That would not be origin/origins in the first place.

31 'The strategy of domination was meant to replace the life-and-death struggle.' In cannibalism death happened through the violence of self on the other. Hegemonic domination, on the other hand, 'was a way of forcing the other to die *within* the context of life'. (Butler 1997: 1–62; 2000)

32 Or perhaps the other is *within* the self, so inalienably within, that the distinction between the Self and the Other is not apparent. Such that both self and other have not drifted apart yet – so far apart that we now find them organized as opposites – binary opposites.

33 Writing *thanatos*? Writing death, writing destruction when faced with possible extinction, with a somewhat real threat to survival. Taking responsibility for death-destruction. Drawing up the contours of death-destruction in the service of survival. Showing up the limits of death-destruction; 'destruction art' is a warning system, an aesthetic response to human emergency that occurs in the lapse between theory and practice in terminal culture; it presents the pain of bodies, the anxiety of minds, the epistemology of technology, the specious claims of ideology, the absence of ecological responsibility, the loss of human integrity and compassion, and the violence that structures both gender and sexual relations.

34 The *auto-bio-graphy* of ethics. Ethics as autobiographical. The bio-graph of the self, of life, of the survival graph of self – how would it remain sutured to ethics? How it must remain sutured to ethics?

References

Amin, S. 1995. *Event Metaphor Memory: Chauri Chaura 1922–1992.* Berkeley: University of California Press.

Bronfen, E. 1998. *The Knotted Subject: Hysteria and its Discontents.* Princeton: Princeton University Press.

Butler, J. 1997. *The Psychic Life of Power: Theories in Subjection.* Stanford: Stanford University Press.

Butler, J., Laclau, E., Zizek, S. 2000. *Contingency, Hegemony, Universality: Contemporary Dialogues on the Left.* London and New York: Verso.

Chaudhury, A. 1994. 'On Colonial Hegemony: Toward a Critique of Brown Orientalism' in *Rethinking Marxism* 7 (4): 44–58.

Chaudhury, A., Das, D., Chakrabarti, A. 2000. *Margin of Margin: Profile of an Unrepentant Postcolonial Collaborator.* Calcutta: Anustup.

Datta, P. K. 1999. *Carving Blocs: Communal Ideology in Early Twentieth-century Bengal.* OUP.

Dawkins, R. 1989. 'The long reach of the gene' in *The Selfish Gene.* Oxford: Oxford University Press.

Derrida, J. 1987. *The Post Card: From Socrates to Freud and Beyond,* trans. Bass, A. Chicago: University of Chicago Press.

_______ 1993. *Aporias,* trans. Dutoit, T. Stanford: Stanford University Press.

_______ 1994. *Specters of Marx: the state of the debt, the work of mourning, a nd the new international*, trans. Kamuf, P. with an introduction by Magnus, B. and Cullenberg, S. New York and London: Routledge.

_______ 2002. *Negotiations: Interventions and Interviews, 1971–2001*, ed., trans., and with an introduction by Elizabeth Rottenberg. Stanford: Stanford University Press.

Freud, S. 1957. 'Mourning and Melancholia' in *The Standard Edition of the Complete Psychological Works of Sigmund Freud* vol. 14, trans. & ed. Strachey, J. London: Hogarth Press: 237–58.

Gupta, C. 1998. 'Articulating Hindu Masculinity and Femininity: "Shuddhi" and "Sangathan" Movements in United Provinces in the 1920s' in *Economic and Political Weekly* March 28, 1998.

Hegel, G. 1998. *Phenomenology of Spirit.* Delhi: Motilal Banarasidass Publishers.

Lacan, J. 1977a. *Ecrits.* London: Tavistock.

_______ 1977b. *The Four Fundamental Concepts of Psychoanalysis.* London: Hogarth Press.

Laclau, E., Mouffe, C. 1985. *Hegemony and Socialist Strategy.* London and New York: Verso.

Deutscher, P. *Mourning the Other, Cultural Cannibalism, and the Politics of Friendship (Jacques Derrida and Luce Irigaray) – http://muse.jhu.edu/journals/differences/v010/10.3deutscher.html.*

Corning, P. A. 1996. 'Evolution and Ethics: An Idea Whose Time Has Come?' (Part I) in *Journal of Social and Evolutionary Systems* 19(3): 277–285. (http://www.complexsystems.org/essays/evoleth1.html).

Mr. and Mrs. Iyer (http://en.wikipedia.org/wiki/Mr._and_Mrs._Iyer).

Resnick, S. and Wolff, R. 1987. *Knowledge and Class.* Chicago: University of Chicago Press.

Semprun, J. 1998. *Literature of Life*, trans. Linda Coverdale. New York: Penguin Books.

Spivak, G. C. 1988. 'Can the Subaltern Speak?' in *Marxism and the Interpretation of Culture*, eds Nelson, C. and Grossberg, L. Urbana: University of Illinois Press: 271–316.

_______ 1999. *A Critique of Postcolonial Reason.* Calcutta: Seagull.

Theweleit, K. 1987. *Male Fantasies: Women, Floods, Bodies, History* – Minneapolis: University of Minnesota Press (Vol 1).

Chapter 21

'MORAL OBLIGATION' TO FIGHT FOR THE PREVENTION OF GREATER CALAMITY: A DEBATE BETWEEN *SĀDHĀRAṆA DHARMA* AND *SVA DHARMA*

Malabika Majumdar

Most justifications of violence begin with some reference to the principle of self-defence. Suffering of innocents or wrong done to them is also a reason why arms against the wrong doer should be used. Once we cross over the reasons of personal squabbles and ask why nations wage war, not only the magnitude but also the quality of arguments vary. Certain paradigmatic justifications like, 'for the sake of prevention of greater calamity', or 'for the sake of restoration of good over evil' buttresses the argument of ethics in war.

The just war theory faces its biggest challenge from the doctrine of moral pacifism. A pacifist condemns all forms of violence. A warmonger holds forth by arguing that status quo through conflict amelioration is an impotent effort towards conflict resolution. In the context of this debate I have placed the issue of '*dharmayuddha*'. Out of several interpolations of meanings, I have found Gandhi's way of resolving conflict through non-violent means contains the debate between pacifists and just war theorists. However, such was not the case with other interpretations of this term.

As I sketch the history of the concept *dharmayuddha*, from the days of epic, I come across several reasons why retributive justice has demanded actual and mythical wars in the Indian context. In the *Mahābhārata* a paradigmatic argument is given to justify a family feud over inheritance right to the throne and it is backed by Krishna's arguments from *dharma*. Encouraged by Krishna's statement, '*yadā yadā hi dharmasya glānirbhavati bhārata*' ('whenever dharma is at stake, oh Arjuna, I incarnate myself') (Shrimadbhagvadgita: Ch.4.7), the nineteenth-century Bengali urban intellectuals waged a mythical *dharmayuddha* against Muslim misrule and also against British colonisers. I have called it a mythical war, because war in this period was restricted to intellectual debates. However, when Gandhi arrived on the scene, the days of petitioning were almost over, and factions of terrorists had already launched a protracted struggle by adopting guerrilla war tactics. Gandhi's pacifism, though still within the scope of *dharmayuddha*, was a timely effort to bring forth a mass revolution. He was able to win the desired independence for the Indians without bloodshed.

Gandhi's strategic interventions as a champion of just war through moral means, opens a vista of debate. Most thinkers would agree that in undertaking moral evaluation of war it is natural to distinguish rules that determine when it is permissible to wage a war (*jus ad bellum*) from how war is to be carried out (*jus in bello*). In the first case a competent authority, after applying the principle, can decide when to say, 'enough is enough'. *Jus in bello* rules apply to the soldiers who decide on the means that is appropriate or legitimate in a war. Both deserve moral attention. Gandhi was no doubt more concerned about the cognitive power of the means, at the same time he was concerned about *dharma* or moral ground for which alone war was to be waged. Hence *satyāgraha* was the first cause as well as the last cause for waging a war.

Gandhi's notion of *dharma* as well as *yuddha* is ideationally at variance with the concept of *dharmayuddha* as it appears in *Mahābhārata* or as the nineteenth-century thinkers conceive it to be. A historiography of this concept will reveal that while the Kurukshetra battle was fought keeping *retribution* in mind, Gandhi was keen to *reform* the wrong doer by waging a morally designed war. I have in this essay tried to highlight three different notions of *dharmayuddha*. At the same time I also wish to point out that retribution and reform are qualitatively different goals especially in the Indian context. The moral pressure or *satyāgraha*, as Gandhi felt, was conscience directed, which generated a certain compulsion to tell the British that their policies were objectionable at a time when he was convinced that his dissatisfaction did not extend to the people of Britain. Thus Gandhi separated the crime and the criminal. Such was not the view in *Mahābhārata* and *Gita*. Not even does it appear in Bankim Chandra Chatterjee's essays and novels, which are otherwise volatile sources of *dharmayuddha* concept.

The common theme that ran right from the days of *Mahābhārata* is to back morally obligatory war with an ideology. One can imagine, by following Gandhi, that a just war can lead to peaceful co-existence. Intentions of this kind may resemble quaint relics of an idealistic world. Nonetheless, his vision appears to be radically different from the gains made by the Pandavas in the Kurukshetra war. *Gita's* concern about *dharma glāni* (decay of *dharma*) and restoration of *dharma*, may appear to have a *niśkāma* motive as being the ideal reason for waging the Kurukshetra war, yet in real terms, the moral sanction came to the Pandava side largely as a self defence measure to counter Duryodhana's plan to vanquish them.

The term *dharmayuddha* is a compounded word – dharma and *yuddha* are the two constituents that demand separate attention. *Dharma* relates to a set of rules that govern largely the ordering of the way of life, particularly for trans-mortal gains. Many of these laws, which have received scriptural sanction, were meant to foster the *svadharma* of the *brāhman* as a caste. However, from the works of *Mahābhārata*, we receive another set of *dharma* that decided for the *kshatriyas* certain behavioural rules. These were framed keeping in mind the moral welfare of any society. In the *Gita* we come across a *sādhārana dharma* concept as a pre-requisite for *lokasangraha* (conservation of society and people). It is presumed that the *svadharma* of the *kshatriya* king was to protect his tribe and for this he was justified in destroying the enemy. Even though destruction of enemies meant *lokakshaya* (destroying life in general), it did not cause a dichotomous relation with *lokasangraha*. The reason for this is complex and at times unclear too.

I have been able to find contradictory opinions within *Mahābhārata* itself. Contentious views appear, for one, because *yuddha* formed part of the natural necessity particularly for the *kshatriyas*, as it was a means through which surplus was generated. Secondly, the kings were expected to utilise the spoils of war for the welfare of their own people. At the same time, it is also true that reasons for justifying the Kurukshetra War went way beyond this commonplace reason. Accentuated debates take place as to whether the *lokasngraha dharma* of the *kshatriya* permit hostilities to such a degree that it can take up arms against one's own kin and yet refer to it as *dharmāṛthayuddha (yuddha* for the sake of perpetration of welfare).

In the *Gita*, the *dharmāṛthayuddha* concept takes yet another twist, because dharma is restricted to mean *kshatriya* caste duty in specific. *Svadharmammapi chāvekshya…na vidyate* (*Shrimadbhagvadgita*: Ch. 2.31) (by taking care of *svadharma*, you should not be perturbed too, as there is nothing more glorious than *dharmayuddha* for a *kshatriya*) or *svadharme nidhanam śreya paradharma bhayābaha* (*Shrimadbhagvadgita*: Ch. 3.35) (penalty of death by following one's *svadharma* is superior to following the path of *paradharma*) are morally valid arguments in the context of *kshatriyadharma* as framed within the *varnāshramadharma*. One wonders whether *loksangraha* too was similarly connoted.

The other interesting point about *Gita* and *Mahābhārata* notion of *dharmārthayuddha* is that it did not resemble a religious crusade of the Christian variety. The reason could be that *dharma* in the ancient period did not signify institutionalised religion. In the Pauranic texts mythical wars of Gods and Goddesses suggest fight against evil. In the works of Bankim and Gandhi, though, the term *dharma* had a religious overtone, when it came to *dharmayuddha*, they both conceived it as fight against evil. Bankim understood the concept *svadharma* as socio-ethical compulsion of a man to destroy the undeserving or else the *dharma* or social equilibrium would be in jeopardy. If one took a moral posture in war, then as Bankim argued, there was no conflict of interest between *sādhāranadharma* of *lokasangraha* and the *svadharma* or the individual's compulsions to wage a war.

In Gandhi once again, there appears to be a thin line of distinction between the religious and the moral. He shared the concern that Bankim's generation felt towards the British policy of exploitation. However, Gandhi's philosophy of war was unique in many senses. He thought the path of non-cooperation was a gentleman's way of resolving the conflict between *lokasangraha* and *lokakshaya*. Consequently, there is no dichotomy between *sādhāranadharma* and *svadharma*.

In this discussion, I will try to restrict my analysis to text-based material to exemplify my views on *dharmayuddha*. It is therefore largely an impressionistic generalisation. At the same time, I also recognise that history of ideas of any particular period could not have come up in abstraction from the material conditions of the same period. I have tried to recognise the symbiotic relation between sociological conditions and the ideational development of any period. This approach makes the meaning of the term *dharmayuddha* context specific. Hence the *dharmayuddha* for which the Pandavas fought the Kauravas cannot be the same for the Indians fighting the British. In other words, the *artha* or purpose of the two sets of wars was not the same.

Yuddha or war has a history quite independent of *dharma*. Archaeological evidences are quoted by historians to show that the Indo-Iranian tribe who settled by occupying the upper-Gangetic belt and who were subsequently called the Aryans, were a warrior and a nomadic tribe. (Sharma, 1996: 36–38) As food gatherers, they survived by waging wars to settle their disputes. In the early Rgvedic period war was waged chiefly for economic necessities particularly to generate surplus (Sharma, 1996: 38). Propitiation to Indra for waging mythical wars against the Dasyus abounds in the *Rgveda*. (Sharma, 1996: 37–38) The word *loptra* as mentioned in the *Rgveda* means loot (*Rgveda Samhita*: Mandala V.61.5). It is assumed to be the spoils of war in passages that mention distribution of wealth as the Gods and the kings practised. *Vṛijanasya rājā*, for instance, refers to the king as the destroyer of enemies and captor of their wealth, and distributor of it among his people. (*Rgveda Samhita*: Mandala X 97. 10) During the Yajus period, war was fought for economic as well as political control. Through *Ashvamedha yajña* the king virtually attained superior status over sundry kings and forced them to pay taxes.

However, there is no reference to intra-tribe dispute through war anywhere in the *Ṛgveda*. Protection of the *Kula* was a primary consideration for not indulging in family feuds. Though there is no direct reference, but there is a possibility that war within *kula, grām, goshti gana* was a taboo. In *Mahābhārata* we find references to show how important the *kula* is. To protect the *Kula*,

Krishna is known to have killed Kansha and re-established Ugrasen on the throne of Mathura. *Tyajet kularthe purusham* (for the sake of (protection) of the *kula* the person can be sacrificed), etc. proves the point that one who defames the *kula* ought to be shunned. (*Mahābhārata*, vol. III *Udyogaparva* 'Bhagavadyanasandhiparvodhaya')

Coercive method as a form of settlement of disputes came under scrutiny in the age of Buddha. In the same period Aryans moved from the upper Gangetic to the middle Gangetic belt. (Sharma, 1996: 89 and Chakravarty, 1987: 19 and Thapar, 1976: 139) Agriculture was now the mainstay of their economy. The economy in the Buddhist states, sustained largely by trade, which generated a considerable surplus, made wars redundant. (Thapar, 1976: 48–49) Either because of urbane attitude or because traders expected peaceful settlement of disputes, in the age of Buddha *ahimsā* was the most popular *āchara dharma*. (Thapar, 1976: 46–48)

Early Buddhism dates between 600–500 BC. But a few centuries later in Kautilya's Arthashastra, we once again find that war is not only justified, but also glorified.[1] One reason for this could be that through war territorial expansion was expected to take place, which in turn expedited political and economic gains. We also find that both Kautilya and Manu stressed the productiion activity and not trading as means of livelihood. This is supported by the fact that both Kautilya and Manu looked down upon usury as a profession. (Kangle, 1960: 176 and Manu Dharmashastra, 1958: 124–125 and Thapar, 1997: 54–60)

The analysis so far reveals that there existed two schools of thought that decided on the necessity of war, particularly as an economic measure. It is evident that Buddhists had only sectoral control. After Asoka's death, the Buddhist stronghold in the Mauryan Empire slackened, and under the Satabahana rulers resurgent Brahminism surfaced. (Thapar, 1996: vol. I, 131–132) Laws of this period were now controlling advanced urban settlements. *Dharmaśāstra* and *Dharmasutra* texts that form the core of Brahmanical rule based social order, in the same period adopted a quasi-legal status. In these *śāstras*, we get a clear idea about *dharma* and its scope. Though many of the *Dharmaśāstras* were compiled in the age of the Buddha, in the Satabahana period the gamut of the rules expanded to include the duties of the kings, rules relating to inheritance, marriage rules, rules that determine the caste order. (Thapar, 1966: 123 and Thapar, 1976: 48–49) But no rule was there for just war.

Dharma is a syncretic concept that upholds or strings together in the form of codes, divergent behavioural aspects (*varnāśramadharma*) within a society. (Dey, 1970: vol. II, 314) *Śruti śāstra* is of the view that *dharma* is the basis of *dharma*. (*Jaimini Sutra Sabara Bhasya: Adhyaya* I.1.1) The first *dharma* refers to the inviolable propensity of things. (*Jaimini Sutra Sabara Bhasya*: I.1.5) According to this view, the individual's desires (*codanā*) must be in the harmony with the rule of law. (*Jaimini Sutra Sabara Bhasya*: I.1.2) The *Smṛiti* laws that emphasise the ascendance of goals (*purushārthas*) by individuals by following the path of *dharma*, derive their mandate not just from hearing the *śāstra*, but also from other sources like custom and the opinions of learned men. (*Jaimini Sutra Sabara Bhasya*: I. III.1)

In the *Mahābhārata*, we come across gross violations of prescriptions of *dharma*. Shankar, the *Advaitavada* thinker has categorised *Mahābhārat* and *Gita* under *Smṛiti Śāstra*. (Daya Krishna, 2002: 28) Violation of customary laws relating to *varnāśrama dharma*, is the cause of several *dharmasamkats* (crisis of dharma). Shantanu's love and marriage to Dhibar's daughter Satyavati, Panchali's marriage to five Pandavas are obvious instances of flouting of *varna* and marriage rules.[2] Bhishma's decision to remain unmarried goes against the *ashrama dharma*. Subsequent to the death of his two half brothers, Bhishma arranged for a *niyoga* conception for the widows of the deceased kings. Manu discouraged *niyoga*. (*Manu Dhrmashastras*, 1958: IX, 64–69) Pandavas were either *kānina* (Karna) (out of wedlock) or *sahoda* children (children procured from persons other than the legally wedded husband). The lawmakers of the same period did not approve of birth of such children. (*Manu Dharmashastras*, 1958: IX, 166)

These *dharmasamkat* cases were resolved *ex post facto* by referring to custom alone. There is a possibility that though the epic stories were written under advanced urban conditions, the society retained many of their tribal customs. (Sharma, 1996: 142, 157) There is yet another possibility that during the epic period, the *kshatriya* kings rose to prominence as a result they flouted brahmanical *śāstra* laws and replaced them with their own set of laws. (Sharma, 1996: 127) This is evidenced from Kunti's (mother of the Pandavas) statement in *Udyogparva*. Worried about her son Yudhisthira's inaction in crisis, she sends a message, 'son, you are acting foolishly. As your mind is clouded by the *śāstras* of sacrificing brahmins, you have failed to appreciate the *dharma* of the *kshatriya*. Physical strength is the asset of the kshatriya. With that he settles disputes and also wields justice with an even hand.' (*Mahābhārata*, vol. III *Udyogaparva*, Ch. 133 'Bhagvadyanasandhi Parvodhyaya-viduraupakhyana')

An argument stemming from natural necessity overtakes the view that war is ethically justified. The difficulty is that natural necessity often bypasses ethical debates such as, do *kshatriyas* need to prioritise *yuddha dharma* over *sādharana dharma* such as *lokasangraha*? In Kunti's opinion, the *rājdharma* of the *kshatriya*, as stated by their forefathers, is that a weakling or a believer of non-violence could never be a good king. (*Mahābhārata*, vol. III *Udyogparva* Ch. 133) On the other hand, when Gandhari chided her son Duryodhana for perpetrating war and slandering *dharma*, she argued like a pacifist. War, she felt, was a retrogressive step as it led to needless *lokakshaya*. Neither the victor nor the vanquished can make a real gain. (*Mahābhārata* vol. III, Ch. 129 'Bhagavadyanasandhiparvodhyaya') Gandhari's prediction raises a general ethical debate. Are wars, which are of mammoth stature like the Kurukshetra war, backed by a sense of collective responsibility that the warriors recognised, even when they declared it as *dharmayuddha*? This seems a pertinent issue since tales about mindless destruction of life, property and weaponry abound in the cantos describing this war. In the *Stŗparva* we read of thousands of weeping widows, carrying lamps at night, searching for the bodies of their husbands, mothers their sons. (*Mahābhārata* vol. VI *Striparva,* Ch. 16 'Jalapradanik Parva Adhyaya') The Kaurava widows cursed the victors and prayed for their doom. (*Mahābhārata* vol. VI *Striparva* Ch.20)

In the *Stŗparva,* Gandhari directs her ire towards Krishna. Having lost all her sons in the war, she felt that Krishna, even after foreseeing the ravages of this war, did not prevent it. (*Mahābhārata* vol. VI Ch. 24) These questions seem irrelevant on the face of the fact that Ksrishna had already declared this war as *dharmayuddha* in *Bhishmaparva.* (*Mahābhārata,* vol. IV *Bhishmaparva,* Ch. 27–28 'Bhagavadgita Parvodhyaya') The entire objective of *Gita* has been to convince Arjuna that restoration of *dharma* is enough of a moral reason why this war ought to be fought, even at the cost of killing one's own relatives. He also argued that it was Arjuna's *svadharma* dictate that makes it obligatory for him to fight this war.

Some unavoidable incongruities relating to moral necessity of fighting this war in particular arise when Krishna in *Gita*, countering Arjuna's apprehensions about *kulanāsh,* states, *Svadharmammapi chāvekshya na vikampitumarhasi dharmāddhi yuddhāt śreya anyat kshatryiyasya na vidyate.* ('By taking care of *Svadharma*, you should not be perturbed too, as there is nothing more glorious than *dharmayuddha* for a *Kshatriya.*') (*Shrimadbhagvadgita*: Ch. 2.31) Krishna also says the reasons of *lābha* and *alābha* (gain and loss) or *jaya* and *ajaya* (success and defeat) are not the conditions for waging this war. The obligation has to be entirely *nishkāma karma* (*Shrimadbhagvadgita*: Ch. 2.47). There are some inconsistent statements that mar the idea of *nishkāma karma.* For instance, *hatovā prāpsyasi svarga*, etc. ('If you die you will attain heaven, or if you win you will rule the earth') (*Shrimadbhagavadgita*: Ch. 2.37) embarrass the much eulogised statement, *karmanyevādhikārastu mā phaleshu kadāchana.* ('You have duty only to perform the action, may the results of karma never attract you') (*Shrimadbhagavadgita*: Ch. 2.47) *Nishkāmakarma*, for that matter, cannot be justified when Krishna says to Arjuna, *yogakshemam bahāmyaham* ('I will bear the fruits of your labour') (*Shrimadbhagavadgita*: Ch. 9.22) or, *aham twām sarva pāpebhya mokshyaishyami mā sucha* ('I will deliver you from all sinful deeds'). (*Shrimadbhagavadgita*: Ch. 18.66)

The Kurukshetra War had caused a *dharmasamkat*. For restoration of *dharma*, Krishna had persuaded Arjuna to fight this war. At the same time the larger issue raised by Gandhari leads us to enquire about the virtual gain made by the Pandavas in this war. Yudhistira's remorse in the Shantiparva bares open the question about the gains through war by using violent means to establish a morally sanctioned king. Yudhisthira at the end of this war was heartbroken, so much so that he wanted to quit the throne and retire. (*Mahābhārata,* vol. V, Chs 1–29 'Rajaddharmaparvodhyaya') It is said that at the end of this war Kaliyuga had set in. (Sharma, 1996: 147). It is also difficult to assimilate the morals of this war, because at the end of this war his own community secretly murdered Krishna. (*Mahābhārata* vol. VI, Ch. 7)[1] Also, a fighting broke out within the Vrishni community, and it was justified on grounds that Kuru Pandava war showed the way. (*Mahābhārata* vol.VI Ch. 1–2) Lack of administrative control and appearance of greedy princes on the scene led to robbery and other crimes. (Sharma, 1996: 148) If this was the aftermath of the Kurukshetra War, then in real terms it had brought good to no one.

Dharmasamkat also arose when Arjuna refused to wage a war against his *svajana* (relatives). Should the *svadharma* of a *kshatriya* supersede the reasons for protecting the *kuladharma* needs deliberation. (*Shrimadbhagvadgita* Ch.1.37) Customarily the *kula* is to be protected for the sake of maintaining the *varnavyāvasthā*. Particularly since there are no annals of *svajanahatyā* in any of the Vedic and *Dharmaśāstra* texts. It is only under special condition that *svadharma* of *kshatriya* has to violate the *kuladharma*. Krishna's opinion appears rather strange. His insistence on *svadharma* as the only motive to fight a *dharmayuddha* and its potency to lead to *moksha*, seems to contravene the *sādhārana dharma* relating to the welfare of the tribe. Also, there is a logical incongruity, because *kula* is a higher principle, and *svadharma* with its *varna* peculiarities are subsumed within it. Hence, destruction of the *kula* at the cost of maintaining the *svadharma* was probably not a correct decision.

Krishna is of the opinion that *svadharma* has to be performed with the purest of intention, *sukhé dukkhé samé kritvā lābhālābhayu jayājayu tato yudhāya yuddhasva naivam pāpamavāpsyasi.* ('By treating happiness and unhappiness, gain and loss with equal significance, be prepared for war. By fighting a war (with this attitude in mind), you will never be a sinner.') (*Shrimadbhagvadgita*: Ch. 2.38) The intention to fight a war for its own sake and not for the sake of making a gain in war is backed by two principal points made in *Gita*. First, it refers to the notion of conscience of the warrior: the *sādhārana dharma* that he is morally obliged to destroy evil. Then, action has to be pursued without the intention of enjoying the consequent benefits. The point about this *yuddha* is that it is fought with retribution as a desiderative motive; hence neither objective could have been attained through this war.

Further, the principle of *jus ad bellum* is at variance here. Retribution through war becomes obligatory and not just morally permissible when the aggrieved person can say: 'Enough is enough'. In any case, we have to search for the original sinner because of whom the war is necessary. Duryodhana insulted Krishna in *Udyog Parvah* (*Mahābhārata*, Vol. III *Udyogaparva* 'Bhagavadyanaparvodhyaya' Ch.128) and that snapped his limit of tolerance and provoked him to declare *dharmayuddha* against the Kauravas. It is strange that no war was declared against Yudhisthira when he gambled, gleefully waging his kingdom, brothers as well as his wife over a game of dice. By conventional standard, he had contravened *sādhārana dharma* and created a *dharmasamkat*. First of all, gamble, was looked down upon as an indiscreet act right from Rgvedic period. (*Rgvedasamhita*: Mandala X.32) Secondly, the violation of dignity and self-respect that Draupadi suffered because her husband was indiscreet could itself have been a more potent cause of *dharmayuddha*. Lastly, Yudhisthira had knowingly played for high stakes. Going by Kautilya's *śāstra,* promise has a certain writ – it is made with the presumption that the person has given consent after knowing the consequences. (*Kautilya Arthashastra*, vol. I, Book III 'Determination of Forms of Agreement') Where then is the moral clout of the Pandavas to wage a *dharmayuddha*?

The incidence of remorse of Arjuna and the questions he raised about *svajanahatyā* and Krishna's advice to him to fight despite the moral dilemma can be summarised in four sentences. The first is, *svadharme nidhanam Pārtha* (*Srimadbhagvadgita*: Ch. 3.35), the second, *yuddhāya yujjasva* (*Srimadbhagvadgita*: Ch.2.38), the third, *yuddhasva*, (*Srimadbhagavadgita*: Ch. 2.50) and the fourth, *mā phaleshu*. (*Srimadbhagvadgita*: Ch. 2.47) These have attracted the attention of many commentators, ancient as well as modern. Arjuna's *śoka* is interpreted as an instance of what *śoka* in *samsāra* can be. Following the philosophies of Samkhya and Vedanta, we come to know that *tri tāpa* is inevitable. Commentators of the stature of Śankaracharya have used Krishna's fourfold *upadeshas* as ways of removing the barrier of the mind pre-disposed with *śoka. Yuddhasva,* says Śankara is not a *vidhi,* but merely a means of removing the *pratibandhas* such as *śoka* so that *svadharma* or spiritual development can be carried out in an unimpaired manner (Panoli, 1980: *Sloka* 2.18)

Most modern commentators are of the opinion that in the backdrop of Kurukshetra war Gitopadesh contains three sections, Arjuna's *vishāda,* Krishna's *tattva jñāna* and Arjuna's *mohanāsh* and resolve to fight. These are the primary three parts of an ethical debate. Hence, spiritual discourse is of incidental significance in *Gita.* In the nineteenth century many scholars who have attempted to develop a national consciousness through cultural regeneration and thereby free India from British colonisers, showed a renewed interest in *Gita* and the concept of *dharmayuddha.* Lokamanya Tilak, for instance, refused to accept the theory that Krishna's pronouncement *tasmāt yuddhasva Bharata* ('out of the reason for this, fight Arjuna') as indicating the *nivritti marga*. The philosophy of *Gita* provides a unique synthesis of karma and *sannyāsa margas,* according to this view. *Naishkarmabhāva* is as much an undesirable concept in Gita's teaching as *sakāmakarma bhāva* is. They considered Niskama karma as an alternative ethical principle that sanctioned their just war theories.

From the works of many nineteenth-century thinkers we gather that they felt a peculiar urgency to establish retributive form of justice by applying the *jus ad bellum* principle. What lent complexity to the nature of the problem was their failure to uniformly identify their enemy. The immediate provocation that disheartened a large section of the intelligentsia was the material disadvantages caused to the Indians by certain unfriendly British administrative policies that in due course set the colonising process. In this section, I have attempted to examine the views of Bankim Chandra Chattopadhyaya, a mid-nineteenth-century novelist and scholar, in particular for an overt reason that relates to his preoccupations with *Gita* and its philosophy that preached campaign against evil with a selfless motive. Alongside, I have also found many of Bankim's ideas depict the complexities that otherwise plagued his contemporaries, while addressing the issue of the object of their struggle.

In the early decades of the nineteenth century, actual war was confined to a localised revolt against white man's tyranny. The Indigo revolt in Bengal was one such aborted effort. Nevertheless, it attracted considerable scholarly attention in the same period. One of the fallout of intellectualisation of such revolts was the renewed interest in the *dharmayuddha* concept of *Gita.* The resurrection of some key concept of *Gita* like *svadharme nidhanam Partha, mā phaleshu kadāchana* or *tasmāt yuddhasva Bharata,* now contained innovated meanings directed largely towards development of secular morality.

The material history of the present *dharmayuddha* dates back to the period of battle of Plassey (1757), through which the British made a formidable political entry in Bengal. Bankim Chandra Chatterjee in the prologue of his novel *Anandamath* recounts the days from the Battle of Plassey to the days of Warren Hasting's reforms as a period of 'power without responsibility'. (Chattopadhyaya, 1964: 56) Bankim takes us back to those anarchical days of 1770s when diarchical form of government prevailed in Bengal. The Nawab of Bengal was powerless, while East India Company men were mercilessly collecting revenue. Against this ruthless rapacity, the common people had neither protection nor any court of appeal. (Chattopadhyaya, 1964: 56)

The story of English advent in India, however, began a century from this period. It is linked with the landing of the East India Company a trading company on the Indian soil in the year 1650. After obtaining a grant of 'Diwani' from the then Mughal emperor to have accessibility to collect revenue, the company made inroad to economic control. (Chatterjee, 1990: 3) The Indian traders (*banians*) supplied the capital for investment to the Company's servants. As a result the company's trade flourished till as late as end of the eighteenth century. (Chaterjee, 1990: 3) The British government within a century's time started to politically control India through this Company. By the end of the eighteenth century, the passage of two memorable Acts by the British Parliament soured the minds of Indians.

In the wake of Pitts India Act of 1784 followed by Cornwallis' Reform, the company started to operate as a private trader, and their chief source of revenue came from indigo trade. The Company's policies with regard to trade and to land revenue system had inter-related aspects. One of the adverse outcomes was the decline in the Eastern Seas' trade of the company's servant. Another unfriendly Act from the point of view of the Indian trading partners was passing of the Charter of 1813, by which monopoly trade of the East India Company was abolished. The Indo-British commercial relation suffered as the nascent Indian trading partners were now subjected to the rough weathers of Industrial Revolution, without British arm of friendship supporting them.

To the common man, The India Act, that came from the Parliament of England and mainly proposed by the English landlords whose sympathies lay with the Indian landed community, had caused considerable disappointments. (Spear, 1990: 332) The Act insisted on the abandonment of annual leases and directed the preparation of 'permanent rulers' as revenue collectors. These decisions preceded the passing of the historic Permanent Settlement Act in 1793. (Spear, 1990: 333) One reads about endless incidents of exploitation of the poor peasants by the new zamindars in the role of revenue collectors. (Chatterjee, 1990: 4–6) The attitude of the Indian elite was ambivalent towards the British from this period onwards. Though Permanent Settlement was noted as an administrative reform measure, thinkers like Bankim complained that it had not adequately benefited the peasants.[3]

For a section of the intelligentsia residing in the urban locality of Bengal these disappointments appeared not grave enough when compared to the erstwhile Muslim rule who reigned in Bengal before the advent of the British administrators. (Majumdar, 1960: 19) The positive fallout of colonisation, they felt, was the ushering of modernity that included the English administrative reform and new education policy. (Majumdar, 1960: 31) There was a growing feeling among intellectuals like Bankim that British rule had given them political stability, security of life and property. The rule of law was reasonably truncated, he felt, to deliver impartial administration of justice. (Chattopadhyaya, 1964, Vol. II: 394–395) The modernists amongst the nationalists envisioned a strong civil society for India that presupposes industrialization, scientific temper and technological know-how coupled with a nationalist culture. (Majumdar, 1960: 54–55) A sort of crusade against practices that stood in the way of religious and cultural reform was also in the anvil within the environs of change. (Chattopadhyaya, 1964. Vol. I: 76)

It now appears that the reformers of the nineteenth century had opened several battlefronts. British policy of 'unsympathy' that was visible especially in the economic front no doubt had the triggering effect that fanned discontent. However, their own inertia to modernise on the matrix developed by the British was also taken up on a war footing. What strikes as an unusual feature of the history of this period is that due to the ambivalent relation with the British the intelligentsia failed to address the issue of anti-colonialism directly. Rather, they were hovering within the domain of their own social regeneration. (Halbfass, 1990: 217–246).

The Indian reformers, pioneered by Ram Mohan Roy, also developed an antipathy towards certain abhorrent traditional practices that included hook swinging and *Satidaha*. With the co-operation of the British these were suppressed through enactment around the mid-nineteenth century. These bans were otherwise significant too, as they placed a direct threat to the emerging relation between the newly educated members of the upper echelons of the society and their attitude towards popular local religious and social practices. Changing attitude towards religion was also part of a broader process, as the elite was now in search of a new matrix for religio-culture that approximated European norms. The search for new religio-cultural symbol was yet another way of saying what the white man's burden was.

Some aggressive reform process by a section of the elite that disavowed culture in its entirety came under scrutiny from a section of traditionalists within the elite. The latter seemed to have created a third battlefront by flaunting the 'glorious past' as constructed by British Indologists, and wanted the Hindus to emulate these values. (Halbfass, 1990: 62) This gave rise to certain new concept of *dharma*, which placed in Western parlance could be best termed as 'dynamic classicism'. (Van M Baumer, 1976: 46–47) Bankim's concept of *dharma* retains some of these antithetical ideas. He derives his claims to national self-assertion and superiority from the 'inclusivistic' wealth of the religious tradition of Hinduism by drawing inspirations from *Puranas*, *Mahābhārata* and *Srimadbhagvadgita*. He sorted these to weed out the untenable phantasm that is generally associated with Hindu religion. The re-casted Hinduism was simultaneously theistic and secular to the extent of being utilitarian. (Chattopadhyaya, 1964: Vol. II, 589–594) As a self proclaimed neo-Hindu, he searched within the classical tradition to sieve out the husk and retain the kernel which he believed could have instrumental use for developing the national consciousness. (*Bankim Chandra Chatterjee's Works*, 596)

Bankim's kernel or sense of *dharma* created a new semantic situation, as it now became one of the mediating terms for cross-cultural references. Following Mill, Bankim argued that happiness is the end of life. Asceticism and extermination of sensuous feelings are unnatural. Thus, neither *nivritti marga* of *Vedanta* nor sensuous philosophy of the *Vaishnavas*, that describes unbridled love between Radha and Krishna, is worth emulating. According to him, the ideal man makes a rational and harmonious balance of the two. (*Bankim Chandra Chatterjee's Works*, 596–602) His own reconstructed *Krishna Charitra* is an embodiment of rational as well as utilitarian ideal. *Dharma* is the synthesis and a harmonised disposition, (Bankim refers to them as *vrittis*) of all faculties, physical, intellectual, aesthetic and religious. (*Bankim Chandra Chatterjee's Works*, 596–602) Krishna, as depicted by him, has carried these faculties to an exceptional height. (Chattopadhyaya, 1964, vol. II: 565–567)

Bankim was keen to re-establish Hindu religion shorn of all its maladies and portray it as the universal religion of man that cuts across the boundaries of nation, creed and religion. *Svadharma*, that orders *yuddhasva* to the moral person, is not restricted to performing the caste duties. For him, division within society was more occupational (Chattopadhyaya, 1964, vol. II: 693–694). The specific *svadharma* of each individual is applied to a 'crucial instance'. War, he agreed, was no doubt a destructive affair; nevertheless, certain special moral circumstances act as a *crucial instance* that decide on behalf of the agent its moral justification. The moral permission does not mean license to kill indiscriminately. In a war that claims to establish the *dharma* or moral fibre of the society (*dharma sansthāpanārthāya*), the agent is duty bound to fight only that. Hence, *dharma sansthāpan* is the *sādharana dharma*, which the moral agent takes upon him as the crucial instance or his *svadharma* to fight.

The debate of moral necessity of war for Bankim would have remained without much controversy, had these been his concluding remarks. Instead, he combined his moral theory of *dharma* with the spiritual belief that *ātman* is indestructible. Hence the moral person is one who kills with the conviction that it is causing no damage to the soul or the true and eternal existence of man. Through this war the evil doer's body alone is dispensed with. (Chattopadhyaya, 1964: 720) There is a possibility that Bankim was trying to design his *dharmayuddha* concept after the Christian concept of crusade, in which the Holy Spirit wins over the unholy body of the sinner. However, he complicated his view by stating that God's will is sublime and hence the duty of the individual is to follow it unconditionally, that is, in a *nishkāma* manner. (Chattopadhyaya, 1964, Vol. I: 17) A *dharmayuddha* or a morally justified war forbids any form of personal gain whether this worldly or otherworldly.

The question now remains, whom does Bankim list as criminal. Though many thinkers were of the view that his notion of *dharmayuddha* was a much-needed

Hindu face in the nationalist struggle against the British, yet it is also a fact that during Bankim's lifetime no actual revolt had taken place. Nor was any significant seditious behaviour recorded. Nevertheless, there were reasons why around the mid-nineteenth century, the elite had begun to get disenchanted with the British administrative policies. At the fag end of his career, Bankim, too, had expressed doubts about the British sense of liberal justice and equality in his novels *Anadamath, Devi Choudhurani* and *Sitaram*. In each of these, he campaigned in favour of *dharmnayuddha*, keeping Hindu chauvinism in mind. The central theme of these novels is the seizure of political power from the exploiters. Bankim overlooked the need to change the material conditions of the society even when he himself acknowledged that under both Muslim rule and British Raj there was rampant economic exploitation.

The period chosen as the backdrop of these novels, dates back to the days of diarchical rule in Bengal. Both British and their puppet Muslim rulers were exploiting the peasants by demanding excessive revenue. In *Devi Choudhurani*, there is no organised political party that undertook frontal attack against the indifferent rulers. The dacoit queen, Devi Choudhurani, engages in guerrilla warfare that resembled the style of Robin Hood. However, her intention is entirely *nishkāma*, that is, other than routing the British she has no personal gain in this war. In comparison, *Anadamath* is a more advanced political novel. It partly depicts the *Sannāyasi* revolt of 1770s. However, Bankim's heroes were not the *Sannyāsis*, but terrorists who called themselves *Santāns* of *desh mātricā*. Heinous means like dacoity by the Santans was morally justified war strategy. It was argued that robbing the robbers was not really a crime. (Chattopadhyaya, 1964, Vol. I: 17)

Certain common features of these wars are that the mythical characters are craftily woven into a period history to give it an impression that the author is seemingly archiving historical anecdotes. Nevertheless, by applying the *jus ad bellum* principle, these wars were declared by him as *dharmayuddha*s. The search for the original sinner leads us to certain complexities. In *Anandamath* in particular, Bankim gets carried away by his disregard for the Muslims, both as rulers as well as subjects. Together, they robbed, he felt, the Hindus of their kingdom and glory, and also their religious followings. (Chattopadhyaya, 1964, Vol. I: 64–65, 75) British have also been portrayed as enemy of the Hindus, largely because of their turn-coat attitude. The interesting point is that these wars had a retributive motive that in principle goes against the *nishkāma karma* theory that Bankim so seriously wanted his *dharmayuddha* warriors to emulate.

Bankim had envisioned a third kind of *dharmayuddha*, but this was an internal battle that Hindus as moral persons ought to fight. He never wanted Hindus to *en mass* pursue the Vedanta path and renounce the world. Nor did he expect that modern Hindus should needlessly worry about the Vedas and its ritualistic *karma mārga*. The spirit of Hinduism can truly shine when more attention is paid to moral development that balances both the *mārgas*. Sitaram, the hero of his novel *Sitaram*, lost his glory and his kingdom while fighting the Pathans because he faltered as a moral Hindu. Bankim strongly believed that controlling the passion (*kama*) with the help of *dharma* is the Hindu ideal. Thus, the motive of this *yuddha* as depicted in this novel is a moral war in an 'inclusivist' Hindu sense.

It is strange that Bankim, who was so carried away by the notion of *dharmayuddha*, had practically no opinion about morally justified means incorporated in the *jus in bello* principle. There is a hint in the epilogue of *Anandamath* about the necessity of moral means in a just war. This passage is even otherwise significant, because the author is trying to unravel the real reason why this war was fought by the *Santān*s. After initial gain made by *Santāns* in repelling the Muslim and the British, they rejoiced, for now the Hindu *rājya* with all its splendours could be established. At this juncture, Satyananda, the hero among the *Santāns*, is commanded by the 'Doctor' (a mysterious messiah) to repair to the Himalayas. The Doctor argued that the *Santān*s had used wrong means, such as dacoity. He also argued that wrong means couldn't lead to a just cause. Bankim thus wanted the *Santāns* to reform themselves internally as well as externally, by adopting a scientific attitude towards development, as a preliminary means to win the battle against the British. He seems to be vacillating between reform and retribution as a goal for his *dharmayuddha*. (Chattopadhyaya, 1964, Vol. I: 75)

The history behind Gandhi's intention to wage a just war advances to the actual conflict that nationalists had with the British rulers in the early part of the twentieth century. Historians are of the opinion that from the period around 1905, British entered into a new era of governance. The vice royalty of Lord Curzon was the last of the old blaze ruler of imperialism that was so well conceived by Lord Wellesley and strategised by Lord Dalhousie. Among Lord Curzon's notorious deeds was an abortive attempt to partition Bengal Presidency ostensibly for administrative reasons. (Sarkar, 1983: 106–111) This move caused unprecedented adverse reaction from the public. (Majumdar, 1960). The partition of Bengal was intensely opposed with a direct confrontation through civil disobedience movement. (Sarkar, 1983: 112) One of the fallout of this movement was that the days of petitioning had come to an end.

From 1905 onwards, a turbulent phase of national movement had begun. For one, it was marked by a series of *swādeshi* movements, engaging the intellectuals as well as people from the middle class at one level and peasants at another. In the same period, the attitude of the British, too, underwent a qualitative change. Paternalism, on which British governance thrived for century and a half, now gave way to actual brutal repression of the *Swādeshis*.

(Sarkar, 1983:137–140) The leaders of major nationalist groups, especially the Indian National Congress, began negotiations with the British regarding the terms of transfer of power. A growing distrust was noticed between the Hindus and Muslims within the Congress. Vocal members of the Muslim intelligentsia also made an independent bid for power. After the end of First World War, British who were recovering from their wounds, dialogued with leading political groups with a view to augment the process of transfer of power on their terms. (Spear, 1990: 332–333)

In 1905 the intelligentsia spontaneously reacted against the Partition of Bengal. The *Swadeshis* took the movement to the streets. Activities of different terrorist and interventionist groups, too, intensified their activities followed by this initial movement. Congress in the year 1916 formed the Home Rule League whose activities were largely to draw public into debates on nationalist issues. These events preceded the arrival of Gandhi on the Indian political scene. Even though Gandhi disagreed in large measure with the strategies of these movements and intervened to change them, nevertheless he had to address his political will within the existing trends. As for the tactics, the issue lay between direct or constitutional method and within that the means such as peaceful or violent action had to be adjusted. These views were closely related but not identical. For instance one could be unconstitutional and yet remain non-violent, as Gandhi proposed.

After concluding successfully a *Satyāgraha* struggle in South Africa, Gandhi received instruction from Gokhale to return to India to experiment his new found method of applying non-violent means to fight a just war. Gandhi reached India in 1915. During this period, he had earned the reputation of being a thoroughly moral person, and hence he declared that the just war against the British had to be fought, keeping moral means in the forefront. The *Dharma* meaning founded by him was fundamentally a religious belief with the proviso that religious was moral too. 'True morality covers religion for the most part. Anyone who observes the law of morality for their own sake and not for some selfish end can be regarded as religion.' (Narayan, 1968, Vol. IV: 8) God for Gandhi was the highest truth in a holistic sense and not a mere personal idol to be prayed. Like the Platonic God that symbolised all that was good or perfect, Gandhi's Truth too metaphysically represented all that was perfect – perfect society, perfect man and perfect mentality. (Narayan, 1968, Vol. IV: 20–23)

Unlike Bankim, Gandhi's idea of cultural regeneration was entirely pan-Indian in nature. He was opposed to the idea of modernity that was a gift of Western materialistic culture. (Narayan, 1968, Vol. IV: 112) Bankim, on the other hand, had eulogised it. Gandhi was unhappy that the culture of civil society was unwarrantedly imposed on sleepy rural India. (Narayan, 1968,

Vol. IV: 96) He also felt that Indian culture traditionally upheld spiritual development that encouraged amelioration of the ego and abnegation of physical comfort. He felt disturbed that in the name of ushering modernity the Indian reformers had rejected the true Hindu spirit. Thus, while *swarāj* at one level meant capturing political power, at another more substantial level, it meant for him freedom from the British cultural imposition. (Narayan, 1968, Vol. IV: 150–151) For the individual, *swarāj* really means self-control. 'Only he is capable of self-control who observes the rules of morality,' said Gandhi. (Narayan, 1968, Vol. IV: 778)

For Gandhi, the inner battle was morally more compelling than the external battle. At the same time, both had to be synchronised. For a *satyāgrahi*, the preparations were more in tune with spiritual power to say no to immorality. Gandhi felt that even if a single *satyāgrahi* holds out till the end, victory is absolutely certain. 'That is the beauty of *satyāgraha;* it comes up to oneself; one has not to go out and search for it. This is a virtue inherent in itself.' says Gandhi. (Narayan, 1968, Vol. III: 186) It is in this context that he explains his design of *a dharmayuddha*. 'A *dharmayuddha*, in which there are no secrets to be guarded, no scope for cunning and no place for untruth, comes unsought; and a man of religion is ever ready for it. A struggle, which has to be previously planned, is not a righteous struggle. A *dharmayuddha* can be waged only in the name of God, and it is only when the *Satyagrāhi* feels quite helpless that God comes to his help.' (Narayan, 1968, Vol. IIII: Preface xiii)

This longish passage on *dharmayuddha* satisfies the *jus ad bellum* principle but with the proviso that the spirit alone has the right to declare the war. Interestingly, for Gandhi *jus ad bellum* principle is incomplete without taking cognisance of the moral means (*jus in bello*) complimenting it. Gandhi had been interchangeably using two kinds of forces, truth-force and soul-force. Yet he wants to crucially distinguish the two kinds of forces, for he argued that they are not twin forces. (Narayan, 1968, Vol. VI: 150) The first is the force within, that a *satyāgrahi* feels to not to co-operate with evil and immoral laws, the second is the message of concerned appeal that the *satyāgrahi* sends to his contenders.

The second is thus the force of love, which is to be applied gently by conveying the message to the enemy that his policies are wrong, but he is not. (Narayan, 1968, Vol. VI: 154) So, crime does not extend to hating the criminal. This is the principle of *ahimsā* that he innovates so that a completely bloodless battle can be fought. 'I discovered in the earliest stages that the pursuit of truth did not admit of violence being inflicted on one's opponent but that he must be weaned from the error by patience and sympathy. For what appears to be truth to the one may appear error to the other. And patience means self-suffering. So the doctrine came to mean vindication of truth not by infliction of suffering on the opponent but on oneself.' (Narayan, 1968, Vol. VI: 155)

Gandhi's foot soldiers of war are, interestingly, messengers of love too. It is towards these means, that Gandhi paid utmost attention. 'Means and ends are convertible terms in my philosophy.' He felt there was no wall of separation between them. The message of love is carried to the enemies. 'It is no non-violence if we merely love those that love us. It is non-violence only when we love those that hate us.' (Narayan, 1968, Vol. VI: 155) Gandhi believed that a person should bear the pain himself to demonstrate its effect to the enemy, to convince him that he has caused pain by doing wrong. A unique fight or *dharmayuddha* was totally bereft of any retributive motive.

The special treatment that he gave to morally obligatory war has led to certain unprecedented conclusion regarding issues, like who decides, whether an action is morally permissible or not, and is in askance for an impartial spectator. For instance, the crusade of St Augustine was carried out with God's permission. In Gandhi's case, the moral person is *himself* the agent. The truth force is the autonomous agent and also the voice of God, according to Gandhi. God represents the moral person within. Second, in all cases of retribution we search for a referee, which or who stands out as a higher principle of authority. Gandhi's reply is once again unique. The higher principle is man's own conscience. (Narayan, 1968, Vol. IV: 16) The autonomy of the conscience is the impartial spectator, because ultimately man is his best critic. The de-ontic status of the impartial spectator makes it entirely *nishkāma*, for it dwells perennially in the *anāsakta* (impartial) state.

Armed with these moral compulsions, Gandhi waged a real *dharmayuddha* against the British, but with the manners of an impeccable gentleman. After undertaking small-scale dissenting movements, the major launch targeting the British was organising a *hartāl* against the contentious issues in Rowlatt Act in 1919. (Narayan, 1968, Vol. IV: 16) Gandhi's gentlemanly attitudes towards the enemy aroused curious speculations, such that his s*atyāgraha* campaigns were probably not inconsistent with his loyalty for the British. From Gandhi's point, he obsessively followed the path of non-violence and on repeated occasion told the British that though their policies were deplorable, no actual love was lost between them and us. The present *dharmayuddha* under Gandhi's leadership sought to unite culturally the *swādeshis,* cutting across regional groups. (Narayan, 1968, Vol. IV: 178) Second, he tried to hold on to his non-violent means to create a moral pressure (Narayan, 1968, Vol. IV: 179) and third, the movement received an ideology that Gandhi had put down in his book *Hind Swaraj* (Narayan, 1968, Vol. IV: 180)

Succession of events like Jallianwallah Bagh, Khilafat Movement and Gandhi's second phase of *dharmayuddha* in the form of non co-operation movement happened in quick succession. However, Gandhi's qualitative position in all these was rather mysterious. He refused to declare the British as the enemy. In fact he had withdrawn his foot soldiers, after the Chauri Chaura incident, after the movement turned violent. (Chandra, 1989: 193–195) One of the observable fallouts of this movement was that there was an increasing disregard towards constitutional authority, and growth of a dangerous spirit of lawlessness had begun. This momentum continued when Gandhi initiated the spirited move to march to Dandi in 1930 and manufacture salt as a protest measure against the Salt Law. (Chandra, 1989: 270–273) Once again, Gandhi was undaunted in his belief that the war has to be gentlemanly. Prior to the launch of the protest movement, he informed in details to the government about his movement plan. Moreover, he instructed his unarmed foot soldiers to advance without resisting the resisters.

Vindication of Gandhi's non-violent stand came not when British relented after the Dandi march, but with the acclamation it received from world public. Gandhi's method has since been listed as the moral way of waging a war. Gandhi had showed the way that just cause is not the sufficient moral reason why a war should be fought. Equally important he felt are the just means without which the moral battle cannot be won. In fact, Bankim's theory ends with the message that the *dharma* of the aggrieved party is to retaliate and not relent. He universalised the *dharmayuddha* morals of the Kurukshetra War. Wrong had to be righted, or else the social *sāmanjasya* (equilibrium) would get disturbed. Gandhi, on the other hand, by interpolating the meaning of *dharmayuddha* created two domains of battlefields, one internal and the other external. Both can be brought under the principle of *jus ad bellum*.

For Gandhi, it is not enough to say that external war ought to be conscience directed. All moralists would agree to that and so would Bankim. Gandhi goes a step further. His conscience is split in two. The Arjuna aspect of conscience acts, but more importantly, it has to receive instruction from Krishna or pure consciousness. In his Anasaktiyoga, he states that the entire war of Kurukshetra is happening within our conscience. The autonomous will is the voice of Krishna that persuades Arjuna not to be complacent about the enemy (both within and outside, as Gandhi sees it). *Yuddhasva* is the righteous force from within, which acts as the morally autonomous agent in this war. (Gandhi, 1977: *Introduction*) The internal enemy like *himsā* or hatred has to go, and external enemy that perpetrates this *himsā* must also undergo a change, through a change of heart.

These internal and external reforms were not just restricted to notions put forth by Bankim, like control of sexual urge, and followed a patterned idea of *cittasuddhi* (the idea that recurs in his novels particularly Anandamath, Devi Coudhurani and Sitaram). Rather, Gandhi translated his reform measure into a constructive programme that overhauled the body and the soul as well as socio-economic condition. The Ashrama that he repaired to in Wardha, during the lull period of the 'freedom struggle', was one such moral purgatory for him and for his close followers. The Ashrama experiment was to resolve the cultural dilemma that the Indian national consciousness has been facing since Bankim's time, which is to discover a pan-Indian variety of *Indian* gentlemen.

The layers of reform, starting from physical self control to giving a name and a face to the untouchables, to resolving Hindu-Muslim crisis and fighting the adverse policy of the British, were *dharmayuddha* at different levels for Gandhi. The experiment to resolve external conflict by inflicting pain on oneself and purging the body of all kind of ill-feeling towards the enemy was really an attempt to take the *dharmayuddha* concept to a level of *sādhana* (ascetic practice). It is not the way the *nivritti marga* advocated, but one that carried forward the *nishkāmabhāva* in letter and in spirit. Gandhi's two famous fasts and one *padyātra* for Hindu Muslim amity were no less of a *dharmayuddha* than Civil disobedience movement was. There is thus a universal appeal in Gandhi's concept of *dharmayuddha.* Anybody can wage this war without preparation. He is required to say no to the enemy's policy after extending his arm in friendship towards him; and second, purge his own body so that the love within can radiate and convert the wrong doer.

Notes

1 *Arthashastra* was written with the explicit intention of acquisition and protection of earth (*prithivya labhepalanecha*). It is for this reason the role of the *vijigisu* king has been glorified. He is the one who contemplates expansion of the territory. See vol. I.1.1 and vol. III p. 249 of Kangle, *The Kautilya Arthashastra.*

2 About Draupadi's polyandry the *shastrakars* are not happy, as not even customary evidence can be sighted for it. *Tantravarttika by Kumarilabhatta,* translated and edited by Ganganath Jha, states that Draupadi's marriage cannot be cited as a customary case of polyandry as she was like a Divine Being.

3 See *Bankim Rachnabali* p. 287–291. Bankim had an ambivalent opinion about the advent of British in India. He argued that Permanent Settlement had streamlined revenue collection, but its positive impact had not reached the poor.

References

Chatterjee, Bankim Chandra. 1969. *Bankim Chandra Chatterjee's Work,* cent. ed., ed. and trans. Jogesh Chandra Bagh (Calcutta: Bangiya Sahitya Parishad).

Chakravarty Uma. 1987. *The Social dimensions of Early Buddhism* (Delhi: O.U.P).

Chandra, Bipan. 1989. *India's Struggle for Independence* (New Delhi: Penguin Books).

Chatterjee, Dilip Kumar. 1990. *The Dynamics of Social Change in Bengal 1817–1851* (Calcutta: Punthi Pustak).

Chattopadhyaya, Bankim Chandra. 1964. *Bankim Rachanabali* (Calcutta: Sahitya Sansad).

Daya Krishna, ed. 2000. *Development of Philosophy from 18th Century Onward* (Delhi: O.U.P).

Dey, S. K. et al. 1970. *Cultural Heritage of India.* (Calcutta: R.K.Mission of Institute of Culture).

Gandhi, M.K. 1977. *Anasaktiyoga*. (Ahmedabad: Navajivan Publishing House)

Gita in Shankar's Own Words. Vidyavachaspati V. Panoli, ed. and trans. 1980. (Madras: P. S. Paramsivam).

Halbfass, Wilhelm. 1990. *India and Europe: An Essay in Philosophical Understanding* (Delhi: Motilal Banarasidass).

Jaimini Sutra Sabara Bhashya, ed. and trans. Ganganath Jha, 2nd ed. 1973. (Baroda: Oriental Institute Baroda).

Kangle, R. P. 1960. *The Kautilya Arthashastra*. (Bombay: University of Bombay Publications).

Mahābhārata ed. and trans. Ramnarayan Dutta Shastri. 2004. (Gorakhpur: Gita Press).

Majumdar, R. C., ed. 1978. *The History and Culture of the Indian People* (Delhi: Bharatiya Vidyabhavan Publication Delhi).

Majumdar, R. C. 1960. *Glimpses of Bengal in the Nineteenth Century* (Calcutta: FKL Mukhopadhyaya).

Manu Dharmashastra, ed. and trans. by Kewal Motwani. 1958. (Madras: Ganesh and Co.).

Narayan Shriman, ed. 1968. *Selected Works of Mahatma Gandhi* (Ahmedabad: Navajivan Publishing House).

Rachel Van M Baumer, ed. 1976. *Aspects of Bengali History and Society* (Delhi: Vikas Publishing House).

RgvedaSamhita, ed. and trans. H. H. Wilson. 1834. (London: H. Allen).

Sarkar, Sumit. 1983. *Modern India: 1885–1947* (Madras: Macmillan).

Sharma, R. S. 1996. *Material Culture and Social Formation in Ancient India*. (Delhi: Macmillan India Ltd.).

Shrimadbhagavadgita, ed. and trans. Harendranath Choudhuri Roy. 1964. (Baranagar: Munshi House).

Spear, Perceival. 1990. *Oxford History of Modern India 1740–1975*, 2nd ed. (Delhi: O.U.P).

Thapar, Romila. 1966. *A History of India* vol. I (Hammondsworth: Penguin Books).

_______ 1997. *Asoka and the Decline of the Mauryas* (Delhi: OUP).

_______ 1976. *Ancient Indian Social History: Some Interpretations* (Delhi: Orient Longmans).

Chapter 22

GLOBALISATION AND HUMAN RIGHTS

R. P. Singh

The present millennium is different from all earlier such occasions. We have the most delicate and advanced scientific knowledge, the most capable and sophisticated technology, the fifth generation microprocessors with knowledge and information; but do we have wisdom to make use of all these, so that there is human face impressed on these achievements? One of the features of human history has been that people, resources, ideas and consciousness move from one place to another, and in the wake of globalisation they are moving all too fast and getting transformed gradually; but what has been the role of values in such movements and transformations? Is our identity getting lost in the process of globalisation? Since the proclamation of the Universal Declaration of Human Rights on 10th December 1948 by the United Nations Organization, there have been intense and endless debates and discussions so far as the legal, political, cultural, ethnic, social and philosophical aspects are concerned. Indeed, the need for the Declaration of Human Rights has arisen from the sense of insecurity faced by human beings after World War II. Moreover, it raises the questions of human dignity, self-respect, right to live and work in the world that has become the driving force and furtherance of human rights. As a matter of fact, globalisation has intervened human life and activity since 1975 onwards, and since 1990 it has become unavoidable and inevitable. With globalisation, human life is affected not only in so far as market is concerned, but also in our ethnic, cultural and linguistic identities. A study shows that after 15–20 years, 40% of world's languages will have no role in the globalised world. We all know that language is not simply a set of symbols and signs, of words and grammar, but it also is the basis of our identity, culture, ethnicity, values, legends, protagonists, etc. There is an imminent sense of conflict between globalisation and human rights; at the same time globalisation enhances people's sensitivity towards their identity. Through Internet and Cyberspace we can easily access the violation and oppression of the state, suppression of the poor and the weak, atrocities committed on women, child labour and so on. Globalisation therefore creates obstructions to human rights on the one hand and, on the other, it enhances sensitivity towards the practices of human rights.

In this paper, I will first formulate the basic principles of human rights, the philosophical underpinnings, especially with reference to Kant. Secondly, I will try to reassess the realm of human rights in the wake of globalisation. I will not only catalogue the resemblances between human rights and globalisation but also pave the way for their mutual transformation, so that a healthy philosophic growth can be achieved.

Human Rights: A Historical Perspective

As a matter of fact, human rights are as old as the human society itself but, historically speaking, the first mentioned instance of them can be found in the Magna Carta, or the Great Charter (1215). 'Barons in opposition to John (ruled 1199–1216) forced him to put his great seal to this charter on 15th June 1215 at Runnymede, near Windsor. Many of its 63 clauses dealt with the barons' grievances but some were of wider importance, e.g. no freeman was to be punished without a trial and the king could not demand taxes without the Great Council's consent. So important was it that copies, of which four survive, were sent into every shire. Though John repudiated it, the Charter was confirmed by later Kings.' (*Longman Illustrated Encyclopaedia of World History*: 547) It included such rights as the freedom of the Church from government influence, freedom for citizens, including widows, to own and inherit property, equality before law, prohibition of bribery, etc. In the course of time and historical developments those rights developed in human rights. After Magna Carta, there came many accords to substantiate and elaborate the rights of the people, such as the Petition of Rights (1628) and the Bill of Rights (1689). During eighteenth century, natural rights as legal rights started getting written into national constitutions. (Levin 1998: 5) But the basic question is: what is a right? The answer to this question is given by Immanuel Kant (1724–1804) in the treatise *Rechtslehre*, 'The only original Right, belonging to each man in virtue of his humanity is Freedom.'[1] 'Every action is in accordance with Right which enables the freedom of each man's will to assist side by side with the freedom of every other man, according to an universal law.' (Kant, *Rechtslehre Einleitung*. Quotation from Vaughan 1939: 77) We can then suppose that when Kant develops freedom as the only original right of man and proposes to limit that freedom in the case of each individual solely by the demand for an equal freedom on the part of all other individuals, it is evidently clear that for Kant an action would be contrary to right, if it interferes with the formal freedom of one's neighbour. It may also be pointed out that freedom is not lawlessness. Instead, it has certain laws and those are the laws of categorical imperatives.

It may, however, be pointed out that Kant in *Rechtslehre* has ruled out any distinction between laws imperative, i.e. moral laws, and laws permissive, i.e. political rights. In that treatise the doctrine of the permissive nature of right is silently dropped, the law of the Right is definitely stated to be a special branch of moral law: its maxims, like the maxims of the moral law, are nothing if not imperative and universal, and it is of their essence to be enforced, when necessary, by compulsion. (Kant, *Rechtslehre Einleitung*. Vaughan 1939: 78)

Behind this notion of right, there is a deeper philosophy and that is the philosophy of European Enlightenment. There is, however, a lack of a sufficiently broad, accurate, comprehensible and useable definition of the early Enlightenment. Part of the reason of this lack is that during Enlightenment there have been complex and quite often contradictory views on such issues as democracy, modernity, secularism, religion and scientific knowledge, etc. It is very difficult to provide one definition of the enlightenment, which fits all the men usually assumed to belong to it. Generally among the enlightenment thinkers we have Voltaire, Rousseau, Hume, Condercet and others. This is, however, not the occasion to go into the details of their specific philosophical systems, their mutual agreements and disagreements. I am basically concerned with the concept of freedom as the key concept of Enlightenment and as the ultimate source of human rights. Notwithstanding the mutual difference between one philosopher and another in the Enlightenment, they have a fundamental preoccupation, i.e. freedom. It was Kant, one of its earliest prophets, who asked that question and answered it in his article in the *Berlinischer Monatsschrift*, December 1783 issue, entitled *Beanwortung der Frage: Was ist Aufklaerung*? Or 'Answer to the Question: What is the Enlightenment?'

His answer is: *Aufklaerung ist der Ausgang des Menschen aus seiner Selbst-verschuldeten Unmuendigkeit.* Let me give his full answer in English, although I confess my inability to give a total word-to-word translation: 'Enlightenment is the coming out of man from his self-imposed immaturity. Immaturity is the incapacity to serve one's own understanding without direction (*Leitung*) from another. This immaturity is self-imposed; Reason itself languishes, not because it lacks understanding; what it lacks is resolution and courage; it is unwilling to serve itself (*Sapere Aude! Hebe Mut*). Take courage to serve your own understanding! This is therefore the Motto (*Walspruch*) of the Enlightenment.'[2] It is in this rather general framework of the Enlightenment rationality that the concept of humanity has evolved and it gets its elaborations in the categorical imperatives.

Kant is the first philosopher who has tried to give a definition of how a moral action ought to be in terms of individual's rights in conformity with the Enlightenment rationality. These are the *principles* of human actions such as 'universality', 'end in itself' and 'kingdom of ends'. These principles could be prescribed to any study of human rights anywhere. There have been certain attempts to define human rights in terms of the constitution of a nation/state, ethnic, cultural and religious identities, etc. But if we wish to define human rights in the most general sense of the term, including all specificities, Kant's categorical imperative is the only principle that could be taken into account. The Maxims, of course, go as follows:

> The first maxim: 'Act only on that maxim through which you can at the same time will that it should become a Universal Law'. (Paton 1969: 67)
>
> The second Maxim: 'Act in such a way that you always treat humanity, whether in your own person or in the person of any other, never simply as a means, but always at the same time as an end'. (Paton 1969: 91)
>
> The third Maxim: 'So act as if you were through your maxim a law making member of a kingdom of ends'. (Paton 1969: 34)

These maxims cannot be strange to any culture, though they could be naïve to every culture, as they are universal. One can easily imagine that the absence of any of these maxims could be tantamount to the denial of human dignity. Therefore these maxims could be regarded as the necessary principles for any study of human rights.

It is well known that Kant proceeds on Copernicus' primary hypothesis in the sphere of epistemology and morality. To recapitulate the basic issue in this regard – what makes Kant's position closer to Copernicus' hypothesis is that Kant makes 'man' the 'law-giver of nature', saying that, 'the order and regularity in the field of appearances, which we entitle nature, we ourselves introduce. We could never find them in appearances, had not we ourselves, or the nature of our mind, originally set them there.' In the same way, Kant places free will at the centre of his morality and states that ought statements are the expressions of that free will. Similarly, the fundamental idea of human rights amounts to another Copernican revolution, analogous in every respect to what we find in his epistemology and morality.

The Copernican revolution is, thus, the fundamental radical movement in the critical philosophy of Kant. The revolution quite literally shifts the direction of epistemology, morality and human rights from the nature of reality outside there, to the essential structure of human consciousness, will and freedom.

With Kant's Copernican revolution, the question about the structure of the world becomes the question of the structure of the 'transcendental self', and the question of ought pursuits, including those of human rights, becomes the question of the 'freedom of will'. Both are activities, but the first is concerned with knowing and the second with doing. Kant places man at the centre of epistemology, morality and human rights and asks, 'what must the world of knowledge, morality and Human Rights be like in order for us to know and act?' The world must be like we know it. Kant thus humanizes not only the problems of epistemology but also those of morality and human rights.

These maxims have created the broad vision of human rights that the United Nations Organization seeks to attain in its global mission of peaceful co-existence and mutual development. Even the very title of the draft has been greatly under Kantian influence, i.e. 'Universal Declaration of Human Rights.' It is a far-reaching document trying to protect human rights and to integrate the fabric of national and international life both ethically and juristically.

It will, however, not be totally futile to briefly reflect upon some of the Clauses of the draft that the General Assembly adopted as the Universal Declaration of Human Rights. These are as follows:

> *Whereas* recognition of the inherent dignity and of the equal and inalienable rights of all members of the human family is the foundation of freedom, justice and peace in the world.
>
> *Whereas* disregard and contempt for human rights have resulted in barbarous acts which have outraged the conscience of mankind, and the advent of a world in which human beings shall enjoy freedom of speech and belief and freedom from fear and want has been proclaimed as the highest aspiration of the common people.
>
> *Whereas* it is essential, if man is not to be compelled to have recourse, as a last resort, to rebellion against tyranny and oppression, that human rights should be protected by the rule of law.
>
> *Whereas* it is essential to promote the development of friendly relations between nations,
>
> *Whereas* the people of the United Nations have in the Charter reaffirmed their faith in fundamental human rights, in the dignity and worth of the human person and in the rights of men and women and have determined to promote social progress and better standard of life in larger freedom.
>
> *Whereas* Member States have pledged themselves to achieve in cooperation with United Nations the promotion of universal respect for and observance of human rights and fundamental freedom.
>
> *Whereas* a common understanding of these rights and freedom is one of the greatest importance for the full realization of this pledge.
>
> Now, therefore, the general Assembly Proclaims the Universal Declaration of Human Rights as a common standard of achievement for all people and all nations, to the end that every individual and every

> organ of society keeping this Declaration constantly in mind shall strive by teaching and education to promote respect for these rights and freedoms and by progressive measures, national and international, to secure their universal and effective recognition and observance, both among the peoples of members states themselves and among the peoples of territory under their jurisdiction.[3]

'Thirty articles of the Universal Declaration of Human Rights provide an overview of the principal rights and freedom that are every person's birthright.' (*Human Rights Today – A United Nations Priority*, United Nations Department of Public Information 1998: 59) Some of those articles are as follows:

1. Right to Freedom and equality in dignity and right
2. Freedom from discrimination
3. Right to life, liberty and security of person
4. Freedom from slavery and servitude
5. Freedom from torture or degrading treatment
6. Right to recognition as a person before the law
7. Right to equal consideration before the law
8. Right to remedy through competent tribunal
9. Freedom from arbitrary arrest or exile
10. Right to a fair trial or public hearing
11. Etc....

The first two articles are fundamental principles underlying all human rights. Articles 3 to 21 comprise civil and political rights. Articles 22 to 27 refer to economic, social and cultural rights. The last three articles provide a framework of solidarity, safeguarding the universal enjoyment of all human rights. (*Human Rights Today – A United Nations Priority*, United Nations Department of Public Information 1998: 5)

Impact of Globalisation

It is in the light of these human rights that we can reassess the impact of globalisation. One of the major achievements towards the end of the last century has been the emergence and development of globalisation. Globalisation started during mid 1970s in the developed countries, and since 1990s the world has moved towards globalisation in a big way. Globalisation has evolved out of the golden period of capitalism, i.e. 1940 to 1975. Origin of globalisation involves economic factors with trade and finance liberalisation, trade linked technology and political situation helping it. Globalisation has challenged the nation/state territorial sovereignty, the institutional autonomy and shrinking of the concepts of space and time. With the collapse of socialism in the Central and East European countries during 1990s, from which the People's Republic of China just managed to escape, the world has moved towards defining values of universalism set out in the Universal Declaration of Human Rights and in setting development goals in the United Nations conferences on environment, population, social development, women and human settlement.

Globalisation is essentially a product of technological advancement. It is a broad mindset that believes that broad world structures are possible. One way of looking at globalisation is to look at the history of social and economic revolutions and the emergence of state in relation to technological advancements and transformations. As we know, in feudal society there is a land-based economy. Infrastructure, like roads, transport, means of communications, etc., is not much developed. There is local production and local consumption. Religion has a rigid control over every walk of feudal life. Religion has three basic functions to perform in a feudal society: (a) it has a way of explaining the reality around us, natural reality, life as such, the relationship with other lives, and so on, (b) it has given rise to highest virtues and value systems in the world like universal compassion, love, ahimsa, sacrifice, etc. (c) it has given rise to aesthetic experiences like music, dance, drama, composition of epics and so on.

Technologically the horse or the bullock cart is the basis of the feudal society. Centralised government marks capitalist society. Infrastructure has to be developed with constant renewal of technology and availability of markets, etc. With secularization, the control of property and the ideas by the Church are given public openness. The dominant value of capitalist society is freedom with the developmentalist ideology. The steam engine is the basis of capitalism or industrial society. Electricity, nuclear energy and electronics lead to the advancement of capitalism towards post-industrial society. And subsequently, computer chips, micro technology of electronics and automations define the present phase, i.e. post-capitalist society. This is also called the 'information society'. These three stages are generally characterized as industrial, technological and financing phases of capitalism. We know that today only Hong Kong Bank, Taipei Bank and Tokyo Bank alone possess 30 per cent of the world's wealth.

Globalisation is by no means uniform; it always means different things to different people. Globalisation means media, rapid transmission of messages and symbols. It is a deregulation of domestic as well as external markets: goods and services. It appreciates the total capital market with the need to promote investment. This is done with Cyberspace and the Internet. It can describe the expansion of economic activities across national boundaries. Later on, it is converted into trade and commerce, banking, rural institutions and so on. All these are necessary beyond the State, because globalisation means global banking, trade and commerce, global migration of population, etc. All these require certain rules, institutions and infrastructures, which can go beyond the nation/state. So we have organizations like World Trade Organization (WTO), General Agreement on Traffics and Trade (GATT), new definitions of the UN and other UN funded organizations. With these institutional mechanisms global reality is regulated and managed. Globalisation also has structural prerequisites and imperatives. One such imperative is that people will 'move' and you have a 'free market'. Market is a very important term of globalisation and it is equivalent to the Internet.

Positive and Negative Factors of Globalisation

Globalisation means liberalisation and free movement of goods, services, capital and finance across national boundaries. In the world currency market more than $1.6 trillion is now exchanged each day and about 1/5 of the goods and services produced each year are traded; hence offering several opportunities for individual countries to achieve higher growth rates. In the last decade, there have been several discussions on the implications (with its positive and negative factors) that globalisation is going to have on development process, particularly in developing and underdeveloped countries. In these countries, development is defined as a 'composite reality'; it is not only economic development but also involves several human rights aspects besides cultural development, philosophical development and development of morals, ethos and values. In these developments, local cultures and local identities are recognized as the valid elements of any design of human kind. So much so that the Copenhagen Summit on Development, which was held in the early 1990s, dealt very clearly on this theme that somehow the kind of change that is taking place in the world today is leading to massive mobility of human kinds, human resources, ideas and consciousness. There is a global worry on the process of globalisation and the consequences of the globalisation on local cultures, local identities, the philosophical heritage and the very diversities that constitute the cultural matrix of human kind. I feel that globalisation of technology, trade and commerce and the optimization of these factors may not be of much help unless we revitalise local identities. In fact, globalisation, by its very process, enhances people's sensitivity to their local identities. There is a view that globalisation triggers, on one hand, massive movement of people, resources and values from one part of the globe to another part. To this extent there is interaction and homogenization between globalisation and local cultures.

On the other hand, the technology of globalisation encourages and helps the formation of local cultures. This is an obvious fact. If we are on Cyberspace or on the Internet, we have teleconferencing. Even sitting in this hall, we can have dialogues with students and teachers in Europe and USA. But the question is – will this technology help preserve local identities? There is a feeling that local identities may not be 'real identities' but only 'virtual reality'. The Internet and Cyberspace have a different language. By computerization and digital system of Cyberprocesses one can create realities that are not found in real life. By simple amalgamation of parameters, which are pre structured and defined, you can create a 'virtual reality'. Thus, technology can help in fostering local identities. People, who are in minority at one place, can search for like-minded people throughout the globe. This way, they can all come together through teleconferencing, without physical movement from one place to another. So, globalisation technologically does not prevent local identities.

The negative factors of globalisation are at two different levels. It threatens the interests of both the powerful and the weak nations. This is the dilemma of globalisation. It is generally criticized in terms of economic Darwinism, implying survival of the fittest. Globalisation is also the coming together of rich entrepreneurs of the whole world with the belief, or rather make-belief, that they do not need the poor. It threatens the power of those who are very strong, especially totalitarian countries. We have examples of the Soviet Union, Romania, Bulgaria, Poland, Czechoslovakia, Hungary, and so on in the late 1980s and early 1990s. I am not saying that media was totally responsible for the collapse of socialism. That would be too simplistic. There were many other factors involved. Like the Soviet Union being a simple Union of Republics, but never becoming a State. In the 70 years of socialist experience, socialism itself became vacuous, mechanical and undynamic. It may happen anywhere. Even in India, democracy is getting vacuous. There are such signs. We have to be vigilant. But facts of the matter remain. Media did play an important role in shaping public opinion of the post second world war Soviets. People in these countries got exposed to new views, new value systems and new life styles. People see what is happening around thc world and this, with the inefficiency of the State, threatens powerful and vested interests. When this threat comes about, there is counter resurgence of ideas. All it does, is to narrow down the process of globalisation. It gives rise to different forms of fundamentalism. There may be ideological fundamentalism or cultural fundamentalism; there will even be a benign fundamentalism, a consumer fundamentalism, an environmental fundamentalism, an industrial fundamentalism, and so on. This way globalisation creates turmoil at the top.

Globalisation also hurts the weak and the poor nations. They are hurt because they have no say or share in the process of globalisation. This is what worries the developing countries. There are many developing countries where the political system is not conducive for encountering globalisation. So there are examples of barring disk antennas, transponders, satellites, etc. And this is a very hopeless task. Many countries have tried it. But they all have failed. So this is a losing game. The poorer countries, which are not at all prepared to face globalisation, face problems in different ways. In such countries, market is always restrained. If a large number of people are illiterate and below the poverty line, and have no access to new jobs and new ways of understanding global situations, they are out of market. So globalisation, which brings free market, creates this problem for the weaker people.

India is the world's largest democracy and has a long history of democratic functioning with pluralistic values and philosophic universal concepts (holistic values included). India cannot remain indifferent to development in terms of globalisation and the New World Order, which has raised serious questions to the foundations of our traditionally established philosophic doctrines. The need is to expose us to our own cultural traditions in the wake of current development at the international scenario. It is urgent in view of the onslaught of western culture on our impressionistic minds, which creates a cultural dilemma and leads to cultural amnesia. The new millennium is different from all earlier occasions. It has new markets – foreign exchange and globally linked capital markets – new tools – the Internet, Cyberspace – new institutions – WTO, GATT, etc. – new rules – multilateral agreements on trade, services, intellectual property rights and patenting rights, backed by strong enforcement mechanisms and binding on the national governments, reducing the scope of national policies. Global markets, global technology, global ideas and global solidarity can enrich the lives of the people everywhere, expanding their choices.

In conclusion we can say that we cannot stop the process of globalisation. But globalisation is not forever; history has not come to an end. Despite the lofty claims that the State has withered away in the era of globalisation I believe that it still exists and is accountable to the people and their human rights. Where people are left out they will not sit back quietly. There will be counter resurgence of struggles, which may take the shape of crimes, like drug related crimes, ethnic struggles, terrorism, and so on. Therefore the State has to come forward to make strategic decisions. The State can certainly and strongly find and frame rules and institutions for governance to provide enough space for local identities, communities and environmental resources to ensure globalisation. Re-defining such values as in the adopting of human rights and setting development goals on environment, population, social development, etc., globalisation should be with regards for pluralistic value systems and without violations of human rights. Without marginalizing local identities, the reward of globalisation should go towards creating equity between nations.

Notes

1 Kant, Immanuel. *Rechtslehre Einleitung*, p. 40. Quotation taken from Vaughan, C. E. *Studies in the History of Political Philosophy before and after Rousseau*. Manchester: Manchester University Press 1939: 77.

2 Kant, Immanuel. *Was ist Aufklaerung: Thesen und Definitionen*. Stuttgart: Reclam 1986: 9 (translation mine).

3 See *The Universal Declaration of Human Rights*. United Nations Department of Public Information 1988: 5.

References

Levin, L. 1998. *Human Rights: Questions and Answers*. New Delhi: National Book Trust.

Longman Illustrated Encyclopaedia of World History. London: Ivy Leaf 1989.

Paton, H. J. 1969. *The Moral Law: Kant's Groundwork of Metaphysic of Morals*. London: Hutchinson University Library.

Vaughan, C. E. 1939. *Studies in the History of Political Philosophy before and after Rousseau*. Manchester: Manchester University Press.

NOTES ON CONTRIBUTORS

Rajendra Prasad was Senior Professor and Head of the Department of Humanities and Social Sciences, Indian Institute of Technology, Kanpur. He has been a Fulbright/Smith Mundt Fellow, a Fellow of the Rockefeller Foundation, USA, and until very recently a Senior Fellow of the Indian Council of Philosophical Research. He has authored many scholarly papers and several books. He was the editor of *Indian Review of Philosophy* and *Darsanika Traimasika* and is currently co-editor of *Indian Philosophical Quarterly* and *Paramarsa.*

Abhik Majumdar is Faculty in the National Law University, Orissa. He has a keen interest in issues of Legal and Moral Philosophy. His other areas of interest include constitutional law and intellectual property. He is also deeply involved with Hindustani classical music.

R. C. Pradhan is Professor of Philosophy at the University of Hyderabad. His research area includes Philosophy of Language and Philosophy of Mind. He has published a number of books and articles in philosophy. His most recent books are: *Language, Reality and Transcendence: An Essay on the Main Strands of Wittgenstein's Later Philosophy* (2009) and *Metaphysics* (2009).

Krishna Menon is Associate Professor in the Department of Political Science, Lady Shri Ram College for Women, University of Delhi. Her areas of interest include political theory, Indian politics and feminist theory and politics. She is co-author of *Human Rights Gender and Environment* (2009).

Shashi Motilal is Associate Professor in the Department of Philosophy, University of Delhi. Her research interests include Ethics, Applied Ethics and issues in Human Rights. She is the co-author of *Human Rights, Gender and Environment* (2006) and the co-editor of *Understanding Social Inequalities: Concerns of Human Rights, Gender and Environment* (2009). She is also currently member of CPCSEA, Ministry of Environment and Forests, Government of India.

Pratap Bhanu Mehta is presently President of the Centre for Policy Research, New Delhi. He is also a participant in the Global Faculty Program of NYU Law School, USA. He was previously Visiting Professor of Government at Harvard University and Professor of Philosophy and Law and Governance in the School of Social Sciences, Jawahar Lal Nehru University, New Delhi. He has published several scholarly articles on Social and Political Philosophy in journals of international repute. His columns have also appeared in a number of national and international dailies.

S. R. Bhatt taught Philosophy at the University of Delhi. He is an eminent philosopher and sanskritist. He has been the General President of Akhil Bhartiya Darshan Parishad and Indian Philosophical Congress. He has a number of scholarly papers and several books to his credit.

Shashi Prabha Kumar is Professor and Former Chairperson of the Special Centre for Sanskrit Studies, Jawahar Lal Nehru University, New Delhi. Prior to this, she taught in the Department of Philosophy, University of Delhi. She is an acclaimed Sanskrit scholar and has 17 books and scores of research papers in reputed journals and edited volumes. She is the recipient of Sri Ramakrishna Sanskrit Award and Shankar Puraskar.

Saral Jhingran, formerly an UGC Research Scientist affiliated to the Nehru Memorial Museum and Library is an erudite scholar of Indian Philosophy. She has several scholarly papers published in journals of Philosophy, Religion and Socio-political thought.

Rakesh Chandra is Head of the Department of Philosophy and Women Studies, Lucknow University. He has worked on Child Rights and Gender issues in India and Nepal. His most recent work is *Necessity, Identity and Conceptual Structures* (2007).

Madhucchanda Sen is Faculty in the Department of Philosophy, Rabindra Bharati University, Kolkata. She is co-editor of *Empiricism and the Two Dogmas* (2006) and *Language and Communication: A Philosophical Study* (2005) and co-author of *Logic* (2009).

Ashley Tellis is Assistant Professor in the Department of Liberal Arts at the Indian Institute of Technology, Hyderabad. He is also a same-sex rights activist, freelance journalist and editor.

Bhagat Oinam is Associate Professor of Philosophy and the current Chairperson of the Centre for Philosophy, School of Social Sciences, Jawaharlal Nehru University, New Delhi. Earlier, he taught philosophy at IIT Bombay, and NEHU, Shillong. He has been writing on the issues related to moral philosophy, philosophy of culture, social and political philosophy.

He has contributed scholarly articles in reputed journals. He is also Executive Editor of the journal *Eastern Quarterly*.

Ruplekha Khullar is Associate Professor in the Department of Philosophy, Janaki Devi Memorial College, University of Delhi.

Ranjita Biswas is a medical professional and consultant psychiatrist. She is a lecturer in the Department of Women's Studies, Jadavpur University and Assistant Editor of *Bengal Journal of Psychiatry*.

Anup Dhar has a professional degree in Medicine and is currently Associate Fellow at Centre for the Study of Culture and Society (CSCS), Bangalore. He is coordinator of an applied research programme 'Culture-Subjectivity-Psyche: Rethinking Mental Health' (CUSP@CSCS), Bangalore, India. He has contributed scholarly articles in several journals and edited volumes. His latest co-authored book is *Global Capitalism and the World of the Third* (2009).

Anirban Das has a professional degree in Medicine and is currently a Fellow in Cultural Studies at the Centre for Studies in Social Sciences, Calcutta. He teaches feminist theory as Visiting Faculty at the Women's Studies programs in the Jadavpur University and the University of Calcutta. He has published essays at the intersections of feminist theory, postcolonial theory and continental philosophy and on the history of medical epistemology.

Rekha Basu is Associate Professor in the Department of Philosophy, Hindu College, University of Delhi.

Nirmalya Narayan Chakraborty is Associate Professor in the Department of Philosophy, Rabindra Bharati University, Kolkata. He is author of *Pursuit of Meaning* (2004) and *In Defense of Intrinsic Value of Nature*(2004). He is also editor of *Empiricism and The Two Dogmas* (2006) and *Perspectives on Radhakrishnan* (2007).

Maushumi Guha is Faculty in the Department of Philosophy and Centre for Cognitive Science, Jadavpur University, Kolkatga. Her research interests include Folk Psychology and Theory of Mind, Cognitive Development, Ethics and the Machine.

Amita Chatterjee is Professor of Philosophy and Coordinator of the Centre for Cognitive Science, Jadavpur University, Kolkata. Her areas of specializations are: Logic and Navya-Nyaya, Analytic Philosophy, Philosophy of Mind and Cognitive Science. She is the author of *Understanding Vagueness*

(1994) and co-author of *Mental Reasoning: Experiments and Theories* (2009). She is the editor of *Bharatiya Dharmaniti* (1998) and *Perspectives on Consciousness* (2003). She has published articles in national and international journals of repute and her articles have been included in important anthologies.

Malabika Majumdar is Associate Professor in the Department of Philosophy, Kamala Nehru College, University of Delhi.

R. P. Singh is Professor and former Chairperson, Centre for Philosophy, School of Social Sciences, Jawaharlal Nehru University, New Delhi. His area of research and expertise is Modern Western Philosophy, Critical Theory and Indian Philosophy. In his long teaching career he has contributed immensely in many national and international journals and has several books to his credit.

www.ingramcontent.com/pod-product-compliance
Lightning Source LLC
Chambersburg PA
CBHW022346280326
41935CB00007B/97
* 9 7 8 9 3 8 0 6 0 1 1 5 1 *